Waterbird Population Estimates

Third Edition

D1394389

Compiled and edited by
Simon Delany and Derek Scott

Wetlands International Global Series No. 12
2002

Copyright 2002 Wetlands International

ISBN 90 5882 012 2

This publication should be cited as follows:
Wetlands International. 2002. *Waterbird Population Estimates – Third Edition*.
Wetlands International Global Series No. 12, Wageningen, The Netherlands

Published by Wetlands International
www.wetlands.org

Available from Natural History Book Service
2–3 Wills Road, Totnes, Devon TQ9 5XN, United Kingdom
www.nhbs.co.uk

Cover photograph:
Snow Geese, Canada Geese and Greater White-Fronted Geese erupting into flight,
Klamath Basin, California USA
© Frans Lanting/Foto Natura

Design by Naturebureau International
36 Kingfisher Court, Hambridge Road, Newbury
Berkshire RG14 5SJ, United Kingdom

Printed by H. Charlesworth & Co Ltd., Huddersfield, United Kingdom.
Printed on 100gsm Chromomat Club.

Names used for geographical entities do not imply recognition by Wetlands International,
or organisations funding this publication, of the political status or boundaries of any
particular territory. Names of territories used (and any alternatives) are included solely to
help users of this publication apply these data for waterbird conservation purposes.

Waterbird Population Estimates – Third Edition

Editors:
Simon Delany[1] and Derek Scott[1]

Regional Editors:
Africa and associated islands: Tim Dodman[2]
Asia-Pacific: David Li[3] and Taej Mundkur[3]; shorebirds, Doug Watkins[4]
Europe, North Africa, Middle East, Central Asia: Derek Scott, Simon Delany, Niels Gilissen[1]
North America, Central America, Caribbean: Melanie Steinkamp[5]
South America: Daniel Blanco[6]

Technical assistants:
Lieuwe Haanstra and Niels Gilissen

Special Contributors:
The following BirdLife International staff:
Stuart Butchart, Des Callaghan, Simba Chan, Mike Crosby, Guy Dutson, Angelica Estrada, Lincoln Fishpool, Umberto Gallo-Orsi, Melanie Heath, Jeremy Speck, Alison Stattersfield, David Wege

The International Coordinators of the following Wetlands International Specialist Groups:
Diver/Loon Specialist Group – Joe Kerekes
Pelican Specialist Group – Alain Crivelli
Heron Specialist Group – Heinz Hafner and James Kushlan
Storks, Ibises & Spoonbills Specialist Group – Malcolm Coulter and Wim Van Den Bossche
Flamingo Specialist Group – Alan Johnson
Swan Specialist Group – Jan Beekman and Roberto Schlatter
Threatened Waterfowl Specialist Group – Baz Hughes and Andy Green
International Crane Foundation – George Archibald
Wader Study Group – David Stroud
Woodcock & Snipe Specialist Group – Yves Ferrand and Herby Kalchreuter
Waterbird Harvest Specialist Group – Gilles Deplanque

[1] Wetlands International Headquarters, Wageningen, The Netherlands
[2] Wetlands International Office, Dakar, Senegal
[3] Wetlands International Office, Kuala Lumpur, Malaysia
[4] Wetlands International Office, Canberra, Australia
[5] United States Geological Survey Patuxent Wildlife Research Center, Laurel, Maryland, USA
[6] Wetlands International Office, Buenos Aires, Argentina

Funders:

Directorate for Nature Management, Ministry of Agriculture, Nature Management and Fisheries, The Netherlands

landbouw, natuurbeheer en visserij

Department for Environment, Food & Rural Affairs, United Kingdom

DEFRA
Department for **Environment, Food & Rural Affairs**

The Joint Nature Conservation Committee (JNCC), United Kingdom

JOINT NATURE CONSERVATION COMMITTEE

Alterra Green World Research, The Netherlands

ALTERRA
GREEN WORLD RESEARCH

National Environmental Research Institute (NERI), Denmark

Ministry of Environment and Energy
National Environmental Research Institute

The Wetland Trust, United Kingdom

Department of Hunting, Ministry of Agriculture, Finland

MINISTRY OF AGRICULTURE AND FORESTRY

Bundesamt für Umwelt, Wald und Landschaft, Switzerland

Swiss Agency for the Environment, Forests and Landscape SAEFL

Ministère de la Région Wallonie, Direction Nature et Espaces Vertes, Belgium

Environmental Protection Agency, Sweden

NATUR VÅRDS VERKET

Duchas, The Heritage Service, Ireland

Dúchas The Heritage Service

Contents

Foreword

Both the Ramsar Convention on Wetlands and the Bonn Convention on Migratory Species belong to the family of international treaties which have been developed in the past three decades. During this period we have seen the first global gathering on the environment, the 1972 Stockholm Conference, followed by the Earth Summit in Rio de Janeiro in 1992, which stimulated the development of another family of environmental treaties addressing a much wider scope of environmental problems. Most recently, the World Summit on Sustainable Development in Johannesburg set the goal of achieving by 2010 a significant reduction in the current rate of loss of biodiversity. Other environment and development issues have also been the subject of major world gatherings in recent years.

This all may seem a bit far away from the aims and goals of the first international conservation treaties, but it is less far than one may think. The natural environment has throughout been an essential element in the discussions in these new developments and challenges for the world community. The need for conserving the flora and fauna of the planet, and for making a sustainable use of their resources, has never been challenged within the wider range of environmental and human issues setting today's agenda.

This was not least because good and objectively collected data were available to underpin this continuous effort for conservation and wise use. The work of the Intergovernmental Panel on Climate Change, which has served to inform the deliberations of the Climate Change Convention, has shown how important it is to have reliable long-term data. For our Conventions, the Global Waterbird Population Estimates is one of these reliable data sets and it is, with its supporting mechanism of the International Waterbird Census, probably the longest term data set in place. Aware of their value and importance, our Conventions have been already supporting in the past the IWC and the publication of the data sets it produces.

This Third Edition of the Global Waterbird Population Estimates is a major achievement by Wetlands International. More populations than ever have been included and the networks providing the data are substantially expanded. It provides a solid basis for the use of important criteria for protecting sites, such as the 1% criterion, and the management of populations within entire flyways. It is now up to the countries and to us to stimulate the use of the data to support their conservation and wise use activities within the framework of our Conventions and agreed implementation plans. This common interest will not fail to be reflected in the Joint Work Programme between our Conventions, currently being elaborated, and the future cooperative arrangements between our Secretariats and Wetlands International.

On behalf of both Conventions we wish to record our deep appreciation for the long-term technical support and competent input by Wetlands International and its staff in ensuring that the best available information is made available in this publication.

Delmar Blasco
Secretary General
Convention on Wetlands
(Ramsar, Iran, 1971)

Arnulf Müller-Helmbrecht
Executive Secretary
Convention on Migratory Species
(Bonn, Germany, 1979)

Acknowledgements

Work on this publication was a team effort and we are extremely grateful to all the people named on the title page for making this work so productive and enjoyable. We are also indebted to the colleagues and friends listed below for their dedication, expertise, enthusiasm and hard work in compiling and sending information, often at short notice. We salute the inestimable contribution of over 10,000 mainly voluntary waterbird counters who participate in the International Waterbird Census and similar large-scale bird monitoring efforts to produce the data which form the basis of a high proportion of these estimates. David Stroud provided valuable comments on the text, and staff in the Wetlands International Wageningen office who contributed beyond the call of duty were Dineke Beintema, Gerard Boere and Ward Hagemeijer. Thank you one and all.

Josep del Hoyo and staff at Lynx Edicions, Barcelona, generously facilitated the inclusion of the maps from *Handbook of the Birds of the World* Volume 1 (1992) and Volume 3 (1996) which are a key improvement on the first and second editions.

Grateful thanks also to Peter Creed and the team at Naturebureau International who turned a difficult manuscript into a clear and attractive publication with utmost professionalism.

Funding for this work from the following donors is gratefully acknowledged:
The Directorate for Nature Management, Ministry of Agriculture, Nature Management and Fisheries, The Netherlands
The Joint Nature Conservation Committee, United Kingdom
The Department of Environment, Food and Rural Affairs, United Kingdom
Alterra Green World Research, The Netherlands
The National Environmental Research Institute, Denmark
The Wetland Trust, United Kingdom
Department of Hunting, Ministry of Agriculture, Finland
Bundesamt für Umwelt, Wald und Landschaft, Switzerland
Ministère de la Région Wallonie Direction Nature et Espaces Vertes, Belgium
Environmental Protection Agency, Sweden
Dúchas, The Heritage Service, Ireland

The following experts contributed information or helped in other ways:
Ghisselle Alvarado, Ellen Amting, Daniel Anderson, Brad Andres, George Archibald, Alejandro Perez Arteaga, Gerhard Aubrecht, Liz Baker, Neil Baker, Jack Barr, Nicolas Barré, Jeb Barzen, Jan Beekman, Rich Beilfuss, Vincent van den Berk, Martina Bernhard, Daniel Blanco, Daniel Bordage, Tim Bowman, Vincent Bretagnolle, Dan Brooks, Joost Brouwer, Stephen Brown, David Boertmann, Axel Braunlich, Seb Buckton, Stuart Butchart, Greg Butcher, Des Callaghan, Geoff Carey, Simba Chan, Brooks Childress, Anwaruddin Choudhury, Kendrew Colhoun, John Cooper, Malcolm Coulter, Peter Cranswick, Rob Crawford, Alain Crivelli, Mike Crosby, Nick Davidson, Bernard Deceuninck, Wim van Den Bossche, Gilles Deplanque, Sergey Dereliev, Kathryn Dickson, Betsy Didrickson, Lars Dineson, Ding Changqing, Tim Dodman, Garry Donaldson, Will Duckworth, Bruce Dugger, Guy Dutson, Bart Ebbinge, Árni Einarsson, Ólafur Einarsson, Mats Ericson, Angelica Estrada, Yves Ferrand, Jason Ferris, Brendan Finch, Lincoln Fishpool, Carol Fouque, Tony Fox, Scott Frazier, Holly Freifeld, Umberto Gallo-Orsi, Patricia Gandini, Arnthór Gardarsson, Grant Gilchrist, Niels Gilissen, Dagny Gingrich, Christian Glahder, Patricia González, Andy Green, Klaus Günther, Lieuwe Haanstra, Heinz Hafner, Susan Haig, Helen Hands, Doug Harebottle, Brian Harrington, David Haukos, Frank Hawkins, Melanie Heath, Saskia Henderikse, Colleen Henson, T.W. Hoffman, Edith Hubert, Baz Hughes, Colleen Hyslop, Zafar ul-Islam, Roger Jaensch, Joe Jehl, Alan Johnson, Scott Johnston, Herby Kalchreuter, Verena Keller, Joe Kerekes, Jeff Kirby, Kees Koffijberg, Arun Kumar, James Kushlan, Hansoo Lee, Pete Leonard, David Li, Warren Lee Long, Ma Ming, Gernant Magnin, Gabor Magyar, Mark Mallory, Richard Maloney, Jim Mattson, Eric Meek, Marlynn Mendoza, Bob Milko, Tino Mischler, Yoshihiko Miyabayashi, Jean-Yves Mondain Monval, Johan Mooij, Nial Moores, Guy Morrison, Mike Moser, Tim Moser, Wim Mullié, Taej Mundkur, Andy Musgrove, Dan Neiman, Steve Newton, Leif Nilsson, Jantien van Oord, Dennis Orthmeyer, Otto Overdijk, Kathy Parsons, Don Paul, Christian Perennou, Bruce Peterjohn, Theunis Piersma, Stefan Pihl, Jon Plissner, Rivo Rabarisoa, Eileen Rees, Cecilia Reyes, Danny Rogers, Marc van Roomen, Paul Rose, Rui Rufino, Yus Rusila Noor, Bob Russell, Roger Safford, Mark Sanders, Jean-Pierre Savard, Tineke Scalzotto, Roberto Schlatter, Jevgeni Shergalin, Marcel Silvius, Rob Simmons, H.S. Singh, U. Sirivardena, Mike Smart, Graham Smith, Jeremy Speck, Peter Spierenburg, Alison Stattersfield, Melanie Steinkamp, David Stroud, Gopi Sundar, Per Ole Syvertsen, Jugal Tiwiri, Pavel Tomkovich, José Torres, John Trapp, Bob Trost, Stephanie Tyler, Les Underhill, Janine van Vessem, Milan Vogrin, Wang Qishan, Deepal Warakagoda, Doug Watkins, David Wege, Steve Wilcox, Khristi Wilkins, Emmanuel Williams, Yeap Chin Aik, Pierre Yésou, Pablo Yorio, Glyn Young, Christoph Zöckler.

Contributing photographers:

The following photographers are thanked for responding to a request for photographs of waterbirds:
Nils Anthes, Hichem Azafzaf, Gerard Boere, Dennis Bright, Nancy Camel, Chaitra M.R./Rajesh B.P., Chung Yu Chiang, Peter Creed, Nick Davidson, Simon Delany, Dileep P.V., Tim Dodman, Ali El Hili, Marc Fasol, Arne Follestad, Niels Gilissen, Paul Goriup, Manie Grobler, Klaus Günther, Baz Hughes, Kazuhiko Ichimi, Per Jordhoy, David Kjaer, Elena Kreuzberg Mukhina, Lena Lebedeva, Gernant Magnin, Atanu Mondal, Ian Montgomery, Hitomi Morohashi, Jun Morohashi, Mike Moser, Nandy Kousik, Christian Perennou, Vasu Rao, Ivan Rusev, Marcel Silvius, Brendan Sloan, Johan Verbanck, Adam Welz, Johanna Winkelman, H. Glyn Young.

Introduction

Waterbirds[1] occur on wetlands, often in spectacular concentrations, and are one of the most obvious indicators of the richness and diversity of these productive ecosystems. The long migrations of some waterbirds, and the fact that some species are the prized quarry of hunters, have made these birds a favoured subject for research, survey, education and recreation throughout the world. Networks of experts on every continent contribute to co-ordinated waterbird monitoring programmes, making waterbirds one of the most comprehensively studied groups of animals on earth, and the first to be mentioned in the title of an important inter-governmental treaty: "The Convention on Wetlands of International Importance, especially as Waterfowl Habitat", now better known as the Ramsar Convention on Wetlands.

Objectives of *Waterbird Population Estimates*

The first edition of *Waterfowl Population Estimates* (Rose and Scott 1994) provided a first global overview of the status of the world's waterbird populations. It was prepared with four objectives, and these objectives have not changed in subsequent editions:
(i)   to assist in the identification of wetlands of international importance using waterbirds as bio-indicators, and especially to provide the basis of the so-called 1% criterion, whereby any site which regularly holds 1% or more of a waterbird population qualifies as being internationally important under the Ramsar Convention on Wetlands;
(ii) to identify priorities for conservation and research to maintain global waterbird biodiversity;
(iii) to identify gaps in knowledge of the world's waterbird populations; and
(iv) to support the development of the Ramsar, Bonn and Biodiversity Conventions.

Background to the Third Edition

The second edition of *Waterfowl Population Estimates* (Rose and Scott 1997) followed a similar format to the first edition, but included many more population estimates and much more information on population trends. The completion of this third edition (now renamed *Waterbird Population Estimates*) has been delayed, and now coincides with the eighth Conference of the Parties to the Ramsar Convention. One benefit of this delay in publication has been that it has been possible to provide more information in the tables and to include distribution maps for all species, generously provided by the editors and publishers of the *Handbook of the Birds of the World* (del Hoyo *et al.* 1996 & 1999). Other new features of this third edition include English vernacular names for all species and some distinctive subspecies, and short descriptions of both the breeding and non-

1   The term 'waterbirds' has been adopted by Wetlands International in preference to the term 'waterfowl' because of the different meanings of that word in different parts of the English speaking world.

Sooty Tern colony, Michaelmas Cay, Australia. Gerard Boere

breeding ('wintering') ranges of all populations, insofar as this is known. A 'Notes' column has been added to the tables, and this has permitted the presentation of many more explanatory notes, particularly with regard to taxonomic treatment and the derivation of population estimates.

Sources of information

Since the second edition of *Waterfowl Population Estimates*, a great deal of new information on waterbird populations has become available. The International Waterbird Census (IWC), co-ordinated by Wetlands International, now covers over 100 countries in five continents, and continues to provide much of the raw data on which many of the estimates and trends are based. Additional census schemes and atlas projects have contributed a wealth of new information on population sizes in many parts of the world. Some of the most significant publications to have appeared since 1997 include:

- *The EBCC Atlas of European Breeding Birds* (Hagemeijer & Blair 1997)
- *The Atlas of Southern African Birds* (Harrison *et al.* 1997)
- *Rails: a Guide to the Rails, Crakes, Gallinules and Coots of the World* (Taylor & van Perlo. 1998)
- *Results from the International Waterbird Census in the Western Palearctic and Southwest Asia 1995 and 1996* (Delany *et al.* 1999)
- *Goose Populations of the Western Palearctic* (Madsen *et al.*1999)
- *Threatened Birds of the World* (BirdLife International 2000)
- *European Bird Populations: Estimates and trends* (BirdLife International/European Bird Census Council 2000)
- *The Action Plan for Australian Birds 2000* (Garnet & Crowley 2000)
- *The Neotropical Waterbird Census – The first 10 years: 1990–1999* (Blanco & Carbonell 2001)
- *Important Bird Areas in Africa and associated islands* (Fishpool & Evans 2001)
- *Estimates of shorebird populations in North America* (Morrison *et al.* 2001)
- *Sea Duck Joint Venture Strategic Plan: 2001–2006* (Sea Duck Joint Venture Management Board. 2001)
- *Numbers and distribution of wintering waterbirds in the Western Palearctic and Southwest Asia in 1997, 1998 and 1999* (Gilissen *et al.* 2002)
- *North American Waterbird Conservation Plan, Version 1.* (Kushlan *et al.* 2002)
- *Action Plan for Herons of the World*, (Hafner *et al.* in prep. 2002)
- *Waterbird Population Estimates in Africa* (Dodman, in review. 2002)
- *Status of Migratory Wader Populations in Africa and Western Eurasia in the 1990s* (Stroud *et al.* in review, 2002)
- *Breeding Waders in Europe 2000* (Thorup in review, 2002).

In addition to these major works, a literature review resulted in over 350 published and unpublished sources (listed on pages 209–219) being used to compile the population estimates and trends presented.

Wetlands International's Specialist Groups have provided valuable updated information on a number of taxa, most notably the Ardeidae: the Heron Specialist Group provided details of a complete review of the world's herons, including a modernisation of taxonomy. The Wader Study Group has undertaken a review of wader populations in Africa and western Eurasia (Stroud *et al.* in review. 2002). Similar work in North America (Morrison *et al.* 2001) and Australia (Bamford & Watkins in prep. 2002) has enabled us to present new population estimates for a majority of the world's wader (shorebird) populations.

Cooperation with BirdLife International has resulted in extremely helpful additional material from data deficient regions, particularly Asia and Oceania.

Ensuring a flow of up-to-date information to the compilers was a major networking exercise in which Wetlands International's regional offices in Buenos Aires, Canberra, Dakar and Kuala Lumpur played a crucial role. In North America, fruitful relations were established with the US Geological Survey Wildlife Research Center in Patuxent, Maryland, who ensured that experts on all waterbird groups were consulted, and their expertise included.

The compilation of information for this edition of *Waterbird Population Estimates* has coincided with the compilation by Wetlands International of information for the second edition of the *Report on the Conservation Status of Migratory Waterbirds in the Agreement Area* (Scott, in review, 2002) for the Second Meeting of the Parties to the African-Eurasian Migratory Waterbird Agreement (AEWA) in Bonn, Germany, in September 2002. This report contains many new estimates derived from a number of published sources, and constitutes a valuable source of additional information on the trends in populations of migratory waterbirds in Africa and Western Eurasia.

Improvements on earlier editions

This publication covers the same families as earlier editions, but the incomplete coverage of two groups in those editions has been rectified. The Rallidae are the second largest waterbird family, and the publication of a comprehensive guide to the family (Taylor & van Perlo 1998) has allowed complete coverage of this group for the first time. Secondly, species which have become extinct since 1600 have been added from *Threatened Birds of the World* (BirdLife International 2000), improving the formerly incomplete coverage of this group. The Heron Specialist Group completed a comprehensive review of the family Ardeidae in 2002, and this has resulted in recognition of many new populations and the presentation of new estimates and trends.

It had already become apparent, even before the second edition of *Waterfowl Population Estimates* was produced, that interpretation of the geographical descriptions of the populations was probably the commonest source of confusion when applying 1% thresholds to identify wetlands of international importance. Some attempt was made in the second edition to give more detailed range descriptions, but the problem remained. It was therefore decided in the present edition to include wherever possible a brief description of both the breeding and non-breeding (or 'wintering') ranges of migratory populations. It is hoped that these range descriptions at the population level, along with the distribution maps, at species level, will help to alleviate this problem. The actual biogeographical ranges of individual populations are, however, often difficult to define, and the boundaries between adjacent 'flyway' populations are often imprecisely known, especially when these populations overlap at some stage during their annual cycle. Only when the limits of each population have been shown on a map will it be possible to determine with any certainty the full suite of range states that are included in each population. The provision of maps showing the limits of individual populations is clearly a priority for the future. A start has been made with addressing this priority by the publication of Flyway Atlases (e.g. Scott & Rose 1996, Miyabayashi & Mundkur 1999). At least one further Flyway Atlas is in preparation, covering waders (shorebirds) in Africa and western Eurasia and the production of similar atlases for additional species in this part of the world is identified as being important in the AEWA Implementation Priorities. The *Waterbird Population Estimates* project has a bright future on the internet, where digital formats have obvious advantages in the presentation of spatial data, which will further enhance its use for the identification of internationally important sites.

Constraints

The task we have set ourselves in assessing global population sizes of all waterbirds is a difficult one, described in the introduction to Morrison *et al.* (2001) as "the process of attempting to know the unknowable". Hugh Boyd in the Foreword to the 1999 publication *Population modelling and management of Snow Geese* expressed the dilemma faced by scientists attempting to present the information needed by policy makers and others involved in the conservation and management of these populations: "Many other considerations in addition to scientific ones are involved in scientific policy making and decision making. Scientists can play their part by providing the best available information and advice. That will rarely be as complete and reliable as they would wish, but making a "best guess" is much better than remaining aloof because perfection has not been achieved".

Our aim has been to use the best available information to set the global standard for knowledge of waterbird population estimates and trends. This publication also highlights gaps in our knowledge of the world's waterbirds and should be used to prioritise further research and survey. Many waterbird populations are poorly known or of unknown size, and for many more, knowledge of whether numbers are stable, declining or increasing is lacking. The biogeographical delimitation of populations is itself often a difficult exercise, and the identification of populations beyond the subspecies level will often be open to re-interpretation in the light of improved knowledge. Wetlands International is committed to deliver the best information and advice available within the limit of available resources. The widest possible consultation of people-networks and published sources has guided the estimates presented in this book. We invite anybody that feels well-placed to contribute to the improvement of these figures to provide information and become involved in the continuing process of revising and refining the information presented.

The Ramsar Criteria and 1% thresholds

The Ramsar Convention (Convention on Wetlands of International Importance especially as Waterfowl Habitat, Ramsar, 1971) has become an important tool by which governments agree common standards for the conservation and wise use of wetlands. One mechanism by which this is achieved is the designation of internationally important wetlands to the Ramsar List. These so-called 'Ramsar sites' must meet at least one of eight criteria by which the wetland can be adjudged to be of international importance. Most of these criteria rely on expert judgement. However two of the criteria, which relate specifically to waterbird populations, are more objective and have been very widely applied.

The first of these waterbird criteria, Criterion 5, states that "a wetland should be considered internationally important if it regularly supports 20,000 or more waterbirds". The second, Criterion 6, states that "a wetland should be considered internationally important if it regularly supports 1% of the individuals in a population of one species or subspecies of waterbird." Of the two criteria, Criterion 5 is the most simple to use, requiring no additional information beyond that which can be collected at the site itself. Criterion 6 is also easy to apply, although it requires a numerical estimate of population size to be available for the appropriate waterbird species or population to act as the basis of a 1% threshold. A major aim of this publication is to provide the quantitative information necessary for the use of Criterion 6. It draws together existing population estimates of the world's waterbirds, and sets the 1% thresholds that are to be used in the application of Criterion 6 in the designation of sites under the Ramsar Convention.

It is generally accepted that the 1% thresholds used to apply Criterion 6 are most useful if they are not changed too frequently, even though the population estimates on which they are based will change, both through improvements in the understanding of the populations and through real changes in population size. It is important that there is an agreed mechanism for changing the 1% thresholds for the application of Criterion 6. The following guidelines have been suggested:

1. Changes to 1% thresholds for application of Ramsar Criterion 6 should not be made for variations in population status within agreed limits of natural fluctuation. In this respect, all future analysis and discussion of waterbird population status should, wherever possible, try to define limits of natural fluctuation.
2. Published population estimates from a technically competent source should be the only justification for changing the 1% thresholds for application of Ramsar Criterion 6 suggested in this publication and in subsequent updates.
3. 1% thresholds for application of Ramsar Criterion 6 should be suggested for waterbird populations of unknown or poorly known status as soon as suitable information becomes available, through the triennial update of this publication.

Morandava, Madagascar. H. Glyn Young

4. Wherever possible, population estimates and 1% thresholds of well monitored species should be reviewed on a regular (nine yearly) basis.

In Resolution VI.4 of the 6th Meeting of the Conference of the Contracting Parties to the Ramsar Convention, the Conference of the Contracting Parties agreed, *inter alia*, that "unless waterfowl populations are poorly known or are known to be rapidly changing, 1% threshold levels should be revised not more frequently than every third ordinary meeting of the Conference of the Contracting Parties", and called on Contracting Parties to use these estimates and thresholds, upon their publication, as a basis for designation of sites for the List of Wetlands of International Importance in the succeeding three triennia.

In this edition of *Waterbird Population Estimates*, 1% thresholds have not been changed if the estimates for the populations concerned have not changed by more than 20% since the second edition (1997). However, it is now almost nine years since the first edition of *Waterfowl Population Estimates* was published, and therefore any 1% thresholds in that edition which were not updated in the 1997 edition have been revised to reflect the latest population estimates, irrespective of the extent of the change in population size. In practice, there are very few well-monitored populations outside Europe and North America, and many of the revised estimates given in this edition of *Waterbird Population Estimates* reflect an improvement in knowledge, rather than any known change in population size. In such cases, the new 1% thresholds have been set on the basis of the improved estimates, irrespective of the percentage change from the previous estimate.

Application of the 1% criterion has already been extensively discussed by Atkinson-Willes *et al.* (1982) and Stroud *et al.* (1990), and guidelines for the application of the criterion have been provided by the Ramsar Convention Bureau and are available on its web site. Once a site has been delimited, the number of birds of each population occurring regularly at the site can be compared with the thresholds given in the tables which form the bulk of this publication. If the site regularly supports more than the given 1% threshold for any population, it is considered to be internationally important for that population.

Migratory waterbirds pass through many wetlands *en route* to their breeding or wintering grounds, so although the number of waterbirds present at any one time may never exceed the 1% threshold, the wetland may still support internationally important numbers of a population because of the total number of birds which use the site during the whole migration period. This can only be substantiated by an estimation of the rate at which the individuals present are changing (turnover rate). Special techniques, such as direct observation of migratory flocks, or indirect observation through studies of marked (ringed) individuals, are usually required to measure turnover. The Ramsar Convention urges the use of turnover estimates, where these data are available, in application of Criterion 6.

If, at any time, a site supports two populations of the same species, problems in applying Criterion 6 can arise if individuals of the two populations are indistinguishable. In such cases, every effort should be made to apply the appropriate 1% threshold to each population by investigating the origin and destination of individuals at the site, or through determining the seasonal patterns of occurrence for each population using the site. Meininger *et al.* (1995) suggested that when two or more populations of a species occur at a site and separation is impossible, the 1% threshold relating to the largest population should be used for site designation purposes.

Methodology

What are waterbirds?

The Ramsar Convention defines 'waterfowl' as species of birds that are "ecologically dependent upon wetlands" and has defined "waterbird" as being synonymous with "waterfowl" for the purposes of the application of the Convention. However, in the second edition of *Waterfowl Population Estimates*, 'waterfowl' were defined more precisely as all species of the families Gaviidae, Podicipedidae, Pelecanidae, Phalacrocoracidae, Anhingidae, Ardeidae, Balaenicipitidae, Scopidae, Ciconiidae, Threskiornithidae, Phoenicopteridae, Anhimidae, Anatidae, Pedionomidae, Gruidae, Aramidae, Rallidae, Heliornithidae, Eurypygidae, Jacanidae, Rostratulidae, Dromadidae, Haematopodidae, Ibidorhynchidae, Recurvirostridae, Burhinidae, Glareolidae, Charadriidae, Scolopacidae, Thinocoridae, Laridae, Sternidae and Rynchopidae. Only a minority of wetland bird populations are excluded by this approach. Conversely, the inclusion of whole families resulted in the waterfowl list containing a few non-wetland species such as some seabirds and stone-curlews. These rather minor anomalies were thought to be outweighed by the convenience of a whole-taxon approach to the definition of 'waterfowl' and, in particular, considering the complications that would arise from applying the definition rigidly to every species.

This edition of *Waterbird Population Estimates* considers the same families of birds as were covered in the two earlier editions. However, the term 'waterbird' implies a broader meaning than the strict definition of 'waterfowl' given in the second edition, and more in keeping with the Ramsar definition of 'waterfowl', *i.e.* birds that are ecologically dependent on wetlands. Many participants in the International Waterbird Census already submit counts of wetland birds additional to the families listed above, and it has been proposed that future editions of *Waterbird Population Estimates* should include population estimates for these, wherever possible. One of the most logical expansions would be to include additional families of birds traditionally regarded as seabirds. Many of the species of 'waterbirds' currently included in *Waterbird Population Estimates* are strictly marine species that would equally merit the name 'seabird', notably many species of cormorants (Phalacrocoracidae), gulls (Laridae) and terns (Sternidae), while many of the 'seabirds', currently excluded, might equally be termed 'waterbirds', as they make extensive use of shallow, inshore waters. Of the seabird groups, perhaps only the four families of Procellariiformes (Diomedeidae, Procellariidae, Hydrobatidae and Pelecanoididae) do not include any species that can be regarded as waterbirds. A majority of species in these families are exclusively pelagic away from the breeding sites, rarely straying into inshore waters except when storm driven. At least some of the species in the other 'seabird' families (Spheniscidae, Phaethontidae, Sulidae, Fregatidae, Stercorariidae and Alcidae) make use of shallow, inshore waters, and could therefore be considered 'waterbirds' appropriate for inclusion in *Waterbird Population Estimates*. It has therefore been proposed that, for the sake of consistency, future editions of *Waterbird Population Estimates* should include at least these groups of seabirds.

Ruddy-headed Geese. H. Glyn Young

The first two editions of *Waterfowl Population Estimates* were restricted to native populations of waterbirds occurring in a natural, wild state, and did not include those populations of waterbirds that have been introduced outside their natural range, either deliberately or accidentally, by humans. This approach has been retained in the present edition. However, it is now widely acknowledged that some artificially introduced populations of waterbirds can have a negative impact on native populations of other species. The accidental introduction of the North American Ruddy Duck *Oxyura jamaicensis* into the wild in Europe and the threat which this is now posing to the already globally threatened White-headed Duck *Oxyura leucocephala* has been well documented. It has therefore been proposed that future editions of *Waterbird Population Estimates* will include established populations of non-native waterbirds, so that their status can be monitored more closely. Established populations of non-native species could be defined as those populations that have been self-supporting in the wild state for at least 10–15 generations, to exclude those frequent but unsuccessful breeding attempts by recent escapes from captivity. All participants in the International Waterbird Census are encouraged to submit counts of non-native waterbirds, and contributors to the fourth edition of *Waterbird Population Estimates* will be requested to provide estimates for these populations. For such populations, however, 1% thresholds will not be published, since the Ramsar Convention has indicated (Resolution VII II) that such non-native species should not be used as part of a supporting case for classification of a wetland of international importance.

What is a waterbird population?

For a full and detailed discussion of this question, readers are referred to the introductory chapters of the *Atlas of Anatidae Populations in Africa and Western Eurasia* (Scott and Rose 1996; see: http://www.wetlands.org/IWC/wpal&swa/atlas/AEAatlas.htm) A waterbird population can be defined as a distinct assemblage of individuals which does not experience significant emigration or immigration. This definition can only be fulfilled if the interchange of individuals between populations remains at a low level. The degree to which exchange of individuals occurs will determine gene flow and hence the justification for recognising subspecies or merely populations.

Given the current information available for waterbirds, it is rarely possible to define ideal populations. There is often overlap of populations at some stage of the annual cycle, and it is even possible for populations to mix yet maintain independence through behavioural isolating mechanisms. Many species have a limited geographical range and can be considered as one population, while others have a cosmopolitan distribution making the consideration of one population inappropriate for conservation and management purposes. For these species, biogeographical units have to be defined taking into consideration all aspects of biology and the practicalities of conserving the populations. In these cases it is often beneficial to use a particular geographic region for more than one species (e.g. East Asia/Australasia, Northwest Europe, Southern Africa). To date, the term 'flyway' has most commonly been used to describe zones common to many species, based on the approximate separation of populations. Within this publication, biogeographical populations have been defined, as far as possible, on the basis of the biology of each species, although it has been necessary to present data using traditional 'flyway' boundaries where more precise information is lacking.

For sedentary species it becomes more difficult to apply the definitions suggested for populations. It is often possible to demonstrate that the dynamics of almost every population fragment are relatively independent of each other. This is especially true for sedentary island populations. In such situations, these smaller populations are best considered as part of a more extensive meta-population. The alternative is to treat every sedentary species as one population which is often equally difficult to justify. In the absence of practical guidelines or principles for defining populations of sedentary species, decisions have been made according to subspecific divisions (usually following del Hoyo *et al.* 1992 and 1996) and with respect to practical implementation of the 1% thresholds. Some anomalies still occur in the treatment of sedentary waterbird species in this publication because of differences between species in morphological variation and consequent taxonomic treatment. For example, the Striated Heron *Butorides striatus* is a sedentary species that exhibits a high degree of morphological variation over its very wide range. Over 30 subspecies have been described, and 23 of these are widely recognised. In this case, estimates (where available) have been provided for each distinct subspecies in line with current taxonomic understanding.

How to use this book

Data presentation

In order to avoid misinterpretation of the tables, we strongly recommend that the following section on data presentation is read thoroughly before the tables are consulted. The results for each waterbird family are presented in the tables. The nature of this publication requires that a great deal of information is presented in a limited amount of space. Despite the care taken to present the data in a way that minimises the possibilities for misinterpretation, some important general clarifications are necessary. The greatest problems are likely to be encountered in determining the geographical limits of a population from the necessarily very concise range descriptions given in the tables.

The data in each column of the tables are presented in a standardised way wherever possible. This process is described for each data category (column) of the tables in the following subsections. Throughout the tables, a primary source reference has been given for each population estimate and trend. Whenever the estimate or trend has been derived from two or more sources, codes for all sources are given and an explanation is given in the Notes column.

Table headers

The Table headers include the scientific and English names of each species. A colour-coding system is used to indicate the threat status of each species, as follows:

Blue header – Species not known to have unfavourable conservation status

Red header – Globally threatened species. IUCN threat status appears after the scientific name, using the following codes:
CR   Critically Endangered
EN   Endangered
VU   Vulnerable

Orange header – Threatened Species considered to be at lower risk of extinction. IUCN threat status appears after the scientific name, using the following codes:
CD   Conservation Dependent
NT   Near Threatened
LC   Least Concern
Also included under orange headers are species in the following IUCN threat category:
DD   Data Deficient

Black header – Extinct species.

For details of the threat status categories, readers are referred to Hilton-Taylor (2000) and BirdLife International (2000).

Maps

Global distribution maps at species level from *Handbook of the Birds of the World*, Volumes 1 and 3 (del Hoyo *et al.* 1992, 1996) have been generously provided by the publisher, Lynx Edicions. The purpose of the maps is to illustrate the geographical range occupied by each species, although the small size of the maps does not allow extreme precision. The maps show the natural range of each species and do not include populations that have been introduced outside their natural range. There are two exceptions to this: Canada Goose *Branta canadensis* and Black Swan *Cygnus atratus.* Three colours are used on the maps: yellow represents the geographical area normally used by the species for breeding, blue represents the geographical area used ouside the breeding season, and green indicates areas where the species is present all year round. Arrows are used to prevent small areas isolated from the main range (especially small islands) passing unnoticed. A few of the species do not have their own maps because of occasional differences in taxonomic approach between *Waterbird Population Estimates* and *Handbook of the Birds of the World.* These species usually have their ranges included on the map of the preceding species, and information in the Notes column gives details of the difference in taxonomic approach. A small number of waterbird species have been discovered and described since publication of *Handbook of the Birds of the World*, and for these it has not been possible to provide maps.

Scientific names

The sequence of families and the treatment at species level follow the *Handbook of the Birds of the World* (del Hoyo *et al.* 1992, 1996) except for two families. Treatment of the grebes follows the sequence preferred by the Grebe Specialist Group (O'Donnell & Fjeldså 1995). Nomenclature and population analysis of the herons follow the approaches of the Heron Specialist Group *Action Plan for Herons of the World* (Hafner *et al.* in prep. 2002) which incorporated recent advances in heron taxonomy and phylogeny, especially recent molecular studies (McCracken and Sheldon, 2002).

English names

English vernacular names are given for all species and some distinctive subspecies, *e.g.* the Bewick's Swan *Cygnus columbianus bewickii*. These names follow the *Handbook of the Birds of the World* (del Hoyo *et al.* 1992, 1996), with the addition, in many cases, of alternative names that are still in common usage over much of the species' range. When the English name in common usage in North America differs from that used in the Old

World, both names are given. Alternative names are separated from the preferred name by a comma.

Subspecies and population

The subspecies and population column contains the name of the subspecies concerned and/or a brief geographical description to separate the population from other populations of the same subspecies (or other populations of a monotypic species). The primary source for treatment of species at subspecific level has been the *Handbook of the Birds of the World* (del Hoyo *et al.* 1992, 1996). However, the treatment of the grebes follows O'Donnell & Fjeldså 1995, and the herons follow Hafner *et al.* in prep (see above). Some additional subspecies that are recognised by other sources but not listed in the *Handbook of the Birds of the World* have been included in brackets, as have newly recognised subspecies. Subspecies that are considered by most modern authorities to be invalid are omitted. Populations that have been identified primarily on the basis of their breeding ranges have been identified with the suffix (br); those identified primarily on the basis of their non-breeding ('wintering') ranges with the suffix (non-br).

Breeding range and non-breeding range

Two columns define the main breeding range and core non-breeding ('wintering') range of every recognised population of a species or subspecies. Many migratory species, especially the long-distance migrants, stray far outside their normal ranges. The occurrence of these vagrants has not been taken into account in the range descriptions, which are intended to indicate where the great bulk of the population occurs during its normal annual cycle. In the case of sedentary species, a single entry in the Breeding range column describes the overall range of the population concerned.

It will be noticed that in many cases there is considerable similarity between the breeding ranges or non-breeding ranges of two or more populations of the same species. In some cases, this is because of a genuine overlap in the distribution of the populations. Thus, many populations defined on the basis of their breeding ranges are known to mix extensively with other populations of the same species in their non-breeding ('wintering') range, while many populations defined on the basis of their non-breeding ranges are known to overlap extensively with other populations on their breeding grounds. In many other cases, however, the main reason for an apparent similarity in ranges during the non-breeding season is uncertainty as to the limits of the non-breeding range of a particular population within the non-breeding range of the species or subspecies as a whole. In these cases, the non-breeding range is given only in very general terms, and will need refining as further information becomes available.

The larger geographical regions most commonly used to describe the ranges of populations in the range description columns are listed below alongside the range states that they usually encompass. This list does not attempt to conform to any other definitions of these regions, and the groupings of states have been defined with no purpose other than to describe the boundaries of waterbird populations. Furthermore, these groupings are intended only as a guideline to the countries in which the population in question may occur. Depending on the species concerned, a minority of countries might be excluded from each region, or one or more additional countries might be added. In most cases, the geographical division of populations is discussed more fully in the source references.

North Africa – Algeria, Egypt, Libyan Arab Jamahiriya, Morocco, Tunisia.

West Africa – Benin, Burkina Faso, Cameroon, Cape Verde, Chad, Côte d'Ivoire, The Gambia, Ghana, Guinea, Guinea-Bissau, Liberia, Mali, Mauritania, Niger, Nigeria, Senegal, Sierra Leone, Togo.

Eastern Africa – Burundi, Djibouti, Eritrea, Ethiopia, Kenya, Rwanda, Somalia, Sudan, Uganda, United Republic of Tanzania.

North-east Africa – Djibouti, Egypt, Eritrea, Ethiopia, Somalia, Sudan.

Southern Africa – Angola, Botswana, Lesotho, Madagascar, Malawi, Mozambique, Namibia, South Africa, Swaziland, Zambia, Zimbabwe.

Central Africa – Cameroon, Central African Republic, Congo, Democratic Republic of Congo, Equatorial Guinea, Gabon, Sao Tome and Principe.

Sub-Saharan Africa – All African states excluding North Africa, as defined above.

Tropical Africa – Sub-Saharan Africa excluding Lesotho, Namibia, South Africa and Swaziland.

North-west Europe – Belgium, Denmark, Finland, France, Germany, Iceland, Ireland, Luxembourg, The Netherlands, Norway, Sweden, Switzerland, United Kingdom of Great Britain and Northern Ireland.

North-east Europe – The northern part of the Russian Federation west of the Urals.

Central Europe – Austria, Czech Republic, Estonia, Germany, Hungary, Latvia, Liechtenstein, Lithuania, Poland, the Russian Federation around the Gulf of Finland and Kaliningrad, Slovakia, Switzerland.

Eastern Europe – Belarus, the Russian Federation west of the Urals, Ukraine.

Western Siberia – The Russian Federation from the Urals to the Yenisey River and south to the Kazakhstan border.

Central Siberia – The Russian Federation from the Yenisey River to the Lena River and south to the Altai Mountains.

West Mediterranean – Algeria, France, Italy, Malta, Monaco, Morocco, Portugal, Spain, Tunisia.

East Mediterranean – Albania, Bosnia and Herzegovina, Croatia, Cyprus, Egypt, Greece, Israel, Lebanon, Libyan Arab Jamahiriya, Slovenia, Syrian Arab Republic, the former Yugoslav Republic of Macedonia, Turkey, Yugoslavia.

Black Sea – Armenia, Bulgaria, Georgia, Republic of Moldova, Romania, Russian Federation, Turkey, Ukraine.

Caspian – Azerbaijan, Islamic Republic of Iran, Kazakhstan, Russian Federation, Turkmenistan, Uzbekistan.

South-west Asia – Bahrain, Islamic Republic of Iran, Iraq, Israel, Jordan, Kazakhstan, Kuwait, Lebanon, Oman, Qatar, Saudi Arabia, Syrian Arab Republic, eastern Turkey, Turkmenistan, United Arab Emirates, Uzbekistan, Yemen.

Western Asia – The western part of the Russian Federation east of the Urals and the states bordering on the Caspian Sea.

Central Asia – Afghanistan, Kazakhstan, Kyrgyzstan, Tajikistan, Turkmenistan, Uzbekistan.

South Asia – Bangladesh, Bhutan, India, Maldives, Nepal, Pakistan, Sri Lanka.

Eastern Asia – China (Mainland and Taiwan Island), Democratic People's Republic of Korea, Japan, Mongolia, Republic of Korea, Russian Federation from the eastern edge of the Taimyr to the Sea of Okhotsk and the Bering Sea.

South-east Asia – Brunei Darussalam, Cambodia, Indonesia, Lao People's Democratic Republic, Malaysia, Myanmar, the Philippines, Singapore, Thailand, Vietnam.

Australasia – Australia, New Zealand, New Guinea and outlying islands, Solomon Islands.

Oceania – Australasia (as defined above) and Pacific island states and dependencies including Hawaii.

North America – Canada, Greenland, Mexico, United States of America.

Central America – Belize, Costa Rica, El Salvador, Guatemala, Honduras, Nicaragua, Panama.

South America – All states of the South American continent, Falklands/Malvinas, Netherlands Antilles, Trinidad and Tobago.

Caribbean – Caribbean island states and dependencies (excluding Netherlands Antilles and Trinidad and Tobago).

NW South America – Bolivia, north-western Brazil, Colombia, Ecuador, Peru, Venezuela.

NE South America – North-eastern Brazil, French Guiana, Guyana, Suriname, Venezuela.

Southern South America – Argentina, southern Brazil, Chile, Paraguay, Uruguay.

Neotropics – South American states, Caribbean island states and dependencies, Central American states.

The division of species into populations should not be regarded as definitive. When a population is defined and an estimate given, we consider the population to be a valid unit for the species concerned. The consequences of this approach will be that populations might be split into smaller geographical units in future editions of *Waterbird Population Estimates*, but would be less likely to be merged into larger units.

Ramsar regions

Columns following the range description indicate the distribution of each species, subspecies or population within the six administrative regions of the Ramsar Convention. These regions are as follows: Africa, Europe, Asia, Oceania, Neotropics and North America. For the purposes of this publication, Asia is taken to include the Philippines and Indonesia east to, and including, the Lesser Sundas. Oceania, the Neotropics and North America are defined as in the preceding section.

Population size

Estimate
All estimates refer to the total number of individuals in the population, including immature birds, and are the most recent estimates available. In most cases, the estimates given in the tables are taken directly from the source references. However, all estimates have been rounded to a maximum of three significant figures, and rough estimates, particularly those given as a broad range, have been rounded to two significant figures.

Most population estimates included in this publication have been derived from censuses made towards the end of the non-breeding season or from estimations of breeding pairs. Waterbird populations tend to be at their lowest and most stable at these times. Individual numbers usually peak after the breeding season due to first year recruitment and suffer high and variable mortality over the non-breeding season making these times unsuitable for population estimation. To allow for the element of immature birds in each population, estimates given by original sources in the form of number of breeding pairs were multiplied by three to give the total population size, as suggested by Meininger *et al.* (1995). Estimates given in the form of breeding adults or mature individuals (*i.e.* twice the number of breeding pairs) have been multiplied by a factor of 1.5. There is no intentional overlap between the populations of a species, and therefore all estimates for the populations of a species can be added to produce a species total.

The population estimates are presented in one of four ways:

i.   **Blank** indicates no information available or widely conflicting sources of data.

ii. **Coded Ranges** are used when only best-guess information is available rather than census data, or where census data or published information imply no greater accuracy than a coded range. The coded ranges are as follows:
A   <10,000
B   10,000–25,000
C   25,000–100,000
D   100,000–1,000,000
E   >1,000,000

iii. **Numerical Ranges** are given when stated in the source reference or to cover the variation implied by two similar estimates. In a few cases, numerical ranges have been replaced by coded ranges when the upper and lower limits are equal to or exceed the coded ranges given above.

iv. **Precise Estimates** are given if stated in the source.

When two widely differing estimates exist for the same population and it is unclear which is the more reliable, either no estimate has been given, or the maximum and mimimum of the two estimates have been combined to give a broad range.

The tables in the first two editions of *Waterfowl Population Estimates* included a column headed 'Type', in which each population estimate was very simply assessed in terms of its reliability through three codes:

1. Well justified and published source reference for the information.
2. Summary publication of data from a variety of sources, or an assimilation of various source references undertaken for this publication.
3. Best-guess type of estimate, often based on only very small amounts of data.

There is much overlap between these categories, especially between types 1 and 3, as many of the well justified, published estimates are little more than informed guesses. Furthermore, estimates of type 2 could be extremely precise estimates, based on several complementary published sources, or simply best-guess type estimates. Given these flaws, this system of qualifying estimates is now thought to be of little value and has been dropped from the present edition. Clearly, however, there would be

value in providing a clear indication of the reliability of each estimate, and it is intended that a more useful system will be developed for presentation in the fourth edition of this work.

Source
The source reference for trends is coded by a two symbol alphanumeric code corresponding to the codes given to the left of the references listed in the References section at the end of the book. In cases where numerous sources have been used to calculate the estimate, all sources are given, and explanation is provided in the Notes column.

Population status

Trend
As an additional indication of the conservation status of each population, an indication of the recent trend in the population is given. This is expressed very simply by one of the following five categories:
STA   Stable
DEC   Decreasing
INC   Increasing
FLU   Fluctuating
EXT   Extinct

Uncertainty is expressed with a question mark. A blank in the column indicates that no definitive information is available.

It has not been possible to standardise the time base for the trend. Instead, the trend stated in the source has been used regardless of the time base. The most recent trend has been chosen if more than one is available. There are also no recommended standards regarding the magnitude of change necessary before a population trend can be stated as increasing or decreasing. An effort will be made in future editions to standardise the assessment of trends as far as possible, but this will always be problematical because of the differences in the ecology of the species being considered, and the inherent effect this variation has on the most sensible time-base for assessing population trends. Generation length will in future be an important parameter to include in the time-basis for assessing population trends.

Source
The source reference for trends is coded by a two symbol alphanumeric code corresponding to the codes given to the left of references in the References section at the end of the book.

One percent thresholds for use in Ramsar Convention Criterion 6

The "1% level" column gives the 1% thresholds to be used in the application of the Ramsar Convention Criterion 6. For virtually all estimates given as a single figure or numerical range, the 1% threshold is equal to 1% of the estimate or 1% of the mid-point of the range. 1% thresholds based on population estimates that have not changed since the second edition of *Waterfowl Population Estimates* have been retained in exactly the form in which they appeared in that publication. However, all new 1% thresholds have been rounded according to the following standard:

1% thresholds between 1 and 10	:	rounded to nearest 1
1% thresholds between 11 and 100	:	rounded to nearest 5
1% thresholds between 101 and 1,000	:	rounded to nearest 10
1% thresholds over 1,000	:	rounded to nearest 100

In a very few cases, the 1% threshold presented in the tables differs from the calculated value, reflecting an expert judgement that the most recent population estimate may no longer be valid. In all such cases, the discrepancy is explained in the Notes column. For all populations of 2,000,000 or more individuals, the 1% threshold is set at 20,000, as all sites which regularly hold 20,000 or more waterbirds of any species qualify as wetlands of international importance under Ramsar Criterion 5.

In the first two editions of *Waterfowl Population Estimates*, no attempt was made to set 1% thresholds on the basis of estimates given in the form of a coded range. Certainly, a 1% threshold set on the basis of the mid-point of such broad and poorly known ranges would be unsafe. For example, a 1% threshold based on the mid-point of a range D estimate (100,000–1,000,000) could be as much as 45% below the true value. However, a 1% threshold based on the top end of a coded range would constitute a maximum value, and would be safe to use in the identification of wetlands of international importance. While such a provisional 1% threshold might be expected to change as better information becomes available, it would only be likely to come down. The provisional 1% thresholds set on the basis of coded ranges are as follows:

A (<10,000)	:	1% threshold	100
B (10,000–25,000)	:		250
C (25,000–100,000)	:		1,000
D (100,000–1,000,000)	:		10,000
A/B (<25,000)	:		250
B/C (10,000–100,000)	:		1,000

No 1% thresholds have been set on the basis of coded ranges C/D (25,000–1,000,000), D/E (100,000–>1,000,000) or E (>1,000,000) because of the considerable uncertainty in these estimates. Obviously, however, the maximum 1% threshold of 20,000 could be applied to all populations with estimates of this type, and indeed to all those populations for which no estimate is available.

Notes

The final column in the tables contains a variety of short notes to explain possible sources of confusion and to provide additional information on taxonomy. The two symbol alphanumeric codes which appear in the notes column are the same as those used in the "source" columns, and correspond to the codes used to identify references and sources at the end of the book. In many cases, this column has been used to explain the derivation of a population estimate when the estimate given in the tables differs in form from that in the source reference (*i.e.* is given as individuals in the table rather than as breeding pairs or mature adults in the source reference), or when the estimate has been derived from a combination of information from two or more sources. This column has also been used to draw attention to those 1% thresholds set at 20,000 for populations with more than 2,000,000 individuals, *i.e.* those populations to which Ramsar Criterion 5 applies.

Globally threatened and near-threatened species

All globally threatened species, as listed in *Threatened Birds of the World* (BirdLife International 2000), are highlighted by the use of a red header in the table and all near-threatened species by the use of orange. Obviously, all populations of a globally threatened (or near-threatened) species are themselves globally threatened (or near-threatened). However, if globally-threatened status were to be assessed at subspecies or even population level, many more populations would be identified as being at risk. It has not as yet been possible to apply such an assessment to all the subspecies, or the 2,271 populations of waterbirds now included in *Waterbird Population Estimates*, but it is hoped that this can be be given priority in future.

Abbreviations used in the tables

Abbreviations used in the range descriptions in Columns 3, 4 and 5 include the following:

AWC	Asian Waterbird Census		NW	North-western
BBS	Breeding Bird Survey		NWC	Neotropical Waterbird Census
br	Breeding		non-br	Non-breeding
C	Central		S	Southern
CWS	Canadian Wildlife Service		SE	South-eastern
E	Eastern		SW	South-western
IBA	Important Bird Area		UK	United Kingdom
IWC	International Waterbird Census		USA	United States of America
Is	Island(s)		USFWS	United States Fish & Wildlife Service
N	Northern			
NE	North-eastern		W	Western

Discussion and conclusions

Number of species and populations

This edition summarises waterbird populations of 868 species compared with only 840 in the second edition and 833 in the first edition. The principal reason for this increase in the number of species considered is the inclusion of all waterbird species which have become extinct since the year 1600, and a second reason is the inclusion of a small number of recent taxonomic splits. A total of 2,271 biogeographic populations are now recognised, compared with only 1,924 in the second edition and 1,824 in the first. The increase in the present edition is largely due to the inclusion of all subspecies of Rallidae (many of which were omitted from the first two editions) and also to further sub-divisions of some populations.

Population estimates are presented for 1,725 of the 2,271 populations, a total of 76%. This compares with 1,342 of the 1924 populations (70%) presented in the second edition. Population trends are presented for 1,138 of the 2,271 populations, a total of 50%. This compares with 792 of the 1924 populations (41%) presented in the second edition. Many of the estimates presented consist of ranges, which makes presentation of simple summaries of numbers difficult. Summing the estimates is itself of limited value because the highest proportion of unknown populations are probably the largest ones. The sum of all the populations presented in the tables has a range from 350 million to 980 million birds, and a geometric mean of just over 500 million.

Summary of population estimates by Ramsar region

Figure 1 is a summary of waterbird population sizes in each of the world's six Ramsar regions. The equivalent population size distributions presented in the second edition (Rose & Scott 1997) are also shown for comparison. The information is also presented in Table 1. In the Europe Ramsar Region, direct comparison is not possible because of a change in the recognised Ramsar regions between 1997 and 2002: East and West Europe were formerly considered separately. The graph presents these two regions separately for 1997.

Table 1 shows that the largest number of waterbird populations (697) is found in Asia, followed by Africa (611) and the Neotropics (540). Fewer waterbird populations are found in Oceania (379), Europe (346) and North America (344). These totals reflect the biogeography of the regions, with the tropics supporting greater biodiversity, and also the land area of the different regions, with Oceania, despite its extension into the tropics, having a disproportionately small land area, and a relatively small extent of permanent wetlands.

The best-known populations occur in Europe, where estimates are now available for 97% of populations, and Africa (91%). These are followed by North America (81%), Asia (79%) Oceania (66%) and the Neotropics (59%). The high proportion of populations in Africa for which estimates are now available reflects the attention given to waterbirds on the continent by Wetlands International and BirdLife International in the 1990s, with a publication prepared in 2002 providing a detailed summary of the state of knowledge of every waterbird population in Africa (Dodman, in review). It should be borne in mind that the quality of estimates in the different regions is just as variable as their quantity, and in Africa, for example, a relatively high proportion of the new estimates are imprecise, covering broad ranges. Such estimates provide a valuable starting point in the population estimation process. Work stimulated by the African-Eurasian Migratory Waterbird Agreement (AEWA) will ensure an increasingly sound basis for the conservation of

Table 1. Waterbird population sizes in the six Ramsar regions (the "%" columns give percentage of populations of known size).

Ramsar region	Total of population lacking estimate No.	%	Number of populations in each size category (Population sizes as number of individuals) <10,001 No.	%	10,001–25,000 No.	%	25,001–100,000 No.	%	100,001–1,000,000 No.	%	>1,000,000 No.	%	Total of populations with known size No.	%	Total number of populations
Africa	52	9	183	33	61	11	148	26	140	25	38	7	559	91	611
Europe	12	3	36	11	41	12	106	32	120	36	46	14	334	97	346
Asia	145	21	132	24	57	10	179	32	174	32	35	6	552	79	697
Oceania	129	34	135	54	23	9	41	16	47	19	9	4	250	66	379
Neotropics	221	41	102	32	33	10	76	24	85	27	32	10	319	59	540
North America	64	19	51	18	31	11	51	18	122	44	36	13	280	81	344
Global Total	**546**	**24**	**591**	**34**	**184**	**11**	**432**	**25**	**457**	**26**	**114**	**7**	**1,725**	**76**	**2,271**

Global totals do not equal the sum of the respective columns because a population is often distributed in more than one Ramsar region.

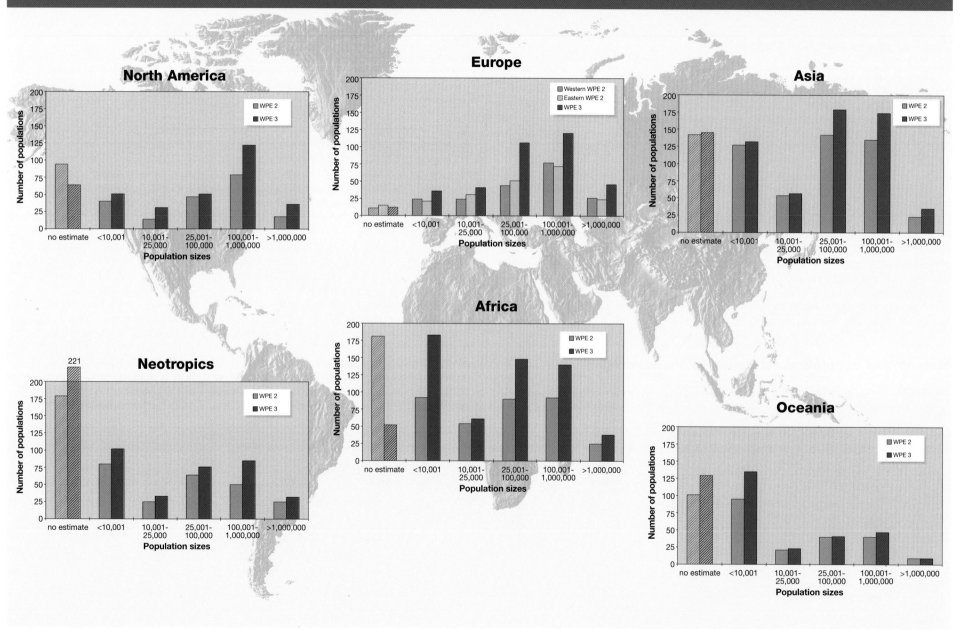

Figure 1. Waterbird population sizes in the six Ramsar regions – second and third editions of *Waterbird Population Estimates* compared.

Figure 2. Waterbird population trends in the six Ramsar regions.

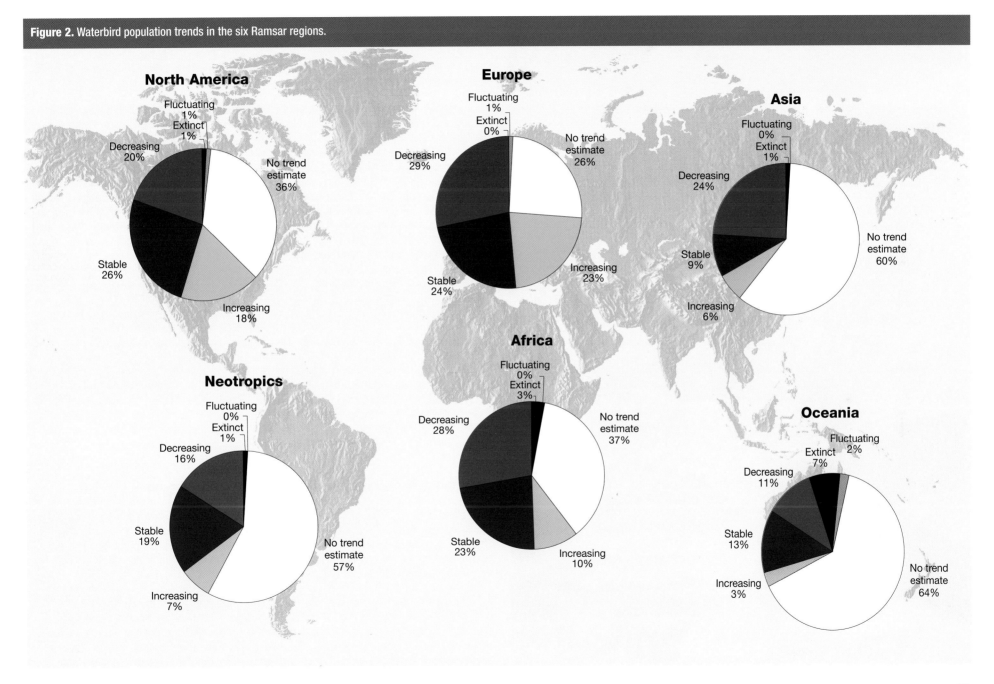

Bar-tailed Godwits, Terek Sandpipers, Wandering Tattlers and a Ruddy Turnstone, Roebuck Bay, Australia. Gerard Boere

waterbird populations in this region. The Asia-Pacific Migratory Waterbird Conservation Strategy (Asia-Pacific Migratory Waterbird Conservation Committee, 2001) is covering similar ground, and it is to be hoped that a similar approach can be adopted in the New World to improve the conservation of waterbirds in the region where they are least well known of all: the Neotropics.

The graphs in Figure 1 illustrate the state of knowledge in the different regions described above, and compare the findings of this third edition of Waterbird Population Estimates with the second edition published in 1997. The most noteworthy change over this 5 year period has been the considerable decrease in the number of populations in Africa for which no information was available in 2002 compared with 1997. The number of populations for which no estimates are available also decreased over this period in North America, and slightly, in Europe. The number of populations for which no information is available in Asia, Oceania and the Neotropics actually increased between 1997and 2002. This is largely explained by the complete coverage in this third edition of the large and little-known waterbird family the Rallidae, which has a high proportion of unknown populations, especially in the tropics and on islands.

The frequency of occurrence of populations of different size ranges in every region shows small numbers of populations in the low and high categories (ranges 10,001–25,000, and >1,000,000) and relatively high numbers of populations in the intervening categories (25,001–100,000 and 100,001–1,000,000). The exception to this distribution is that in all regions except Europe, a disproportionately high proportion of populations fall in the lowest range (<10,001). This is partly explained by the fact that the small populations have the highest priority for conservation action. The small populations are therefore usually the best known populations, and the recent summary of knowledge of all the world's threatened bird species in one publication (BirdLife International 2000) has allowed ready access to this information. The particulary high proportion of small populations in the tropical regions, which have the highest overall biodiversity, is to be expected, as is the highest proportion of all in Oceania, with its many specialised island forms.

Summary of population trends by Ramsar region

Figure 2 is a summary on pie charts of the proportion of waterbird populations in each of the world's six Ramsar regions exhibiting the following population trends: Increasing, Stable, Decreasing, Extinct, and Fluctuating. The (relatively high) proportion of populations for which this population trend information is lacking is also shown. This information is also presented in Table 2.

Table 2 shows that the highest proportion of waterbird population trends have been estimated in Europe (257, 74% of those in the region), followed by North America (220, 64%) and Africa (384, 63%). A smaller proportion of waterbird population trends have been estimated in the Neotropics (234, 43%), Asia, (279, 40%) and Oceania (138, 36%). These totals reflect the state of knowledge of waterbird demography in the different regions.

Table 2. Waterbird population trends in the six Ramsar regions (the "%" columns give percentage of populations with known trend).

Ramsar region	Total of population lacking trend		Number of populations in each trend category												Total of populations with known trends		Total number of populations
			Increasing		Stable		Decreasing		Extinct		Fluctuating						
	No.	%	No.	%	No.	%	No.	%	No.	%	No.	%			No.	%	
Africa	227	37	62	16	141	37	172	45	18[1]	5	3	1			384	63	611
Europe	89	26	81	32	83	32	100	39	0	0	2	1			257	74	346
Asia	418	60	44	16	65	23	164	59	6	2	1	0			279	40	697
Oceania	241	64	11	8	51	37	42	30	28	20	6	4			138	36	379
Neotropics	306	57	39	17	100	43	88	38	6	3	1	0			234	43	540
North America	124	36	62	28	88	40	68	31	2	1	2	1			220	64	344
Global Total	**1,133**	**50**	**216**	**19**	**404**	**36**	**461**	**41**	**60**	**5**	**12**	**1**			**1,138**	**50**	**2,271**

Global totals do not equal the sum of the respective columns because a population is often distributed in more than one Ramsar region.
1. Most extinctions in Africa have been on associated islands.

The relatively high proportion of populations lacking trend information make synthesis of this information difficult, and means that conclusions should be treated with caution. In particular, bias is introduced into the discussion by the fact that, as detailed above, more is known about small populations than large ones, and these small populations are perhaps more likely to be in decline. It is clear from Figure 2 that in every region, the proportion of known populations exhibiting a decreasing trend exceeds the proportion exhibiting an increasing trend. In Europe and North America, where data quality are best and where waterbird conservation policy is most advanced, the proportion of decreasing populations is only a little higher than the proportion which are increasing. In the Neotropics and Africa, more than twice as many known populations are decreasing than increasing, whilst in both Asia and Oceania, nearly four times as many known populations are decreasing than increasing. At global level, the fact that 41% of known populations are declining, 36% are stable and only 19% increasing gives considerable cause for concern and highlights the need for an increase in efforts to conserve these species.

Summary of population estimates by family

Table 3 gives a summary of the frequency distribution of population size categories in each of the world's 33 waterbird families.

Relatively well-known families, for which 90% or more of populations have population size estimates, are as follows: Podicipedidae, Scopidae, Ciconiidae, Balaenicipitidae, Phoenicopteridae, Anhimidae, Anatidae, Gruidae, Dromadidae, Haematopodidae, Recurvirostridae, Pedionomidae and Laridae.

Relatively poorly-known families, for which two-thirds or fewer of populations have population size estimates are as follows: Anhingidae, Aramidae, Rallidae, Eurypigidae, Rostratulidae, Ibidorhynchidae, Burhinidae and Thinocoridae.

Families with a high proportion (half or more) of estimated populations which are known to be small (10,000 or fewer) are as follows: Anhingidae, Ciconiidae, Balaenicipitidae, Threskiornithidae, Gruidae, Rallidae, Heliornithidae, Rostratulidae, Haematopodidae, Pedionomidae and Rynchopidae.

Summary of population trends by family

Table 4 gives a summary of the number and proportion of populations in each of the world's 33 waterbird families which are estimated to have Increasing, Stable, Decreasing or Fluctuating population trends, and the number of species in each family which are known to have become extinct since 1600.

Relatively well-known families, for which more than 70% of populations have population trend estimates available, are as follows: Pelecanidae, Anhingidae, Ciconiidae, Balaenicipitidae, Phoenicopteridae, Anhimidae, Anatidae, Gruidae, Dromadidae, Pedionomidae and Rynchopidae.

Relatively poorly known families, for which one third or fewer of populations have population trend estimates available, are as follows: Scopidae, Aramidae, Heliornithidae, Eurypigidae, Jacanidae, Rostratulidae, Ibidorhynchidae, Burhinidae, Glareolidae, Thinocoridae and Sternidae.

Table 3. Waterbird population sizes by family (the "%" columns give percentage of populations of known size).

| Family | Number of populations lacking estimate | | Number of populations in each size category (Population sizes as numbers of individuals) | | | | | | | | | | | Total of populations with known size | | Total number of populations |
| | No. | % | <10,001 | | 10,001–25,000 | | 25,001–100,000 | | 100,001–1,000,000 | | >1,000,000 | | No. | % | |
			No.	%	No.	%	No.	%	No.	%	No.	%			
Gaviidae	2	15	3	27	0	0	2	18	5	45	1	9	11	85	13
Podicipedidae	6	8	33	49	11	16	15	22	13	19	1	1	67	92	73
Pelecanidae	3	15	6	35	3	18	3	18	5	29	0	0	17	85	20
Phalacrocoracidae	10	13	21	31	9	13	17	25	19	28	3	4	67	87	77
Anhingidae	4	44	4	80	0	0	1	20	0	0	0	0	5	56	9
Ardeidae	99	38	65	40	13	8	39	24	47	29	5	3	162	62	261
Scopidae	0	0	0	0	1	33	1	33	1	33	0	0	3	100	3
Ciconiidae	3	8	21	58	4	11	6	17	5	14	0	0	36	92	39
Balaenicipitidae	0	0	1	100	0	0	0	0	0	0	0	0	1	100	1
Threskiornithidae	9	13	32	55	9	16	8	14	9	16	2	3	58	87	67
Phoenicopteridae	0	0	2	12	1	6	9	53	5	29	1	6	17	100	17
Anhimidae	0	0	1	33	0	0	1	33	1	33	0	0	3	100	3
Anatidae	26	6	116	27	44	10	105	24	143	33	43	10	436	94	462
Gruidae	2	4	31	66	4	9	11	23	2	4	0	0	47	96	49
Aramidae	3	75	0	0	0	0	0	0	0	0	1	100	1	25	4
Rallidae	221	63	87	66	4	3	11	8	17	13	12	9	131	37	352
Heliornithidae	1	14	3	50	0	0	2	33	1	17	0	0	6	86	7
Eurypygidae	3	100	0	0	0	0	0	0	0	0	0	0	0	0	3
Jacanidae	13	76	1	25	0	0	2	50	0	0	1	25	4	24	17
Rostratulidae	2	50	1	50	0	0	0	0	1	50	0	0	2	50	4
Dromadidae	0	0	0	0	0	0	1	100	0	0	0	0	1	100	1
Haematopodidae	1	5	11	55	3	15	4	20	2	10	1	5	20	95	21
Ibidorhynchidae	1	100	0	0	0	0	0	0	0	0	0	0	0	0	1
Recurvirostridae	2	8	3	13	3	13	9	39	8	35	0	0	23	92	25
Burhinidae	11	44	5	36	4	29	4	29	1	7	0	0	14	56	25
Glareolidae	13	28	10	30	6	18	12	36	5	15	0	0	33	72	46
Charadriidae	22	14	47	35	16	12	48	36	23	17	5	4	134	86	156
Scolopacidae	24	11	29	15	16	8	64	32	77	39	19	10	197	89	221
Pedionomidae	0	0	1	100	0	0	0	0	0	0	0	0	1	100	1
Thinocoridae	7	70	1	33	1	33	0	0	1	33	0	0	3	30	10
Laridae	9	9	13	14	9	10	24	26	40	43	11	12	94	91	103
Sternidae	48	28	39	31	23	18	31	25	26	21	8	6	125	72	173
Rynchopidae	1	14	4	67	0	0	2	33	0	0	0	0	6	86	7
Global Total	**546**	**24**	**591**	**34**	**184**	**11**	**432**	**25**	**457**	**26**	**114**	**7**	**1,725**	**76**	**2,271**

Table 4. Waterbird population trends by family (the "%" columns give percentage of populations with known trend).

Family	Number of populations lacking trend		Increasing		Stable		Decreasing		Extinct		Fluctuating		Total of populations with known trend		Total number of populations
	No.	%	No.	%	No.	%	No.	%	No.	%	No.	%	No.	%	
Gaviidae	8	62	0	0	2	40	4	80	0	0	0	0	5	38	13
Podicipedidae	35	48	9	24	17	45	12	32	3	8	0	0	38	52	73
Pelecanidae	5	25	5	33	5	33	5	33	0	0	0	0	15	75	20
Phalacrocoracidae	37	48	9	22	21	52	8	20	1	2	1	2	40	52	77
Anhingidae	2	22	0	0	2	29	5	71	0	0	0	0	7	78	9
Ardeidae	161	62	18	18	42	42	36	36	4	4	0	0	100	38	261
Scopidae	2	67	1	100	1	100	0	0	0	0	0	0	1	33	3
Ciconiidae	10	26	4	14	8	28	17	59	0	0	0	0	29	74	39
Balaenicipitidae	0	0	0	0	0	0	1	100	0	0	0	0	1	100	1
Threskiornithidae	27	40	4	10	16	40	19	48	2	5	1	2	40	60	67
Phoenicopteridae	0	0	6	35	8	47	3	18	0	0	0	0	17	100	17
Anhimidae	0	0	0	0	1	33	2	67	0	0	0	0	3	100	3
Anatidae	116	25	75	22	121	35	130	38	13	4	7	2	346	75	462
Gruidae	6	12	9	21	14	33	20	47	0	0	0	0	43	88	49
Aramidae	3	75	0	0	1	100	0	0	0	0	0	0	1	25	4
Rallidae	226	64	8	6	25	20	63	50	30	24	0	0	126	36	352
Heliornithidae	5	71	0	0	0	0	2	100	0	0	0	0	2	29	7
Eurypygidae	3	100	0	0	0	0	0	0	0	0	0	0	0	0	3
Jacanidae	13	76	0	0	2	50	2	50	0	0	0	0	4	24	17
Rostratulidae	3	75	0	0	0	0	1	100	0	0	0	0	1	25	4
Dromadidae	0	0	0	0	1	100	0	0	0	0	0	0	1	100	1
Haematopodidae	12	57	5	56	3	33	0	0	1	11	0	0	9	43	21
Ibidorhynchidae	1	100	0	0	0	0	0	0	0	0	0	0	0	0	1
Recurvirostridae	11	44	4	29	8	57	2	14	0	0	0	0	14	56	25
Burhinidae	20	80	0	0	0	0	5	100	0	0	0	0	5	20	25
Glareolidae	34	74	0	0	6	50	6	50	0	0	0	0	12	26	46
Charadriidae	95	61	12	20	18	30	31	51	1	2	0	0	61	39	156
Scolopacidae	115	52	12	11	43	41	51	48	5	5	0	0	106	48	221
Pedionomidae	0	0	0	0	0	0	1	100	0	0	0	0	1	100	1
Thinocoridae	10	100	0	0	0	0	0	0	0	0	0	0	0	0	10
Laridae	54	52	23	47	15	31	9	18	0	0	2	4	49	48	103
Sternidae	117	68	11	20	23	41	23	41	0	0	1	2	56	32	173
Rynchopidae	2	29	1	20	1	20	3	60	0	0	0	0	5	71	7
Global Total	**1,133**	**50**	**216**	**19**	**404**	**36**	**461**	**41**	**60**	**5**	**12**	**1**	**1,138**	**50**	**2,271**

19

Nine out of the 33 families include species which have become extinct since 1600; in order of the proportion of species in the family which have become extinct, these are: Rallidae, Haematopodidae, Podicipedidae, Threskiornithidae, Scolopacidae, Ardeidae, Anatidae, Charadriidae and Phalacrocoracidae.

Families with a high proportion (half or more) of estimated populations showing a decreasing trend are as follows: Gaviidae, Anhingidae, Ciconiidae, Balaenicipitidae, Anhimidae, Gruidae, Rallidae, Heliornithidae, Jacanidae, Rostratulidae, Burhinidae, Glareolidae, Charadriidae, Pedionomidae and Rynchopidae.

Future priorities

It is intended to update this publication every three years, in time for each meeting of the Conference of Contracting Parties to the Ramsar Convention.

Wetlands International is committed to increasing the effort it puts into waterbird monitoring, and to making the International Waterbird Census (IWC) a truly global programme. This will result in the collection of ever more data of ever improving quality from an ever increasing number of sites and countries. This activity will provide the basis for the long-term improvements we are seeking in the quantity and quality of waterbird population estimates.

This publication is already available for downloading from the World Wide Web, and it is hoped that in future, interactive web-based dissemination will be possible, so that users can query the Waterbird Population Estimates database to obtain the information that they need. The internet offers many possibilities for the dissemination of Waterbird Population Estimates data and information which will be explored in future planning.

Only when the limits of each population have been shown on a map will it be possible to determine with any certainty the full suite of range states that are included in each population. The provision of maps showing the limits of individual populations is clearly a priority for the future. A start has been made with addressing this priority by the publication of Flyway Atlases (e.g. Scott & Rose 1996, Miyabayashi & Mundkur 1999). At least one further Flyway Atlas is in preparation, covering waders (shorebirds) in Africa and western Eurasia and the production of similar atlases for additional species in this part of the world is identified as being important in the AEWA Implementation Priorities. The *Waterbird Population Estimates* project has a bright future on the internet, where digital formats have obvious advantages in the presentation of spatial data, which will further enhance its use for the identification of internationally important sites.

Cooperation with Wetlands International networks and partner organisations will continue, as will use of the internet to stimulate interest and contributions to the process of estimation of waterbird populations. There remain many gaps in information which future editions will gradually fill. Any reader with information or data which will facilitate this process is invited to contact the Wetlands International Wageningen office: post@wetlands.agro.nl

Waterbird Population Estimates, 2002

In order to avoid misinterpretation of the tables, we strongly recommend that the section on Data Presentation (page 8) is read thoroughly.

Snow Geese. Nancy Camel

GAVIIDAE DIVERS/LOONS

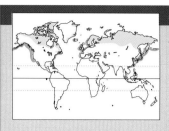

Gavia stellata — Red-throated Diver, Red-throated Loon

Subspecies/Population	Breeding range	Wintering, or core non-breeding range	Afr	Eu	Asia	Oc	Neo	NA	Estimate	Source	Trend	Source	1% level	Notes
NW Europe (non-br)	Arctic West Eurasia, Greenland	NW Europe		●					D	SA	DEC	KQ	10,000	BE: European breeding population 61,000–140,000 pairs (183,000–420,000 individuals).
Caspian, Black Sea, E Mediterranean (non-br)	Arctic Central Eurasia	Caspian, Black Sea, E Mediterranean		●	●									
E Asia (non-br)	Arctic East Asia	E Asia			●				B/C	YA			1,000	
North America	Arctic North America	Coastal North America						●	375,000	B4	DEC	B4	3,800	B4: Continental population estimated at 125,000 pairs (375,000 individuals). GZ: Alaskan breeding population 7,396–12,290 in early 1990s, a decline of nearly 50% since the 1970s.

Gavia arctica — Black-throated Diver, Arctic Loon

Subspecies/Population	Breeding range	Wintering, or core non-breeding range	Afr	Eu	Asia	Oc	Neo	NA	Estimate	Source	Trend	Source	1% level	Notes
arctica	N Europe & W Siberia	Coastal NW Europe, Mediterranean, Black & Caspian Seas		●	●				D	BE	DEC	HC	10,000	BE: European breeding population 120,000–230,000 pairs (360,000–690,000 individuals).
(suschkini)	W Siberia – E Central Asia	Caspian			●									
viridigularis	NE Asia E of Lena R, W Alaska	NW Pacific			●			●	C/D	PE				Fewer than 100 pairs (300 individuals) in Alaska (WC).

Gavia pacifica — Pacific Diver, Pacific Loon

Subspecies/Population	Breeding range	Wintering, or core non-breeding range	Afr	Eu	Asia	Oc	Neo	NA	Estimate	Source	Trend	Source	1% level	Notes
E Asia	Coastal NE Siberia	Coastal E Asia			●				C	PE			1,000	Often considered conspecific with G. arctica.
North America	Arctic North America	Pacific coast of North America						●	900,000–1,500,000	WC	STA	GZ	12,000	WC estimate Continental American population at 300,000–500,000 pairs (900,000–1,500,000 individuals).

Gavia immer — Great Northern Diver, Common Loon

Subspecies/Population	Breeding range	Wintering, or core non-breeding range	Afr	Eu	Asia	Oc	Neo	NA	Estimate	Source	Trend	Source	1% level	Notes
N Europe (non-br)	N America, Greenland, Iceland, Bear Island	Coastal NW Europe		●				●	5,000	LA			50	European breeding population (Greenland + Iceland) 500–2,300 pairs (1,500–6,900 individuals) (BE).
North America	N US, Canada and Alaska	Coastal regions, Great Lakes and Southern states						●	575,000	GZ EV S7	STA/DEC	M9	5,800	GZ: Alaskan breeding population 8,043–9,729 in early 1990s; Breeding population in lower 48 states c 20,000 (North American Loon Fund). Breeding population in Canada c.545,000 (EV + S7).

Gavia adamsii — White-billed Diver, Yellow-billed Loon

Subspecies/Population	Breeding range	Wintering, or core non-breeding range	Afr	Eu	Asia	Oc	Neo	NA	Estimate	Source	Trend	Source	1% level	Notes
Europe, Asia	Arctic Europe, Asia	Coastal NE Atlantic, NW Pacific		●	●				A	SR			100	BE: European breeding population 50–100 pairs (150–300 individuals).
North America	Arctic North America	NE Pacific						●	12,000–15,000	WC			140	WC estimate 4,000–5,000 pairs (12,000–15,000 individuals).

Rollandia rolland — White-tufted Grebe

Subspecies/Population	Breeding range	Wintering, or core non-breeding range	Afr	Eu	Asia	Oc	Neo	NA	Estimate	Source	Trend	Source	1% level	Notes
rolland	Falkland/Malvinas Is						●		2,250–4,200	WS			30	WS estimate 750–1,400 pairs (2,250–4,200 individuals).
chilensis	S South America	Coastal S South America					●		100,000	OF	STA	S8	1,000	
morrisoni	Peru, Bolivia						●		1,000	OF	DEC	OF	10	

Rollandia microptera — Titicaca Flightless Grebe, Short-winged Grebe

Subspecies/Population	Breeding range	Wintering, or core non-breeding range	Afr	Eu	Asia	Oc	Neo	NA	Estimate	Source	Trend	Source	1% level	Notes
Peru, Bolivia	SE Peru, W Bolivia, mainly L Titicaca						●		2,000–10,000	OF	DEC	OF BB	60	

Tachybaptus ruficollis — Little Grebe

Subspecies/Population	Breeding range	Wintering, or core non-breeding range	Afr	Eu	Asia	Oc	Neo	NA	Estimate	Source	Trend	Source	1% level	Notes
ruficollis	Europe E to Urals, NW Africa		●	●					230,000–450,000	BE	STA	BE	3,400	BE: European breeding population 77,000–150,000 pairs (231,000–450,000 individuals).
iraquensis	Iraq, SW Iran				●				6,000	OF			60	
capensis, Sub-Saharan Africa	Sub-Saharan Africa		●						C	OF			1,000	
capensis, SW, S Asia	SW, S Asia				●				D	DO	INC	DO	10,000	
poggei	E, SE Asia				●				D	CE	DEC	WI	10,000	WI: Decline in Japan of 50% in 20 years to 1990s. OF: Includes "kunikyonis" (Ryukyu Is).
philippensis	N Philippines				●									
cotabato	SE Philippines				●									
tricolor	E Indonesia, New Guinea				●									
vulcanorum	Java–Timor				●									Includes "javanicus" (Java).
collaris	NE New Guinea, Solomon Is					●			A	DX			100	DX: <100 estimated for New Guinea Islands+ Solomons; total population likely to be very small but numbers in NE New Guinea unknown.

Tachybaptus rufolavatus CR — Alaotra Grebe, Rusty Grebe

Subspecies/Population	Breeding range	Wintering, or core non-breeding range	Afr	Eu	Asia	Oc	Neo	NA	Estimate	Source	Trend	Source	1% level	Notes
Madagascar	N Central Madagascar		●						0–10	HK	DEC/EXT	HK	1	Sometimes treated as a subspecies of T.ruficollis.

Lac Alaotra, Madagascar.

H. Glyn Young

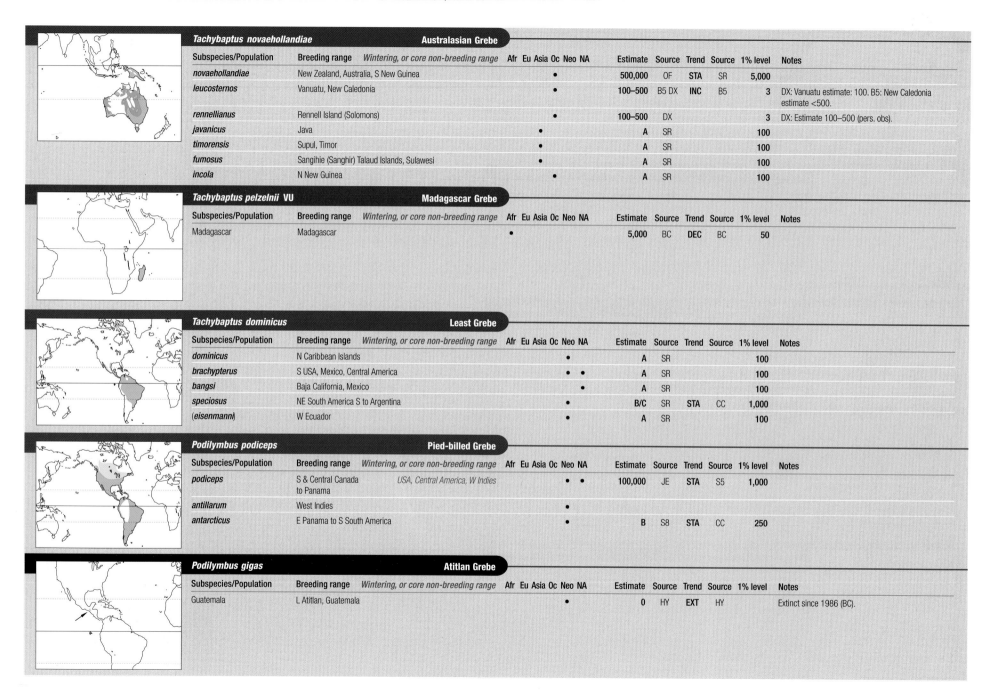

Tachybaptus novaehollandiae — Australasian Grebe

Subspecies/Population	Breeding range	Wintering, or core non-breeding range	Afr	Eu	Asia	Oc	Neo	NA	Estimate	Source	Trend	Source	1% level	Notes
novaehollandiae	New Zealand, Australia, S New Guinea					•			500,000	OF	STA	SR	5,000	
leucosternos	Vanuatu, New Caledonia					•			100–500	B5 DX	INC	B5	3	DX: Vanuatu estimate: 100. B5: New Caledonia estimate <500.
rennellianus	Rennell Island (Solomons)					•			100–500	DX			3	DX: Estimate 100–500 (pers. obs).
javanicus	Java				•				A	SR			100	
timorensis	Supul, Timor				•				A	SR			100	
fumosus	Sangihie (Sanghir) Talaud Islands, Sulawesi				•				A	SR			100	
incola	N New Guinea					•			A	SR			100	

Tachybaptus pelzelnii VU — Madagascar Grebe

Subspecies/Population	Breeding range	Wintering, or core non-breeding range	Afr	Eu	Asia	Oc	Neo	NA	Estimate	Source	Trend	Source	1% level	Notes
Madagascar	Madagascar		•						5,000	BC	DEC	BC	50	

Tachybaptus dominicus — Least Grebe

Subspecies/Population	Breeding range	Wintering, or core non-breeding range	Afr	Eu	Asia	Oc	Neo	NA	Estimate	Source	Trend	Source	1% level	Notes
dominicus	N Caribbean Islands							•	A	SR			100	
brachypterus	S USA, Mexico, Central America						•	•	A	SR			100	
bangsi	Baja California, Mexico							•	A	SR			100	
speciosus	NE South America S to Argentina						•		B/C	SR	STA	CC	1,000	
(eisenmanni)	W Ecuador						•		A	SR			100	

Podilymbus podiceps — Pied-billed Grebe

Subspecies/Population	Breeding range	Wintering, or core non-breeding range	Afr	Eu	Asia	Oc	Neo	NA	Estimate	Source	Trend	Source	1% level	Notes
podiceps	S & Central Canada to Panama	USA, Central America, W Indies					•	•	100,000	JE	STA	S5	1,000	
antillarum	West Indies						•							
antarcticus	E Panama to S South America						•		B	S8	STA	CC	250	

Podilymbus gigas — Atitlan Grebe

Subspecies/Population	Breeding range	Wintering, or core non-breeding range	Afr	Eu	Asia	Oc	Neo	NA	Estimate	Source	Trend	Source	1% level	Notes
Guatemala	L Atitlan, Guatemala						•		0	HY	EXT	HY		Extinct since 1986 (BC).

Poliocephalus poliocephalus — Hoary-headed Grebe

Subspecies/Population	Breeding range	Wintering, or core non-breeding range	Afr	Eu	Asia	Oc	Neo	NA	Estimate	Source	Trend	Source	1% level	Notes
Australia, New Zealand	Australia, S Island New Zealand					●			500,000	FH	STA	FH	5,000	Birds from mid-west & NW Australia have been assigned to *cloatesi* (Peters 1931).

Poliocephalus rufopectus VU — New Zealand Grebe

Subspecies/Population	Breeding range	Wintering, or core non-breeding range	Afr	Eu	Asia	Oc	Neo	NA	Estimate	Source	Trend	Source	1% level	Notes
New Zealand	N Island New Zealand					●			1,700–1,800	BC	DEC	BC	20	

Podiceps major — Great Grebe

Subspecies/Population	Breeding range	Wintering, or core non-breeding range	Afr	Eu	Asia	Oc	Neo	NA	Estimate	Source	Trend	Source	1% level	Notes
major, Brazil–C Chile	S Brazil–Central Chile & Central Argentina						●		B	S8			250	
major, Peru	Coastal Peru						●		<1,000	SR			10	
navasi	S Chile & S Argentina	Coastal S Chile & S Argentina					●		C	S8	STA	S8	1,000	

Podiceps grisegena — Red-necked Grebe

Subspecies/Population	Breeding range	Wintering, or core non-breeding range	Afr	Eu	Asia	Oc	Neo	NA	Estimate	Source	Trend	Source	1% level	Notes
grisegena, NW Europe (non-br)	E Europe	Coastal NW Europe		●					C	OF SA	STA	SA	1,000	BE: European breeding population 31,000–140,000 pairs (90,000–420,000 individuals).
grisegena, Black Sea, Mediterranean (non-br)	E Europe, W Asia	Black Sea, Mediterranean		●					C	OF SA	STA	BE	1,000	
grisegena, Caspian (non-br)	W Asia	Caspian		●	●				15,000	OF			150	
grisegena (*balchashensis*)	Probably Central Asia	S Asia			●				A	OF			100	
holboellii, E Asia	N E Asia	Coastal E Asia			●				C	PE			1,000	
holboellii, North America	N USA, Canada, Alaska	Pacific & Atlantic North America						●	45,000	JE			450	

Podiceps cristatus — Great Crested Grebe

Subspecies/Population	Breeding range	Wintering, or core non-breeding range	Afr	Eu	Asia	Oc	Neo	NA	Estimate	Source	Trend	Source	1% level	Notes
cristatus,	NW Europe			●					370,000–580,000	SA BE	INC	OF BE	4,800	BE: Breeding population in relevant countries 122,700–193,000 pairs (368,000–579,000 individuals).
cristatus, Black Sea, Mediterranean (non-br)	Central & E Europe	Black Sea, Mediterranean		●	●				D	SA	INC	HW	10,000	BE: At least 200,000 pairs (600,000 individuals) breed in C & E Europe.

Podiceps cristatus ... continued

Subspecies/Population	Breeding range	Wintering, or core non-breeding range	Afr	Eu	Asia	Oc	Neo	NA	Estimate	Source	Trend	Source	1% level	Notes
cristatus, Caspian Sea (non-br)	W Asia	*Caspian Sea*	●	●					10,000	OF			100	
cristatus, South Asia (non-br)	Central Asia	*S Asia*			●				B	PE	INC	PE	250	
cristatus, E Asia (non-br)	NE Asia	*E Asia*			●				25,000	OF			250	
infuscatus, E Africa	Eastern Africa: Ethiopia to N Zambia		●						<1,000	DH	DEC	OF	10	
infuscatus, S Africa	Southern Africa		●						A	SR	INC	DH	100	
"Southern Crested Grebe" *australis*, Australia	Australia					●			3,000–10,000	OF			65	Sometimes assigned to *christiani* (Peters, 1931).
australis, New Zealand	New Zealand					●			200–300	ON	DEC	ON	3	

Podiceps auritus — Slavonian Grebe, Horned Grebe

Subspecies/Population	Breeding range	Wintering, or core non-breeding range	Afr	Eu	Asia	Oc	Neo	NA	Estimate	Source	Trend	Source	1% level	Notes
auritus, NW Europe (large billed)	NW Europe	*Coastal NW Europe*		●					2,600–4,100	BE	STA	HC	35	BE: European breeding numbers (both populations 16,000–110,000 pairs (48,000–330,000 individuals).
auritus, NE Europe (small billed)	NE Europe	*Mediterranean, Black Sea*		●					C	HC SA	STA?	SA	1,000	
auritus, Caspian, S Asia (non-br)	E Europe, Central Asia	*Caspian, S Asia*		●	●				B	OF			250	
auritus, E Asia (non-br)	E Asia	*Coastal E Asia*			●				C	PE			1,000	
cornutus	N USA, Canada, Alaska	*Coastal North America*						●	D	OF JE			10,000	JE estimates >100,000.

Slavonian Grebe with young.

Johan Verbanck

Podiceps nigricollis — Black-necked Grebe, Eared Grebe

Subspecies/Population	Breeding range	Wintering, or core non-breeding range	Afr	Eu	Asia	Oc	Neo	NA	Estimate	Source	Trend	Source	1% level	Notes
nigricollis, Europe, N Africa	Europe	*S & W Europe to N & W Africa*	●	●					117,000–450,000	BE	STA/INC	BE	2,800	BE: European breeding population 39,000–150,000 pairs (117,000–450,000 individuals).
nigricollis, E Africa	Eastern Africa		●						B	DO	STA	DO	250	
nigricollis, SW & S Asia (non-br)	W & Central Asia	*SW, S Asia, Caspian, Persian Gulf*	●	●					25,000	PE	INC	PE	250	
nigricollis, E Asia (non-br)	E Asia	*Coastal E Asia*			●				B/C	PE			1,000	
gurneyi	Southern Africa		●						10,000–20,000	HF	INC	SA	150	
californicus	W & Central North America	*S North America, Pacific USA coast*						●	3,700,000	JE	STA	JE	20,000	KS estimate the "fall population" at 3,500,000–4,100,000 individuals. For populations over 2 million birds, Ramsar criterion 5 (20,000 or more waterbirds) applies.

Podiceps andinus — Colombian Grebe

Subspecies/Population	Breeding range	Wintering, or core non-breeding range	Afr	Eu	Asia	Oc	Neo	NA	Estimate	Source	Trend	Source	1% level	Notes
Colombia	Colombia						●		0	OF	EXT	OF		Last confirmed record in 1977 (BC)

Podiceps occipitalis — Silvery Grebe

Subspecies/Population	Breeding range	Wintering, or core non-breeding range	Afr	Eu	Asia	Oc	Neo	NA	Estimate	Source	Trend	Source	1% level	Notes
occipitalis, S South America	Central & S Chile & Argentina						●		100,000	OF	STA	OF	1,000	
occipitalis, Falkland/Malvinas Is	Falkland/Malvinas Is						●		1,500–2,700	WS			20	WS estimate 500–900 pairs (1,500–2,700 individuals).
juninensis	Andes of Colombia, N Chile, NW Argentina						●				DEC	OF		

Podiceps taczanowskii CR — Junin Grebe, Puna (Flightless) Grebe

Subspecies/Population	Breeding range	Wintering, or core non-breeding range	Afr	Eu	Asia	Oc	Neo	NA	Estimate	Source	Trend	Source	1% level	Notes
Peru	Lake Junin, Peru						●		50–250	BC	DEC	BC	2	

Podiceps gallardoi NT — Hooded Grebe

Subspecies/Population	Breeding range	Wintering, or core non-breeding range	Afr	Eu	Asia	Oc	Neo	NA	Estimate	Source	Trend	Source	1% level	Notes
Argentina & Chile	SW Santa Cruz province, Argentina	*Coastal Santa Cruz in Argentina and S Chile*					●		3,000–5,000	OF BC	STA	FG	40	

Aechmophorus occidentalis — Western Grebe

Subspecies/Population	Breeding range	Wintering, or core non-breeding range	Afr	Eu	Asia	Oc	Neo	NA	Estimate	Source	Trend	Source	1% level	Notes
occidentalis	Central W North America	*S & Pacific USA to Baja California*						●	>120,000	JE	DEC	S12	1,200	KS estimate breeding population of both subspecies combined at >110,000 adults (165,000 individuals).
ephemeralis	Central Mexico	*W coastal Mexico*						●	<10,000	SR			100	

Aechmophorus clarkii — Clark's Grebe

Subspecies/Population	Breeding range	Wintering, or core non-breeding range	Afr	Eu	Asia	Oc	Neo	NA	Estimate	Source	Trend	Source	1% level	Notes
clarkii	Central Mexico	*W coastal Mexico*						●	<1,000	SR			10	KS estimate population of both subspecies combined at 10,000–20,000 individuals.
transitionalis	W North America	*S & Pacific USA to Baja California*						●	10,000–20,000	JE			150	

PELECANIDAE PELICANS

Pelecanus onocrotalus — Great White Pelican

Subspecies/Population	Breeding range	Wintering, or core non-breeding range	Afr	Eu	Asia	Oc	Neo	NA	Estimate	Source	Trend	Source	1% level	Notes
W Africa	W Africa		●						60,000	DO	STA	DO	600	
Eastern Africa	Eastern Africa (Ethiopia to Zambia)		●						150,000	CT	STA	DO	1,500	
Southern Africa	Southern Africa S of the Zambezi River		●						20,000	TO	INC	TO	200	
Europe, W Asia (br)	E Europe, W Asia	NE Africa, SW Asia	●	●					20,100–32,900	CU	DEC	SR	270	CU estimate 6,703–10,964 breeding pairs (20,109–32,892 individuals).
South Asia (non-br)	W Central Asia	S Asia			●				15,000–30,000	KR			230	

Pelecanus rufescens — Pink-backed Pelican

Subspecies/Population	Breeding range	Wintering, or core non-breeding range	Afr	Eu	Asia	Oc	Neo	NA	Estimate	Source	Trend	Source	1% level	Notes
Africa	Tropical Africa & the Red Sea		●						50,000–100,000	DO	STA	SR	750	

Pelecanus philippensis VU — Spot-billed Pelican

Subspecies/Population	Breeding range	Wintering, or core non-breeding range	Afr	Eu	Asia	Oc	Neo	NA	Estimate	Source	Trend	Source	1% level	Notes
South Asia	NE & SE India, Sri Lanka	E India, Sri Lanka			●				2,500–5,000	BC	DEC	PE	40	
SE Asia	Cambodia	Cambodia, Laos, Vietnam, Thailand, S China?			●				3,000–5,000	BD	DEC	BD	40	
Sumatra	Sumatra				●				<25	HU	DEC	HU	1	

Pelecanus crispus CD — Dalmatian Pelican

Subspecies/Population	Breeding range	Wintering, or core non-breeding range	Afr	Eu	Asia	Oc	Neo	NA	Estimate	Source	Trend	Source	1% level	Notes
Black Sea, Mediterranean (non-br)	SE Europe	Black Sea, Mediterranean	●	●					2,300–3,200	CU	STA	CU	30	CU estimates summed from appropriate countries give 769–1,071 breeding pairs (2,307–3,213 individuals).
SW, S Asia (non-br)	SW, Central Asia	SW, S Asia			●				9,800–12,400	CU	STA	CU	110	CU estimates summed from appropriate countries give 3,265–4,125 breeding pairs (9,795–12,375 individuals).
E Asia	W Mongolia	S & E China			●				<130	MJ	DEC	MJ	1	MJ consider this population to be critically endangered.

Pelecanus conspicillatus — Australian Pelican

Subspecies/Population	Breeding range	Wintering, or core non-breeding range	Afr	Eu	Asia	Oc	Neo	NA	Estimate	Source	Trend	Source	1% level	Notes
Australia	Australia	Australia & New Guinea				●			D	RS			10,000	

Australian Pelicans (captive).

Marcel Silvius

Pelecanus erythrorhynchos — American White Pelican

Subspecies/Population	Breeding range	Wintering, or core non-breeding range	Afr	Eu	Asia	Oc	Neo	NA	Estimate	Source	Trend	Source	1% level	Notes
North America	Inland W & Central N America	Coastal N & Central America					●	●	>180,000	KS	INC	AN	1,800	KS estimate >120,000 breeding adults (180,000 individuals.

Pelecanus occidentalis — Brown Pelican

Subspecies/Population	Breeding range	Wintering, or core non-breeding range	Afr	Eu	Asia	Oc	Neo	NA	Estimate	Source	Trend	Source	1% level	Notes
occidentalis	Caribbean						●		290,000	KS			2,900	KS estimate (all North American breeding populations combined) 191,600–193,700 breeding adults (287,400–290,550).
carolinensis	Atlantic Coast of tropical Americas						●	●			INC	AN		
californicus	Pacific Coast California–Mexico						●	●			INC	AN		
murphyi	Coastal Colombia, N Peru						●							
urinator	Galapagos Islands						●		5,000	CX			50	

Pelecanus thagus — Peruvian Pelican

Subspecies/Population	Breeding range	Wintering, or core non-breeding range	Afr	Eu	Asia	Oc	Neo	NA	Estimate	Source	Trend	Source	1% level	Notes
Peru, Chile	Coastal Peru, Chile						●		D	S8	INC	S8	10,000	Sometimes treated as conspecific with occidentalis. Population increasing and range expanding.

Phalacrocorax auritus — Double-crested Cormorant

Subspecies/Population	Breeding range	Wintering, or core non-breeding range	Afr	Eu	Asia	Oc	Neo	NA	Estimate	Source	Trend	Source	1% level	Notes
auritus	NE & Central North America	Gulf of Mexico, Florida						●	943,000–1,890,000	HH	INC	S5	14,000	
cincinatus	NW North America							●	10,800–21,600	HH			160	
albociliatus	SW North America							●	90,000–179,000	HH	STA	S5	1,350	
floridanus	SE North America							●	37,000–73,000	HH	INC	S5	550	

Phalacrocorax brasiliensis (olivaceus) — Neotropic Cormorant

Subspecies/Population	Breeding range	Wintering, or core non-breeding range	Afr	Eu	Asia	Oc	Neo	NA	Estimate	Source	Trend	Source	1% level	Notes
brasiliensis	South America						●		>2,000,000	CC	INC	S8	20,000	Now widely known as olivaceus. For populations over 2 million birds, Ramsar Convention criterion 5 (20,000 or more waterbirds) applies.
"Mexican Cormorant" mexicanus	S USA, Lowland E Mexico, Central America, Caribbean						●	●			INC	TC		KS estimate US breeding population at 16,000 adults, (24,000 individuals).
(hornensis)	Tierra del Fuego						●		A	S8			100	

PHALACROCORACIDAE CORMORANTS

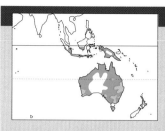

Phalacrocorax sulcirostris — Little Black Cormorant

Subspecies/Population	Breeding range	Wintering, or core non-breeding range	Afr	Eu	Asia	Oc	Neo	NA	Estimate	Source	Trend	Source	1% level	Notes
sulcirostris	E, S & SW Australia					•								B5: 10–100 in New Caledonia, subspecies unknown.
purpuragula	New Zealand					•			B	CX			250	
territori	SE Asia, N Australia				•	•								

Phalacrocorax carbo — Great Cormorant

Subspecies/Population	Breeding range	Wintering, or core non-breeding range	Afr	Eu	Asia	Oc	Neo	NA	Estimate	Source	Trend	Source	1% level	Notes
carbo, North America	NE North America south to Maine	*Atlantic North America*						•	17,400	KS	STA	HG	170	KS estimate 11,600 breeding adults (17,400 individuals).
carbo, Greenland	West Greenland			•					15,000	BH	INC	BH	150	Estimate derived from BH & BJ.
carbo, NW Europe	Iceland, Norway, Britain, Ireland			•					120,000	H2	INC	DF	1,200	
sinensis, N, C Europe	N, Central Europe	*N, Central Europe to Mediterranean*		•					275,000–340,000	BE	INC	BE	3,100	BE – Breeding population in relevant countries 92,000–114,000 pairs (276,000–342,000 individuals).
sinensis, Black Sea, Mediterranean	Black Sea, Mediterranean			•	•				130,000–160,000	BE	INC	BE	1,450	BE – Breeding population in relevant countries 42,400–52,000 pairs (127,200–156,000 individuals).
sinensis, SW Asia (non-br)	West and Central Asia	*SW Asia, Caspian*		•	•				100,000	PE			1,000	
sinensis, South Asia (non-br)	Central & S Asia	*S Asia*			•				C	LL			1,000	Up to 31,000 birds at Qinghai Lake in July–August in the late 1990s (LL).
sinensis, E, SE Asia (non-br)	E, SE Asia				•				C	LZ			1,000	23,222 counted in E Asia in 1996 (LZ).
hanedae	Japan				•				50,000–60,000	FU	INC	FU	550	
(*carboides*)	Australia					•								*carboides* and *steadi* sometimes lumped under the name *novaehollandiae* (HV).
(*steadi*)	New Zealand					•			B	CX			250	
"White-breasted Cormorant" *lucidus*, C & E Africa	Central & E Eastern Africa to Zambia & Malawi		•						200,000–500,000	DO	STA	DO	3,500	
lucidus, Coastal W Africa	Coastal Mauritania to Guinea		•						35,000	DO	STA	DO	350	
lucidus, S Africa	Southern Africa		•						11,000–13,000	CS	STA	TO	120	
maroccanus	NW Africa		•						A	DO	STA	DO	100	

Phalacrocorax fuscicollis — Indian Cormorant

Subspecies/Population	Breeding range	Wintering, or core non-breeding range	Afr	Eu	Asia	Oc	Neo	NA	Estimate	Source	Trend	Source	1% level	Notes
S & SE Asia	S & SE Asia				•				30,000	PE			300	Maximum AWC total 9,238 in 1994.

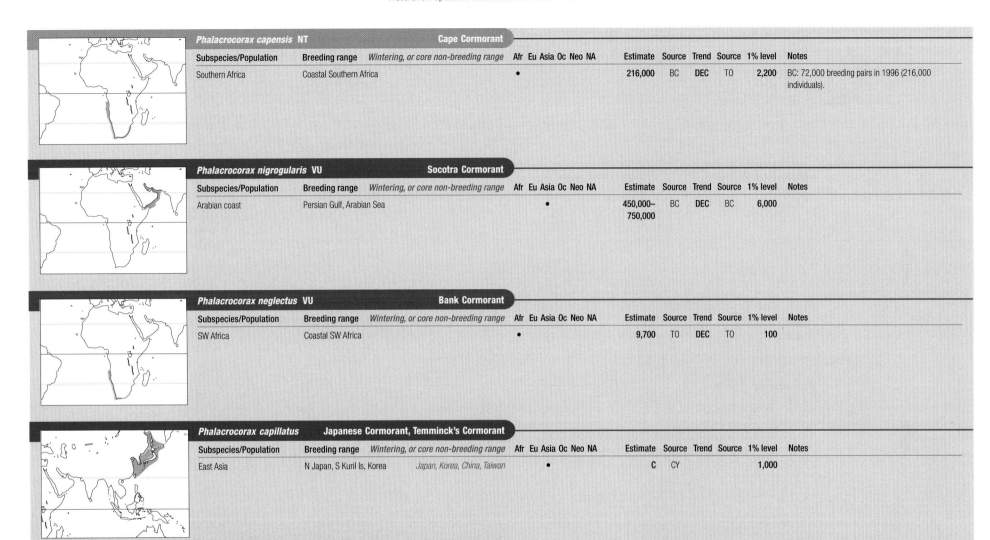

Phalacrocorax capensis NT — Cape Cormorant

Subspecies/Population	Breeding range	Wintering, or core non-breeding range	Afr	Eu	Asia	Oc	Neo	NA	Estimate	Source	Trend	Source	1% level	Notes
Southern Africa	Coastal Southern Africa		•						216,000	BC	DEC	TO	2,200	BC: 72,000 breeding pairs in 1996 (216,000 individuals).

Phalacrocorax nigrogularis VU — Socotra Cormorant

Subspecies/Population	Breeding range	Wintering, or core non-breeding range	Afr	Eu	Asia	Oc	Neo	NA	Estimate	Source	Trend	Source	1% level	Notes
Arabian coast	Persian Gulf, Arabian Sea				•				450,000–750,000	BC	DEC	BC	6,000	

Phalacrocorax neglectus VU — Bank Cormorant

Subspecies/Population	Breeding range	Wintering, or core non-breeding range	Afr	Eu	Asia	Oc	Neo	NA	Estimate	Source	Trend	Source	1% level	Notes
SW Africa	Coastal SW Africa		•						9,700	TO	DEC	TO	100	

Phalacrocorax capillatus — Japanese Cormorant, Temminck's Cormorant

Subspecies/Population	Breeding range	Wintering, or core non-breeding range	Afr	Eu	Asia	Oc	Neo	NA	Estimate	Source	Trend	Source	1% level	Notes
East Asia	N Japan, S Kuril Is, Korea	Japan, Korea, China, Taiwan			•				C	CY			1,000	

Phalacrocorax penicillatus — Brandt's Cormorant

Subspecies/Population	Breeding range	Wintering, or core non-breeding range	Afr	Eu	Asia	Oc	Neo	NA	Estimate	Source	Trend	Source	1% level	Notes
W North America	Coastal Pacific North America							•	227,000	KS	DEC	KS	2,300	KS estimate 151,200 breeding adults (226,800 individuals).

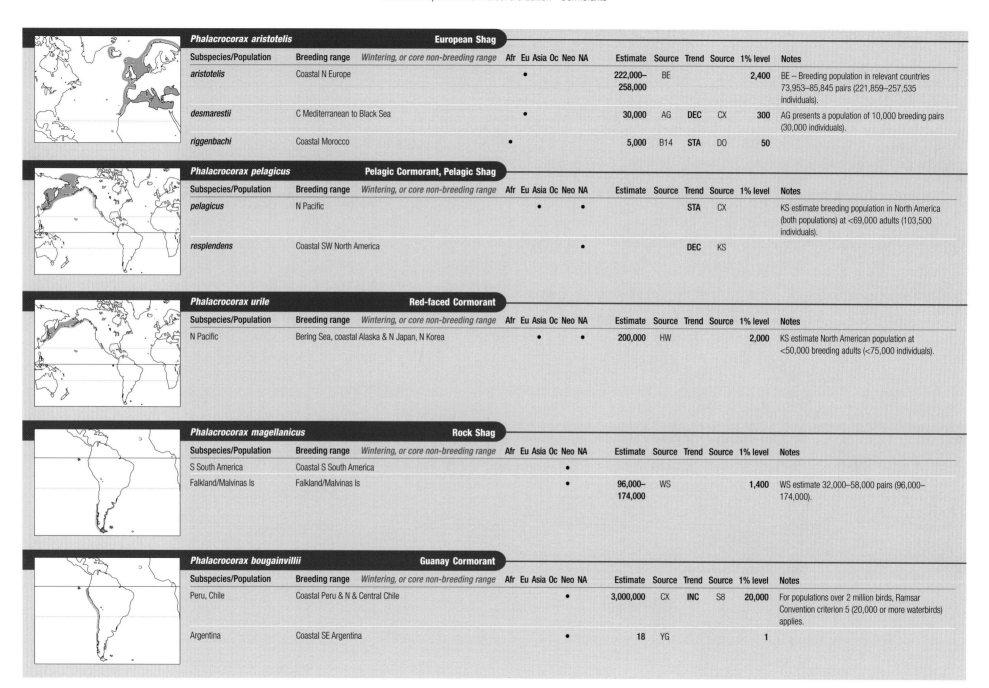

Phalacrocorax aristotelis — European Shag

Subspecies/Population	Breeding range	Wintering, or core non-breeding range	Afr	Eu	Asia	Oc	Neo	NA	Estimate	Source	Trend	Source	1% level	Notes
aristotelis	Coastal N Europe			•					222,000–258,000	BE			2,400	BE – Breeding population in relevant countries 73,953–85,845 pairs (221,859–257,535 individuals).
desmarestii	C Mediterranean to Black Sea			•					30,000	AG	DEC	CX	300	AG presents a population of 10,000 breeding pairs (30,000 individuals).
riggenbachi	Coastal Morocco		•						5,000	B14	STA	DO	50	

Phalacrocorax pelagicus — Pelagic Cormorant, Pelagic Shag

Subspecies/Population	Breeding range	Wintering, or core non-breeding range	Afr	Eu	Asia	Oc	Neo	NA	Estimate	Source	Trend	Source	1% level	Notes
pelagicus	N Pacific				•			•			STA	CX		KS estimate breeding population in North America (both populations) at <69,000 adults (103,500 individuals).
resplendens	Coastal SW North America							•			DEC	KS		

Phalacrocorax urile — Red-faced Cormorant

Subspecies/Population	Breeding range	Wintering, or core non-breeding range	Afr	Eu	Asia	Oc	Neo	NA	Estimate	Source	Trend	Source	1% level	Notes
N Pacific	Bering Sea, coastal Alaska & N Japan, N Korea				•			•	200,000	HW			2,000	KS estimate North American population at <50,000 breeding adults (<75,000 individuals).

Phalacrocorax magellanicus — Rock Shag

Subspecies/Population	Breeding range	Wintering, or core non-breeding range	Afr	Eu	Asia	Oc	Neo	NA	Estimate	Source	Trend	Source	1% level	Notes
S South America	Coastal S South America						•							
Falkland/Malvinas Is	Falkland/Malvinas Is						•		96,000–174,000	WS			1,400	WS estimate 32,000–58,000 pairs (96,000–174,000).

Phalacrocorax bougainvillii — Guanay Cormorant

Subspecies/Population	Breeding range	Wintering, or core non-breeding range	Afr	Eu	Asia	Oc	Neo	NA	Estimate	Source	Trend	Source	1% level	Notes
Peru, Chile	Coastal Peru & N & Central Chile						•		3,000,000	CX	INC	S8	20,000	For populations over 2 million birds, Ramsar Convention criterion 5 (20,000 or more waterbirds) applies.
Argentina	Coastal SE Argentina						•		18	YG			1	

Phalacrocorax varius — Pied Cormorant

Subspecies/Population	Breeding range	Wintering, or core non-breeding range	Afr	Eu	Asia	Oc	Neo	NA	Estimate	Source	Trend	Source	1% level
varius	New Zealand					●			B	CX			250
hypoleucos	Australia					●							

Pied Cormorant.

Nils Anthes

Phalacrocorax fuscescens — Black-faced Cormorant

Subspecies/Population	Breeding range	Wintering, or core non-breeding range	Afr	Eu	Asia	Oc	Neo	NA	Estimate	Source	Trend	Source	1% level	Notes
S Australia	Coastal S Australia					●								

Phalacrocorax carunculatus VU — Rough-faced Shag, New Zealand King Shag

Subspecies/Population	Breeding range	Wintering, or core non-breeding range	Afr	Eu	Asia	Oc	Neo	NA	Estimate	Source	Trend	Source	1% level	Notes
New Zealand	Cook Strait New Zealand					●			600	BC	STA	BC	6	

Phalacrocorax chalconotus VU — Stewart Shag, Bronze Shag

Subspecies/Population	Breeding range	Wintering, or core non-breeding range	Afr	Eu	Asia	Oc	Neo	NA	Estimate	Source	Trend	Source	1% level	Notes
Stewart Is	Stewart Island					●			5,000–8,000	BC			65	

Phalacrocorax onslowi EN — Chatham Island Shag

Subspecies/Population	Breeding range	Wintering, or core non-breeding range	Afr	Eu	Asia	Oc	Neo	NA	Estimate	Source	Trend	Source	1% level	Notes
Chatham Is	Chatham Island					●			1,700	BC			15	

Phalacrocorax colensoi VU — Auckland Island Shag

Subspecies/Population	Breeding range	Wintering, or core non-breeding range	Afr	Eu	Asia	Oc	Neo	NA	Estimate	Source	Trend	Source	1% level	Notes
Auckland Is	Auckland Islands					●			2,000	BC	STA	BC	20	

Phalacrocorax campbelli VU — Campbell Island Cormorant, Campbell Island Shag

Subspecies/Population	Breeding range	Wintering, or core non-breeding range	Afr	Eu	Asia	Oc	Neo	NA	Estimate	Source	Trend	Source	1% level	Notes
Campbell Is	Campbell Island					●			8,000	BC	STA	BC	80	

Phalacrocorax ranfurlyi VU — Bounty Island Shag

Subspecies/Population	Breeding range	Wintering, or core non-breeding range	Afr	Eu	Asia	Oc	Neo	NA	Estimate	Source	Trend	Source	1% level	Notes
Bounty Is	Bounty Island					●			1,140	BC	STA	BC	10	

Phalacrocorax atriceps — Imperial Shag, Blue-eyed Shag

Subspecies/Population	Breeding range	Wintering, or core non-breeding range	Afr	Eu	Asia	Oc	Neo	NA	Estimate	Source	Trend	Source	1% level	Notes
atriceps	S South America						●		D	YG	DEC	YG	10,000	Includes a few *albiventer* in S Argentina & Tierra del Fuego.
albiventer	Falkland/Malvinas Islands						●		135,000–252,000	WS			1,900	WS estimate 45,000–84,000 pairs (135,000–252,000).

Phalacrocorax bransfieldensis — Antarctic Shag

Subspecies/Population	Breeding range	Wintering, or core non-breeding range	Afr	Eu	Asia	Oc	Neo	NA	Estimate	Source	Trend	Source	1% level	Notes
Antarctic Peninsula	Antarctic Peninsula & Islands						●		40,000	CX			400	

Phalacrocorax georgianus — South Georgia Shag

Subspecies/Population	Breeding range	Wintering, or core non-breeding range	Afr	Eu	Asia	Oc	Neo	NA	Estimate	Source	Trend	Source	1% level	Notes
South Georgia	South Georgia, S Orkney Is						●		20,000	CX			200	

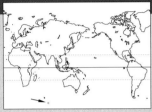

Phalacrocorax nivalis — Heard Shag

Subspecies/Population	Breeding range	Wintering, or core non-breeding range	Afr	Eu	Asia	Oc	Neo	NA	Estimate	Source	Trend	Source	1% level	Notes
Heard Is	Heard Island						●		3,270–3,600	BB	STA	GC	35	BB: Reported discovery of a colony of 1,000 nests at Cape Pillar. Existing known pop was 90–200 pairs. 1,090–1,200 pairs x 3, 3,270–3,600 individuals. Sometimes included in *atriceps*, or in genus *Leucocarbo*.

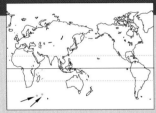

Phalacrocorax melanogenis — Crozet Shag

Subspecies/Population	Breeding range	Wintering, or core non-breeding range	Afr	Eu	Asia	Oc	Neo	NA	Estimate	Source	Trend	Source	1% level	Notes
Crozet	Crozet, Prince Edward Is		●						3,425	DO	STA	DO	35	Sometimes included in *atriceps*.

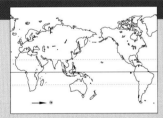

Phalacrocorax verrucosus — Kerguelen Shag

Subspecies/Population	Breeding range	Wintering, or core non-breeding range	Afr	Eu	Asia	Oc	Neo	NA	Estimate	Source	Trend	Source	1% level	Notes
Kerguelen	Kerguelen Islands						●		30,000–35,000	TG			330	

Phalacrocorax purpurascens — Macquarie Shag

Subspecies/Population	Breeding range	Wintering, or core non-breeding range	Afr	Eu	Asia	Oc	Neo	NA	Estimate	Source	Trend	Source	1% level	Notes
Macquarie	Macquarie Island						●		3,750	GC	FLU	GC	40	GC estimate 2,500 breeding adults (3,750 individuals). Sometimes included in *atriceps* or in genus *Leucocarbo*.

Phalacrocorax gaimardi NT — Red-legged Cormorant, Red-legged Shag

Subspecies/Population	Breeding range	Wintering, or core non-breeding range	Afr	Eu	Asia	Oc	Neo	NA	Estimate	Source	Trend	Source	1% level	Notes
Pacific South America	Pacific South America						●		D	S8	STA	S8	10,000	
Atlantic Argentina	Atlantic SE Argentina						●		2,200	GA YG			22	Sometimes assigned to *cirriger*.

Phalacrocorax punctatus — Spotted Shag

Subspecies/Population	Breeding range	Wintering, or core non-breeding range	Afr	Eu	Asia	Oc	Neo	NA	Estimate	Source	Trend	Source	1% level	Notes
punctatus	New Zealand						●		C	CX			1,000	
oliveri	Stewart Island						●		10,000–50,000	CX			300	

Phalacrocorax featherstoni VU — Pitt Island Shag

Subspecies/Population	Breeding range	Wintering, or core non-breeding range	Afr	Eu	Asia	Oc	Neo	NA	Estimate	Source	Trend	Source	1% level	Notes
Chatham Is	Chatham Islands						●		1,400	BC	STA	BC	15	

Phalacrocorax melanoleucos — Little Pied Cormorant

Subspecies/Population	Breeding range	Wintering, or core non-breeding range	Afr	Eu	Asia	Oc	Neo	NA	Estimate	Source	Trend	Source	1% level	Notes
melanoleucos	S Australia, New Caledonia						●							B5: New Caledonia estimate 2,000–5,000 and increasing.
(*melvillensis*)	Australia, Indonesia, Melanesia					●	●							DX: Melanesian population very small (hundreds).
brevicauda	Rennell Island						●		1,000	DX			10	DX: pers. obs.
brevirostris	New Zealand						●		C	CX			1,000	

Phalacrocorax africanus — Long-tailed Cormorant

Subspecies/Population	Breeding range	Wintering, or core non-breeding range	Afr	Eu	Asia	Oc	Neo	NA	Estimate	Source	Trend	Source	1% level	Notes
africanus, W Africa	W & Central Africa		●						100,000	DO	STA	DO	1,000	
africanus, S, E Africa	Southern, Eastern Africa		●						D	DO	STA	DO	10,000	
pictilis	Madagascar		●						A	HJ	DEC	HJ	100	

Phalacrocorax coronatus NT — Crowned Cormorant

Subspecies/Population	Breeding range	Wintering, or core non-breeding range	Afr	Eu	Asia	Oc	Neo	NA	Estimate	Source	Trend	Source	1% level	Notes
SW Africa	Coastal SW Africa Walvis Bay – Cape Agulhas		•						8,700	TO	STA	TO	85	2,665 pairs in 1977–81 (7,995 individuals) (BC).

Phalacrocorax niger — Little Cormorant

Subspecies/Population	Breeding range	Wintering, or core non-breeding range	Afr	Eu	Asia	Oc	Neo	NA	Estimate	Source	Trend	Source	1% level	Notes
South Asia	S Asia				•				150,000	PE			1,500	
SE Asia	SE Asia				•				C	CE			1,000	

Phalacrocorax pygmeus NT — Pygmy Cormorant

Subspecies/Population	Breeding range	Wintering, or core non-breeding range	Afr	Eu	Asia	Oc	Neo	NA	Estimate	Source	Trend	Source	1% level	Notes
SE Europe, Turkey	SE Europe, Turkey			•					40,000	GI	STA?	BC	400	GI: IWC count January 1998 37,225 (Special Survey in Greece). CV: Number of estimated breeding pairs gives a range of 21,393–37,323 individuals.
SW Asia (non-br)	SW & Central Asia	SW Asia, Caspian	•		•				C	SA			1,000	Population in Azerbaijan "probably in the high tens of thousands" (PB).

Phalacrocorax harrisi EN — Galapagos (Flightless) Cormorant

Subspecies/Population	Breeding range	Wintering, or core non-breeding range	Afr	Eu	Asia	Oc	Neo	NA	Estimate	Source	Trend	Source	1% level	Notes
Galapagos Is	Galapagos Islands						•		900	BC	STA	BC	9	BC: Between 1977 and 1999, numbers fluctuated between 650 and 1,000, falling to 400 during 1983 El Niño.

Phalacrocorax perspicillatus — Spectacled Cormorant, Pallas's Cormorant

Subspecies/Population	Breeding range	Wintering, or core non-breeding range	Afr	Eu	Asia	Oc	Neo	NA	Estimate	Source	Trend	Source	1% level	Notes
Commander Is	Commander Islands, Bering Sea				•				0	GY	EXT	GY		Extinct since c.1852, last specimen 1850 (BC).

ANHINGIDAE DARTERS

Anhinga anhinga — Anhinga

Subspecies/Population	Breeding range	Wintering, or core non-breeding range	Afr	Eu	Asia	Oc	Neo	NA	Estimate	Source	Trend	Source	1% level	Notes
anhinga	S America south to N Argentina						•							
leucogaster	SE USA, Mexico, Cuba, Central America							•	•			DEC	FR		FR presents a population of 10,000–17,000 breeding pairs (30,000–51,000 individuals) in the USA.

Anhinga rufa — African Darter

Subspecies/Population	Breeding range	Wintering, or core non-breeding range	Afr	Eu	Asia	Oc	Neo	NA	Estimate	Source	Trend	Source	1% level	Notes
rufa, W Africa	W & Central Africa		•						A/B	DO	STA	DO	250	Often included in melanogaster.
rufa, S & E Africa	Southern, Eastern Africa		•						C	DO	STA	DO	1,000	
vulsini	Madagascar		•						A	HJ	DEC	HJ	50	HJ estimate 1,000–10,000.
(chantrei)	Iraq, Iran				•				<50	PE	DEC	PE	1	

Anhinga melanogaster NT — Oriental Darter

Subspecies/Population	Breeding range	Wintering, or core non-breeding range	Afr	Eu	Asia	Oc	Neo	NA	Estimate	Source	Trend	Source	1% level	Notes
South Asia	South Asia				•				4,000	PE	DEC	BC	40	
SE Asia	Myanmar, Indochina, Singapore, Brunei, Indonesia, Philippines				•						DEC	BC		

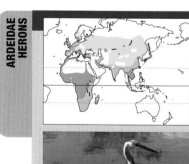

Oriental Darter.

Paul Goriup

Anhinga novaehollandiae — Australian Darter

Subspecies/Population	Breeding range	Wintering, or core non-breeding range	Afr	Eu	Asia	Oc	Neo	NA	Estimate	Source	Trend	Source	1% level	Notes
Australia, New Guinea	Australia, New Guinea					•								Often included in melanogaster.

ARDEIDAE HERONS

Ardea cinerea — Grey Heron

Subspecies/Population	Breeding range	Wintering, or core non-breeding range	Afr	Eu	Asia	Oc	Neo	NA	Estimate	Source	Trend	Source	1% level	Notes
cinerea, Sub-saharan Africa (br)	Sub-Saharan Africa		•						D	FE	STA	DO	10,000	Increasing in southern Africa (HF).
cinerea, W Europe, NW Africa (br)	Europe W of and including Sweden, Germany, Switzerland, Italy NW Africa	Some migration to S of breeding range	•	•					263,000–286,000	M5	INC	SR	2,700	M5 estimate 87,640–95,400 pairs (263,000–286,000 individuals). SR recognises a separate population in Tunisia, Algeria & Morocco of 45–120 individuals.
cinerea, C & E Europe (br)	C & E Europe, Black Sea, Mediterranean	Some migration to S of breeding range	•	•					189,000–256,000	M5 HA	INC	SR	2,200	LM & HA estimate 62,960–85,270 pairs (189,000–256,000 individuals)
cinerea, Central & SW Asia	Central & SW Asia,	E Black Sea & W, SW Asia, Caspian		•	•				C/D	SA				
cinerea, South Asia	S Asia				•				20,000	PE			200	Sometimes assigned to rectirostris.
jouyi, E, SE Asia	Japan to N Myanmar S to Java	Northern birds migrate south in winter			•				D	PE CE			10,000	
jouyi, Sumatra	Sumatra				•				1,000–2,000	LG			15	Sometimes assigned to altirostris.
monicae	Banc d'Arguin, coastal Mauritania		•						7,500–12,500	CB HA	STA	HA	100	4,188 nests (12,564 individuals), in 1997 (HA). Sometimes considered a separate species.
firasa	Madagascar		•						5,000	DO	DEC	HJ	50	

Grey Heron. Marcel Silvius

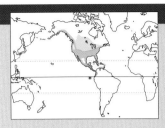

Ardea herodias — Great Blue Heron

Subspecies/Population	Breeding range	Wintering, or core non-breeding range	Afr	Eu	Asia	Oc	Neo	NA	Estimate	Source	Trend	Source	1% level	Notes
herodias, C & NE North America	Central & NE NorthAmerica	Many migrate to S of breeding range					●	●			INC	S5		KS estimate population of all subspecies in North America at 83,000 breeding adults (124,500 individuals).
herodias, W North America	W North America	Many migrate to S of breeding range					●				STA	S5		Sometimes ascribed to *hyperonca*.
herodias, W North America, N Mexico	W North America, N Mexico	Some migrate to S of breeding range					●							Sometimes ascribed to *treganzai*.
herodias, Baja California, Mexico	Baja California, Mexico	Some migrate to S of breeding range					●							Sometimes ascribed to *sanctilucae*.
fannini	NW North America	Most migrate to S of breeding range					●		6,500	HB			65	
wardi	SE North America	Some migrate to S of breeding range					●				INC	S5		
occidentalis, Florida	S Florida, Caribbean	Some migrate to S of breeding range					●	●						BT estimates 1,500 individuals in Florida.
occidentalis, Caribbean	Caribbean						●							
occidentalis, Central America	Central America						●							
cognata	Galapagos Islands						●							

Ardea cocoi — Cocoi Heron

Subspecies/Population	Breeding range	Wintering, or core non-breeding range	Afr	Eu	Asia	Oc	Neo	NA	Estimate	Source	Trend	Source	1% level	Notes
South America	South America except Andes and extreme south						●		D	CC	INC	S8	10,000	

Ardea pacifica — White-necked Heron, Pacific Heron

Subspecies/Population	Breeding range	Wintering, or core non-breeding range	Afr	Eu	Asia	Oc	Neo	NA	Estimate	Source	Trend	Source	1% level	Notes
Australia	Australia & Tasmania	Nomadic, Australia to S New Guinea				●			D	M1			10,000	

Ardea alba (Casmerodius albus, Egretta alba) — Great (White) Egret

Subspecies/Population	Breeding range	Wintering, or core non-breeding range	Afr	Eu	Asia	Oc	Neo	NA	Estimate	Source	Trend	Source	1% level	Notes
alba, W, C & E Europe, Black Sea & E Mediterranean (br)	W, C & E Europe, Black Sea & E Mediterranean (br)	Partial migration to S & W Europe & N Africa	●	●					38,800–54,300	SR	INC	SR	470	A pioneering breeding population of 180–210 individuals is becoming established in France, The Netherlands and Italy. Up to 5,000 present in France & Italy in winter (HA). Often assigned to genus *Casmerodius*, occasionaly *Egretta*.
alba, SW Asia (non-br)	Caspian, Central & SW Asia	SW Asia, Caspian	●	●					B/C	SA			1,000	
melanorhynchos	Sub-Saharan Africa, Madagascar		●						100,000–500,000	DO	STA	DO	3,000	
egretta, North America	North America	Partial migrant south of range						●	270,000	KS	INC	S5	2,700	KS estimate North American population at >180,000 breeding adults (270,000 individuals).

Great (White) Egret.   Nancy Camel

Ardea alba (*Casmerodius albus*, *Egretta alba*) ... continued

Subspecies/Population	Breeding range	Wintering, or core non-breeding range	Afr	Eu	Asia	Oc	Neo	NA	Estimate	Source	Trend	Source	1% level	Notes
egretta, Mexico	Mexico							•						M8 give incomplete estimates: Mexico E coast, 20,400 pairs; Mexico W coast, 6,700 pairs (81,300 individuals).
egretta, Central America	Central America						•							
egretta, Caribbean	Caribbean						•							
egretta, South America	South America						•		D/E	MP				MP estimate 82,000–305,000 pairs (246,000–915,000 individuals) in Venezuela, the Guianas and Argentina.

Ardea modesta   Eastern Great Egret

Subspecies/Population	Breeding range	Wintering, or core non-breeding range	Afr	Eu	Asia	Oc	Neo	NA	Estimate	Source	Trend	Source	1% level	Notes
South Asia (non-br)	Central & S Asia	*S Asia*			•				25,000	PE	STA	PE	250	
E Asia (non-br)	E Asia	*E Asia, SE Asia, Philippines*			•				B/C	PE	DEC	PE	1,000	
Indonesia	Indonesia				•									
Australia	Australia					•								
New Zealand	New Zealand					•			100	MH PW			1	Sometimes ascribed to *maorianus*.

Ardea intermedia   Intermediate Egret

Subspecies/Population	Breeding range	Wintering, or core non-breeding range	Afr	Eu	Asia	Oc	Neo	NA	Estimate	Source	Trend	Source	1% level	Notes
intermedia, South Asia	S Asia				•				25,000	PE			250	Often included in the genus *Mesophyx* or *Egretta*.
intermedia, E, SE Asia	E & SE Asia C Japan S to Indonesia	*Birds breeding in N of range migrate to S China & S Japan*			•				B/C	PE			1,000	
brachyrhyncha	Sub-Saharan Africa		•						C	DO	STA	DO	1,000	
plumifera	E Indonesia–New Guinea–Australia					•	•		C/D	PE				

Ardea melanocephala   Black-headed Heron

Subspecies/Population	Breeding range	Wintering, or core non-breeding range	Afr	Eu	Asia	Oc	Neo	NA	Estimate	Source	Trend	Source	1% level	Notes
Africa	Sub-Saharan Africa		•						100,000–500,000	DO	INC	DO	3,000	

Ardea humbloti VU   Madagascar Heron

Subspecies/Population	Breeding range	Wintering, or core non-breeding range	Afr	Eu	Asia	Oc	Neo	NA	Estimate	Source	Trend	Source	1% level	Notes
Madagascar	W Madagascar		•						1,000–3,000	HJ	DEC	BC	20	

Ardea insignis EN — White-bellied Heron

Subspecies/Population	Breeding range	Wintering, or core non-breeding range	Afr	Eu	Asia	Oc	Neo	NA	Estimate	Source	Trend	Source	1% level	Notes
S–SE Asia	Nepal to NE India & Myanmar				•				250–1,000	BC	DEC	SR	6	

Ardea sumatrana — Sumatran Heron, Great-billed Heron

Subspecies/Population	Breeding range	Wintering, or core non-breeding range	Afr	Eu	Asia	Oc	Neo	NA	Estimate	Source	Trend	Source	1% level	Notes
SE Asia	Myanmar, Thailand, S Vietnam, Singapore, Indonesia, Philippines, New Guinea				•	•			B/C	LF	DEC	LF	1,000	
Australia	N Australia					•			7,500	GC	STA	GC	75	GC estimate 5,000 breeding adults (7,500 individuals). Sometimes ascribed to *mathewsae*.

Ardea goliath — Goliath Heron

Subspecies/Population	Breeding range	Wintering, or core non-breeding range	Afr	Eu	Asia	Oc	Neo	NA	Estimate	Source	Trend	Source	1% level	Notes
Sub-Saharan Africa	Sub-Saharan Africa		•						B/C	HW	STA	DO	1,000	Estimate of 3,000 and trend increasing in southern Africa (HF).
SW Asia	S Iraq, S Iran				•				50	PE			1	
S Asia	Pakistan to Bangladesh, S to Sri Lanka				•				20	PE			1	

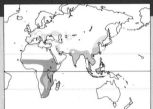

Ardea purpurea — Purple Heron

Subspecies/Population	Breeding range	Wintering, or core non-breeding range	Afr	Eu	Asia	Oc	Neo	NA	Estimate	Source	Trend	Source	1% level	Notes
purpurea, Tropical Africa (br)	Tropical Africa		•						75,000–100,000	DO	STA	DO	880	Declining in southern Africa (HF).
purpurea, SW & NW Europe, NW Africa (br)	Italy, Mallorca, Iberia, France, Netherlands, Germany + NW Africa	*Sub-Saharan (mainly West) Africa*	•	•					11,500–12,100	M5	DEC	SG	120	M5 estimates 3,760–3,930 pairs (11,300–11,900 individuals). SR recognises separate populations in Tunisia, Algeria & Morocco of 150–300 individuals and in The Netherlands and Germany of 690–1,020 individuals.
purpurea, C & E Europe, Black Sea, Mediterranean	C & E Europe, Black Sea, Mediterranean	*Sub-Saharan Africa; some winter within breeding range*	•	•	•				135,000–300,000	SR	DEC	BE	2,200	M5 estimate 45,000–99,460 pairs (135,000–298,300 individuals). Russian population poorly known.
purpurea, SW Asia (br)	Russia 55–80 E, Central & SW Asia	*Persian Gulf, Nile Valley, Sub-Saharan Africa*	•	•	•				B	SR			250	
madagascariensis	Madagascar		•						5,000–10,000	HJ	STA	DO	75	
bournei	Cape Verde Islands		•						<50	HN	DEC	HN	1	May merit full specific status (HW).
manilensis, South Asia	S Asia				•				25,000	PE	STA	PE	250	
manilensis, E & SE Asia	E & SE Asia, Ryukyu Is (Japan)	*Birds breeding in N China migrate south in winter, when range includes Korea, Taiwan*			•				B/C	PE			1,000	

Ardea ibis — Cattle Egret

Subspecies/Population	Breeding range	Wintering, or core non-breeding range	Afr	Eu	Asia	Oc	Neo	NA	Estimate	Source	Trend	Source	1% level	Notes
ibis, S Africa	Southern Africa		•						D	SA	INC	HF	10,000	Usually placed in genus *Bubulcus*.
ibis, Tropical Africa	Tropical Africa		•						E	SA				
ibis, NW Africa	Tunisia, Algeria, Morocco		•						100,000–150,000	HA			1,300	
ibis, SW Europe,	SW Europe		•	•					250,000–310,000	SR	INC	SR	2,800	
ibis, E Mediterranean, SW Asia (br)	E Mediterranean & SW Asia	SW Asia to Caspian Sea, Persian Gulf & NE Africa	•	•	•				B/C	SR	INC	SR	1,000	
ibis, North America	S Canada, USA,	S USA, Caribbean & Central America					•	•	E	KS BU	STA	S5		BU estimate 250,000–500,000 pairs (750,000–1,500,000 individuals) in the USA.
ibis, Mexico	Mexico						•							
ibis, Central America	Caribbean, Central America	S USA, Caribbean & Central America					•	•						
ibis, Caribbean	Caribbean						•							
ibis, South America	S America S to Central Argentina, Chile						•		E	CC	INC	NA		MP estimates 11,000–80,000 pairs in Venezuela, Suriname and Argentina (33,000–240,000 individuals).
ibis, Falkland/Malvinas Is	Falkland/Malvinas Is						•							
seychellarum	Seychelles granitic islands		•						A	DO	STA	DO	100	
coromandus, South Asia	S Asia				•				D/E	PE				
coromandus, E, SE Asia	E & SE Asia				•				D	CE	STA	CE	10,000	
coromandus, Oceania	New Zealand, Australia, New Guinea					•			100,000	M1			1,000	

Butorides virescens — Green Heron

Subspecies/Population	Breeding range	Wintering, or core non-breeding range	Afr	Eu	Asia	Oc	Neo	NA	Estimate	Source	Trend	Source	1% level	Notes
virescens, Central & E North America	Central & E North America	S USA, to Panama, Caribbean, Ecuador, Suriname					•	•			DEC	S5		Sometimes considered conspecific with *striatus* (e.g. HW).
virescens, Mexico	Mexico						•							Sometimes ascribed to *maculatus*.
virescens, Centrlal America	Central America						•							
virescens, Caribbean	Caribbean						•							
bahamensis	Bahamas Islands						•							
anthonyi	W North America to N Baja California	W Mexico					•				INC	S5		
frazari	S Baja California, Mexico						•							

Butorides striatus — Striated Heron

Subspecies/Population	Breeding range	Wintering, or core non-breeding range	Afr	Eu	Asia	Oc	Neo	NA	Estimate	Source	Trend	Source	1% level	Notes
striatus, Central & South America	E Panama to N Chile & N Argentina						•							MP estimates 250–500 pairs (750–1,500 individuals) in Venezuela.
striatus, South America	Central South America						•				STA	AT		Sometimes ascribed to *cyanurus*.
striatus, Bolivia	Bolivia						•							
sundevalli	Galapagos Islands						•							Sometimes considered separate species *Butorides sundevalli*.
brevipes	Red Sea, N Somalia		•		•				A	DO			100	

Green Heron. *Nancy Camel*

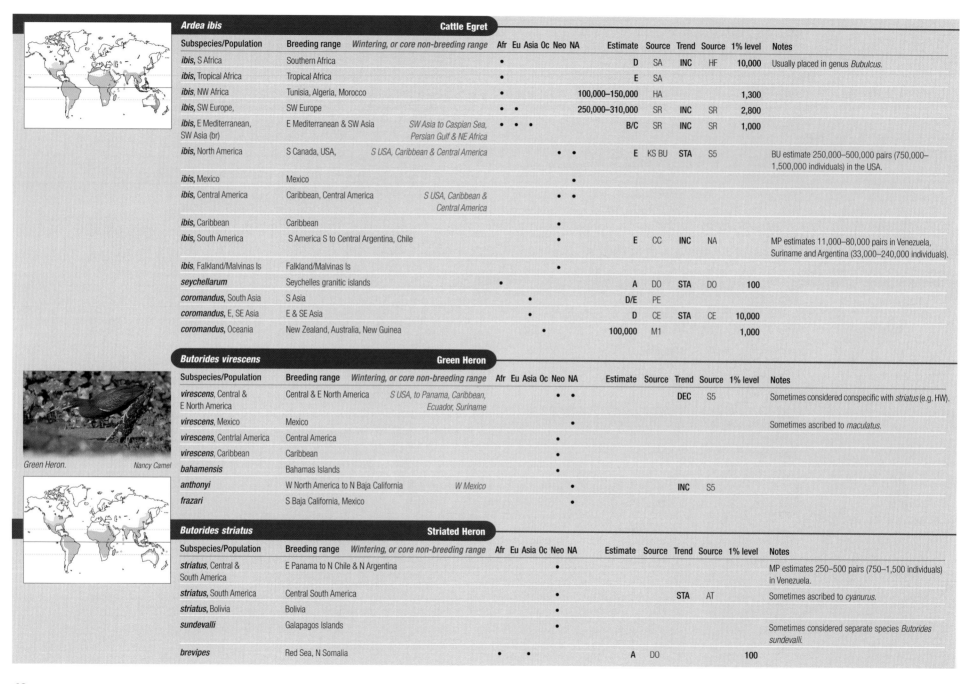

42

Butorides striatus... continued

Subspecies/Population	Breeding range	Wintering, or core non-breeding range	Afr	Eu	Asia	Oc	Neo	NA	Estimate	Source	Trend	Source	1% level	Notes
atricapillus	Sub-Saharan Africa		•						D	DO	STA	DO	10,000	
rutenbergi	Madagascar		•						A/B	DO	STA	DO	250	
rhizophorae	Comoros Islands		•						A	DO			100	
degens	Seychelles granitic islands		•						A	DO			100	
crawfordi	Aldabra & Amirante Is		•						<5,000	DO	STA	DO	50	
albolimbatus	Chagos Is, Maldives, Diego Garcia				•				A	LG			100	
chloriceps	India, Sri Lanka				•				25,000	HT	DEC	HT	250	
spodiogaster	W Sumatra, Andaman, Nicobar Islands				•									
amurensis	NE China, SE Russia S to Shandong & Korea, Japan, Ryukyu & Bonin Is, Taiwan & S China	_S China to Sumatra & Philippines_			•									
actophilus	S China to N Indochina & N Myanmar	_S Nicobar Is, Sumatra, Borneo_			•									Includes "_connectens_".
javanicus	Mauritius, Rodrigues, W Indonesia, Malay Peninsula Myanmar, Thailand		•		•				B/C	SR			1,000	Includes "_abbotti_".
moluccarus, Moluccas	Moluccas				•									
moluccarus, NW New Guinea	NW New Guinea, Aru Is					•								Sometimes ascribed to _papuensis_.
solomonensis	New Ireland, Solomon Islands, Vanuatu, W Fiji Is					•			A/B	DX			250	
idenburgi	West Papua					•								
flyensis	New Guinea (South Coast)					•								
stagnatilis, N Australia	N Australia					•								
stagnatilis, NW Australia	NW Western Australia					•								Sometimes ascribed to _rogersi_.
stagnatilis, NE Western Australia	NE Western Australia					•								Sometimes ascribed to _cinereus_.
patruelis	Tahiti, Society Is					•			100–200	TG	DEC	TG	2	
macrorhynchus, E Australia	E Queensland, New Caledonia, Loyalty Is					•								B5: Extinct in New Caledonia since 1980s.
macrorhynchus, SC New Guinea, NE Queensland	SC New Guinea, NE Queensland					•								Sometimes ascribed to _littleri_.
carcinophilus	Taiwan, Philippines, Sulawesi				•									
steini	Lesser Sundas Is, Indonesia				•									

Ardeola ralloides — Squacco Heron

Subspecies/Population	Breeding range	Wintering, or core non-breeding range	Afr	Eu	Asia	Oc	Neo	NA	Estimate	Source	Trend	Source	1% level	Notes
SW Europe, NW Africa (br)	SW Europe, W Mediterranean, NW Africa	_Sub-Saharan (mainly W) Africa_	•	•					2,700–5,600	SR	INC	SR	40	Increased during 1990s in France, Spain, Italy. SR recognises a separate population in Tunisia, Algeria & Morocco of 120–300 individuals.
C & E Europe, Black Sea & E Mediterranean (br)	C & E Europe, Black Sea & E Mediterranean	_Persian Gulf, Nile Valley, Sub-Saharan Africa_	•	•	•				42,000–76,000	SR	DEC	SR	600	
SW Asia (br)	Central Asian Republics, Azerbaijan, Iran	_Persian Gulf, Nile Valley, Sub-Saharan Africa_	•	•	•				C	PE			1,000	Breeding population in Azerbaijan estimated at 15,000–18,000 pairs (SP).
Sub-Saharan Africa	Sub-Saharan Africa, Madagascar		•						100,000–500,000	DO	STA	DO	3,000	Sometimes ascribed to _paludivaga_.

Ardeola grayii — Indian Pond-Heron

Subspecies/Population	Breeding range	Wintering, or core non-breeding range	Afr	Eu	Asia	Oc	Neo	NA	Estimate	Source	Trend	Source	1% level	Notes
grayii, SW, S Asia	N Persian Gulf E through South Asia, Sri Lanka				•				D	PE			10,000	
grayii, Myanmar, Bay of Bengal	Myanmar, Andaman & Nicobar Is				•									
(*phillipsi*)	Maldives				•									

Ardeola bacchus — Chinese Pond-Heron

Subspecies/Population	Breeding range	Wintering, or core non-breeding range	Afr	Eu	Asia	Oc	Neo	NA	Estimate	Source	Trend	Source	1% level	Notes
E, SE & S Asia	NE & E China W to Assam; occasional Japan	*S China, Taiwan, Indochina, Borneo, Sumatra, Ryukyu Is, Philippines*			•				C/D	CE	**STA**	CE		

Ardeola speciosa — Javan Pond-Heron

Subspecies/Population	Breeding range	Wintering, or core non-breeding range	Afr	Eu	Asia	Oc	Neo	NA	Estimate	Source	Trend	Source	1% level	Notes
speciosa	W & Central Indonesia, S Philippines				•									
continentalis	C Thailand, S Indochina				•				B/C	PE			1,000	

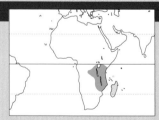

Ardeola idae VU — Madagascar Pond-Heron

Subspecies/Population	Breeding range	Wintering, or core non-breeding range	Afr	Eu	Asia	Oc	Neo	NA	Estimate	Source	Trend	Source	1% level	Notes
Madagascar	Madagascar, Aldabra, Europa	*Central & E Africa*	•						2,000–6,000	DO	**DEC**	BC	40	5,000 according to Rabarisoa in litt. (SA).

Ardeola rufiventris — Rufous-bellied Heron

Subspecies/Population	Breeding range	Wintering, or core non-breeding range	Afr	Eu	Asia	Oc	Neo	NA	Estimate	Source	Trend	Source	1% level	Notes
E & S Africa	Uganda & Kenya S to E South Africa, W to Angola, Zambia, N Namibia, N Botswana		•						B/C	SR			1,000	Possibly declining in southern Africa (HF).

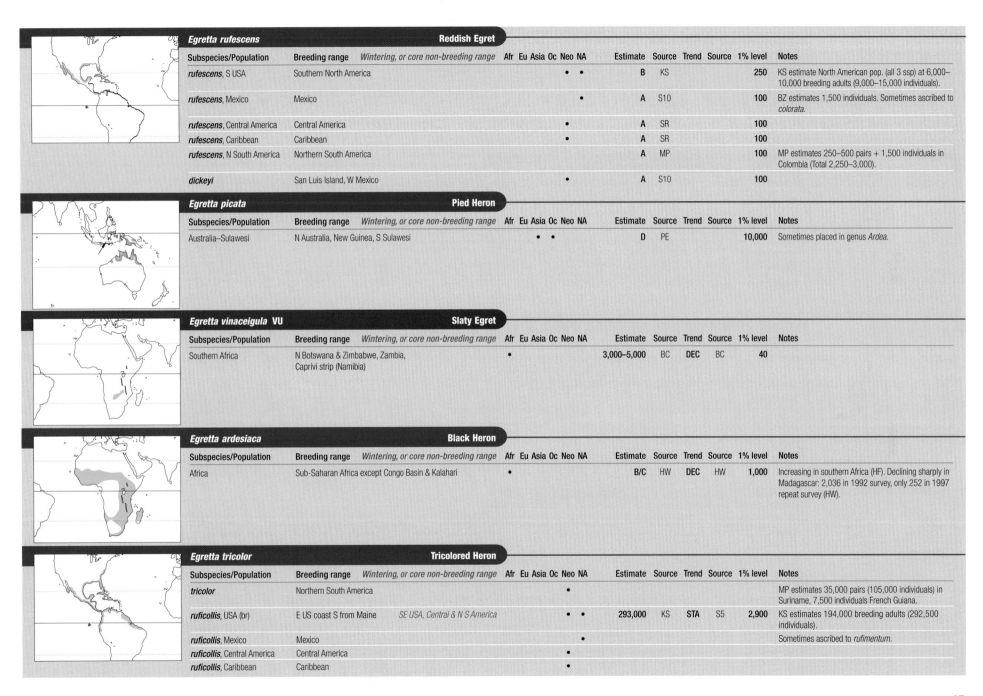

Egretta rufescens — Reddish Egret

Subspecies/Population	Breeding range	Wintering, or core non-breeding range	Afr	Eu	Asia	Oc	Neo	NA	Estimate	Source	Trend	Source	1% level	Notes
rufescens, S USA	Southern North America						●	●	B	KS			250	KS estimate North American pop. (all 3 ssp) at 6,000–10,000 breeding adults (9,000–15,000 individuals).
rufescens, Mexico	Mexico							●	A	S10			100	BZ estimates 1,500 individuals. Sometimes ascribed to *colorata*.
rufescens, Central America	Central America							●	A	SR			100	
rufescens, Caribbean	Caribbean							●	A	SR			100	
rufescens, N South America	Northern South America								A	MP			100	MP estimates 250–500 pairs + 1,500 individuals in Colombia (Total 2,250–3,000).
dickeyi		San Luis Island, W Mexico						●	A	S10			100	

Egretta picata — Pied Heron

Subspecies/Population	Breeding range	Wintering, or core non-breeding range	Afr	Eu	Asia	Oc	Neo	NA	Estimate	Source	Trend	Source	1% level	Notes
Australia–Sulawesi	N Australia, New Guinea, S Sulawesi					●	●		D	PE			10,000	Sometimes placed in genus *Ardea*.

Egretta vinaceigula VU — Slaty Egret

Subspecies/Population	Breeding range	Wintering, or core non-breeding range	Afr	Eu	Asia	Oc	Neo	NA	Estimate	Source	Trend	Source	1% level	Notes
Southern Africa	N Botswana & Zimbabwe, Zambia, Caprivi strip (Namibia)		●						3,000–5,000	BC	DEC	BC	40	

Egretta ardesiaca — Black Heron

Subspecies/Population	Breeding range	Wintering, or core non-breeding range	Afr	Eu	Asia	Oc	Neo	NA	Estimate	Source	Trend	Source	1% level	Notes
Africa	Sub-Saharan Africa except Congo Basin & Kalahari		●						B/C	HW	DEC	HW	1,000	Increasing in southern Africa (HF). Declining sharply in Madagascar: 2,036 in 1992 survey, only 252 in 1997 repeat survey (HW).

Egretta tricolor — Tricolored Heron

Subspecies/Population	Breeding range	Wintering, or core non-breeding range	Afr	Eu	Asia	Oc	Neo	NA	Estimate	Source	Trend	Source	1% level	Notes
tricolor	Northern South America						●							MP estimates 35,000 pairs (105,000 individuals) in Suriname, 7,500 individuals French Guiana.
ruficollis, USA (br)	E US coast S from Maine	SE USA, Central & N S America					●	●	293,000	KS	STA	S5	2,900	KS estimates 194,000 breeding adults (292,500 individuals).
ruficollis, Mexico	Mexico						●							Sometimes ascribed to *rufimentum*.
ruficollis, Central America	Central America						●							
ruficollis, Caribbean	Caribbean						●							

Egretta novaehollandiae — White-faced Heron

Subspecies/Population	Breeding range	Wintering, or core non-breeding range	Afr	Eu	Asia	Oc	Neo	NA	Estimate	Source	Trend	Source	1% level	Notes
novaehollandiae	New Zealand, Australia, New Guinea, E Indonesia				•	•			E	M1				B5: >5,000 in New Caledonia.
parryi	NW Australia					•								

Egretta caerulea — Little Blue Heron

Subspecies/Population	Breeding range	Wintering, or core non-breeding range	Afr	Eu	Asia	Oc	Neo	NA	Estimate	Source	Trend	Source	1% level	Notes
North America	North America	S USA, Central America					•	•	225,000–300,000	BU	DEC	S5	2,600	BU estimates 75,000–100,000 pairs (225,000–300,000 individuals).
Mexico	Mexico						•		75,000–150,000	BU MP			1,100	BU estimates 25,000–50,000 pairs (75,000–150,000 individuals).
Central America	Central America						•							
Caribbean	Caribbean						•							
South America	South America						•							MP estimates 50,000–95,000 pairs (150,000–285,000 individuals) in Venezuela, Suriname, French Guiana & Argentina.

Egretta thula — Snowy Egret

Subspecies/Population	Breeding range	Wintering, or core non-breeding range	Afr	Eu	Asia	Oc	Neo	NA	Estimate	Source	Trend	Source	1% level	Notes
thula	Central & E North America	Coastal E & S USA, Caribbean, Central & N S America						•	215,000	KS	STA	CC	2,100	KS estimate >143,000 breeding adults (214,500 individuals).
brewsteri	W USA, Baja California	Central America						•	D	SR	INC	S5	10,000	
thula, Mexico	Mexico							•		75,000–150,000	BU			1,100	BU estimates 25,000–50,000 pairs (75,000–150,000 individuals).
thula, Central America	Central America							•						
thula, Caribbean	Caribbean							•						
thula, South America	South America							•						MP estimates 180,000–390,000 pairs (390,000–1,170,000 individuals) in Venezuela, Suriname, French Guiana & Argentina.

Egretta garzetta — Little Egret

Subspecies/Population	Breeding range	Wintering, or core non-breeding range	Afr	Eu	Asia	Oc	Neo	NA	Estimate	Source	Trend	Source	1% level	Notes
garzetta, Sub-Saharan Africa (br)	Scattered distribution in Sub-Saharan Africa		•						200,000–500,000	DO			3,500	
garzetta, W Europe, NW Africa	Ireland, UK, SE to Italy, Tunisia, Algeria, Morocco	Breeding range to W Africa	•	•					125,000–143,000	HA	INC	HA	1,300	Details in BWP Update 2002, Vol 4. (1), 1–19. SR recognises a separate population in Tunisia, Algeria & Morocco of 1,200–3,000 individuals.
garzetta, C & E Europe, Black Sea, E Mediterranean (br)	C & E Europe, Mediterranean & Black Sea basins	Sub-Saharan Africa, Mediterranean, SW Asia	•	•					44,000–72,400	HA	STA?	HA	580	Details in BWP Update 2002, Vol 4. (1), 1–19.
garzetta, West Indies	Barbados	Barbados & adjacent islands					•		30–60	SR	INC	PJ	1	Colonised in early 1990s, (PJ). 10–20 pairs (30–60 individuals). See BU.
garzetta, W Asia (br)	W Asia	W & SW Asia	•		•				C	PE			1,000	H2: 6,200–11,200 pairs (18,600–33,600 individuals) in Azerbaijan.

Little Egret. *Johan Verbanck*

Egretta garzetta... continued

Subspecies/Population	Breeding range	Wintering, or core non-breeding range	Afr	Eu	Asia	Oc	Neo	NA	Estimate	Source	Trend	Source	1% level	Notes
garzetta, South Asia	South Asia				•				60,000	PE			600	
garzetta, E, SE Asia	E, SE Asia	Northern breeding birds migrate south in winter			•				D	CE	STA	CE	10,000	
nigripes	Java, New Guinea, associated Islands SE Asia & SW Pacific				•	•			C/D	PE				
immaculata	New Zealand, Australia				•	•								
gularis	Coastal W Africa Mauritania–Gabon		•						B/C	FE	STA	DO	1,000	1,897 nests in 1997 in Mauritania (5,691 individuals). Sometimes treated as separate species, Reef Heron.
schistacea, NE Africa, Red Sea	Coastal NE Africa, Red Sea		•		•				B/C	FE			1,000	
schistacea, SW, South Asia	Coastal SW, S Asia				•				17,000	PE			170	Sometimes assigned to asha.
dimorpha, Madagascar	Madagascar		•						6,000–20,000	HJ	DEC	HJ	130	Sometimes treated as separate species, Madagascar Reef Heron.
dimorpha, Aldabra & Amirante Is	Aldabra & Amirante Is		•						3,000–9,000	RO	STA	DO	60	
dimorpha, E African coast	Coastal E Africa S Kenya–N Mozambique		•						10,000	DO	STA	DO	100	

Egretta eulophotes VU — Chinese Egret, Swinhoe's Egret

Subspecies/Population	Breeding range	Wintering, or core non-breeding range	Afr	Eu	Asia	Oc	Neo	NA	Estimate	Source	Trend	Source	1% level	Notes
E, SE Asia	Korea, NE China, Furugelm Island (Russian far East)	China, Japan, Taiwan, SE Asia			•				2,600–3,400	BD	STA?	BD	30	

Egretta sacra — Eastern Reef Heron, Pacific Reef-Egret

Subspecies/Population	Breeding range	Wintering, or core non-breeding range	Afr	Eu	Asia	Oc	Neo	NA	Estimate	Source	Trend	Source	1% level	Notes
sacra	Coastal SE Asia, Andaman & Nicobar Is, China, Taiwan, Korea, Japan, Indonesia, Philippines, SW & S Pacific islands, Australia, New Zealand				•	•			D	SR	STA?	SR	10,000	Regarded as 'rapidly declining and very rare' in China (CE).
albolineata	New Caledonia, Loyalty Is					•			1,000–2,000	B5	STA	B5	15	

Syrigma sibilatrix — Whistling Heron

Subspecies/Population	Breeding range	Wintering, or core non-breeding range	Afr	Eu	Asia	Oc	Neo	NA	Estimate	Source	Trend	Source	1% level	Notes
sibilatrix	Bolivia to SE Brazil & NE Argentina						•							MP estimates 250–500 pairs (750–1,500 individuals) in Argentina.
forstersmithi	E Colombia, Venezuela						•							MP estimates 5,000–25,000 pairs (15,000–75,000) individuals in Venezuela.

Pilherodius pileatus — Capped Heron

Subspecies/Population	Breeding range	Wintering, or core non-breeding range	Afr	Eu	Asia	Oc	Neo	NA	Estimate	Source	Trend	Source	1% level	Notes
C & S America	Panama to Guianas & E Brazil, S to E Ecuador, S Bolivia, Paraguay						•							

Nyctanassa violacea/Nycticorax violaceus — Yellow-crowned Night-Heron

Subspecies/Population	Breeding range	Wintering, or core non-breeding range	Afr	Eu	Asia	Oc	Neo	NA	Estimate	Source	Trend	Source	1% level	Notes
violacea, North America	E Central USA, E Mexico to Honduras	S USA, Caribbean, Central America					•	•	75,000–150,000	BU	STA	S5	1,100	BU estimate 25,000–50,000 pairs (75,000–150,000 individuals) in USA. Often placed in genus Nycticorax.
violacea, Mexico to Honduras	Mexico & Central America to Honduras						•	•						
violacea, Socorro Island	Socorro Island, W Mexico						•							Sometimes ascribed to gravirostris.
caliginis	Panama to Peru						•		A	NA	STA	NA	100	
cayennensis	Colombia to NE & E Brazil						•							MP estimates 13,500–16,000 pairs (40,500–48,000 individuals) in Colombia and Suriname.
bancrofti	Baja California to El Salvador & West Indies							•						
pauper	Galapagos Islands						•							

Nycticorax nycticorax — Black-crowned Night-Heron

Subspecies/Population	Breeding range	Wintering, or core non-breeding range	Afr	Eu	Asia	Oc	Neo	NA	Estimate	Source	Trend	Source	1% level	Notes
nycticorax, W Europe, NW Africa (br)	W, C & S Europe, NW Africa	Sub-Saharan Africa, Mediterranean	•	•					61,000–97,000	M5	DEC	SA	790	M5 estimates 19,800–30,700 pairs (59,400–92,100 individuals). SR recognises a separate population in Tunisia, Algeria & Morocco of 1,600–4,650 individuals.
nycticorax, C & E Europe, Black Sea, E Mediterranean (br)	C & E Europe, Black Sea, E Mediterranean	E Mediterranean, Sub-Saharan Africa	•	•					92,100–138,000	SR	DEC	SR	1,200	M5 & HA estimate 30,700–45,900 pairs (92,100–137,700 individuals).
nycticorax, W Asia (br)	Caspian, Central Asia	Sub-Saharan Africa	•	•	•				C	SA			1,000	
nycticorax, Sub-Saharan Africa, Madagascar (br)	Sub-Saharan Africa, Madagascar		•						C/D	DO	STA	DO		Increasing in southern Africa (HF).
nycticorax, South Asia	S Asia				•				C	PE	STA	PE	1,000	
nycticorax, E, SE Asia	Japan, Korea E & S China, Taiwan, Indochina, Malaysia, Indonesia, Philippines	Japan, SE China, Indochina, Taiwan, Philippines, Indonesia			•				D	SR	STA	CE	10,000	
nycticorax, North America (br)	North America	S USA, Caribbean, C America, S America					•	•	75,000–150,000	BU	STA	S8	1,100	BU estimate 25,000–50,000 pairs (75,000–150,000 individuals). Sometimes ascribed to hoactli.
nycticorax, Mexico	Mexico							•						
nycticorax, Central America	Central America						•							
nycticorax, Caribbean	Caribbean						•							
nyccticorax, northern South America (br)	South America to N Chile & N Argentina						•							MP estimates 50,000–250,000 pairs (150,000–750,000 individuals) in Venezuela and 2,500–5,000 pairs (7,500–15,000) individuals in Suriname.
obscurus, S South America	N Chile & NC Argentina to Tierra del Fuego						•		C/D	S8				
obscurus, Falkland/Malvinas Islands	Falkland/Malvinas Islands						•		5,700–10,500	WS			80	WS estimate 1,900–3,500 pairs (5,700–10,500).

Nycticorax duboisi — Réunion Night-Heron

Subspecies/Population	Breeding range	Wintering, or core non-breeding range	Afr	Eu	Asia	Oc	Neo	NA	Estimate	Source	Trend	Source	1% level	Notes
Réunion	Réunion Island		•						0	BC	EXT	BC		Described and last recorded in 1674 (BC).

Nycticorax mauritianus — Mauritius Night-Heron

Subspecies/Population	Breeding range	Wintering, or core non-breeding range	Afr	Eu	Asia	Oc	Neo	NA	Estimate	Source	Trend	Source	1% level	Notes
Mauritius	Mauritius		•						0	BC	EXT	BC		Described and last recorded in 1693 (BC).

Nycticorax megacephalusus — Rodrigues Night-Heron

Subspecies/Population	Breeding range	Wintering, or core non-breeding range	Afr	Eu	Asia	Oc	Neo	NA	Estimate	Source	Trend	Source	1% level	Notes
Rodrigues	Rodrigues		•						0	BC	EXT	BC		Described and last recorded in 1726 (BC).

Nycticorax caledonicus — Rufous Night-Heron

Subspecies/Population	Breeding range	Wintering, or core non-breeding range	Afr	Eu	Asia	Oc	Neo	NA	Estimate	Source	Trend	Source	1% level	Notes
caledonicus	New Caledonia					•			2,000–4,000	B5	STA	B5	30	
manillensis	Philippines, NE Borneo, Sulawesi				•									
pelewensis	Palau & Caroline Islands					•			A	DX			100	
mandibularis	Solomon Islands, Bismarck Archipelago					•			B/C	DX			1,000	Bismarck birds sometimes separated as *cancrivorus*.
hilli	Java, New Guinea, Australia					•								

Nycticorax leuconotus — White-backed Night-Heron

Subspecies/Population	Breeding range	Wintering, or core non-breeding range	Afr	Eu	Asia	Oc	Neo	NA	Estimate	Source	Trend	Source	1% level	Notes
Africa	Tropical Africa to NE South Africa		•						C/D	DO	STA	DO		Declining in southern Africa (HF). Sometimes included in genus *Gorsachius*.

Gorsachius magnificus EN — White-eared Night-Heron

Subspecies/Population	Breeding range	Wintering, or core non-breeding range	Afr	Eu	Asia	Oc	Neo	NA	Estimate	Source	Trend	Source	1% level	Notes
SE Asia	S & E China, Hainan, Vietnam				•				<50	SR	DEC	BC	1	BC estimate 250–1,000. Habitat detrimentally transformed at principal site, Shennongjia in Hubei province, China, in 1990s.

Gorsachius goisagi EN — Japanese Night-Heron

Subspecies/Population	Breeding range	Wintering, or core non-breeding range	Afr	Eu	Asia	Oc	Neo	NA	Estimate	Source	Trend	Source	1% level	Notes
E & SE Asia	Japan	Ryukyu Is, SE China, Taiwan, Philippines, Indonesia			•				250–1,000	BC	DEC	BC	6	

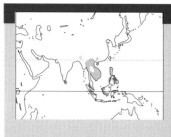

Gorsachius melanolophus — Malayan Night-Heron

Subspecies/Population	Breeding range	Wintering, or core non-breeding range	Afr	Eu	Asia	Oc	Neo	NA	Estimate	Source	Trend	Source	1% level	Notes
South Asia	SW India	Sri Lanka			•									
SE Asia	Indochina, SW China	NE India, Malaysia, W Indonesia			•									
Philippines	Philippines				•									Sometimes ascribed to kutteri. Probably this subspecies on Ryukyu Is and Taiwan.
Palawan, Philippines	Palawan, Philippines				•				A	LG			100	Sometimes ascribed to rufolineatus.
Nicobar Is	Nicobar Islands				•				A	LG			100	Sometimes ascribed to minor.

Botaurus pinnatus — South American Bittern, Pinnated Bittern

Subspecies/Population	Breeding range	Wintering, or core non-breeding range	Afr	Eu	Asia	Oc	Neo	NA	Estimate	Source	Trend	Source	1% level	Notes
pinnatus	Nicaragua–Ecuador & Guianas S through Brazil & Paraguay to NE Argentina						•							
caribaeus	E Mexico, Belize						•							

Botaurus lentiginosus — North American Bittern, American Bittern

Subspecies/Population	Breeding range	Wintering, or core non-breeding range	Afr	Eu	Asia	Oc	Neo	NA	Estimate	Source	Trend	Source	1% level	Notes
North America	S & C Canada, USA,	S USA, Central America & Caribbean					•	•	2,976,000	WC	STA	S5	20,000	Estimate from BBS 992,000 pairs (2,976,000 individuals). For populations over 2 million birds, Ramsar criterion 5 (20,000 or more waterbirds) applies.

Botaurus stellaris — Eurasian Bittern, Great Bittern

Subspecies/Population	Breeding range	Wintering, or core non-breeding range	Afr	Eu	Asia	Oc	Neo	NA	Estimate	Source	Trend	Source	1% level	Notes
stellaris, W Europe, NW Africa (br)	W Europe, NW Africa	W Europe, Mediterranean, Sub-Saharan Africa	•	•					5,880–6,730	M5	DEC	SG	65	M5 estimates 1,950–2,235 pairs (5,850–6,700 individuals). SR recognises a separate population in Tunisia, Algeria & Morocco of 30 individuals.
stellaris, C & E Europe, Black Sea, E Mediterranean (br)	C & E Europe, Black Sea, E Mediterranean (br)	Breeding range to Sub-saharan Africa	•	•					53,800–124,200	M5	DEC	SR	900	M5 estimates 17,956–41,400 pairs (53,800–124,200 individuals).
stellaris, W & Central Asia (br)	Russia E of 55° E to 80° E, Azerbaijan, Iran, Central Asian Republics	S Central Asia, Caspian, Persian Gulf, Turkey to Sub-Saharan Africa	•	•					C		SR		1,000	
stellaris, South Asia (non-br)	Central Asia	South Asia			•									
stellaris, S & E Asia (non-br)	S & SE Russia, Mongolia, N China, Japan	N India–Myanmar, S & E China, Taiwan, Korea, S Japan			•				C	CE	DEC	CE	1,000	Sometimes ascribed to orientalis.
capensis	Southern Africa (including Zambia)		•						5,000	FE	DEC	HF	50	

Botaurus poiciloptilus VU — Australasian Bittern

Subspecies/Population	Breeding range	Wintering, or core non-breeding range	Afr	Eu	Asia	Oc	Neo	NA	Estimate	Source	Trend	Source	1% level	Notes
SW Australia	SW Australia					•			500	CK BC	DEC	BC	5	BC estimates 2,500 for both populations, mostly in SE Australia. Proportion of populations in SW and SE Australia assume a similar ratio to that presented in CK.
SE Australia	SE Australia					•			2,000	CK BC	DEC	BC	20	
New Zealand	New Zealand					•			<725	BC	DEC	BC	7	BC estimates 580–725 in 1980, possibly many more.
New Caledonia	New Caledonia & Loyalty Island					•			0–50	B5	DEC	B5	1	Only two recent records (BC). Possibly extinct (DX).

Ixobrychus involucris — Streaked Bittern, Stripe-backed Bittern

Subspecies/Population	Breeding range	Wintering, or core non-breeding range	Afr	Eu	Asia	Oc	Neo	NA	Estimate	Source	Trend	Source	1% level	Notes
N South America	N Colombia, N Venezuela, Guyana, Surinam						•		D	CC	STA	CC	10,000	
S South America	S Bolivia & S Brazil to C Argentina, C Chile						•							

Ixobrychus exilis — Least Bittern

Subspecies/Population	Breeding range	Wintering, or core non-breeding range	Afr	Eu	Asia	Oc	Neo	NA	Estimate	Source	Trend	Source	1% level	Notes
exilis	SE Canada & E USA W USA to Central America, Caribbean	S USA to N South America					•	•	128,000	WC			1,300	Information developed by WC: Estimate from BBS 42,700 pairs (128,100 individuals).
pullus	Sonora (NW Mexico)							•						
bogotensis	Central Colombia							•	150–750	MP			5	MP estimates 50–250 pairs (150–750 individuals).
erythromelas	E Panama to Guianas SE to Brazil & Paraguay							•						
peruvianus	Central W Peru							•						

Ixobrychus minutus — Little Bittern

Subspecies/Population	Breeding range	Wintering, or core non-breeding range	Afr	Eu	Asia	Oc	Neo	NA	Estimate	Source	Trend	Source	1% level	Notes
minutus, W Europe, NW Africa	W Europe, Algeria, Tunisia, Morocco	Sub-Saharan Africa	•	•					11,900–17,900	M5	DEC	SR	150	M5 estimates 3,850–5,880 pairs (11,550–17,640 individuals). SR recognises a separate population in Tunisia, Algeria & Morocco of 300 individuals.
minutus, C & E Europe, Black Sea, E Mediterranean (br)	C & E Europe, Black Sea & E Mediterranean, Nile Valley	Some winter in Nile Delta, most in Sub-Saharan Africa	•	•					110,000–325,000	SR	DEC	SR	2,200	SR recognises a separate population in Nile Valley & Delta & Israel of <10,000 birds.
minutus, W & SW Asia (br)	W, Central & SW Asia, Caspian	Sub-Saharan Africa	•	•	•				C	PE			1,000	
minutus, South Asia	Central & S Asia	S Asia			•				B	PE			250	
payesii	Sub-Saharan Africa		•						C	FE			1,000	
podiceps	Madagascar		•						3,000–15,000	HJ			90	
novaezelandiae	New Zealand					•			0	PW	EXT	PW		Sometimes ascribed to separate species, I. novaezelandiae. Became extinct before 1900 (BC).
dubius	SW & E Australia, S New Guinea					•			7,500	GC	STA	GC	75	GC estimate 5,000 breeding birds (7,500 individuals).

Ixobrychus sinensis — **Yellow Bittern**

Subspecies/Population	Breeding range	Wintering, or core non-breeding range	Afr	Eu	Asia	Oc	Neo	NA	Estimate	Source	Trend	Source	1% level	Notes
Seychelles	Seychelles		•						<300	RO	DEC	SW	3	Principal site recently drained (SR).
South Asia	South Asia				•									
E & SE Asia	E & SE Asia	*E & SE Asia to New Guinea, Micronesia*			•				D	SR	INC	SR	10,000	B5: Recently colonised New Caledonia.

Ixobrychus eurhythmus — **Schrenck's Bittern**

Subspecies/Population	Breeding range	Wintering, or core non-breeding range	Afr	Eu	Asia	Oc	Neo	NA	Estimate	Source	Trend	Source	1% level	Notes
E & SE Asia	SE Siberia, Japan, Korea, NE & E China	*S China, S Japan, Indochina, Malay Peninsula, Greater Sundas, Sulawesi & Philippines*			•				A/B	LG	DEC	LG	250	

Ixobrychus cinnamomeus — **Cinnamon Bittern**

Subspecies/Population	Breeding range	Wintering, or core non-breeding range	Afr	Eu	Asia	Oc	Neo	NA	Estimate	Source	Trend	Source	1% level	Notes
South Asia	South Asia				•				C/D	PE				Trend declining in Sri Lanka (HT).
E, SE Asia	SE Asia to NE China, Taiwan, S Japan	*SE Asia to S Japan*			•				D	SR	STA	SR	10,000	

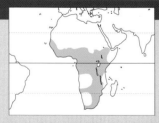

Ixobrychus sturmii — **Dwarf Bittern**

Subspecies/Population	Breeding range	Wintering, or core non-breeding range	Afr	Eu	Asia	Oc	Neo	NA	Estimate	Source	Trend	Source	1% level	Notes
Africa	Sub-Saharan Africa except arid areas		•						C	FE			1,000	

Ixobrychus flavicollis — **Black Bittern**

Subspecies/Population	Breeding range	Wintering, or core non-breeding range	Afr	Eu	Asia	Oc	Neo	NA	Estimate	Source	Trend	Source	1% level	Notes
flavicollis, South Asia	Pakistan, India, Bangladesh				•				C	PE			1,000	Sometimes ascribed to genus *Dupetor*.
flavicollis, E, SE Asia	Myanmar, Thailand, Indochina, S China, Philippines	*Myanmar, Thailand, Indochina, S China, Malaysia, Indonesia, Philippines*			•				B/C	SR			1,000	
australis, Australia, New Guinea	W, N & E Australia, New Guinea, Bismarck Archipelago					•					DEC	GC		GC estimate Australian population at 20,000 breeding adults (30,000 individuals). Declining trend on basis of decline in Australia. Sometimes ascribed to *gouldi*.
australis, Timor	Timor					•								

Ixobrychus flavicollis... continued

Subspecies/Population	Breeding range	*Wintering, or core non-breeding range*	Afr	Eu	Asia	Oc	Neo	NA	Estimate	Source	Trend	Source	1% level	Notes
australis	Rennell Island					•			<500	DX			5	Sometimes included in *woodfordi*, or as separate subspecies, *pallidor*.
australis, New Britain, New Ireland	New Britain, New Ireland					•			A	DX			100	Sometimes ascribed to *nesophilus*.
woodfordi	Solomon Islands					•			A	DX			100	

Zebrilus undulatus — **Zigzag Heron**

Subspecies/Population	Breeding range	*Wintering, or core non-breeding range*	Afr	Eu	Asia	Oc	Neo	NA	Estimate	Source	Trend	Source	1% level	Notes
South America	E Colombia to Guianas, NC Brazil, E Peru, NE Bolivia						•							

Tigrisoma mexicanum — **Bare-throated Tiger-Heron**

Subspecies/Population	Breeding range	*Wintering, or core non-breeding range*	Afr	Eu	Asia	Oc	Neo	NA	Estimate	Source	Trend	Source	1% level	Notes
Colombia to Mexico	Colombia, Central America, Coastal Mexico						•	•	10,000	KS			100	KS estimate 10,000.
S Mexico	Sonora & Sinaloa uplands (S Mexico)						•							Sometimes ascribed to *fremitus*.

Tigrisoma fasciatum — **Fasciated Tiger-Heron**

Subspecies/Population	Breeding range	*Wintering, or core non-breeding range*	Afr	Eu	Asia	Oc	Neo	NA	Estimate	Source	Trend	Source	1% level	Notes
fasciatum	SE Brazil, NE Argentina						•		A	AT			100	
salmoni	E Costa Rica, E Panama, Venezuela, E Colombia to N Bolivia, Argentina						•							
pallescens	NW Argentina						•							

Tigrisoma lineatum — **Rufescent Tiger-Heron**

Subspecies/Population	Breeding range	*Wintering, or core non-breeding range*	Afr	Eu	Asia	Oc	Neo	NA	Estimate	Source	Trend	Source	1% level	Notes
lineatum	SE Mexico to W Ecuador + Guianas & upper Amazonia						•							MP estimates 5,000–50,000 pairs (15,000–150,000 individuals) in Venezuela.
marmoratum	Central Bolivia to E Brazil & S to NE Argentina & Paraguay						•							

Zonerodius heliosylus NT   New Guinea Tiger-Heron, New Guinea Forest Bittern

Subspecies/Population	Breeding range	Wintering, or core non-breeding range	Afr	Eu	Asia	Oc	Neo	NA	Estimate	Source	Trend	Source	1% level	Notes
New Guinea	New Guinea					•			A	SR	DEC	SR	100	

Tigriornis leucolophus DD   White-crested Tiger-Heron, White-crested Bittern

Subspecies/Population	Breeding range	Wintering, or core non-breeding range	Afr	Eu	Asia	Oc	Neo	NA	Estimate	Source	Trend	Source	1% level	Notes
W & C Africa	African forest & Mangrove: The Gambia to the Congo Basin		•						C	SR			1,000	

Agamia agami   Agami Heron

Subspecies/Population	Breeding range	Wintering, or core non-breeding range	Afr	Eu	Asia	Oc	Neo	NA	Estimate	Source	Trend	Source	1% level	Notes
C & S America	E Mexico to N & C Brazil, E Bolivia						•	•						

Cochlearius cochlearius   Boat-billed Heron

Subspecies/Population	Breeding range	Wintering, or core non-breeding range	Afr	Eu	Asia	Oc	Neo	NA	Estimate	Source	Trend	Source	1% level	Notes
cochlearius	E Panama SE to Guianas, Amazonia, NE Argentina						•							MP estimates 3,250 pairs (9,750 individuals) in Suriname.
zeledoni	W Central Mexico						•							
phillipsi	E Mexico, Belize						•							
ridgwayi	S Mexico to W Honduras & El Salvador						•							
panamensis	Costa Rica & Panama						•							

SCOPIDAE
HAMERKOP

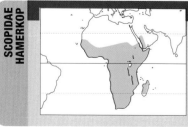

Scopus umbretta   Hamerkop

Subspecies/Population	Breeding range	Wintering, or core non-breeding range	Afr	Eu	Asia	Oc	Neo	NA	Estimate	Source	Trend	Source	1% level	Notes
umbretta	Tropical & sub-tropical Africa to SW Arabia		•	•					D	FE			10,000	Assigned to bannermanni by Peters (1931).
minor	Coast Sierra Leone to E Nigeria		•						B	DO			250	Assigned to nominate by Peters (1931).
(bannermanni)	Madagascar		•						60,000–90,000	HJ	STA/INC	HJ	750	

Mycteria americana — Wood Stork

Subspecies/Population	Breeding range	Wintering, or core non-breeding range	Afr	Eu	Asia	Oc	Neo	NA	Estimate	Source	Trend	Source	1% level	Notes
South America	Tropical & E South America	*N & E South America*					•							BW estimates 50,000–100,000 for all 3 populations combined.
Mexico, Caribbean, Central America	Mexico, Caribbean, C America						•	•	B/C	SR			1,000	KS estimate 32,000–46,000 breeding adults in Americas N of the equator (48,000–69,000 individuals).
North America	SE USA							•	20,000–25,000	CN	DEC	SR	230	CN estimates 7,853 breeding pairs (23,559 individuals).

Mycteria cinerea VU — Milky Stork

Subspecies/Population	Breeding range	Wintering, or core non-breeding range	Afr	Eu	Asia	Oc	Neo	NA	Estimate	Source	Trend	Source	1% level	Notes
Indonesia	W Indonesia				•				5,400	BC	DEC	BC	55	BC details 5,000 in Sumatra and 400 in W Java. SH suggests there maybe as few as 100–150 in Java.
Malaysia	Malaysia				•				100	SH	DEC	BC	1	
Cambodia	S Cambodia				•				50	SH	DEC	BC	1	

Mycteria ibis — Yellow-billed Stork

Subspecies/Population	Breeding range	Wintering, or core non-breeding range	Afr	Eu	Asia	Oc	Neo	NA	Estimate	Source	Trend	Source	1% level	Notes
Africa	Sub-Saharan Africa		•						50,000–100,000	DO	STA	BN	750	

Yellow-billed Stork.

Johan Verbanck

Mycteria leucocephala NT — Painted Stork

Subspecies/Population	Breeding range	Wintering, or core non-breeding range	Afr	Eu	Asia	Oc	Neo	NA	Estimate	Source	Trend	Source	1% level	Notes
South Asia	Pakistan, India, Nepal	*Pakistan, India, Nepal, Sri Lanka, Bangladesh*			•				15,000	PE	DEC	BC	150	BW estimates 15,000–20,000 for both populations.
SE Asia	Cambodia, Thailand	*Cambodia, Myanmar, Thailand, Laos, Vietnam*			•				<10,000	PE	DEC	PE	100	Free-flying population re-established in parks in Thailand.

Anastomus oscitans — Asian Openbill

Subspecies/Population	Breeding range	Wintering, or core non-breeding range	Afr	Eu	Asia	Oc	Neo	NA	Estimate	Source	Trend	Source	1% level	Notes
S, SE Asia	S & SE Asia				•				>125,000	SR			1,250	

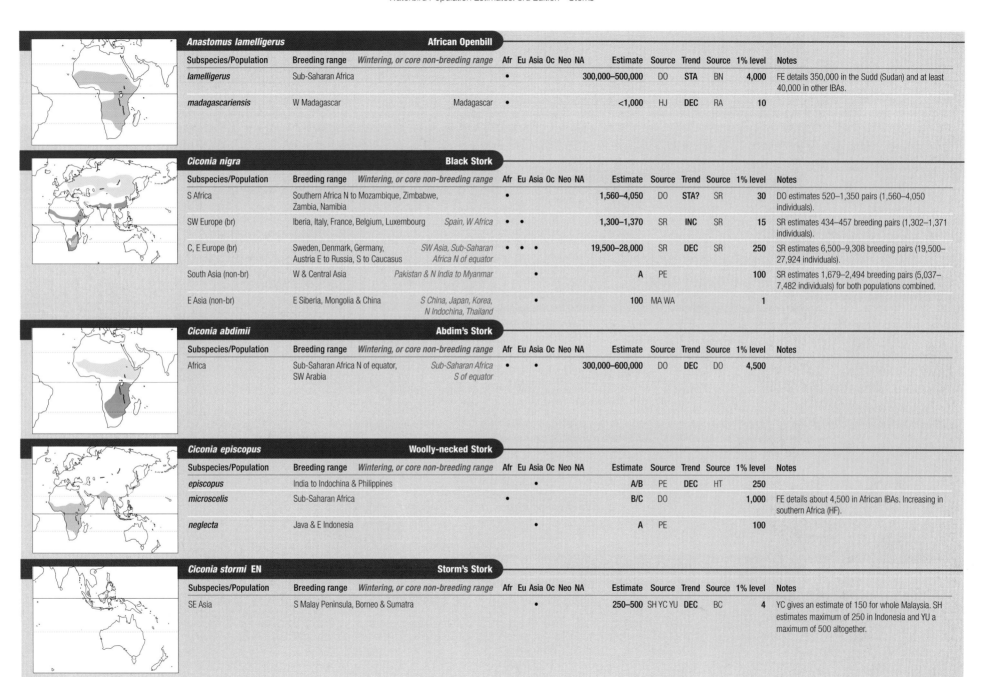

Anastomus lamelligerus — African Openbill

Subspecies/Population	Breeding range	Wintering, or core non-breeding range	Afr	Eu	Asia	Oc	Neo	NA	Estimate	Source	Trend	Source	1% level	Notes
lamelligerus	Sub-Saharan Africa		•						300,000–500,000	DO	STA	BN	4,000	FE details 350,000 in the Sudd (Sudan) and at least 40,000 in other IBAs.
madagascariensis	W Madagascar	Madagascar	•						<1,000	HJ	DEC	RA	10	

Ciconia nigra — Black Stork

Subspecies/Population	Breeding range	Wintering, or core non-breeding range	Afr	Eu	Asia	Oc	Neo	NA	Estimate	Source	Trend	Source	1% level	Notes
S Africa	Southern Africa N to Mozambique, Zimbabwe, Zambia, Namibia		•						1,560–4,050	DO	STA?	SR	30	DO estimates 520–1,350 pairs (1,560–4,050 individuals).
SW Europe (br)	Iberia, Italy, France, Belgium, Luxembourg	Spain, W Africa	•	•					1,300–1,370	SR	INC	SR	15	SR estimates 434–457 breeding pairs (1,302–1,371 individuals).
C, E Europe (br)	Sweden, Denmark, Germany, Austria E to Russia, S to Caucasus	SW Asia, Sub-Saharan Africa N of equator	•	•	•				19,500–28,000	SR	DEC	SR	250	SR estimates 6,500–9,308 breeding pairs (19,500–27,924 individuals).
South Asia (non-br)	W & Central Asia	Pakistan & N India to Myanmar			•				A	PE			100	SR estimates 1,679–2,494 breeding pairs (5,037–7,482 individuals) for both populations combined.
E Asia (non-br)	E Siberia, Mongolia & China	S China, Japan, Korea, N Indochina, Thailand			•				100	MA WA			1	

Ciconia abdimii — Abdim's Stork

Subspecies/Population	Breeding range	Wintering, or core non-breeding range	Afr	Eu	Asia	Oc	Neo	NA	Estimate	Source	Trend	Source	1% level	Notes
Africa	Sub-Saharan Africa N of equator, SW Arabia	Sub-Saharan Africa S of equator	•	•					300,000–600,000	DO	DEC	DO	4,500	

Ciconia episcopus — Woolly-necked Stork

Subspecies/Population	Breeding range	Wintering, or core non-breeding range	Afr	Eu	Asia	Oc	Neo	NA	Estimate	Source	Trend	Source	1% level	Notes
episcopus	India to Indochina & Philippines				•				A/B	PE	DEC	HT	250	
microscelis	Sub-Saharan Africa		•						B/C	DO			1,000	FE details about 4,500 in African IBAs. Increasing in southern Africa (HF).
neglecta	Java & E Indonesia				•				A	PE			100	

Ciconia stormi EN — Storm's Stork

Subspecies/Population	Breeding range	Wintering, or core non-breeding range	Afr	Eu	Asia	Oc	Neo	NA	Estimate	Source	Trend	Source	1% level	Notes
SE Asia	S Malay Peninsula, Borneo & Sumatra				•				250–500	SH YC YU	DEC	BC	4	YC gives an estimate of 150 for whole Malaysia. SH estimates maximum of 250 in Indonesia and YU a maximum of 500 altogether.

Ciconia maguari — Maguari Stork

Subspecies/Population	Breeding range	Wintering, or core non-breeding range	Afr	Eu	Asia	Oc	Neo	NA	Estimate	Source	Trend	Source	1% level	Notes
S America	N, Central South America E of Andes						•		50,000–100,000	BW	STA	CC	750	

Ciconia ciconia — European White Stork

Subspecies/Population	Breeding range	Wintering, or core non-breeding range	Afr	Eu	Asia	Oc	Neo	NA	Estimate	Source	Trend	Source	1% level	Notes
ciconia, South Africa (br)	South Africa	Southern to NE Africa	•						20	UL	STA	UL	1	Population established since at least the 1930s. 7 out of 8 breeding pairs at Tygerberg Zoo, Cape Town. (SR).
ciconia, SW & W Europe (br)	NW Africa, Iberia, Italy, France, Belgium, Netherlands, W Germany, Switzerland	Iberia, West Africa	•	•					93,000	S9 KA SR	INC	S9	930	Summed national breeding totals updated from S9 by SR, dividing Germany as recommended by KA, 30,974 breeding pairs (92,922 individuals).
ciconia, C & E Europe + Syria, Israel (br)	Poland, Ukraine, Belarus, Baltic States, Russia, W to Denmark, E Germany, Austria, S to Balkans, W Turkey, Syria, Israel	SW Asia, Sub-Saharan Africa	•	•	•				390,000–400,000	S9 DG SR	STA	S9	4,000	Summed national breeding totals updated from S9 by SR and DG, dividing Germany as recommended by KA, 131,073–133,573 breeding pairs (393,219–400,719 individuals).
ciconia, W Asia & Caucasus (br)	Iran, Armenia, Georgia	?SW Asia		•	•				B	SA	DEC	S9	250	Summed national breeding totals updated from S9 by SR, 2,937 breeding pairs (8,811individuals, incomplete total).
asiatica	Central Asian Republics	S Asia			•				4,350	SF	INC	SF	45	SE presents details of 1,400 pairs in Uzbekistan, 35–40 pairs in Kazakhstan, 5–6 pairs in Tajikistan and 1–2 pairs in Kyrgyzstan. Total: 1,440–1,450 pairs (4,320–4,350 individuals).

European White Stork.   Paul Goriup

Ciconia boyciana EN — Oriental White Stork

Subspecies/Population	Breeding range	Wintering, or core non-breeding range	Afr	Eu	Asia	Oc	Neo	NA	Estimate	Source	Trend	Source	1% level	Notes
E Asia	SE Siberia, NE China	S & SE China, Taiwan, Japan, Korea			•				3,000	XL ZL	DEC	BC	30	2,919 recorded by AWC in China in 1999 (2,832 at Poyang Lake) (XL, ZL).

Ephippiorhynchus asiaticus NT — Black-necked Stork

Subspecies/Population	Breeding range	Wintering, or core non-breeding range	Afr	Eu	Asia	Oc	Neo	NA	Estimate	Source	Trend	Source	1% level	Notes
asiaticus	S, SE Asia				•				1,000	SY	DEC	RC	10	SY reports 200–250 in 2 districts of Uttar Pradesh and suggests a total population of 1,000.
australis	Australia, S New Guinea					•			30,000	GC	STA	GC	300	GC estimates 20,000 breeding adults in Australia (30,000 individuals) Most of the population occurs in Australia (GC).

Ephippiorhynchus senegalensis — Saddle-billed Stork, Saddlebill

Subspecies/Population	Breeding range	Wintering, or core non-breeding range	Afr	Eu	Asia	Oc	Neo	NA	Estimate	Source	Trend	Source	1% level	Notes
Africa	Sub-Saharan Africa		•						A/B	DO	STA	PC	250	FE details 7,000 in African IBAs.

Jabiru mycteria — Jabiru

Subspecies/Population	Breeding range	Wintering, or core non-breeding range	Afr	Eu	Asia	Oc	Neo	NA	Estimate	Source	Trend	Source	1% level	Notes
Central America	Central America						•		675	KS			7	BW estimates 10,000–25,000 for all three populations. KS estimate 450 breeding adults for Central America (675 individuals).
N South America	N South America						•							
C South America	Central South America						•							

Leptoptilos javanicus VU — Lesser Adjutant

Subspecies/Population	Breeding range	Wintering, or core non-breeding range	Afr	Eu	Asia	Oc	Neo	NA	Estimate	Source	Trend	Source	1% level	Notes
S & SE Asia	S & SE Asia				•				5,000	BC	DEC	BC	50	Estimate may require upward revision in the light of recent estimate of 2,000 in Assam (CJ).

Lesser Adjutant (in Matang).

Marcel Silvius

Leptoptilos dubius EN — Greater Adjutant

Subspecies/Population	Breeding range	Wintering, or core non-breeding range	Afr	Eu	Asia	Oc	Neo	NA	Estimate	Source	Trend	Source	1% level	Notes
Assam, India (br)	Assam, India	India, Nepal, Bangladesh			•				650–800	CJ BD	DEC	BC	7	BD estimates 650–700 individuals, CJ estimates over 800.
Cambodia (br)	Cambodia	Cambodia, Myanmar, Thailand, S Laos, S Vietnam			•				150–200	BD	DEC	BC	2	BD: Estimate assumes majority at Tonle Sap Lake.

Leptoptilos crumeniferus — Marabou (Stork)

Subspecies/Population	Breeding range	Wintering, or core non-breeding range	Afr	Eu	Asia	Oc	Neo	NA	Estimate	Source	Trend	Source	1% level	Notes
Africa	Sub-Saharan Africa		•						100,000–300,000	DO	INC	BN	2,000	FE details 360,000 in The Sudd, Sudan, alone.

Balaeniceps rex NT — Shoebill

Subspecies/Population	Breeding range	*Wintering, or core non-breeding range*	Afr	Eu	Asia	Oc	Neo	NA	Estimate	Source	Trend	Source	1% level
C Africa	Central Tropical Africa		•						5,000–8,000	DO	DEC	DO	65

Shoebill.

Johan Verbanck

Threskiornis aethiopicus — Sacred Ibis

Subspecies/Population	Breeding range	*Wintering, or core non-breeding range*	Afr	Eu	Asia	Oc	Neo	NA	Estimate	Source	Trend	Source	1% level
aethiopicus, Sub-Saharan Africa	Sub-Saharan Africa		•						200,000–450,000	DO	STA	SR	3,300
aethiopicus, Iraq, Iran	SE Iraq	Iraq, Iran			•				200	PE	DEC	PE	2
abbotti	Aldabra		•						300–750	RO	STA	DO	5
bernieri	Madagascar		•						2,500	HJ	DEC	SR	25

Sacred Ibis.

Johan Verbanck

Threskiornis melanocephalus NT — Black-headed Ibis

Subspecies/Population	Breeding range	*Wintering, or core non-breeding range*	Afr	Eu	Asia	Oc	Neo	NA	Estimate	Source	Trend	Source	1% level	Notes
South Asia	S Asia				•				A	BW	STA	HT	100	BW estimates <10,000 for all three populations.
SE Asia	SE Asia				•				A	BW			100	
E Asia	NE China	*China, Taiwan, Korea, Japan*			•				<100	WA	DEC	PE	1	

Threskiornis molucca — Australian White Ibis

Subspecies/Population	Breeding range	*Wintering, or core non-breeding range*	Afr	Eu	Asia	Oc	Neo	NA	Estimate	Source	Trend	Source	1% level	Notes
molucca	Moluccas, Lesser Sundas and possibly New Guinea				•	•			A	SR	STA	SR	100	SR estimates 80,000 for 3 populations combined, a majority probably belonging to *strictipennis*.
(*strictipennis*)	Australia, ?S New Guinea					•			<70,000	HP			700	Recognised by Peters (1931). Often included in nominate (*molucca*).
pygmeus	Rennell, Bellona, (Solomon) Is					•			A	DX			100	

Threskiornis spinicollis — Straw-necked Ibis

Subspecies/Population	Breeding range	*Wintering, or core non-breeding range*	Afr	Eu	Asia	Oc	Neo	NA	Estimate	Source	Trend	Source	1% level
Australia	Australia	*Australia, S New Guinea*				•			500,000	SR			5,000

Straw-necked Ibis.

Paul Goriup

Threskiornis solitarius — Réunion Flightless Ibis

Subspecies/Population	Breeding range	*Wintering, or core non-breeding range*	Afr	Eu	Asia	Oc	Neo	NA	Estimate	Source	Trend	Source	1% level	Notes
Réunion	Réunion		•						0	BC	**EXT**	BC		Last account in 1705 (BC).

Pseudibis papillosa — Indian Black Ibis, Red-naped Ibis

Subspecies/Population	Breeding range	*Wintering, or core non-breeding range*	Afr	Eu	Asia	Oc	Neo	NA	Estimate	Source	Trend	Source	1% level	Notes
S Asia	India, S Pakistan, S Nepal				•				10,000	PE			100	

Pseudibis davisoni CR — White-shouldered Ibis

Subspecies/Population	Breeding range	*Wintering, or core non-breeding range*	Afr	Eu	Asia	Oc	Neo	NA	Estimate	Source	Trend	Source	1% level	Notes
Indochina	S Vietnam, S Laos, Cambodia,				•				<100	SR	**DEC**	BC	1	
Borneo	Borneo				•				<50	YU SH	**DEC**	BC	1	YU reports only one individual in Indonesia in recent years.

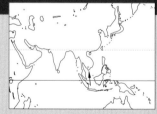

Pseudibis (Thaumatibis) gigantea CR — Giant Ibis

Subspecies/Population	Breeding range	*Wintering, or core non-breeding range*	Afr	Eu	Asia	Oc	Neo	NA	Estimate	Source	Trend	Source	1% level	Notes
Indochina	Cambodia, marginally in S Laos, Thailand, & S Vietnam				•				100–200	SR	**DEC**	BC	2	

Geronticus eremita CR — Northern Bald Ibis, Waldrapp

Subspecies/Population	Breeding range	*Wintering, or core non-breeding range*	Afr	Eu	Asia	Oc	Neo	NA	Estimate	Source	Trend	Source	1% level	Notes
Morocco	Morocco		•						220	BC	**FLU**	SP BC	2	BC estimates 220; FE estimates 63 pairs (189 individuals) and STA trend. SP gives trend as DEC; BC gives trend as INC. Long term trend is DEC.
SW Asia	SW Asia	*SW Asia, NE Africa*			•				7	B13	**DEC**	PE	1	In the 1990s, this population was reduced to the artificially maintained colony at Birecik, Turkey. In 2002, 3 pairs with eggs and a seventh adult were discovered at a breeding colony in central Syria.

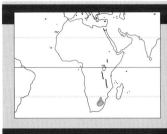

Geronticus calvus VU — Southern Bald Ibis

Subspecies/Population	Breeding range	Wintering, or core non-breeding range	Afr	Eu	Asia	Oc	Neo	NA	Estimate	Source	Trend	Source	1% level	Notes
calvus	S African highlands		•						8,000–10,000	BC HF	DEC?	BC HF	90	

Nipponia nippon EN — Crested Ibis

Subspecies/Population	Breeding range	Wintering, or core non-breeding range	Afr	Eu	Asia	Oc	Neo	NA	Estimate	Source	Trend	Source	1% level	Notes
China	Central China				•				140	BB CE	INC	BC	1	There are an additional 100 Nipponia nippon in captivity (BC).

Bostrychia olivacea — Olive Ibis

Subspecies/Population	Breeding range	Wintering, or core non-breeding range	Afr	Eu	Asia	Oc	Neo	NA	Estimate	Source	Trend	Source	1% level	Notes
olivacea	West African Tropical forest, Sierra Leone to Ghana		•						A	BW			100	
cupreipennis	Central African tropical forest, Cameroon to DR Congo		•						A	BW			100	
akleyorum	Mountains of Kenya & Tanzania		•						A	BW	DEC	DO	100	
bocagei CR Sao Tomé Ibis, Dwarf Olive Ibis	Sao Tomé		•						<50	BC			1	BC treats this population (Bostrychia olivacea bocagei) as a full species (Bostrychis bocagei) to which they assign Critically Endangered status.
rothschildi	Principe		•						0–10	S4	EXT/DEC	GY	1	

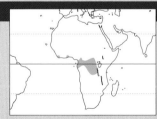

Bostrychia rara — Spot-breasted Ibis

Subspecies/Population	Breeding range	Wintering, or core non-breeding range	Afr	Eu	Asia	Oc	Neo	NA	Estimate	Source	Trend	Source	1% level	Notes
W & C Africa	Tropical forest of West & Central Africa		•						A	SR			100	

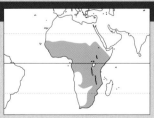

Bostrychia hagedash — Hadada Ibis

Subspecies/Population	Breeding range	Wintering, or core non-breeding range	Afr	Eu	Asia	Oc	Neo	NA	Estimate	Source	Trend	Source	1% level	Notes
hagedash	Southern Africa S of Zambezi R		•											BW estimate 100,000–250,000 for all four subspecies combined.
brevirostris	West Africa from Gambia to DR Congo		•											
nilotica	NE Africa (Sudan, Ethiopia)		•											
(erlangeri)	E Africa Somalia–Malawi		•											

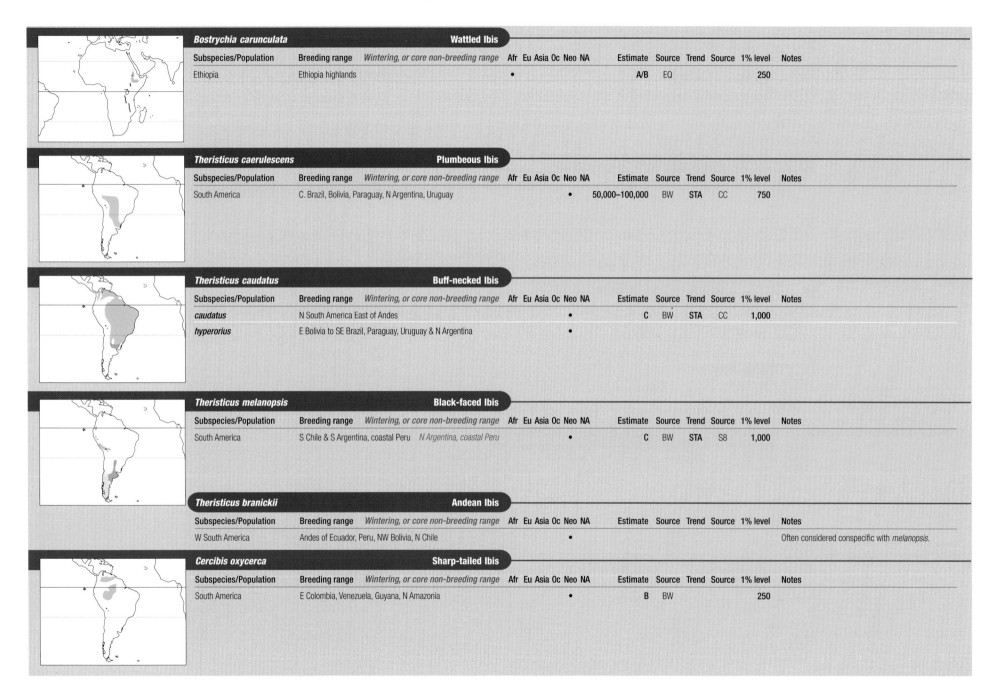

Bostrychia carunculata — Wattled Ibis

Subspecies/Population	Breeding range	Wintering, or core non-breeding range	Afr	Eu	Asia	Oc	Neo	NA	Estimate	Source	Trend	Source	1% level	Notes
Ethiopia	Ethiopia highlands		•						A/B	EQ			250	

Theristicus caerulescens — Plumbeous Ibis

Subspecies/Population	Breeding range	Wintering, or core non-breeding range	Afr	Eu	Asia	Oc	Neo	NA	Estimate	Source	Trend	Source	1% level	Notes
South America	C. Brazil, Bolivia, Paraguay, N Argentina, Uruguay						•		50,000–100,000	BW	STA	CC	750	

Theristicus caudatus — Buff-necked Ibis

Subspecies/Population	Breeding range	Wintering, or core non-breeding range	Afr	Eu	Asia	Oc	Neo	NA	Estimate	Source	Trend	Source	1% level	Notes
caudatus	N South America East of Andes						•		C	BW	STA	CC	1,000	
hyperorius	E Bolivia to SE Brazil, Paraguay, Uruguay & N Argentina						•							

Theristicus melanopsis — Black-faced Ibis

Subspecies/Population	Breeding range	Wintering, or core non-breeding range	Afr	Eu	Asia	Oc	Neo	NA	Estimate	Source	Trend	Source	1% level	Notes
South America	S Chile & S Argentina, coastal Peru	N Argentina, coastal Peru					•		C	BW	STA	S8	1,000	

Theristicus branickii — Andean Ibis

Subspecies/Population	Breeding range	Wintering, or core non-breeding range	Afr	Eu	Asia	Oc	Neo	NA	Estimate	Source	Trend	Source	1% level	Notes
W South America	Andes of Ecuador, Peru, NW Bolivia, N Chile						•							Often considered conspecific with melanopsis.

Cercibis oxycerca — Sharp-tailed Ibis

Subspecies/Population	Breeding range	Wintering, or core non-breeding range	Afr	Eu	Asia	Oc	Neo	NA	Estimate	Source	Trend	Source	1% level	Notes
South America	E Colombia, Venezuela, Guyana, N Amazonia						•		B	BW			250	

Mesembrinibis cayennensis — Green Ibis

Subspecies/Population	Breeding range	Wintering, or core non-breeding range	Afr	Eu	Asia	Oc	Neo	NA	Estimate	Source	Trend	Source	1% level	Notes
South America	N & Central South America E of Andes, Central America						•		50,000–100,000	BW			750	

Phimosus infuscatus — Bare-faced Ibis, Whispering Ibis

Subspecies/Population	Breeding range	Wintering, or core non-breeding range	Afr	Eu	Asia	Oc	Neo	NA	Estimate	Source	Trend	Source	1% level	Notes
berlepschi	E Colombia to Guianas, Suriname & NW Brazil						•							
nudifrons	Brazil S of Amazon						•							
infuscatus	E Bolivia to Paraguay, NE Argentina & Uruguay						•		D	AT	STA	CC	10,000	

Eudocimus albus — American White Ibis

Subspecies/Population	Breeding range	Wintering, or core non-breeding range	Afr	Eu	Asia	Oc	Neo	NA	Estimate	Source	Trend	Source	1% level	Notes
Central & South America	C America, NW South America						•							
North America	SE North America							•	150,000	SR	STA	S5	1,500	KS estimate >100,000 breeding adults in the USA (150,000 individuals).

Eudocimus ruber — Scarlet Ibis

Subspecies/Population	Breeding range	Wintering, or core non-breeding range	Afr	Eu	Asia	Oc	Neo	NA	Estimate	Source	Trend	Source	1% level	Notes
NE South America	NE Neotropics						•		100,000–150,000	BW	DEC	FT	1,300	

Plegadis falcinellus — Glossy Ibis

Subspecies/Population	Breeding range	Wintering, or core non-breeding range	Afr	Eu	Asia	Oc	Neo	NA	Estimate	Source	Trend	Source	1% level	Notes
falcinellus, Sub-Saharan Africa (br)	Sub-Saharan Africa		•						1,000,000–2,000,000	DO			15,000	FE details 1,500,000 in the Sudd, Sudan, alone. Increasing in Southern Africa (HF).
falcinellus, Madagascar	Madagascar		•						<5,000	HJ	DEC	HJ	50	Sometimes included in peregrinus.
falcinellus, E & S Europe (br)	E & S Europe	Spain, Sub-Saharan Africa	•	•					49,000–57,000	BE	DEC	SA	530	BE: European breeding population 16,200–18,900 pairs (48,600–56,700 individuals).
falcinellus, SW Asia (br)	SW Asia & Caspian	SW Asia & NE Africa	•	•	•				C	SA			1,000	Minimum Breeding Population 17,000–30,000 pairs, including 4,500–9,500 pairs in European Russia (Volga).

Plegadis falcinellus... continued

Glossy Ibis.   Paul Goriup

Subspecies/Population	Breeding range	Wintering, or core non-breeding range	Afr	Eu	Asia	Oc	Neo	NA	Estimate	Source	Trend	Source	1% level	Notes
falcinellus, S, SE Asia (non-br)	Central, S, SE Asia	S, SE Asia			•				B	PE	DEC	PE	250	
falcinellus, North & Central America, Caribbean	Coastal E USA, Gulf of Mexico, Caribbean						•	•	19,500–22,500	KS	DEC	DB	210	KS estimate 13,000–15,000 breeding adults (19,500–22,500).
(peregrinus), Australia, SE Asia	Australia, Philippines, Indonesia				•	•			C/D	PE				

Plegadis chihi — White-faced Ibis

Subspecies/Population	Breeding range	Wintering, or core non-breeding range	Afr	Eu	Asia	Oc	Neo	NA	Estimate	Source	Trend	Source	1% level	Notes
S USA, Mexico, Central America	W USA, Coastal Mexico S to Nicaragua	Coastal Mexico, Central America					•	•	>150,000	KS	STA	KS	1,500	KS estimate >100,000 breeding adults (>150,000 individuals).
Central South America	S Central South America						•		E	SR	INC	SR		

Plegadis ridgwayi — Puna Ibis

Subspecies/Population	Breeding range	Wintering, or core non-breeding range	Afr	Eu	Asia	Oc	Neo	NA	Estimate	Source	Trend	Source	1% level	Notes
South America	Central South America Andes	Central South America Andes to Peruvian coast					•		10,000–15,000	BW	DEC	S8	130	

Lophotibis cristata NT — Madagascar Crested Ibis

Subspecies/Population	Breeding range	Wintering, or core non-breeding range	Afr	Eu	Asia	Oc	Neo	NA	Estimate	Source	Trend	Source	1% level	Notes
Madagascar	Madagascar		•						10,000	BW	STA	SR	100	

Platalea leucorodia — Eurasian Spoonbill

Subspecies/Population	Breeding range	Wintering, or core non-breeding range	Afr	Eu	Asia	Oc	Neo	NA	Estimate	Source	Trend	Source	1% level	Notes
leucorodia, E Atlantic	Coastal W Europe	W Mediterranean & W African coast	•	•					9,950	OZ	INC	CO	100	
leucorodia, C, SE Europe (br)	Central, SE Europe	Mediterranean, N tropical Africa	•	•					11,700	OZ	DEC	OZ	120	
balsaci	Coastal Mauritania		•						6,000–7,000	OZ	STA	OZ	65	
archeri	Red Sea & Somalia		•		•				1,250	NN SA			15	
(major), SW, S Asia (non-br)	Central & SW & S Asia	SW & S Asia			•				23,000	PE	STA	HT	230	Often included in nominate.
(major), E Asia	NE Asia	China, Taiwan, Korea, Japan			•				6,500	ZL	DEC	PE	65	ZL report a count of 6,362 at Poyang Lake in January 1999.

Platalea minor EN — Black-faced Spoonbill

Subspecies/Population	Breeding range	Wintering, or core non-breeding range	Afr	Eu	Asia	Oc	Neo	NA	Estimate	Source	Trend	Source	1% level	Notes
E & SE Asia	N & S Korea, NE China	Japan, South Korea, South China, Vietnam, Taiwan, Philippines			•				970	DA CE	INC	DA	10	969 in joint census of 2001–2002 (CE).

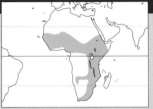

Platalea alba — African Spoonbill

Subspecies/Population	Breeding range	Wintering, or core non-breeding range	Afr	Eu	Asia	Oc	Neo	NA	Estimate	Source	Trend	Source	1% level	Notes
Africa	Sub-Saharan Africa		•						B/C	DO	STA	DO	1,000	Increasing in southern Africa (HF).

Platalea regia — Royal Spoonbill

Subspecies/Population	Breeding range	Wintering, or core non-breeding range	Afr	Eu	Asia	Oc	Neo	NA	Estimate	Source	Trend	Source	1% level	Notes
Australasia (br)	Australia, New Zealand	Australia, New Zealand, New Guinea, E Indonesia			•	•			100,000–250,000	BW	DEC	PE	1,800	

Platalea flavipes — Yellow-billed Spoonbill

Subspecies/Population	Breeding range	Wintering, or core non-breeding range	Afr	Eu	Asia	Oc	Neo	NA	Estimate	Source	Trend	Source	1% level	Notes
Australia	Australia					•			C	BW			1,000	

Ajaia ajaja — Roseate Spoonbill

Subspecies/Population	Breeding range	Wintering, or core non-breeding range	Afr	Eu	Asia	Oc	Neo	NA	Estimate	Source	Trend	Source	1% level	Notes
N Neotropics to S USA	N Neotropics, Mexico, S USA						•	•	100,000–250,000	BW	STA	CC	1,800	KS estimate 20,500 breeding adults in North America (30,750 individuals).
Florida & West Indies	Florida & West Indies						•	•	3,400	DW HW			35	DW: 1,100 pairs (3,300 individuals) in Florida in 1992 and 1998; 50 Bahamas (HW) + some small colonies in Cuba.

PHOENICOPTERIDAE FLAMINGOS

Phoenicopterus ruber — Greater Flamingo

Subspecies/Population	Breeding range	*Wintering, or core non-breeding range*	Afr	Eu	Asia	Oc	Neo	NA	Estimate	Source	Trend	Source	1% level	Notes
roseus, W Africa	W Africa	*Partial dispersion*	•						40,000	SR	STA	DO	400	Breeding population increases in some years when birds from W Mediterranean breed in e.g. Mauritania.
roseus, E Africa	Eastern Africa	*Partial dispersion*	•						35,000	KB	STA	DO	350	
roseus, S Africa	Southern Africa	*Partial dispersion*	•						65,000–87,000	SR	STA	SR HF	760	HF estimate 26,000 pairs (72,000 individuals).
roseus, W Mediterranean	W Mediterranean	*Partial dispersion*	•	•					100,000	SR	INC	SR	1,000	Regular movements to breed as far away as Mauritania.
roseus, E Mediterranean, SW & S Asia	E Mediterranean, SW & S Asia	*Partial dispersion*	•	•	•				290,000	SR	STA	PE	2,900	Former estimates for this population based on estimates in India in 1945 and 1960 now considered to be too high.
roseus, Aldabra	Aldabra		•						25–50	DO	STA	DO	1	
ruber, Galapagos Is	Galapagos Islands						•		435	SR	STA	SR	4	Felicity Arengo in litt. to SR, 2001.
ruber, Bonaire, Venezuela	Bonaire, Venezuela						•		34,000	EP	INC	EP	340	
ruber, Mexico	Mexico							•	30,000	SR	INC	SR	300	R Migoya, pers. comm to SR.
ruber, Bahamas, Cuba	Bahamas, Cuba						•		260,000	MO SR	INC	SR	2,600	MO estimates 200,000 for Cuba, SR give approximate estimate of 60,000 for Bahamas.

Greater Flamingos. — Manie Grobler

Phoenicopterus chilensis NT — Chilean Flamingo

Subspecies/Population	Breeding range	*Wintering, or core non-breeding range*	Afr	Eu	Asia	Oc	Neo	NA	Estimate	Source	Trend	Source	1% level	Notes
S South America	S South America						•		200,000	BC VA	DEC	BC	2,000	

Phoenicopterus minor NT — Lesser Flamingo

Subspecies/Population	Breeding range	*Wintering, or core non-breeding range*	Afr	Eu	Asia	Oc	Neo	NA	Estimate	Source	Trend	Source	1% level	Notes
W Africa	W Africa		•						15,000	PC	STA	BN	150	
E Africa	Eastern Africa		•						2,000,000–4,000,000	DO	DEC	SK	20,000	For populations over 2 million birds, Ramsar criterion 5 (20,000 or more waterbirds) applies.
S Africa	Southern Africa, Madagascar		•						55,000–65,000	DO	STA	DO	600	
S Asia	NW India, SE Pakistan				•				150,000	PE	INC	PE	1,500	

Phoenicopterus andinus VU — Andean Flamingo

Subspecies/Population	Breeding range	*Wintering, or core non-breeding range*	Afr	Eu	Asia	Oc	Neo	NA	Estimate	Source	Trend	Source	1% level	Notes
South American Andes	Central high Andes of Argentina, Bolivia, Chile & Peru						•		34,000	VA	DEC	BC	340	

Phoenicopterus jamesi NT — James's Flamingo, Puna Flamingo

Subspecies/Population	Breeding range	Wintering, or core non-breeding range	Afr	Eu	Asia	Oc	Neo	NA	Estimate	Source	Trend	Source	1% level	Notes
South American Andes		Central high Andes of Argentina, Bolivia, Chile & Peru					•		64,000	VA	INC	BC	640	

Anhima cornuta — Horned Screamer

Subspecies/Population	Breeding range	Wintering, or core non-breeding range	Afr	Eu	Asia	Oc	Neo	NA	Estimate	Source	Trend	Source	1% level	Notes
N South America		Colombia through Brazil to N Argentina					•		C	EJ	DEC	EJ	1,000	

Chauna torquata — Southern Screamer

Subspecies/Population	Breeding range	Wintering, or core non-breeding range	Afr	Eu	Asia	Oc	Neo	NA	Estimate	Source	Trend	Source	1% level	Notes
C South America		Bolivia & S Brazil to N Argentina, Uruguay					•		D	CC	STA	CC	10,000	

Chauna chavaria NT — Northern Screamer

Subspecies/Population	Breeding range	Wintering, or core non-breeding range	Afr	Eu	Asia	Oc	Neo	NA	Estimate	Source	Trend	Source	1% level	Notes
N Colombia, NW Venezuela	N Colombia, NW Venezuela						•		2,000	SD	DEC	EJ	20	

Anseranas semipalmata — Magpie Goose

Subspecies/Population	Breeding range	Wintering, or core non-breeding range	Afr	Eu	Asia	Oc	Neo	NA	Estimate	Source	Trend	Source	1% level	Notes
N Australia, S New Guinea	N Australia, S New Guinea				•	•			E	GC	FLU	GC		GC: Numbers fluctuate in response to rainfall patterns and sometimes exceed 4,000,000 breeding adults (6,000,000 individuals). For populations over 2 million birds, Ramsar Convention criterion 5 (20,000 or more waterbirds), applies.

ANHIMIDAE SCREAMERS

ANATIDAE DUCKS, GEESE & SWANS

Dendrocygna guttata — Spotted Whistling Duck

Subspecies/Population	Breeding range	Wintering, or core non-breeding range	Afr	Eu	Asia	Oc	Neo	NA	Estimate	Source	Trend	Source	1% level	Notes
SE Asia		E Indonesia, S Philippines, New Guinea			●	●			B	PE			250	

Dendrocygna eytoni — Plumed Whistling Duck

Subspecies/Population	Breeding range	Wintering, or core non-breeding range	Afr	Eu	Asia	Oc	Neo	NA	Estimate	Source	Trend	Source	1% level
Australia		N & E Australia				●			D/E	TL	STA	TL	

Plumed Whistling Duck.

Ian Montgomery

Dendrocygna bicolor — Fulvous Whistling Duck

Subspecies/Population	Breeding range	Wintering, or core non-breeding range	Afr	Eu	Asia	Oc	Neo	NA	Estimate	Source	Trend	Source	1% level	Notes
W Africa	W Africa, Senegal to Chad		●						100,000	PC			1,000	
E & S Africa	Eastern, Southern Africa		●						150,000–350,000	DO			2,500	
Madagascar	Madagascar		●						10,000–20,000	DO	DEC	S11	150	
S Asia	S Asia, Myanmar				●				20,000	PE	DEC	PE	200	
Neotropics, S USA	Neotropics, S USA						●	●	E	CC	DEC	AT		

Dendrocygna arcuata — Wandering Whistling Duck

Subspecies/Population	Breeding range	Wintering, or core non-breeding range	Afr	Eu	Asia	Oc	Neo	NA	Estimate	Source	Trend	Source	1% level	Notes
arcuata	E Indonesia, S Philippines					●			D	MM			10,000	
pygmaea	New Britain					●			0	EJ	EXT	EJ		Recorded in 1970s; possibly survives on Fiji (DX).
australis	New Guinea, N Australia					●			D/E	PE	STA	PE		

Dendrocygna javanica — Lesser Whistling Duck

Subspecies/Population	Breeding range	Wintering, or core non-breeding range	Afr	Eu	Asia	Oc	Neo	NA	Estimate	Source	Trend	Source	1% level	Notes
South Asia	South Asia				●				D	PE	DEC	PE	10,000	
E & SE Asia	E & SE Asia, Andaman & Nicobar Islands to W Indonesia				●				D	PE	DEC	PE	10,000	

Dendrocygna viduata — White-faced Whistling Duck

Subspecies/Population	Breeding range	Wintering, or core non-breeding range	Afr	Eu	Asia	Oc	Neo	NA	Estimate	Source	Trend	Source	1% level	Notes
W Africa	W Africa, Senegal to Chad		•						250,000–500,000	DO	INC	S11	3,800	
E & S Africa	Eastern, Southern Africa		•						D	DO	INC	S11	10,000	
Madagascar	Madagascar		•						20,000–50,000	S11	DEC	S11	350	
Central & South America	Costa Rica S to N Argentina & Uruguay						•		E	CC	INC	AT		

Dendrocygna arborea VU — West Indian Whistling Duck

Subspecies/Population	Breeding range	Wintering, or core non-breeding range	Afr	Eu	Asia	Oc	Neo	NA	Estimate	Source	Trend	Source	1% level	Notes
Caribbean	Caribbean Islands						•		>10,000	BC	DEC	BC	100	

Dendrocygna autumnalis — Black-bellied Whistling Duck

Subspecies/Population	Breeding range	Wintering, or core non-breeding range	Afr	Eu	Asia	Oc	Neo	NA	Estimate	Source	Trend	Source	1% level	Notes
autumnalis	Arizona, SE Texas, Louisiana, Arkansas, Florida, Mexico, to Central Panama						•	•	D	EJ	INC	JD	10,000	
fulgens	E Panama S to Ecuador, N Argentina						•		E	CC	INC	AT		Sometimes ascribed to discolor.

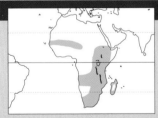

Thalassornis leuconotus — White-backed Duck

Subspecies/Population	Breeding range	Wintering, or core non-breeding range	Afr	Eu	Asia	Oc	Neo	NA	Estimate	Source	Trend	Source	1% level	Notes
leuconotus, W Africa	W Africa		•						<1000	D	DEC	PD	10	
leuconotus, E & S Africa	Eastern, Southern Africa		•						10,000–25,000	CA	STA	CA	180	
insularis	Madagascar		•						2,500–5,000	YO	DEC	S11	40	

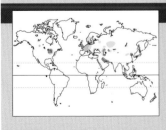

Cygnus olor — Mute Swan

Subspecies/Population	Breeding range	Wintering, or core non-breeding range	Afr	Eu	Asia	Oc	Neo	NA	Estimate	Source	Trend	Source	1% level	Notes
NW, C Europe	NW Mainland & Central Europe			•					250,000	S11 DF	INC	DF	2,500	Population estimated by S11 increased on basis of trends presented in DF.
Britain	Britain			•					37,500	KN	INC	KN	380	Population increased by about 50% in 1990s.
Ireland	Ireland			•					10,000	SE			100	
Black Sea	Black Sea region	Black Sea, SE Europe		•					45,000	S11	INC	S11	450	
W & Central Asia, Caspian	W Central Asia, Caspian			•	•				250,000	S11	INC	S11	2,500	
Central Asia	Central Asia	S Central Asia			•				B	YA			250	
East Asia	L Baykal (Russia), Mongolia, NW & NE China	W & NE China, Korean Peninsula			•				1,000–3,000	MM		MM	20	Introduced population of 100 individuals in Japan.

Cygnus atratus — Black Swan

Subspecies/Population	Breeding range	Wintering, or core non-breeding range	Afr	Eu	Asia	Oc	Neo	NA	Estimate	Source	Trend	Source	1% level	Notes
Australia	Australia					•			300,000–500,000	SR			4,000	The New Zealand population is introduced and has not been included.
Tasmania	Tasmania					•								

Cygnus melanocorypha — Black-necked Swan

Subspecies/Population	Breeding range	Wintering, or core non-breeding range	Afr	Eu	Asia	Oc	Neo	NA	Estimate	Source	Trend	Source	1% level	Notes
South America	S & Central Chile, Argentina, Uruguay	*Some northward movement to Paraguay, SE Brazil*					•		C	AT	STA	S8	1,000	
Falkland/Malvinas Islands	Falkland/Malvinas Islands						•		900–1,800	WS			15	WS estimate 300–600 pairs (900–1,800 individuals).

Cygnus buccinator — Trumpeter Swan

Subspecies/Population	Breeding range	Wintering, or core non-breeding range	Afr	Eu	Asia	Oc	Neo	NA	Estimate	Source	Trend	Source	1% level	Notes
Pacific	Alaska, W Canada	*Coastal S Alaska, British Colombia & NW USA*						•	14,200	C2	INC	C1	140	
Rocky Mountains	Rocky Mountains of N USA							•	2,500	C2	INC	C2	25	
Interior	Mid western USA							•	1,700	C2	INC	C2	15	

Trumpeter Swan.

Nancy Camel

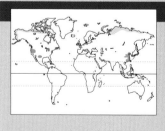

Cygnus cygnus — Whooper Swan

Subspecies/Population	Breeding range	Wintering, or core non-breeding range	Afr	Eu	Asia	Oc	Neo	NA	Estimate	Source	Trend	Source	1% level	Notes
Iceland (br)	Iceland	*Iceland, UK, Ireland*		•					20,900	CQ	INC	CQ	210	Sometimes ascribed to "*islandicus*".
N mainland Europe (br)	Scandinavia, N European Russia	*NW & Central Mainland Europe*		•					59,000	LI	INC	S11	590	
Black Sea, E Mediterranean (non-br)	N Europe, W Siberia	*Black Sea, E Mediterranean*		•	•				17,000	RU	DEC	S11	170	
Caspian, Central Asia (non-br)	W & Cent Siberia	*Caspian, Central Asia*		•	•				20,000	S11	DEC	S11	200	
E Asia	Central & E Siberia to NE China	*E Asia*			•				60,000	MM			600	

Cygnus columbianus — Tundra Swan "Whistling Swan"

Subspecies/Population	Breeding range	Wintering, or core non-breeding range	Afr	Eu	Asia	Oc	Neo	NA	Estimate	Source	Trend	Source	1% level	Notes
columbianus, E North America	E Arctic North America	*Coastal E USA*						•	98,000	U1	STA	U1	980	
"Whistling Swan" *columbianus*, W North America	W Arctic North America	*W USA*						•	90,000	U1	STA	U1	900	
"Bewick's Swan" *bewickii*, NW Europe (non-br)	Arctic N Russia	*NW Europe*		•	•				29,000	B7	DEC	SQ	290	Population increased in 1990s (DF), decreased from late 1990s onwards (SQ).
bewickii, Caspian (non-br)	N Siberia	*Caspian*		•	•				500	S11			5	
jankowskii	Central & E Siberia	*East Asia*			•				86,000	WE MM			860	WE >60,000 reported during aerial survey of Poyang Lake, China, in 2001. MM report an average of 26,00 in Japan.

Coscoroba coscoroba   Coscoroba Swan

Subspecies/Population	Breeding range	Wintering, or core non-breeding range	Afr	Eu	Asia	Oc	Neo	NA	Estimate	Source	Trend	Source	1% level	Notes
S South America	S South America						•		B	SR	STA	CC	250	Last proved to breed on Falkland/Malvinas Is in 1860 (WS).

Anser cygnoides EN   Swan Goose

Subspecies/Population	Breeding range	Wintering, or core non-breeding range	Afr	Eu	Asia	Oc	Neo	NA	Estimate	Source	Trend	Source	1% level	Notes
C & E Asia	S Central Siberia, Mongolia, to NE China	*E China, Korea, Japan, Taiwan*			•				50,000–60,000	LW ZJ	DEC	BC	550	ZJ reports a count of 61,650 at Sha Lake, a part of the Poyang Lake complex in China, in December 2001; 35,000–45,000 is the range of more usual totals at this site in recent years (e.g. LW).

Anser fabalis   Bean Goose "Taiga Bean Goose"

Subspecies/Population	Breeding range	Wintering, or core non-breeding range	Afr	Eu	Asia	Oc	Neo	NA	Estimate	Source	Trend	Source	1% level	Notes
fabalis	Scandinavia E to W Siberia	*NW Europe*		•					100,000	M3	STA	M3	1,000	
"Tundra Bean Goose" *rossicus*	Tundra of N Europe, W & C Siberia	*Central & SW Europe*		•	•				600,000	M3	STA	M3	6,000	
johanseni	Urals–L Baikal (Taiga & wooded tundra)	*? Central Asia*			•									Occupies area between *fabalis* and *middendorfi*, and south of *rossicus*.
middendorffi	Siberian Taiga E of L Baikal	*E Central & E Asia*			•				50,000–70,000	MM	DEC	EB	600	
serrirostris	East Siberian Tundra	*East Asia*			•				45,000–65,000	MM	DEC	GE	550	

Anser brachyrhynchus   Pink-footed Goose

Subspecies/Population	Breeding range	Wintering, or core non-breeding range	Afr	Eu	Asia	Oc	Neo	NA	Estimate	Source	Trend	Source	1% level	Notes
Greenland, Iceland (br)	E Greenland, Iceland	*Scotland, England*		•					240,000	KN	INC	M3	2,400	
Svalbard (br)	Svalbard	*Denmark, Netherlands, Belgium*		•					37,000	M3	STA	M3	370	

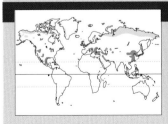

Anser albifrons   Greater White-fronted Goose

Subspecies/Population	Breeding range	Wintering, or core non-breeding range	Afr	Eu	Asia	Oc	Neo	NA	Estimate	Source	Trend	Source	1% level	Notes
albifrons, Baltic–North Sea	European Arctic Russia & NW Siberia	*NW Europe*		•	•				1,000,000	GI	INC	M3	10,000	GI reports the following totals for this pop: 1997: 885,898; 1998: 969,673; 1999: 835,039. This population has undoubtedly increased, but possibly at the expense of populations in C & E Europe (KO).
albifrons, Pannonic	European Arctic Russia & NW Siberia	*Central Europe*		•	•				10,000–40,000	M3	DEC	M3	250	
albifrons, Pontic/Anatolian	European Arctic Russia & NW Siberia	*SE Europe, Turkey*		•	•				350,000–700,000	M3	STA	M3	5,300	

Anser albifrons... continued

Subspecies/Population	Breeding range	Wintering, or core non-breeding range	Afr	Eu	Asia	Oc	Neo	NA	Estimate	Source	Trend	Source	1% level	Notes
albifrons, Caspian, Iran, Iraq (non-br)	European Arctic Russia & NW Siberia	*Caspian, Iran, Iraq*	●	●					15,000	S11	DEC	PE	150	
"Greenland White-fronted Goose" *flavirostris*	W Greenland	*Ireland, Scotland, Wales*		●				●	27,000	FO	DEC	FO	300	Numbers peaked at 35,500 in late 1990s, declined to <27,000 by 2002 (FO). 1% threshold maintained at 1997 level (<20% change).
frontalis, E Asia	E Siberia	*East Asia*			●				100,000–150,000	MM	DEC	KP	1,300	
frontalis, Pacific	Yukon-Kuskokwim Delta, Alaska	*Central Valley, California*						●	310,000	U1	INC	U1	3,100	
frontalis, Mid-Continent	C & NW Alaska across Arctic Canada to Foxe Basin	*Louisiana, Texas & Mexico*						●	1,070,000	U1	STA	U1	10,700	
"Tule White-fronted Goose" *gambelli*	Alaskan Taiga	*California, USA*						●	5,100	OT	INC	CA	50	USFWS estimate (Tim Moser) based on observations of neck-collared birds in 1997: 3,400.
elgasi	SW Alaska	*San Clemente Valley, California*												Recently described; recognised by AOU (1998) and Clements (2000).

Greater White-fronted Geese.   Johan Verbanck

Anser erythropus VU   **Lesser White-fronted Goose**

Subspecies/Population	Breeding range	Wintering, or core non-breeding range	Afr	Eu	Asia	Oc	Neo	NA	Estimate	Source	Trend	Source	1% level	Notes
N Europe, Arctic W Siberia (br)	N Scandinavia, Arctic W Russia	*SE Europe, Caspian*	●	●					8,000–13,000	BC	DEC	BC	110	
E China (non-br)	Arctic N Asia	*E China*			●				14,000	MM	DEC	PE	140	

Anser anser   **Greylag Goose**

Subspecies/Population	Breeding range	Wintering, or core non-breeding range	Afr	Eu	Asia	Oc	Neo	NA	Estimate	Source	Trend	Source	1% level	Notes
anser, Iceland (br)	Iceland	*UK, Ireland*		●					89,100	KN	STA	SA	1,000	1% threshold maintained at 1997 level (<20% change).
anser, NW Scotland	NW Scotland			●					9,000	M3	INC	M3	90	
anser, NW Europe (br)	NW Europe	*NW Europe, SW Europe*		●					400,000	SR	INC	M3	4,000	Information provided by Kees Koffijberg, Leif Nilsson and Johan Mooij, June 2002.
anser, C Europe (br)	Central Europe	*N Africa*	●	●					25,000	M3	INC	M3	250	
rubrirostris, Black Sea, Turkey	Black Sea, Turkey			●					85,000	M3		M3	850	
rubrirostris, Caspian, Iraq (non-br)	W Siberia, Caspian	*S Caspian, Iraq*	●	●					250,000	SA	INC	SA	2,500	
rubrirostris, South Asia (non-br)	Central Asia	*Central & S Asia*			●				15,000	PE	INC	PE	150	
rubrirostris, E Asia (non-br)	N China, Mongolia, SC & SE Russia	*China, Taiwan, N & S Korea, S to Myanmar, N Vietnam*			●				50,000–100,000	MM			750	

Greylag Geese.

Johan Verbanck

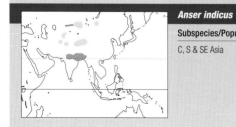

Anser indicus   **Bar-headed Goose**

Subspecies/Population	Breeding range	Wintering, or core non-breeding range	Afr	Eu	Asia	Oc	Neo	NA	Estimate	Source	Trend	Source	1% level	Notes
C, S & SE Asia	Kyrgyzstan, C China, Tibet, Mongolia	*China, India, Pakistan, Bangladesh, Nepal, Myanmar*			●				52,000–60,000	LL MM			560	LL reports a peak count from 1999–2000 of 52,000 breeding at Qinghai Lake.

Chen (Anser) caerulescens — Snow Goose

Subspecies/Population	Breeding range	Wintering, or core non-breeding range	Afr	Eu	Asia	Oc	Neo	NA	Estimate	Source	Trend	Source	1% level	Notes
caerulescens "Lesser", E Asia	N Far East Asia	E China, Korea, Japan			•				<300	GE			3	
caerulescens "Lesser", Hudson Bay (br)	W Hudson Bay, Southampton Is, Baffin Is	Gulf of Mexico coast						•	4,760,000	KL	INC	KL	20,000	For populations over 2 million birds, Ramsar Convention criterion 5 (20,000 or more waterbirds), applies.
caerulescens "Lesser", C Canadian Arctic (br)	Central Canadian Arctic	S USA, N Mexico						•	1,230,000	KL	INC	KL	12,300	
caerulescens "Lesser", W North American Arctic	W North American Arctic	California, Mexico						•	632,000	KM	INC	KM	6,300	
caerulescens "Lesser", Wrangel Is (br)	Wrangel Is, Russia	California, Mexico			•			•	105,000	KM	STA	KM	1,100	
atlanticus "Greater"	E high Arctic Canada, NW Greenland	E USA						•	837,000	U1	INC	U1	8,400	

Snow Geese.

Nancy Camel

Chen (Anser) rossii — Ross's Goose

Subspecies/Population	Breeding range	Wintering, or core non-breeding range	Afr	Eu	Asia	Oc	Neo	NA	Estimate	Source	Trend	Source	1% level	Notes
North America	Central & E Arctic Canada	SW USA, US & Mexican Gulf Coast						•	1,050,000	MX	INC	MX	10,500	

Chen (Anser) canagicus NT — Emperor Goose

Subspecies/Population	Breeding range	Wintering, or core non-breeding range	Afr	Eu	Asia	Oc	Neo	NA	Estimate	Source	Trend	Source	1% level	Notes
N Pacific	Alaska, NE Siberia,	Aleutian Is, Gulf of Alaska & Kamchatka			•			•	84,500	U1	STA	U1	850	

Branta sandvicensis VU — Hawaiian Goose, Nene

Subspecies/Population	Breeding range	Wintering, or core non-breeding range	Afr	Eu	Asia	Oc	Neo	NA	Estimate	Source	Trend	Source	1% level	Notes
Hawaii	Hawaiian Islands					•			1,050	U3	FLU	U3	10	

Branta canadensis — Canada Goose

Subspecies/Population	Breeding range	Wintering, or core non-breeding range	Afr	Eu	Asia	Oc	Neo	NA	Estimate	Source	Trend	Source	1% level	Notes
canadensis / interior, NE Canada (br) "Atlantic"	Quebec, Canada	Coastal E USA, New England–South Carolina						•	637,000	U1	STA	U1	6,400	
canadensis / interior, "North Atlantic"	Newfoundland, Labrador, W Greenland	Coastal E USA						•	130,000	U1	STA	U1	1300	
Atlantic flyway resident (various subspecies)	S Quebec & S Maritime Provinces S through Atlantic states							•	1,010,000	U1	INC	U1	10,100	

Branta canadensis... continued

Subspecies/Population	Breeding range	Wintering, or core non-breeding range	Afr	Eu	Asia	Oc	Neo	NA	Estimate	Source	Trend	Source	1% level	Notes
interior, S James Bay (br)	S James Bay, Ontario/Nunavut	*S & SE USA*						•	103,000	U1	STA	U1	1,000	
interior, Mississippi Valley	N Ontario W of James Bay & S of Hudson Bay	*Wisconsin & Illinois*						•	469,000	U1	STA	U1	4,700	
maxima, Giant (Mississippi flyway)	Mississippi Flyway resident							•	1,370,000	U1	INC	U1	13,700	
interior, Eastern Prairie	Hudson Bay lowlands of Manitoba	*Manitoba & Minnesota to Missouri*						•	215,000	U1	STA	U1	2,200	
moffitti / maxima Western Prairie/Great Plains	Saskatchewan & Manitoba to Oklahoma & Texas	*Kansas to Texas*						•	683,000	U1	INC	U1	6,800	
hutchinsii / parvipes Eastern Tall Grass Prairie	Arctic Canada–Baffin Is to Queen Maud Gulf S to Hudson Bay	*Oklahoma, Texas & New Mexico*						•	149,000	U1	STA	U1	1,500	
hutchinsii / parvipes Western Tall Grass Prairie	Victoria Island & Queen Maud Gulf S to N Alberta	*SE Colorado, NE New Mexico & adjacent Oklahoma & Texas*						•	164,000	U1	DEC	U1	1,600	
moffitti, Hi-line	SE Alberta & SW Saskatchewan S to Wyoming & Colorado	*Colorado to C New Mexico*						•	253,000	U1	INC	U1	2,500	
moffitti, Rocky Mountains	Rocky Mountains	*Montana & Idaho S to S California & Arizona*						•	161,000	U1	INC	U1	1,600	
fulva, Pacific	British Colombia S to California							•	>84,000	U1	INC	U1		U1 gives partial estimate (from Alberta only) of 84,000.
occidentalis Dusky	Copper River Delta, Alaska	*Willamette & Colombia river valleys, Oregon & Washington*						•	17,300	U1	STA	U1	170	
minima Cackling	Yukon-Kuskokwim Delta, Alaska	*W Oregon, W Washington*						•	136,000	U1	INC	U1	1,400	
taverneri/ parvipes Taverner	Interior Alaska	*Washington to California*						•	272,000	U1	STA	U1	2,700	
leucopareia, Aleutian (Buldir–California)	W Aleutian Islands, Alaska	*W coast Canada S to California*			•			•	29,800	U1	INC	U1	300	Some birds of this subspecies still occasionally winter in Japan, Korea and probably China, though the Kuril breeding population is now extinct.

Branta leucopsis — Barnacle Goose

Subspecies/Population	Breeding range	Wintering, or core non-breeding range	Afr	Eu	Asia	Oc	Neo	NA	Estimate	Source	Trend	Source	1% level	Notes
E Greenland (br)	East Greenland	*NW Scotland, Ireland*		•					54,100	CR	INC	M3	540	
Svalbard (br)	Svalbard	*SW Scotland*		•					23,000	M3	INC	M3	230	
N Russia, E Baltic (br)	N Russia, E Baltic	*N Germany, Netherlands*		•					360,000	SR	INC	M3	3,600	Information compiled by Klaus Günther, June 2002.

Branta bernicla — Brent Goose

Subspecies/Population	Breeding range	Wintering, or core non-breeding range	Afr	Eu	Asia	Oc	Neo	NA	Estimate	Source	Trend	Source	1% level	Notes
"Dark-bellied Brent Goose" *bernicla*, W Siberia (br)	W Siberia	*Coastal W Europe*		•	•				215,000	SR	DEC	SR	2,200	Estimate of 190,000 based on 2002 spring migration counts compiled by Klaus Günther, June 2002. Adjusted by Bart Ebbinge to 215,000 to compensate for missing birds. Long-term increase to 260,000 by May 1995; decline thereafter.
"Light-bellied Brent Goose" *hrota*, Svalbard, N Greenland (br)	Svalbard, N Greenland	*Coastal Denmark, NE UK*		•					5,000	M3	INC	M3	50	
"Light-bellied Brent Goose" *hrota*, Ireland (non-br)	E Canadian High Arctic	*Coastal Ireland*		•				•	20,000	M3	STA	M3	200	

Branta bernicla... continued

Subspecies/Population	Breeding range	Wintering, or core non-breeding range	Afr	Eu	Asia	Oc	Neo	NA	Estimate	Source	Trend	Source	1% level	Notes
"Atlantic Brant" *hrota*, US East Coast (non-br)	Arctic NE Canada	*E US coast*						•	181,600	U1	INC	U1	1,800	
"Grey-bellied Brant" *hrota/nigricans*, western Canadian high Arctic (br)	Parry Islands, Canadian NW Territories	*Puget Sound, W Washington & SW British Columbia*						•	7,500	U5			75	Population newly recognised by USFWS, monitored from 2002 onward.
"Black Brant" *nigricans*, E Pacific (non-br)	Low Arctic North America	*E Pacific coast, mainly in Mexico*						•	136,200	U5	INC	U1	1,400	
nigricans, E Asia (non-br	E Siberia, Anadyr Basin eastward	*Coastal Kamchatka, Korea, Japan*			•				5,000	MM			50	

Branta ruficollis VU — Red-breasted Goose

Subspecies/Population	Breeding range	Wintering, or core non-breeding range	Afr	Eu	Asia	Oc	Neo	NA	Estimate	Source	Trend	Source	1% level	Notes
N C Russia to E Europe	Taymyr, Gydan & Yamal Peninsulas N Siberia	*W to N Black Sea, Caspian Sea, SE Europe*		•	•				88,000	BC	INC	M3	880	

Cereopsis novaehollandiae — Cape Barren Goose

Subspecies/Population	Breeding range	Wintering, or core non-breeding range	Afr	Eu	Asia	Oc	Neo	NA	Estimate	Source	Trend	Source	1% level	Notes
novaehollandiae	Islands off S to SE Australia, Tasmania	*Partial dispersal to mainland*				•			15,000–17,000	HW	STA?	HW	160	
griseus	Recherche Island Archipelago and adjacent mainland, SW Australia					•			650	GC	STA	GC	7	Comprehensive survey in 1993 found 631 birds (GC).

Stictonetta naevosa LC — Freckled Duck

Subspecies/Population	Breeding range	Wintering, or core non-breeding range	Afr	Eu	Asia	Oc	Neo	NA	Estimate	Source	Trend	Source	1% level	Notes
SE Australia	SE Australia					•			19,000	GC	FLU	GC	190	Abundance correlated with Southern Oscillation Index (GC).
SW Australia	SW Australia					•			1,000	GC	FLU	GC	10	

Cyanochen cyanopterus NT — Blue-winged Goose

Subspecies/Population	Breeding range	Wintering, or core non-breeding range	Afr	Eu	Asia	Oc	Neo	NA	Estimate	Source	Trend	Source	1% level	Notes
Ethiopia	Ethiopian highlands		•						5,000–15,000	BC	STA	BC	100	

Chloephaga melanoptera — Andean Goose

Subspecies/Population	Breeding range	Wintering, or core non-breeding range	Afr	Eu	Asia	Oc	Neo	NA	Estimate	Source	Trend	Source	1% level	Notes
Andean South America	Central Andes, Central Peru to Central Argentina						•		C	RS	STA	S8	1,000	

Chloephaga picta — Upland Goose

Subspecies/Population	Breeding range	Wintering, or core non-breeding range	Afr	Eu	Asia	Oc	Neo	NA	Estimate	Source	Trend	Source	1% level	Notes
picta	S South America N to Central Chile & Argentina	Population shifts N a little					•		D	CC	DEC	CC	10,000	
leucoptera	Falkland/Malvinas Islands						•		138,000–255,000	WS	STA	SS	2,000	WS estimate 46,000–85,000 pairs (138,000–255,000 individuals).

Chloephaga hybrida — Kelp Goose

Subspecies/Population	Breeding range	Wintering, or core non-breeding range	Afr	Eu	Asia	Oc	Neo	NA	Estimate	Source	Trend	Source	1% level	Notes
hybrida	Mainland S South America						•		C	S8	STA	CC	1,000	
malvinarum	Falkland/Malvinas Islands						•		30,000–54,000	WS			420	WS estimate 10,000–18,000 pairs (30,000–54,000 individuals).

Chloephaga poliocephala — Ashy-headed Goose

Subspecies/Population	Breeding range	Wintering, or core non-breeding range	Afr	Eu	Asia	Oc	Neo	NA	Estimate	Source	Trend	Source	1% level	Notes
South America	S Chile & S Argentina	Partial migrant N to Buenos Aires province					•		C/D	S8	DEC	CC		
Falkland/Malvinas Islands	Falkland/Malvinas Islands						•		150–270	WS				WS estimate 50–90 pairs (150–270 individuals).

Chloephaga rubidiceps — Ruddy-headed Goose

Subspecies/Population	Breeding range	Wintering, or core non-breeding range	Afr	Eu	Asia	Oc	Neo	NA	Estimate	Source	Trend	Source	1% level	Notes
S Chile (br)	S. Chile & Tierra del Fuego	Buenos Aires province, Argentina					•		900	M4	DEC	CC	9	
Falkland/Malvinas Is	Falkland/Malvinas Islands						•		42,000–81,000	WS	STA	HO	620	WS estimate 14,000–27,000 pairs (42,000–81,000 individuals).

Neochen jubata NT — Orinoco Goose

Subspecies/Population	Breeding range	Wintering, or core non-breeding range	Afr	Eu	Asia	Oc	Neo	NA	Estimate	Source	Trend	Source	1% level	Notes
N South America	N South America E of Andes S to N Argentina						•		C	CC	DEC	TL	1,000	

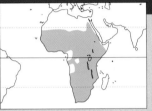

Alopochen aegyptiacus — Egyptian Goose

Subspecies/Population	Breeding range	Wintering, or core non-breeding range	Afr	Eu	Asia	Oc	Neo	NA	Estimate	Source	Trend	Source	1% level	Notes
W Africa	W Africa		•						10,000–25,000	S11	DEC	DO	180	
E & S Africa	Eastern, Southern Africa		•						200,000–500,000	S11	STA	DO	3,500	Increasing in southern Africa (HF).

Alopochen mauritianus — Mauritian Shelduck

Subspecies/Population	Breeding range	Wintering, or core non-breeding range	Afr	Eu	Asia	Oc	Neo	NA	Estimate	Source	Trend	Source	1% level	Notes
Mauritius	Mauritius		•						0	BC	EXT	BC		Extinct between 1693 and 1698 (BC).

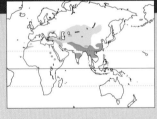

Tadorna ferruginea — Ruddy Shelduck

Subspecies/Population	Breeding range	Wintering, or core non-breeding range	Afr	Eu	Asia	Oc	Neo	NA	Estimate	Source	Trend	Source	1% level	Notes
Ethiopia	Ethiopia		•						30–80	ER	DEC	DO	1	
NW Africa	NW Africa		•						3,000	GX	DEC	GX	30	
E Med, Black Sea, NE Africa	E Mediterranean, Black Sea, NE Africa		•	•					20,000	MN	DEC	S11	200	
W Asia, Caspian, Iran, Iraq	W Asia, Caspian, Iran, Iraq			•	•				50,000	GI	INC	PE	500	GI report count totals in SW Asia of 40,045 in 1997 and 83,762 in 1998, but the latter total was biased by a single abnormally high count of 65,000 at L Uromieh.
S & SE Asia (non-br)	Central Asia	India, Pakistan, Nepal, Bangladesh, SE Asia			•				50,000	PE			500	
E Asia (non-br)	E Central Asia, Mongolia, NE China, Siberia	S China, Korea, Myanmar N Thailand, Laos			•				50,000–100,000	MM			750	

Tadorna cana — Cape Shelduck, South African Shelduck

Subspecies/Population	Breeding range	Wintering, or core non-breeding range	Afr	Eu	Asia	Oc	Neo	NA	Estimate	Source	Trend	Source	1% level	Notes
S Africa	Southern Africa		•						50,000	HF	STA	DO	500	

Tadorna variegata — Paradise Shelduck

Subspecies/Population	Breeding range	Wintering, or core non-breeding range	Afr	Eu	Asia	Oc	Neo	NA	Estimate	Source	Trend	Source	1% level	Notes
New Zealand	New Zealand					•			150,000–180,000	WM	STA	WM	1,700	

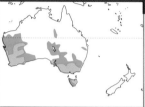

Tadorna tadornoides — Australian Shelduck

Subspecies/Population	Breeding range	Wintering, or core non-breeding range	Afr	Eu	Asia	Oc	Neo	NA	Estimate	Source	Trend	Source	1% level	Notes
SW Australia	SW Australia					•								
SE Australia	SE Australia, including Tasmania					•								

Tadorna cristata CR — Crested Shelduck

Subspecies/Population	Breeding range	Wintering, or core non-breeding range	Afr	Eu	Asia	Oc	Neo	NA	Estimate	Source	Trend	Source	1% level	Notes
NE Asia	SE Russia, NE China?, Korea?, N Japan				•				<50	BC	EXT?		1	Last recorded near Vladivostok in 1964 (BC).

Tadorna tadorna — Common Shelduck

Subspecies/Population	Breeding range	Wintering, or core non-breeding range	Afr	Eu	Asia	Oc	Neo	NA	Estimate	Source	Trend	Source	1% level	Notes
NW Europe (br)	NW Europe	*W Europe*		•					300,000	S11	STA	DF	3,000	DF Report increasing trend 1974–1996; but stable trend 1987–96.
Black Sea, Mediterranean	Black Sea, Mediterranean		•	•					75,000	S11	DEC	DF	750	DF Report increasing trend 1974–1996; but declining trend 1987–96.
Caspian, SW Asia (non-br)	W & SW Asia	*Caspian, SW Asia*	•	•					80,000	PE	INC	PE	800	
South Asia (non-br)	Central Asia	*Bangladesh, Myanmar, Pakistan, N & C India*			•				C	AW			1,000	10,000 winter in NW India & Pakistan (PE), and 10,000 in Myanmar. A count of 120,000 in Bangladesh in 2001 remains unsubstantiated.
E Asia (non-br)	E Central Asia, Mongolia, NE China, Siberia	*E China, Korea, Japan, Taiwan*			•				100,000–150,000	MM			1,300	

Common Shelduck.   Johan Verbanck

Tadorna radjah — Radjah Shelduck

Subspecies/Population	Breeding range	Wintering, or core non-breeding range	Afr	Eu	Asia	Oc	Neo	NA	Estimate	Source	Trend	Source	1% level	Notes
radjah	New Guinea, Moluccas			•	•				B/C	CA	DEC	CA	1,000	
rufitergum	N Australia					•			150,000	GC	STA	GC	1,500	GC estimate 100,000 breeding adults (150,000 individuals).

Tachyeres patachonicus — Flying Steamerduck

Subspecies/Population	Breeding range	Wintering, or core non-breeding range	Afr	Eu	Asia	Oc	Neo	NA	Estimate	Source	Trend	Source	1% level	Notes
S Chile & Argentina	S Chile, S Argentina, Tierra del Fuego						•		A/B	S8	DEC	S8	250	
Falkland/Malvinas Is	Falkland/Malvinas Islands						•		600–1,200	WS			9	WS estimate 200–400 pairs (600–1,200 individuals).

Tachyeres pteneres — Magellanic Steamerduck, Flightless Steamerduck

Subspecies/Population	Breeding range	Wintering, or core non-breeding range	Afr	Eu	Asia	Oc	Neo	NA	Estimate	Source	Trend	Source	1% level	Notes
S South America	S Chile, Tierra del Fuego						•		B/C	EJ	STA	EJ	1,000	

Tachyeres brachypterus — Falkland Steamerduck

Subspecies/Population	Breeding range	Wintering, or core non-breeding range	Afr	Eu	Asia	Oc	Neo	NA	Estimate	Source	Trend	Source	1% level	Notes
Falkland/Malvinas Islands	Falkland/Malvinas Islands						•		27,000–48,000	WS			380	WS estimate 9,000–16,000 pairs (27,000–48,000 individuals).

Tachyeres leucocephalus — NT White-headed Steamerduck, Chubut Steamerduck

Subspecies/Population	Breeding range	Wintering, or core non-breeding range	Afr	Eu	Asia	Oc	Neo	NA	Estimate	Source	Trend	Source	1% level	Notes
Argentina	S Chubut coast Argentina						•		A	CA	STA	CA	100	Possibly only a few hundred (D Scott per obs).

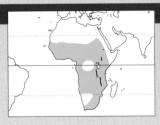

Plectropterus gambensis — Spur-winged Goose

Subspecies/Population	Breeding range	Wintering, or core non-breeding range	Afr	Eu	Asia	Oc	Neo	NA	Estimate	Source	Trend	Source	1% level	Notes
gambensis, W Africa	W Africa		•						100,000	DO	STA	DO	1,000	
gambensis, E Africa	E Africa, Sudan to Zambia		•						200,000–300,000	S11	STA	S11	2,500	
niger	Southern Africa		•						50,000–100,000	S11	INC	UN	750	

Cairina moschata — Muscovy Duck

Subspecies/Population	Breeding range	Wintering, or core non-breeding range	Afr	Eu	Asia	Oc	Neo	NA	Estimate	Source	Trend	Source	1% level	Notes
C & S America	Mexico S to E Peru & N Uruguay						•		D	CC	DEC	CC	10,000	

Cairina scutulata EN — White-winged Duck

Subspecies/Population	Breeding range	Wintering, or core non-breeding range	Afr	Eu	Asia	Oc	Neo	NA	Estimate	Source	Trend	Source	1% level	Notes
India–Myanmar	India–Bangladesh–Myanmar				•				450	SR	DEC	BD	5	
SE Asia	Thailand, Cambodia, Laos, Vietnam				•				200	SR	DEC	BD	2	
W Indonesia	Sumatra				•				150	BD	DEC	BD	2	

Sarkidiornis melanotos — Comb Duck

Subspecies/Population	Breeding range	Wintering, or core non-breeding range	Afr	Eu	Asia	Oc	Neo	NA	Estimate	Source	Trend	Source	1% level	Notes
melanotos, W Africa	W Africa		•						50,000–100,000	DO	STA	PC	750	
melanotos, S & E Africa	Southern & Eastern Africa		•						100,000–500,000	DO	STA	S11	3,000	
melanotos, Madagascar	Madagascar		•						B	S11	DEC	S11	250	
melanotos, S & SE Asia	India, Nepal, Bangladesh, Myanmar, Cambodia, rarely Thailand, Laos, Vietnam				•				6,000	PE	DEC	PE	60	
sylvicola	South America Colombia–N Argentina						•		C	AT	DEC	AT	1,000	

Pteronetta hartlaubi NT — Hartlaub's Duck

Subspecies/Population	Breeding range	Wintering, or core non-breeding range	Afr	Eu	Asia	Oc	Neo	NA	Estimate	Source	Trend	Source	1% level	Notes
W Africa	W Africa (Guinea–Ghana)		•						A	FF	DEC	S11	100	
W Central Africa	W Central Africa		•						B/C	CA	DEC	CA	1,000	

Nettapus pulchellus — Green Pygmy-Goose

Subspecies/Population	Breeding range	Wintering, or core non-breeding range	Afr	Eu	Asia	Oc	Neo	NA	Estimate	Source	Trend	Source	1% level	Notes
New Guinea	New Guinea					•								
N Australia	Tropical N Australia					•								

Nettapus coromandelianus — Cotton Pygmy-Goose

Subspecies/Population	Breeding range	Wintering, or core non-breeding range	Afr	Eu	Asia	Oc	Neo	NA	Estimate	Source	Trend	Source	1% level	Notes
coromandelianus, South Asia	S Asia				•				C	PE			1,000	
coromandelianus, E & SE Asia	E, SE Asia	SE Asia, W Indonesia			•				C/D	PE				
coromandelianus, NE New Guinea	NE New Guinea					•			<1,000	TL	STA	TL	10	
albipennis	NE Australia					•			7,500	GC	STA	GC	75	GC estimate 5,000 breeding adults (7,500 individuals).

Nettapus auritus — African Pygmy- Goose

Subspecies/Population	Breeding range	Wintering, or core non-breeding range	Afr	Eu	Asia	Oc	Neo	NA	Estimate	Source	Trend	Source	1% level	Notes
W Africa	W Africa		•						A	DO	DEC	DO	100	
S & E Africa	Southern & Eastern Africa		•						100,000–250,000	S11			1,750	
Madagascar	Madagascar		•						5,000–10,000	S11	DEC	S11	75	

Callonetta leucophrys — Ringed Teal

Subspecies/Population	Breeding range	Wintering, or core non-breeding range	Afr	Eu	Asia	Oc	Neo	NA	Estimate	Source	Trend	Source	1% level	Notes
C South America	Bolivia & S Brazil to N Argentina, Uruguay						•		B/C	CC	STA	CC	1,000	

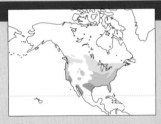

Aix sponsa — (American) Wood Duck

Subspecies/Population	Breeding range	Wintering, or core non-breeding range	Afr	Eu	Asia	Oc	Neo	NA	Estimate	Source	Trend	Source	1% level	Notes
E North America (br)	E North America, W Cuba	Partial migrant S to Mexico						•	2,800,000	B12	INC	S5	20,000	For populations over 2 million birds, Ramsar criterion 5 (20,000 or more waterbirds), applies.
Interior North America (br)	Interior North America	Partial migrant S to Mexico						•	665,100	B11			6,700	
W North America	W North America	Partial migrant S to Mexico						•	66,000	B12	STA	B12	660	

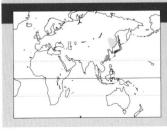

Aix galericulata — Mandarin Duck

Subspecies/Population	Breeding range	Wintering, or core non-breeding range	Afr	Eu	Asia	Oc	Neo	NA	Estimate	Source	Trend	Source	1% level	Notes
China (non-br)	Far East Russia, China, N Korea	China			•				20,000	MM	DEC	CA	200	
Korea (non-br)	E Asia	Korea			•				5,000	CA	DEC	CA	50	
Japan (non-br)	Japan, S Kuril Is	Japan			•				40,000	MM	STA	CA	400	
Taiwan (resident)	Taiwan				•				350–500	YS	STA	YS	4	

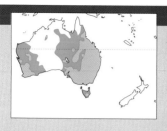

Chenonetta jubata — Maned Duck

Subspecies/Population	Breeding range	Wintering, or core non-breeding range	Afr	Eu	Asia	Oc	Neo	NA	Estimate	Source	Trend	Source	1% level	Notes
SW Australia	SW Australia					•								
E Australia	E Australia, Tasmania					•								

Amazonetta brasiliensis — Brazilian Teal

Subspecies/Population	Breeding range	Wintering, or core non-breeding range	Afr	Eu	Asia	Oc	Neo	NA	Estimate	Source	Trend	Source	1% level	Notes
brasiliensis	E Colombia, N & E Venezuela, Guyana, N & C Brazil						•		D	EJ	STA	EJ	10,000	
ipecutiri	E Bolivia & S Brazil to N Argentina & Uruguay	Some migration to N					•		B/C	EJ	STA	EJ	1,000	

Merganetta armata — Torrent Duck

Subspecies/Population	Breeding range	Wintering, or core non-breeding range	Afr	Eu	Asia	Oc	Neo	NA	Estimate	Source	Trend	Source	1% level	Notes
columbiana	Andes from Venezuela to N Ecuador						•		7,000–12,000	C3	DEC	CA	95	
leucogenis	Andes from C Ecuador to N Chile, Argentina						•		9,000–13,000	C3	DEC	S8	110	
armata	Andes of Chile and Argentina						•		4,000–10,000	C3	DEC	CA	70	

Hymenolaimus malacorhynchos VU — Blue Duck

Subspecies/Population	Breeding range	Wintering, or core non-breeding range	Afr	Eu	Asia	Oc	Neo	NA	Estimate	Source	Trend	Source	1% level	Notes
North Island, New Zealand	North Island, New Zealand					•			1,920	BC	DEC	BC	20	BC estimates 640 breeding pairs (1,920 individuals).
South Island, New Zealand	South Island, New Zealand					•			1,740	BC	DEC	BC	15	BC estimates 580 breeding pairs (1,740 individuals).

Salvadorina waigiuensis VU — Salvadori's Teal

Subspecies/Population	Breeding range	Wintering, or core non-breeding range	Afr	Eu	Asia	Oc	Neo	NA	Estimate	Source	Trend	Source	1% level	Notes
New Guinea	New Guinea highlands					•			A/B	BC	DEC	BC	250	

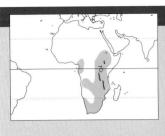

Anas sparsa — African Black Duck

Subspecies/Population	Breeding range	Wintering, or core non-breeding range	Afr	Eu	Asia	Oc	Neo	NA	Estimate	Source	Trend	Source	1% level	Notes
sparsa	Southern Africa		•						B	DO	STA	CA HF	250	
leucostigma, E Africa	Eastern Africa		•						15,000–25,000	DO	DEC	S11	200	
leucostigma, Ethiopian Highlands	Ethiopian highlands		•						2,000–10,000	S11			60	
leucostigma, Cameroon, Nigeria	Cameroon highlands, E Nigeria		•						1,000–5,000	S11			30	
leucostigma?	E highlands of Guinea		•						100	S11			1	
maclatchyi	Equatorial Guinea to Gabon		•						1,000–5,000	S11			30	

Anas penelope — Eurasian Wigeon

Subspecies/Population	Breeding range	Wintering, or core non-breeding range	Afr	Eu	Asia	Oc	Neo	NA	Estimate	Source	Trend	Source	1% level	Notes
NW Europe (non-br)	W Siberia & NW, NE Eur	*NW Europe*	•	•					1,500,000	DF	INC?	DF	15,000	1,400,000 counted in 1995; trend from 1974–1996 applied to this count results in total of 2,000,000 for 2002. However, count totals in 1997–99 ranged from 1.1–1.2 million, suggesting a levelling of the trend (DF, GI).
Black Sea, Mediterranean (non-br)	W Siberia NE Europe	*Black Sea, Mediterranean*	•	•	•				300,000	DF	DEC	DF	3,000	Rate of decrease calculated between 1987 and 1996 (DF) applied to S11 estimate results in 2002 estimate of 290,000.
SW Asia, NE Africa (non-br)	Central & W Siberia	*SW Asia, NE Africa*	•	•	•				250,000	PE	DEC	PE	2,500	
South Asia (non-br)	Central Siberia	*S Asia*			•				250,000	PE	INC	PE	2,500	
E Asia (non-br)	East Siberia, Mongolia, NE China	*E Asia*			•				500,000–1,000,000	MM	DEC	PE	7,500	

Wigeon. — Peter Creed

Anas americana — American Wigeon

Subspecies/Population	Breeding range	Wintering, or core non-breeding range	Afr	Eu	Asia	Oc	Neo	NA	Estimate	Source	Trend	Source	1% level	Notes
N & C America	NW to Central E N America	*N American Atlantic & Pacific coasts, C America, Caribbean*					•	•	2,700,000	U1	STA	U1	20,000	For populations over 2 million birds, Ramsar Convention criterion 5 (20,000 or more waterbirds), applies.

Anas sibilatrix — Chiloe Wigeon

Subspecies/Population	Breeding range	Wintering, or core non-breeding range	Afr	Eu	Asia	Oc	Neo	NA	Estimate	Source	Trend	Source	1% level	Notes
S South America	S South America S of Central Chile, Argentina	*S South America N to Paraguay, S Brazil*					•		D	CC	STA	CC	10,000	
Falkland/Malvinas Is	Falkland/Malvinas Islands						•		1,500–2,700	WS			20	WS estimate 500–900 pairs (1,500–2,700 individuals).

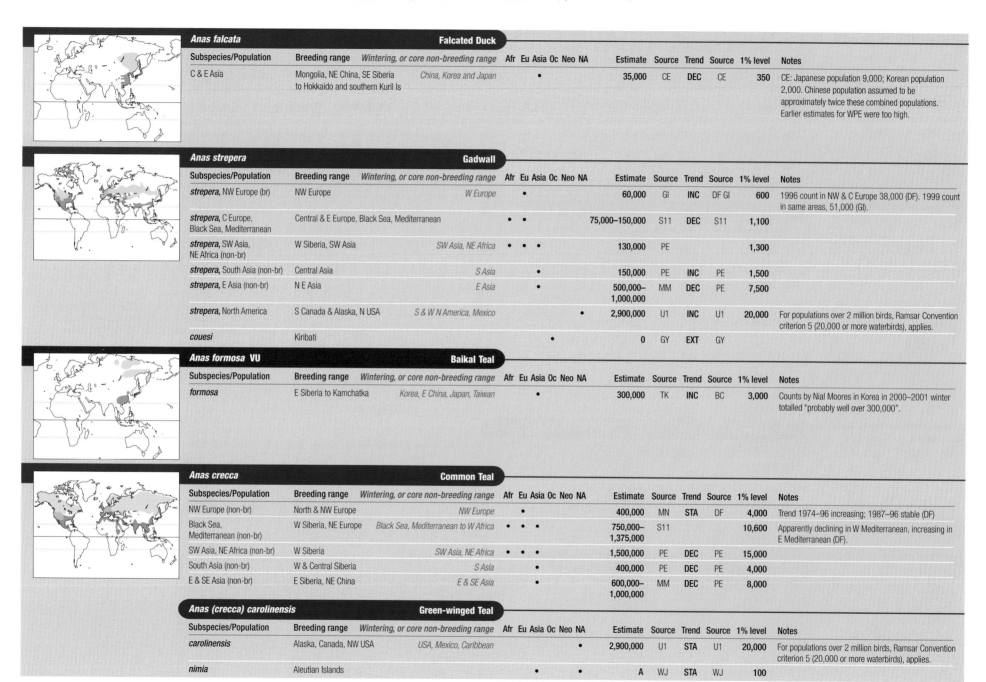

Anas falcata — Falcated Duck

Subspecies/Population	Breeding range	Wintering, or core non-breeding range	Afr	Eu	Asia	Oc	Neo	NA	Estimate	Source	Trend	Source	1% level	Notes
C & E Asia	Mongolia, NE China, SE Siberia to Hokkaido and southern Kuril Is	China, Korea and Japan			•				35,000	CE	DEC	CE	350	CE: Japanese population 9,000; Korean population 2,000. Chinese population assumed to be approximately twice these combined populations. Earlier estimates for WPE were too high.

Anas strepera — Gadwall

Subspecies/Population	Breeding range	Wintering, or core non-breeding range	Afr	Eu	Asia	Oc	Neo	NA	Estimate	Source	Trend	Source	1% level	Notes
strepera, NW Europe (br)	NW Europe	W Europe		•					60,000	GI	INC	DF GI	600	1996 count in NW & C Europe 38,000 (DF). 1999 count in same areas, 51,000 (GI).
strepera, C Europe, Black Sea, Mediterranean	Central & E Europe, Black Sea, Mediterranean			•	•				75,000–150,000	S11	DEC	S11	1,100	
strepera, SW Asia, NE Africa (non-br)	W Siberia, SW Asia	SW Asia, NE Africa	•	•	•				130,000	PE			1,300	
strepera, South Asia (non-br)	Central Asia	S Asia			•				150,000	PE	INC	PE	1,500	
strepera, E Asia (non-br)	N E Asia	E Asia			•				500,000–1,000,000	MM	DEC	PE	7,500	
strepera, North America	S Canada & Alaska, N USA	S & W N America, Mexico						•	2,900,000	U1	INC	U1	20,000	For populations over 2 million birds, Ramsar Convention criterion 5 (20,000 or more waterbirds), applies.
couesi	Kiribati					•			0	GY	EXT	GY		

Anas formosa VU — Baikal Teal

Subspecies/Population	Breeding range	Wintering, or core non-breeding range	Afr	Eu	Asia	Oc	Neo	NA	Estimate	Source	Trend	Source	1% level	Notes
formosa	E Siberia to Kamchatka	Korea, E China, Japan, Taiwan			•				300,000	TK	INC	BC	3,000	Counts by Nial Moores in Korea in 2000–2001 winter totalled "probably well over 300,000".

Anas crecca — Common Teal

Subspecies/Population	Breeding range	Wintering, or core non-breeding range	Afr	Eu	Asia	Oc	Neo	NA	Estimate	Source	Trend	Source	1% level	Notes
NW Europe (non-br)	North & NW Europe	NW Europe		•					400,000	MN	STA	DF	4,000	Trend 1974–96 increasing; 1987–96 stable (DF)
Black Sea, Mediterranean (non-br)	W Siberia, NE Europe	Black Sea, Mediterranean to W Africa	•	•	•				750,000–1,375,000	S11			10,600	Apparently declining in W Mediterranean, increasing in E Mediterranean (DF).
SW Asia, NE Africa (non-br)	W Siberia	SW Asia, NE Africa	•	•	•				1,500,000	PE	DEC	PE	15,000	
South Asia (non-br)	W & Central Siberia	S Asia			•				400,000	PE	DEC	PE	4,000	
E & SE Asia (non-br)	E Siberia, NE China	E & SE Asia			•				600,000–1,000,000	MM	DEC	PE	8,000	

Anas (crecca) carolinensis — Green-winged Teal

Subspecies/Population	Breeding range	Wintering, or core non-breeding range	Afr	Eu	Asia	Oc	Neo	NA	Estimate	Source	Trend	Source	1% level	Notes
carolinensis	Alaska, Canada, NW USA	USA, Mexico, Caribbean						•	2,900,000	U1	STA	U1	20,000	For populations over 2 million birds, Ramsar Convention criterion 5 (20,000 or more waterbirds), applies.
nimia	Aleutian Islands			•		•			A	WJ	STA	WJ	100	

Anas flavirostris — Speckled Teal

Subspecies/Population	Breeding range	Wintering, or core non-breeding range	Afr	Eu	Asia	Oc	Neo	NA	Estimate	Source	Trend	Source	1% level	Notes
flavirostris, S South America	N Argentina S to Tierra del Fuego	C Argentina & Chile N to Paraguay & S Brazil					•		E	CC	STA	AT		
flavirostris, Falkland/Malvinas Islands	Falkland/Malvinas Islands						•		18,000–33,000	WS			260	WS estimate 6,000–11,000 pairs (18,000–33,000 individuals).
oxyptera	Andes Central Peru to NW Argentina						•		C	EJ	STA	EJ	1,000	
andium	N Andes Colombia–Ecuador						•		<20,000	CA	DEC	CA	200	
altipetens	E Andes Colombia–Venezuela						•		<20,000	CA	DEC	CA	200	

Anas capensis — Cape Teal

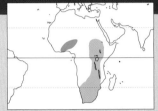

Subspecies/Population	Breeding range	Wintering, or core non-breeding range	Afr	Eu	Asia	Oc	Neo	NA	Estimate	Source	Trend	Source	1% level	Notes
N & E Africa	E African Rift Valley	E Africa W to Chad & N to Libya	•						5,000–10,000	B2	DEC	DO	75	
Lake Chad basin	Lake Chad basin		•						<500	B2	DEC	DO	5	
S Africa	Southern Africa N to Angola & Zambia		•						100,000–250,000	S11	INC	S11	1,750	

Anas bernieri EN — Madagascar Teal, Bernier's Teal

Subspecies/Population	Breeding range	Wintering, or core non-breeding range	Afr	Eu	Asia	Oc	Neo	NA	Estimate	Source	Trend	Source	1% level	Notes
W Madagascar	W Madagascar		•						1,500–2,500	YO	DEC	YO	20	

Anas gibberifrons — Sunda Teal

Subspecies/Population	Breeding range	Wintering, or core non-breeding range	Afr	Eu	Asia	Oc	Neo	NA	Estimate	Source	Trend	Source	1% level	Notes
gibberifrons	E Indonesia					•			B/C	MM	STA	CA	250	Sometimes considered conspecific with gracilis.

Anas gracilis — Grey Teal

Subspecies/Population	Breeding range	Wintering, or core non-breeding range	Afr	Eu	Asia	Oc	Neo	NA	Estimate	Source	Trend	Source	1% level	Notes
gracilis, Australia, New Guinea	Australia, New Guinea, New Britain, New Caledonia					•			C/D					Population of New Britain + New Caledonia 1,500–3,000 (B5). Often considered conspecific with A gibberifrons.
gracilis, New Zealand	New Zealand					•			C	WM	STA	WM	1,000	
remissa	Rennell Island					•			0	M2	EXT	M2		
"Andaman Teal" albogularis	Andaman Islands, Great Coco Island					•			500–1,000	MM	DEC	GT	8	

Grey Teal. Nils Anthes

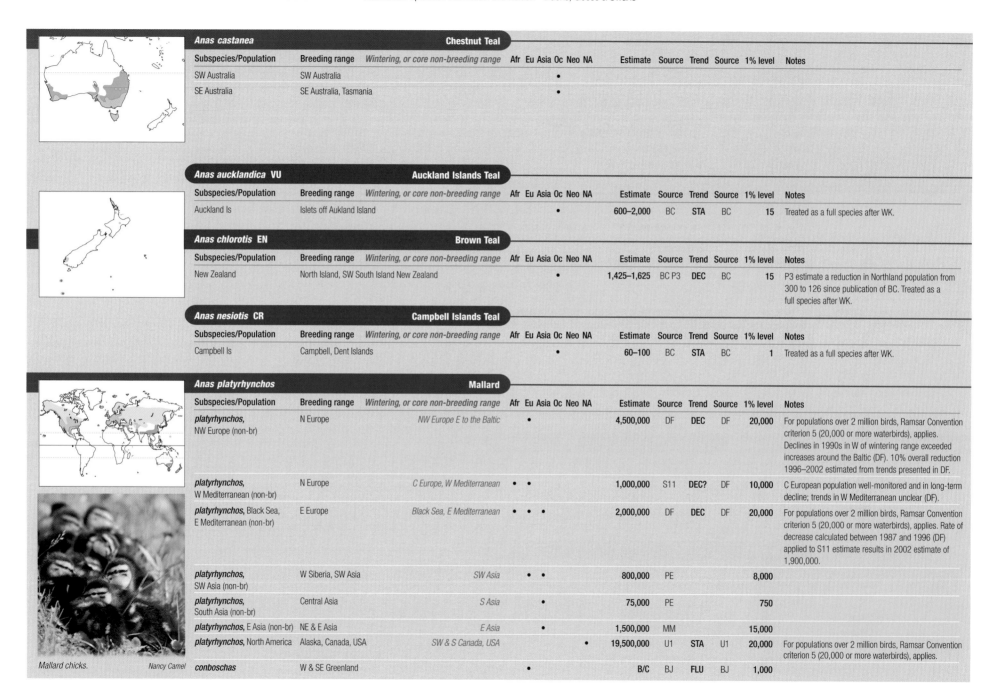

Anas castanea — Chestnut Teal

Subspecies/Population	Breeding range	Wintering, or core non-breeding range	Afr	Eu	Asia	Oc	Neo	NA	Estimate	Source	Trend	Source	1% level	Notes
SW Australia	SW Australia					•								
SE Australia	SE Australia, Tasmania					•								

Anas aucklandica VU — Auckland Islands Teal

Subspecies/Population	Breeding range	Wintering, or core non-breeding range	Afr	Eu	Asia	Oc	Neo	NA	Estimate	Source	Trend	Source	1% level	Notes
Auckland Is	Islets off Aukland Island					•			600–2,000	BC	STA	BC	15	Treated as a full species after WK.

Anas chlorotis EN — Brown Teal

Subspecies/Population	Breeding range	Wintering, or core non-breeding range	Afr	Eu	Asia	Oc	Neo	NA	Estimate	Source	Trend	Source	1% level	Notes
New Zealand	North Island, SW South Island New Zealand					•			1,425–1,625	BC P3	DEC	BC	15	P3 estimate a reduction in Northland population from 300 to 126 since publication of BC. Treated as a full species after WK.

Anas nesiotis CR — Campbell Islands Teal

Subspecies/Population	Breeding range	Wintering, or core non-breeding range	Afr	Eu	Asia	Oc	Neo	NA	Estimate	Source	Trend	Source	1% level	Notes
Campbell Is	Campbell, Dent Islands					•			60–100	BC	STA	BC	1	Treated as a full species after WK.

Anas platyrhynchos — Mallard

Subspecies/Population	Breeding range	Wintering, or core non-breeding range	Afr	Eu	Asia	Oc	Neo	NA	Estimate	Source	Trend	Source	1% level	Notes
platyrhynchos, NW Europe (non-br)	N Europe	NW Europe E to the Baltic		•					4,500,000	DF	DEC	DF	20,000	For populations over 2 million birds, Ramsar Convention criterion 5 (20,000 or more waterbirds), applies. Declines in 1990s in W of wintering range exceeded increases around the Baltic (DF). 10% overall reduction 1996–2002 estimated from trends presented in DF.
platyrhynchos, W Mediterranean (non-br)	N Europe	C Europe, W Mediterranean	•	•					1,000,000	S11	DEC?	DF	10,000	C European population well-monitored and in long-term decline; trends in W Mediterranean unclear (DF).
platyrhynchos, Black Sea, E Mediterranean (non-br)	E Europe	Black Sea, E Mediterranean	•	•	•				2,000,000	DF	DEC	DF	20,000	For populations over 2 million birds, Ramsar Convention criterion 5 (20,000 or more waterbirds), applies. Rate of decrease calculated between 1987 and 1996 (DF) applied to S11 estimate results in 2002 estimate of 1,900,000.
platyrhynchos, SW Asia (non-br)	W Siberia, SW Asia	SW Asia	•	•					800,000	PE			8,000	
platyrhynchos, South Asia (non-br)	Central Asia	S Asia			•				75,000	PE			750	
platyrhynchos, E Asia (non-br)	NE & E Asia	E Asia			•				1,500,000	MM			15,000	
platyrhynchos, North America	Alaska, Canada, USA	SW & S Canada, USA						•	19,500,000	U1	STA	U1	20,000	For populations over 2 million birds, Ramsar Convention criterion 5 (20,000 or more waterbirds), applies.
conboschas	W & SE Greenland			•					B/C	BJ	FLU	BJ	1,000	

Mallard chicks.   Nancy Camel

Anas platyrhynchos... continued

Subspecies/Population	Breeding range	Wintering, or core non-breeding range	Afr	Eu	Asia	Oc	Neo	NA	Estimate	Source	Trend	Source	1% level	Notes
"Mariana Duck" oustaleti	Mariana Islands					•			0	EJ	EXT	EJ		Possibly unstable hybrid between *platyrhynchos* and *superciliosa*.
"Mexican Duck" diazi	Mexico, Arizona, S Texas							•	55,500	S10	INC	PG	560	PG detail a long-term (1960–2000) increase of 2.5% per annum, with large flucatuations throughout the study period.

Anas fulvigula — Mottled Duck

Subspecies/Population	Breeding range	Wintering, or core non-breeding range	Afr	Eu	Asia	Oc	Neo	NA	Estimate	Source	Trend	Source	1% level	Notes
fulvigula	Florida Peninsula							•	35,000	FW			350	Sometimes considered conspecific with *platyrhynchos*.
maculosa	W Gulf Coast, Mississippi, Alabama, Louisiana, Texas, Mexico							•	135,000	HI			1,400	

Anas wyvilliana EN — Hawaiian Duck

Subspecies/Population	Breeding range	Wintering, or core non-breeding range	Afr	Eu	Asia	Oc	Neo	NA	Estimate	Source	Trend	Source	1% level	Notes
Hawaii	Main Hawaiian Islands					•			2,525	U2	STA	U2	25	Sometimes considered conspecific with *platyrhynchos*.

Anas laysanensis VU — Laysan Teal, Laysan Duck

Subspecies/Population	Breeding range	Wintering, or core non-breeding range	Afr	Eu	Asia	Oc	Neo	NA	Estimate	Source	Trend	Source	1% level	Notes
Laysan Island	Laysan Island					•			391–537	U4	FLU	U4	5	BC presents estimate of 375 and trend of increase since 1993.

Anas rubripes — American Black Duck

Subspecies/Population	Breeding range	Wintering, or core non-breeding range	Afr	Eu	Asia	Oc	Neo	NA	Estimate	Source	Trend	Source	1% level	Notes
E USA (non-br)	E Canada, NE USA	*E USA*						•	396,000	U1 SO	STA	U1	4,000	U1 estimates 270,000 for both populations combined, amended with additional data by SO.
Mississippi flyway	Central Canada, N USA	*Mississippi flyway*						•						

Anas melleri EN — Meller's Duck

Subspecies/Population	Breeding range	Wintering, or core non-breeding range	Afr	Eu	Asia	Oc	Neo	NA	Estimate	Source	Trend	Source	1% level	Notes
Madagascar	E & Central Madagascar		•						2,000–5,000	S11 YO	DEC	YO	35	

Meller's Duck.

H. Glyn Young

Anas undulata — Yellow-billed Duck

Subspecies/Population	Breeding range	Wintering, or core non-breeding range	Afr	Eu	Asia	Oc	Neo	NA	Estimate	Source	Trend	Source	1% level	Notes
undulata, E Africa	East Africa		•						20,000–60,000	DO	STA	S11	400	
undulata, S Africa	Southern Africa		•						>100,000	HF	STA	S11	1,000	100,000 in Orange Free State & S Transvaal alone (HF).
rueppelli	N East Africa to S Sudan		•						20,000–50,000	S11	STA	S11	350	
rueppelli?	Highlands of Cameroon & E Nigeria		•						<5,000	DO			50	

Anas poecilorhyncha — Spot-billed Duck

Subspecies/Population	Breeding range	Wintering, or core non-breeding range	Afr	Eu	Asia	Oc	Neo	NA	Estimate	Source	Trend	Source	1% level	Notes
poecilorhyncha	S Asia				●				50,000	PE			500	
"Chinese Spotbill" zonorhyncha	SE Siberia, Japan, Korea, NE & E China, Taiwan	S & E China, Japan, Korea, Taiwan			●				800,000–1,600,000	MM	DEC	PE	12,000	
hartingtoni	E Assam, Myanmar, E to S China & Laos	SE Asia			●					B/C	PE			1,000	

Anas superciliosa — Pacific Black Duck

Subspecies/Population	Breeding range	Wintering, or core non-breeding range	Afr	Eu	Asia	Oc	Neo	NA	Estimate	Source	Trend	Source	1% level	Notes
superciliosa	New Zealand & Islands					●			80,000–150,000	WM	DEC	WM	1,200	
pelewensis	N New Guinea, SW Pacific Is					●				A/B	EJ	STA	EJ	250	B5: 2,500 to 5,000 in New Caledonia.
rogersi	Australia, New Guinea, Indonesia					●	●			D	M4a	DEC	M4a	10,000	

Anas luzonica VU — Philippine Duck

Subspecies/Population	Breeding range	Wintering, or core non-breeding range	Afr	Eu	Asia	Oc	Neo	NA	Estimate	Source	Trend	Source	1% level	Notes
N Philippines	N Philippines				●					A	TL	DEC	TL	100	TL estimate 2,500–10,000.

Anas specularis NT — Spectacled Duck, Bronze-winged Duck

Subspecies/Population	Breeding range	Wintering, or core non-breeding range	Afr	Eu	Asia	Oc	Neo	NA	Estimate	Source	Trend	Source	1% level	Notes
S South America	S Andes to Tierra del Fuego	South America N & E to Buenos Aires					●		A	S8	STA	BC	100	

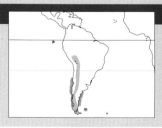

Anas specularioides — Crested Duck

Subspecies/Population	Breeding range	Wintering, or core non-breeding range	Afr	Eu	Asia	Oc	Neo	NA	Estimate	Source	Trend	Source	1% level	Notes
specularioides, S South America	S Andes to Tierra del Fuego	Partial migrant from mountains to coast					●		B	(EJ)	STA	EJ	250	EJ formerly estimated A/B for This population and Falkland/Malvinas population combined.
specularioides, Falkland/Malvinas Is	Falkland/Malvinas Is								21,000–36,000	WS			290	WS estimate 7,000–12,000 pairs (21,000–36,000 individuals).
alticola	Andes Central Peru–N Argentina & Chile						●		B/C	EJ	STA	EJ	1,000	

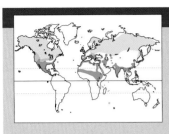

Anas acuta — Northern Pintail

Subspecies/Population	Breeding range	Wintering, or core non-breeding range	Afr	Eu	Asia	Oc	Neo	NA	Estimate	Source	Trend	Source	1% level	Notes
NW Europe (non-br)	N Europe, W Siberia	NW Europe	•						60,000	S11	DEC	DF	600	Trend 1974–96 stable; 1987–96 declining (DF).
Black Sea, Mediterranean, W Africa (non-br)	NE Europe, W Siberia	Black Sea, Mediterranean, West Africa	•	•	•				1,000,000	DF	DEC	DF	10,000	Trend in Africa unknown, but populations in both E & W Mediterranean declined between 1987 and 1996 (DF).
SW Asia, E & NE Africa (non-br)	W Siberia	SW Asia, E & NE Africa	•	•	•				700,000	S11			7,000	
South Asia (non-br)	Central Siberia, Central Asia	S Asia			•				D/E	PE	DEC	PE		
E & SE Asia	E Siberia	E & SE Asia S to Thailand			•				500,000–1,000,000	MM	DEC	PE	7,500	
North America (br)	Alaska, Canada, N USA	SW Canada, USA, Mexico, Caribbean, C America						•	3,700,000	U1	DEC	U1	20,000	For populations over 2 million birds, Ramsar Convention criterion 5 (20,000 or more waterbirds), applies.

Anas eatoni VU — Eaton's Pintail

Subspecies/Population	Breeding range	Wintering, or core non-breeding range	Afr	Eu	Asia	Oc	Neo	NA	Estimate	Source	Trend	Source	1% level	Notes
eatoni	Kerguelen Islands		•						45,000–60,000	BC	DEC	BC	530	Sometimes treated as conspecific with A acuta. 15,000–20,000 pairs in 1982–85 (BC).
drygalski	Crozet Islands		•						1,800–2,100	GT	DEC	GT	20	600–700 pairs in 1980–82 (BC) (1,800–2,100 individuals).

Anas georgica — Yellow-billed Pintail, "South Georgia Pintail"

Subspecies/Population	Breeding range	Wintering, or core non-breeding range	Afr	Eu	Asia	Oc	Neo	NA	Estimate	Source	Trend	Source	1% level	Notes
georgica	South Georgia						•		A	GT	DEC	GT	100	
niceforoi	Central Colombia						•		0	EJ	EXT	EJ		Extinct by 1956 (HW).
spinicauda, mainland South America	S Colombia–Tierra del Fuego	S of range deserted, migration N & E into Brazil					•		D	CC	STA	CC	10,000	
spinicauda, Falkland/Malvinas Is	Falkland/Malvinas Islands						•		1,800–3,000	WS			25	WS estimate 600–1,000 pairs (1,800–3,000 individuals).

Anas bahamensis — White-cheeked Pintail

Subspecies/Population	Breeding range	Wintering, or core non-breeding range	Afr	Eu	Asia	Oc	Neo	NA	Estimate	Source	Trend	Source	1% level	Notes
bahamensis	Caribbean, NE South America						•		75,000	EJ	STA	EJ	750	
galapagensis	Galapagos Islands						•		2,000–5,000	TL			35	
rubrirostris	E Bolivia & S Brazil to N Argentina, Uruguay & Chile	Some dispersal to N of breeding range					•		D	CC	DEC	AT	10,000	

Anas erythrorhyncha — Red-billed Duck

Subspecies/Population	Breeding range	Wintering, or core non-breeding range	Afr	Eu	Asia	Oc	Neo	NA	Estimate	Source	Trend	Source	1% level	Notes
S Africa	Southern Africa		•						500,000–1,000,000	S11	STA	S11	7,500	
E Africa	Eastern Africa		•						100,000–300,000	S11	STA	S11	2,000	
Madagascar	Madagascar		•						15,000–25,000	S11	DEC	S11	200	

Anas versicolor — Silver Teal

Subspecies/Population	Breeding range	Wintering, or core non-breeding range	Afr	Eu	Asia	Oc	Neo	NA	Estimate	Source	Trend	Source	1% level	Notes
versicolor	Bolivia, S Brazil, N Argentina & Chile						●		C	S8	STA	EJ	1,000	
fretensis, S South America	C Chile, C Argentina S to Patagonia	S of range deserted, migration N & E into Brazil					●		C	S8	STA	EJ	1,000	
fretensis, Falkland/Malvinas Is	Falkland/Malvinas Islands						●		2,400–4,500	WS			35	WS estimate 800–1,500 pairs (2,400–4,500 individuals).

Anas puna — Puna Teal

Subspecies/Population	Breeding range	Wintering, or core non-breeding range	Afr	Eu	Asia	Oc	Neo	NA	Estimate	Source	Trend	Source	1% level	Notes
Andean S America	Central Andes: N Chile–Peru						●		D	CC	STA	CC	10,000	Sometimes considered conspecific with versicolor.

Anas hottentota — Hottentot Teal

Subspecies/Population	Breeding range	Wintering, or core non-breeding range	Afr	Eu	Asia	Oc	Neo	NA	Estimate	Source	Trend	Source	1% level	Notes
Chad Basin	Lake Chad Basin,		●						1,000–5,000	DO	DEC	S11	30	
E Africa	Eastern Africa to N Zambia		●						C	DO	STA	S11	1,000	
S Africa	Southern Africa to S Zambia		●						C	DI	STA	S11	1,000	
Madagascar	Madagascar		●						5,000–10,000	S11	DEC	S11	75	

Anas querquedula — Garganey

Subspecies/Population	Breeding range	Wintering, or core non-breeding range	Afr	Eu	Asia	Oc	Neo	NA	Estimate	Source	Trend	Source	1% level	Notes
W Africa (non-br)	Europe, W Siberia	West Africa	●	●	●				>2,000,000–3,300,000	BE	DEC	HC	20,000	BE estimate European breeding population at 650,000–1,100,000 pairs (1,950,000–3,300,000 individuals). Also numerous in W Siberia. For populations over 2 million birds, Ramsar Convention criterion 5 (20,000 or more waterbirds), applies.
SW Asia, NE Africa (non-br)	W Siberia	SW Asia, NE & E Africa	●	●	●				100,000–200,000	S11			1,500	
South Asia (non-br)	W & Central Siberia	S Asia			●				250,000	PE			2,500	
E & SE Asia (non-br)	Central & E Siberia, NE China	E & SE Asia			●				D	PE			10,000	

Anas discors — Blue-winged Teal

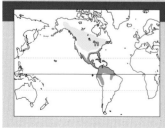

Subspecies/Population	Breeding range	Wintering, or core non-breeding range	Afr	Eu	Asia	Oc	Neo	NA	Estimate	Source	Trend	Source	1% level	Notes
N, C & N South America	N North America	S USA, Central America, N South America					●	●	6,100,000	U1	STA	U1	20,000	For populations over 2 million birds, Ramsar Convention criterion 5 (20,000 or more waterbirds), applies.

Anas cyanoptera — Cinnamon Teal

Subspecies/Population	Breeding range	Wintering, or core non-breeding range	Afr	Eu	Asia	Oc	Neo	NA	Estimate	Source	Trend	Source	1% level	Notes
cyanoptera	South America S of S Peru, S Brazil						•							WS estimate 12–22 pairs (36–66 individuals) in Falkland/Malvinas Is.
orinomus	Central Andes: N Chile–Peru						•		B/C	EJ	STA	EJ	1,000	
septentrianalium	W Central N America to NW Mexico	SW USA, Mexico, Central America					•	•	260,000	RE	STA	RE	2,600	
tropica	NW Colombia						•		A	NA	DEC	NA	100	
borreroi	E Andes of Colombia						•		<250	GT	DEC	GT	3	No records in recent years (HW).

Anas platalea — Red Shoveler

Subspecies/Population	Breeding range	Wintering, or core non-breeding range	Afr	Eu	Asia	Oc	Neo	NA	Estimate	Source	Trend	Source	1% level	Notes
S South America	South America S of Central Chile, N Argentina						•		C/D	S8	STA	CC		WS estimate 8–16 pairs (24–48 individuals) in Falkland/Malvinas Is.

Anas smithii — Cape Shoveler

Subspecies/Population	Breeding range	Wintering, or core non-breeding range	Afr	Eu	Asia	Oc	Neo	NA	Estimate	Source	Trend	Source	1% level	Notes
S Africa	South Africa, Namibia, Botswana, Zimbabwe		•						20,000–50,000	S11	INC	HF	350	

Anas rhynchotis — Australian Shoveler

Subspecies/Population	Breeding range	Wintering, or core non-breeding range	Afr	Eu	Asia	Oc	Neo	NA	Estimate	Source	Trend	Source	1% level	Notes
rhynchotis, SW Australia	SW Australia					•								
rhynchotis, SE Australia	SE Australia, Tasmania					•								
variegata	New Zealand					•			B/C	EJ	STA	EJ	1,000	

Anas clypeata — Northern Shoveler

Subspecies/Population	Breeding range	Wintering, or core non-breeding range	Afr	Eu	Asia	Oc	Neo	NA	Estimate	Source	Trend	Source	1% level	Notes
NW & C Europe (non-br)	N, NW & Central Europe	NW & Central Europe		•					40,000	MN	STA	MN	400	1980s population estimate and trend still apply.
Black Sea, Mediterranean, W Africa (non-br)	W Siberia, NE & E Europe	Black Sea, Mediterranean, West Africa	•	•	•				450,000	S11	DEC	SP	4,500	1990s population estimate and trend still apply.
SW Asia, NE & E Africa (non-br)	W Siberia, Central Asia	SW Asia, NE & E Africa	•	•	•				400,000	S11	DEC	S11	4,000	
South Asia (non-br)	Central Siberia, Central Asia	S Asia			•				D	PE	DEC	PE	10,000	
E & SE Asia (non-br)	E Siberia, NE China	E & SE Asia			•				500,000–1,000,000	MM			7,500	
North America	Alaska, Canada, N USA	SW Canada, USA, Mexico, Central America						•	3,500,000	U1	STA	U1	20,000	For populations over 2 million birds, Ramsar Convention criterion 5 (20,000 or more waterbirds), applies.

Anas marecula — Amsterdam Island Duck

Subspecies/Population	Breeding range	Wintering, or core non-breeding range	Afr	Eu	Asia	Oc	Neo	NA	Estimate	Source	Trend	Source	1% level	Notes
Amsterdam Is	Amsterdam Islands					•			0	BC	EXT	BC		Last record probably 1793, on St Paul Island (BC).

Anas theodori — Mauritian Duck

Subspecies/Population	Breeding range	Wintering, or core non-breeding range	Afr	Eu	Asia	Oc	Neo	NA	Estimate	Source	Trend	Source	1% level	Notes
Mauritius	Mauritius		•						0	BC	EXT	BC		Last recorded 1696 (BC).

Malacorhynchus membranaceus — Pink-eared Duck

Subspecies/Population	Breeding range	Wintering, or core non-breeding range	Afr	Eu	Asia	Oc	Neo	NA	Estimate	Source	Trend	Source	1% level	Notes
SW Australia	SW Australia					•								
SE Australia	SE Australia					•								

Marmaronetta angustirostris VU — Marbled Teal

Subspecies/Population	Breeding range	Wintering, or core non-breeding range	Afr	Eu	Asia	Oc	Neo	NA	Estimate	Source	Trend	Source	1% level	Notes
W Mediterranean, W Africa	W Mediterranean	W Mediterranean, W Africa	•	•					3,000–5,000	DO BM	FLU	GW	40	BM estimated 4,250 based on counts in Tunisia in 1999.
E Mediterranean	E Mediterranean			•					1,000	GU	DEC	GU	10	
SW Asia (non-br)	SW Asia, C Asia, Extreme W China	SW Asia			•				5,000–15,000	S11	DEC	S11	100	
South Asia (non-br)	SW Asia, C Asia, Extreme W China	Pakistan, NW India			•				5,000	PE			50	

Rhodonessa caryophyllacea CR — Pink-headed Duck

Subspecies/Population	Breeding range	Wintering, or core non-breeding range	Afr	Eu	Asia	Oc	Neo	NA	Estimate	Source	Trend	Source	1% level	Notes
NE India, Myanmar	NE India, Myanmar				•				<50	BC	EXT?	BC	1	Last recorded in 1949 (BC).

Netta rufina — Red-crested Pochard

Subspecies/Population	Breeding range	Wintering, or core non-breeding range	Afr	Eu	Asia	Oc	Neo	NA	Estimate	Source	Trend	Source	1% level	Notes
C Europe & W Mediterranean	Central west Europe & W Mediterranean		•	•					50,000	GI	INC	KH	500	37,000 counted in 1999 (GI). The increase on lakes north of the Alps continues.
Black Sea, E Mediterranean (non-br)	SE Europe, S Russia to N Caspian	Black Sea, E Mediterranean		•					20,000–43,500	SP	DEC	SA	320	
C & SW Asia (non-br)	W & Central Asia	Central & SW Asia	•	•					250,000	SA	STA	S11	2,500	
South Asia (non-br)	Central Asia	S Asia			•				C	PE	DEC	PE	1,000	

Netta erythropthalma — Southern Pochard

Subspecies/Population	Breeding range	Wintering, or core non-breeding range	Afr	Eu	Asia	Oc	Neo	NA	Estimate	Source	Trend	Source	1% level	Notes
erythropthalma, Venezuela	Venezuela						•		<2,500	TL	DEC	FK	25	
erythropthalma, E South America	E Brazil to NE Argentina						•		A/B	TL	INC	AO	250	
brunnea	Southern, Eastern Africa		•						30,000–70,000	S11	STA	S11	500	

Netta peposaca — Rosy-billed Pochard

Subspecies/Population	Breeding range	Wintering, or core non-breeding range	Afr	Eu	Asia	Oc	Neo	NA	Estimate	Source	Trend	Source	1% level	Notes
S South America	Central Chile, SE S America	S of range deserted, migration N to S Brazil					•		E	CC	INC	AT		

Aythya valisineria — Canvasback

Subspecies/Population	Breeding range	Wintering, or core non-breeding range	Afr	Eu	Asia	Oc	Neo	NA	Estimate	Source	Trend	Source	1% level	Notes
N America	Alaska, W Canada, NW USA	Lowland USA, N Mexico						•	620,000	U1	STA	U1	6,200	

Aythya ferina — Common Pochard

Subspecies/Population	Breeding range	Wintering, or core non-breeding range	Afr	Eu	Asia	Oc	Neo	NA	Estimate	Source	Trend	Source	1% level	Notes
NE & NW Europe (non-br)	Russia, NE, NW Europe	NE, NW Europe	•						350,000	MN	STA	DF	3,500	Trend stabilised in 1990s; former estimate remains valid (DF).
C Europe, Black Sea, Mediterranean (non-br)	Central & NE Europe	Central Europe, Black Sea, Mediterranean	•	•					1,100,000	DF	INC	DF	10,000	Estimated 10% increase 1997–2002 based on trends in DF. 1% threshold maintained at 1997 level (<20% change).
SW Asia (non-br)	W Siberia	SW Asia	•		•				350,000	PE	DEC	PE	3,500	
South Asia (non-br)	Central Asia	S Asia			•				D	PE	STA	PE	10,000	
E Asia (non-br)	Siberia, Sakhalin, NE China, Hokkaido	(mainly Korea & Japan)			•				600,000–1,000,000	MM			8,000	

Aythya americana — Redhead

Subspecies/Population	Breeding range	Wintering, or core non-breeding range	Afr	Eu	Asia	Oc	Neo	NA	Estimate	Source	Trend	Source	1% level	Notes
N America	Alaska, W & S Canada, W USA	W, S & SE USA, Mexico						•	750,000	U1	STA	U1	7,500	

Aythya collaris — **Ring-necked Duck**

Subspecies/Population	Breeding range	Wintering, or core non-breeding range	Afr	Eu	Asia	Oc	Neo	NA	Estimate	Source	Trend	Source	1% level	Notes
N America	C Alaska, C & E Canada, C & W USA	W, S & SE USA, Mexico						•	1,220,000	U1 SN	STA	U1	12,200	

Aythya australis — **Hardhead**

Subspecies/Population	Breeding range	Wintering, or core non-breeding range	Afr	Eu	Asia	Oc	Neo	NA	Estimate	Source	Trend	Source	1% level	Notes
australis	SW & E Australia	Australia including Tasmania				•			D	M4a	STA	M4a	10,000	
extima	Vanuatu (New Hebrides)					•			<1,000	TL			10	Doubtfully valid population; may be result of brief colonisation from Australia (HW).

Aythya baeri VU — **Baer's Pochard**

Subspecies/Population	Breeding range	Wintering, or core non-breeding range	Afr	Eu	Asia	Oc	Neo	NA	Estimate	Source	Trend	Source	1% level	Notes
C, E, SE & S Asia	SE Siberia, NE China	S China, Korea, Japan, Taiwan, SE Asia S to Thailand & NE India, Bangladesh			•				10,000–20,000	MM	DEC	BC	150	

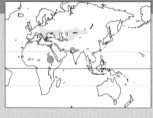

Aythya nyroca NT — **Ferruginous Duck**

Subspecies/Population	Breeding range	Wintering, or core non-breeding range	Afr	Eu	Asia	Oc	Neo	NA	Estimate	Source	Trend	Source	1% level	Notes
N & W Africa (non-br)	W Mediterranean	N & W Africa	•	•					2,000–3,000	SA	DEC	GV	30	
E Europe, E Mediterranean, Black Sea (non-br)	E Europe	E Europe, E Mediterranean, Black Sea, Sahelian Africa	•	•					40,000–65,000	SA	DEC	S11	530	SA (BE): E European breeding population 13,000–22,000 pairs (39,000–66,000 individuals). Nearly 17,000 counted in Mali in 1998–99 (TW).
SW Asia & NE Africa (non-br)	W & SW Asia	SW Asia & NE Africa	•	•	•				C	(BC)	DEC	PE	1,000	Counts in 1990s in Azerbaijan (9,000), Turkmenistan (20,833) & Uzbekistan (7,000) (BC) suggest an estimate of C.
S, E & SE Asia (non-br)	Central Asia to W China & W Mongolia	S, E & SE Asia			•				C/D	LZ BC UH	DEC	PE		LZ, 13,710 S Asia 1994; tens of thousands breed in Inner Mongolia and common on Tibetan Plateau (BC). 70,000 on Hoars of NE Bangladesh, Jan 2002 (UH).

Aythya innotata CR — **Madagascar Pochard**

Subspecies/Population	Breeding range	Wintering, or core non-breeding range	Afr	Eu	Asia	Oc	Neo	NA	Estimate	Source	Trend	Source	1% level	Notes
Madagascar	N Central Madagascar		•						0–10	S11	EXT?	S11	1	

Aythya fuligula — Tufted Duck

Subspecies/Population	Breeding range	Wintering, or core non-breeding range	Afr	Eu	Asia	Oc	Neo	NA	Estimate	Source	Trend	Source	1% level	Notes
NW Europe (non-br)	N & NW Europe	NW Europe		•					1,200,000	DF	INC	DF	12,000	Rate of increase calculated between 1987 and 1996 (DF) applied to S11 estimate results in 2002 estimate of 1,200,000.
C Europe, Black Sea, Mediterranean (non-br)	E & Central Europe, Black Sea, Mediterranean	Central Europe, Black Sea, Mediterranean	•	•	•				700,000	DF	INC	DF	7,000	Rate of increase based on trends in DF.
SW Asia, NE Africa (non-br)	W Siberia, SW Asia, NE Africa	SW Asia, NE Africa	•	•	•				200,000	PE			2,000	
C & South Asia (non-br)	W & Central Siberia	Central & S Asia			•				D	PE	INC	PE	10,000	
E & SE Asia (non-br)	Central & E Siberia, NE China, Hokkaido	E, SE Asia S to Thailand			•				500,000–1,000,000	MM			7,500	

Tufted Duck.   Johan Verbanck

Aythya novaeseelandiae — New Zealand Scaup

Subspecies/Population	Breeding range	Wintering, or core non-breeding range	Afr	Eu	Asia	Oc	Neo	NA	Estimate	Source	Trend	Source	1% level	Notes
New Zealand	New Zealand					•			5,000–10,000	GT	INC	GT	75	

Aythya marila — Greater Scaup

Subspecies/Population	Breeding range	Wintering, or core non-breeding range	Afr	Eu	Asia	Oc	Neo	NA	Estimate	Source	Trend	Source	1% level	Notes
marila, W Europe (non-br)	W Siberia, N Europe	W Europe		•					310,000	LJ	STA	SR	3,100	
marila, Black & Caspian Seas (non-br)	W Siberia	Black & Caspian Seas		•	•				100,000–200,000	S11			1,500	
mariloides, E Asia	E Siberia	E Asia			•				200,000–400,000	MM			3,000	
mariloides, North America	Alaska, Arctic Canada	Coasts of N America, Great Lakes						•	520,000	AL	STA	AL	5,200	

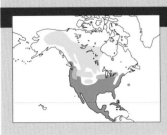

Aythya affinis — Lesser Scaup

Subspecies/Population	Breeding range	Wintering, or core non-breeding range	Afr	Eu	Asia	Oc	Neo	NA	Estimate	Source	Trend	Source	1% level	Notes
N & C America	North America, Central America						•	•	2,994,000	AL	DEC	AL	20,000	For populations over 2 million birds, Ramsar Convention criterion 5 (20,000 or more waterbirds), applies.

Somateria mollissima — Common Eider

Common Eider. — Paul Goriup

Subspecies/Population	Breeding range	Wintering, or core non-breeding range	Afr	Eu	Asia	Oc	Neo	NA	Estimate	Source	Trend	Source	1% level	Notes
mollissima, Britain, Ireland	Britain, Ireland			•					73,000	KN			750	
mollissima, Baltic, Wadden Sea	Baltic, Wadden Sea			•					850,000–1,200,000	PR	DEC	PR	10,300	
mollissima, Norway, NW Russia	Norway, Russia E to Novaya Zemlya	*Norway, NW Russia*		•					300,000–550,000	S11	STA	S11	4,250	
mollissima, White Sea	White Sea			•					20,000–30,000	S11			250	
mollissima, Black Sea	Black Sea			•					5,400	YB	INC	YB	55	YB presents estimate of 1,800 breeding pairs (5,400 individuals).
faeroeensis, Faeroe Is	Faeroe Islands			•					6,000–12,000	S11	STA	S11	90	
faeroeensis, Shetland, Orkney Is	Shetland, Orkney Islands			•					12,000–13,500	S11	STA	S11	130	
borealis, Svalbard, Franz Joseph	Svalbard, Franz Joseph	*Unknown*		•					40,000–80,000	S11	STA	S11	600	
borealis, Iceland	Iceland			•					600,000–900,000	S11	INC	S11	7,500	
borealis, West Greenland	West Greenland	*Coastal SW Greenland*						•	36,000–45,000	MF	DEC	MF	400	MF estimates 12,000–15,000 breeding pairs (36,000–45,000 individuals).
borealis, NE Greenland	NE Greenland	*Iceland*		•					A/B	BJ	STA	BJ	250	
borealis, Arctic NE Canada	Arctic NE Canada	*Atlantic coast Canada & SW Greenland*		•				•	180,000–220,000	SB	DEC	GS	2,000	
dresseri	Atlantic NE Canada	*Atlantic Coast, Canada, N USA*						•	107,000	SB	STA	SB	1,100	
sedentaria	Hudson Bay, Canada	*Atlantic coast, Canada*						•	100,000	GG	DEC	GS GG	1,000	
v-nigra	NE Siberia, NW N America	*Bering Sea, Aleutians to Kamchatka*			•			•	130,000–200,000	MM	DEC	KE	1,700	

Somateria spectabilis — King Eider

Subspecies/Population	Breeding range	Wintering, or core non-breeding range	Afr	Eu	Asia	Oc	Neo	NA	Estimate	Source	Trend	Source	1% level	Notes
N Europe, W Siberia (br)	E Greenland, NE Europe, W Siberia	*Coasts of Iceland, Norway, NW Russia*		•	•				300,000	S11	STA	SP	3,000	
E Asia (br)	Arctic E Asia	*Extreme N Pacific coast*			•									
Alaska, NW Canada (br)	N Alaska, Arctic NW Canada	*Extreme N Pacific coast*						•	340,000–380,000	SB	DEC	SB	3,600	
E Canada, N Greenland (br)	E Canadian Arctic, N Greenland	*Canadian Atlantic coast & SW Greenland*		•				•	150,000–250,000	SB	DEC	SB	2,000	300,000 winter in SW Greenland (MG, MV, MW).

King Eider. — Gerard Boere

Somateria fischeri LC — Spectacled Eider

Subspecies/Population	Breeding range	Wintering, or core non-breeding range	Afr	Eu	Asia	Oc	Neo	NA	Estimate	Source	Trend	Source	1% level	Notes
E Siberia, N & W Alaska	Siberian coast E of Lena, N & W Alaska	*Bering Sea pack ice*			•			•	330,000–390,000	LH			3,600	

Polysticta stelleri LC — Steller's Eider

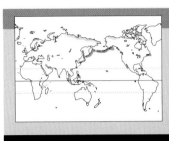

Subspecies/Population	Breeding range	Wintering, or core non-breeding range	Afr	Eu	Asia	Oc	Neo	NA	Estimate	Source	Trend	Source	1% level	Notes
N Norway, SE Baltic (non-br)	N Siberian coast	N Norway, SE Baltic		•	•				40,000	PP	INC	S11	400	BC estimate 30,000–50,000.
N Pacific (non-br)	N Siberian coast, N & W Alaska	SW Alaska, Aleutians, Kamchatka, Kuril Is			•			•	180,000	PP	STA?	BC	1,800	

Camptorhynchus labradorius — Labrador Duck

Subspecies/Population	Breeding range	Wintering, or core non-breeding range	Afr	Eu	Asia	Oc	Neo	NA	Estimate	Source	Trend	Source	1% level	Notes
NE North America	NE North America							•	0	GY	EXT	GY		Last specimens in 1875 (or 1878) (BC).

Histrionicus histrionicus — Harlequin (Duck)

Subspecies/Population	Breeding range	Wintering, or core non-breeding range	Afr	Eu	Asia	Oc	Neo	NA	Estimate	Source	Trend	Source	1% level	Notes
NW North America (br)	Alaska, NW Canada, NW USA	Coasts of S & W Alaska, W Canada, NW USA						•	150,000–250,000	SB	STA	SB	2,000	
E North America	E Canada, W & SE Greenland	Coastal NE Canada & USA, E & SW Greenland						•	10,000–30,000	TH			200	Birds breeding in E Canada and those breeding in Greenland were treated as separate populations in WPE2, but satellite tracking has revealed that many birds from Canada moult and winter in SW Greenland. TH estimate 1,500–1,600 breeding in E Canada.
Iceland	Iceland			•					9,000–12,000	IA			75	IA estimates 3,000–4,000 pairs (9,000–12,000 individuals).
(pacificus) E Siberia, N Japan	E Siberia, N Japan	Coastal W Pacific S to Yellow Sea			•				C	YA			1,000	

Clangula hyemalis — Long-tailed Duck, Oldsquaw

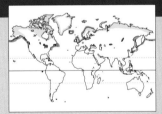

Subspecies/Population	Breeding range	Wintering, or core non-breeding range	Afr	Eu	Asia	Oc	Neo	NA	Estimate	Source	Trend	Source	1% level	Notes
Iceland, Greenland (br)	Iceland, Greenland	N Atlantic		•					100,000–150,000	SR	STA	PS	1,300	Estimate for the wintering population in coastal W Greenland: 94,000 (MF).
W Siberia, N Europe (br)	W Siberia, N Europe	N Atlantic, Baltic, N Seas, C European Lakes		•	•				4,600,000	S11	STA	S11	20,000	For populations over 2 million birds, Ramsar Convention criterion 5 (20,000 or more waterbirds), applies.
E Asia (non-br)	E Siberia	Seas of E Asia			•				500,000–1,000,000	MM			7,500	
N America	Alaska, N Canada	North Pacific, North Atlantic, Great Lakes, SW Greenland		•				•	2,000,000	SB	DEC?	SB	20,000	For populations over 2 million birds, Ramsar Convention criterion 5 (20,000 or more waterbirds), applies. E & W coast birds may merit separate treatment.

Melanitta nigra — Common Scoter, Black Scoter

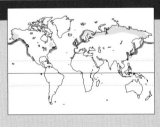

Subspecies/Population	Breeding range	Wintering, or core non-breeding range	Afr	Eu	Asia	Oc	Neo	NA	Estimate	Source	Trend	Source	1% level	Notes
nigra	W Siberia, Scandinavia, Iceland, Scotland, Ireland	Baltic, W Atlantic S to Mauritania	•	•	•				1,600,000	PS	STA	PT	16,000	
americana, E Asia	Siberia E of Lena	Coastal E Asia S to Korea			•				D	GF			10,000	
americana, NE North America	E Canada	Atlantic S Canada–N USA						•	100,000	BK BL	DEC	BK	1,000	Uncertain estimate of 25,800 pairs in BK (77,400 individuals), increased to 100,000 by BL to reflect improved state of knowledge. >200,000 stage on St Lawrence River during migrations (J-P Savard in litt.).
americana, NW North America	Alaska	Pacific Coast N America						•	80,000–120,000	SB	DEC	SB	1,000	

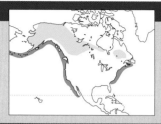

Melanitta perspicillata — Surf Scoter

Subspecies/Population	Breeding range	Wintering, or core non-breeding range	Afr	Eu	Asia	Oc	Neo	NA	Estimate	Source	Trend	Source	1% level	Notes
N America	Alaska, N Canada	Atlantic & Pacific coasts N America						•	400,000–600,000	SB	DEC	SB	5,000	>200,000 stage on St Lawrence River during migrations J-P Savard in litt. E & W Coast populations may merit separate treatment.

Melanitta fusca — Velvet Scoter, White-winged Scoter

Subspecies/Population	Breeding range	Wintering, or core non-breeding range	Afr	Eu	Asia	Oc	Neo	NA	Estimate	Source	Trend	Source	1% level	Notes
fusca, Baltic, W Europe (non-br)	W Siberia, N Europe	Baltic, W Europe	•	•					1,000,000	PS	STA	PS	10,000	
fusca, Black Sea (non-br)	Black Sea, Caucasus	Black Sea		•					1,500	S11			15	
stejnegeri	Central & E Siberia E of Yenisey	Coastal Far East & E Asia			•				600,000–1,000,000	MM			8,000	
deglandi	Alaska, Canada E to Hudson Bay	Atlantic & Pacific coasts N America						•	1,000,000	EJ	STA	EJ	10,000	

Bucephala albeola — Bufflehead

Subspecies/Population	Breeding range	Wintering, or core non-breeding range	Afr	Eu	Asia	Oc	Neo	NA	Estimate	Source	Trend	Source	1% level	Notes
N America	Alaska, W & S Canada	N Mexico, USA, Atlantic & Pacific N America					•	•	1,000,000	U1	STA	U1	10,000	

Bucephala islandica — Barrow's Goldeneye

Subspecies/Population	Breeding range	Wintering, or core non-breeding range	Afr	Eu	Asia	Oc	Neo	NA	Estimate	Source	Trend	Source	1% level	Notes
Iceland	N Iceland	Iceland		•					1,500–1,800	IA	STA	S11	15	IA estimates 500–600 pairs (1,500–1,800 individuals). A census during 1999–2000 winter counted 1,663.
W North America	S Alaska, W Canada, NW USA	Pacific coast S Alaska, W Canada, W USA						•	170,000–200,000	SB	STA	SB	1,900	
E North America	NE Canada	Atlantic coast NE USA, E Canada						•	4,500	RF RM			5	Not observed in Greenland for c.50 years and probably extinct there (BG).

Bucephala clangula — Common Goldeneye

Subspecies/Population	Breeding range	Wintering, or core non-breeding range	Afr	Eu	Asia	Oc	Neo	NA	Estimate	Source	Trend	Source	1% level	Notes
clangula, NW, Central Europe (non-br)	N, NE Europe	NW, Central Europe		•					400,000	DF	INC	DF	4,000	Rate of increase based on trends in DF.
clangula, SE Europe, Adriatic (non-br)	NE Europe	Middle Danube, Adriatic		•					75,000	S11			750	
clangula, Black Sea (non-br)	W Siberia, NE Europe	Black Sea		•	•				20,000	MN			200	
clangula, Caspian Sea (non-br)	W Siberia	Caspian		•	•				25,000	S11			250	
clangula, E Asia (non-br)	E Siberia, N Monglia NE China	E Asia			•				50,000–100,000	MM			750	
americana	Alaska, Canada	USA, Atlantic and Pacific coast of Canada & Alaska						•	1,500,000	U1	STA	U1	15,000	E & W Coast populations may merit separate treatment.

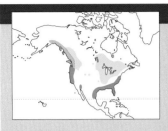

Lophodytes cucullatus — Hooded Merganser

Subspecies/Population	Breeding range	Wintering, or core non-breeding range	Afr	Eu	Asia	Oc	Neo	NA	Estimate	Source	Trend	Source	1% level	Notes
N America	W USA & Canada, S Alaska, SE Canada, E USA	Pacific & Atlantic coasts of North America						•	270,000–385,000	DV	INC	S6	3,300	E & W Coast populations may merit separate treatment.

Mergellus albellus — Smew

Subspecies/Population	Breeding range	Wintering, or core non-breeding range	Afr	Eu	Asia	Oc	Neo	NA	Estimate	Source	Trend	Source	1% level	Notes
NW & C Europe (non-br)	N Scandinavia, N Russia	NW & Central Europe		•					40,000	DF	INC	DF	400	DF presented strongly increasing trend 1987–96, but coverage considered unrepresentative and reduced trend used to derive estimate.
Black Sea, E Mediterranean (non-br)	N Scandinavia, N Russia	Black Sea, E Mediterranean		•					35,000	SA			350	
C & SW Asia (non-br)	W Siberia	Central & SW Asia, Caspian		•	•				30,000	PE	DEC		300	
E Asia (non-br)	Central & E Siberia, Hokkaido	E Asia			•				C	MM			1,000	

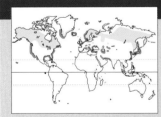

Mergus octosetaceus CR — Brazilian Merganser

Subspecies/Population	Breeding range	Wintering, or core non-breeding range	Afr	Eu	Asia	Oc	Neo	NA	Estimate	Source	Trend	Source	1% level	Notes
C South America	S & C Brazil, NE Argentina & E Paraguay						•		50–250	BC	DEC	BC	2	TK: Found at several new localities in C Brazil in 2002.

Mergus serrator — Red-breasted Merganser

Subspecies/Population	Breeding range	Wintering, or core non-breeding range	Afr	Eu	Asia	Oc	Neo	NA	Estimate	Source	Trend	Source	1% level	Notes
NW & C Europe (non-br)	N & NW Europe, Iceland, E Greenland	N NW & Central Europe, Iceland, E Greenland		•					170,000	PS DF	INC	DF	1,700	DF presented strongly increasing trend 1987–96, but coverage considered unrepresentative and reduced trend used to derive estimate.
Black Sea, Mediterranean (non-br)	NE Europe	Black Sea, E Mediterranean		•	•				50,000	MN			500	
SW & C Asia (non-br)	W Siberia	SW Asia, Central Asia			•				<10,000	S11			100	
E Asia (non-br)	Central & E Siberia, NE China	E Asia			•				C	GD			1,000	
North America	Alaska, Canada, + locally Minnesota, Michigan, Wisconsin, Maine	US Pacific & Atlantic coasts, Mexican Gulf						•	249,000	TN	DEC	TN	2,500	E & W Coast populations may merit separate treatment.
W & SE Greenland	W & SE Greenland	SW Coastal Greenland		•					B	BJ	STA	BJ	250	Sometimes ascribed to *schioleri*, but this form doubtfully valid.

Mergus squamatus VU — Scaly-sided Merganser

Subspecies/Population	Breeding range	Wintering, or core non-breeding range	Afr	Eu	Asia	Oc	Neo	NA	Estimate	Source	Trend	Source	1% level	Notes
E & SE Asia	Extreme SE Russia, NE China, N Korea	S & E to C & S China, N Indochina, Japan, Korea			•				3,600–4,500	BC	DEC	BC	40	

Mergus merganser — Goosander, Common Merganser

Subspecies/Population	Breeding range	Wintering, or core non-breeding range	Afr	Eu	Asia	Oc	Neo	NA	Estimate	Source	Trend	Source	1% level	Notes
merganser, NW & C Europe (non-br)	Scandinavia Baltic, W Russia	NW, Central Europe		•					250,000	DF	INC	DF	2,500	DF presented strongly increasing trend 1987–96, but coverage considered unrepresentative and reduced trend used to derive estimate.
merganser, Iceland	Iceland			•					900	S11			9	
merganser, Scotland, N England, Wales	Scotland, England, Wales			•					16,100	KN	INC	KN	160	
merganser, Central west Europe (br)	Switzerland, SW Germany, E France			•					2,670–3,400	KG LD	INC	S11	30	KG: 620–870 pairs in Switzerland+French part of Lac Leman. LD: 270 breeding pairs in Bavaria. Total 890–1,140 pairs (2,670–3,400 individuals).
merganser, Balkans (br)	Balkans			•					50–100	S11			1	
merganser, Black Sea (non-br)	NE Europe	Black Sea		•					10,000	MN			100	
merganser, Caspian Sea (non-br)	Central & W Siberia	Caspian Sea, central & SW Asia		•	•				20,000	S11			200	
orientalis, S Asia (non-br)	Mountains of Central Asia.	S Asia			•				2,500–10,000	CA	STA	CA	60	Sometimes ascribed to comatus.
orientalis, E Asia (non-br)	Central & E Siberia, NE China, Hokkaido	E Asia			•				50,000–100,000	MM			750	Sometimes ascribed to comatus.
americanus	S Alaska & Canada, N USA	W Canada, USA, N Mexico						•	D	HZ			1,000	

Mergus australis — Auckland Merganser

Subspecies/Population	Breeding range	Wintering, or core non-breeding range	Afr	Eu	Asia	Oc	Neo	NA	Estimate	Source	Trend	Source	1% level	Notes
Auckland Is	Auckland Islands					•			0	GY	EXT	GY		Last recorded specimen in 1902 (BC).

Heteronetta atricapilla — Black-headed Duck

Subspecies/Population	Breeding range	Wintering, or core non-breeding range	Afr	Eu	Asia	Oc	Neo	NA	Estimate	Source	Trend	Source	1% level	Notes
S C South America	C Chile to Paraguay & N Argentina						•							

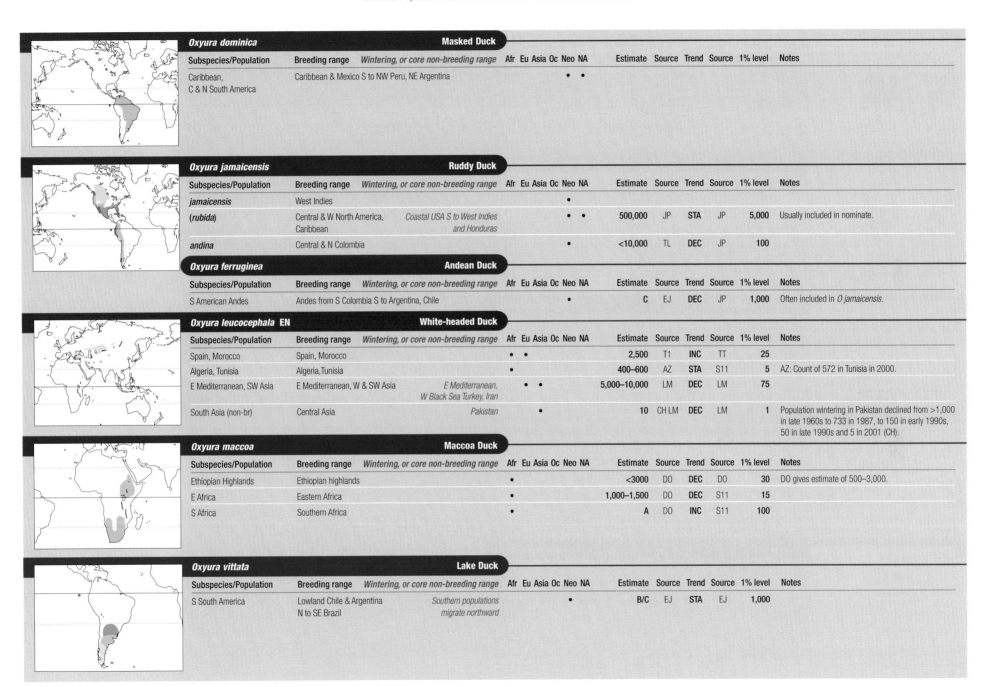

Oxyura dominica — Masked Duck

Subspecies/Population	Breeding range	Wintering, or core non-breeding range	Afr	Eu	Asia	Oc	Neo	NA	Estimate	Source	Trend	Source	1% level	Notes
Caribbean, C & N South America	Caribbean & Mexico S to NW Peru, NE Argentina						•	•						

Oxyura jamaicensis — Ruddy Duck

Subspecies/Population	Breeding range	Wintering, or core non-breeding range	Afr	Eu	Asia	Oc	Neo	NA	Estimate	Source	Trend	Source	1% level	Notes
jamaicensis	West Indies						•							
(*rubida*)	Central & W North America, Caribbean	*Coastal USA S to West Indies and Honduras*					•	•	500,000	JP	STA	JP	5,000	Usually included in nominate.
andina	Central & N Colombia						•		<10,000	TL	DEC	JP	100	

Oxyura ferruginea — Andean Duck

Subspecies/Population	Breeding range	Wintering, or core non-breeding range	Afr	Eu	Asia	Oc	Neo	NA	Estimate	Source	Trend	Source	1% level	Notes
S American Andes	Andes from S Colombia S to Argentina, Chile						•		C	EJ	DEC	JP	1,000	Often included in *O jamaicensis*.

Oxyura leucocephala EN — White-headed Duck

Subspecies/Population	Breeding range	Wintering, or core non-breeding range	Afr	Eu	Asia	Oc	Neo	NA	Estimate	Source	Trend	Source	1% level	Notes
Spain, Morocco	Spain, Morocco		•	•					2,500	T1	INC	TT	25	
Algeria, Tunisia	Algeria, Tunisia		•						400–600	AZ	STA	S11	5	AZ: Count of 572 in Tunisia in 2000.
E Mediterranean, SW Asia	E Mediterranean, W & SW Asia	*E Mediterranean, W Black Sea Turkey, Iran*		•	•				5,000–10,000	LM	DEC	LM	75	
South Asia (non-br)	Central Asia	*Pakistan*			•				10	CH LM	DEC	LM	1	Population wintering in Pakistan declined from >1,000 in late 1960s to 733 in 1987, to 150 in early 1990s, 50 in late 1990s and 5 in 2001 (CH).

Oxyura maccoa — Maccoa Duck

Subspecies/Population	Breeding range	Wintering, or core non-breeding range	Afr	Eu	Asia	Oc	Neo	NA	Estimate	Source	Trend	Source	1% level	Notes
Ethiopian Highlands	Ethiopian highlands		•						<3000	DO	DEC	DO	30	DO gives estimate of 500–3,000.
E Africa	Eastern Africa		•						1,000–1,500	DO	DEC	S11	15	
S Africa	Southern Africa		•						A	DO	INC	S11	100	

Oxyura vittata — Lake Duck

Subspecies/Population	Breeding range	Wintering, or core non-breeding range	Afr	Eu	Asia	Oc	Neo	NA	Estimate	Source	Trend	Source	1% level	Notes
S South America	Lowland Chile & Argentina N to SE Brazil	*Southern populations migrate northward*					•		B/C	EJ	STA	EJ	1,000	

Oxyura australis — Blue-billed Duck

Subspecies/Population	Breeding range	Wintering, or core non-breeding range	Afr	Eu	Asia	Oc	Neo	NA	Estimate	Source	Trend	Source	1% level	Notes
SE Australia	SE Australia	E & SE Australia				•			18,000	GC	DEC	GC	180	GC estimate 12,000 breeding adults (18,000 individuals). (Both populations combined.)
SW Australia	SW Australia	W & SW Australia				•								

Biziura lobata — Musk Duck

Subspecies/Population	Breeding range	Wintering, or core non-breeding range	Afr	Eu	Asia	Oc	Neo	NA	Estimate	Source	Trend	Source	1% level	Notes
SE Australia	SE Australia					•								
SW Australia	SW Australia					•								
Tasmania	Tasmania					•								

GRUIDAE CRANES

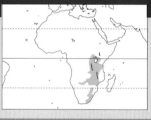

Balearica regulorum — Grey Crowned Crane

Subspecies/Population	Breeding range	Wintering, or core non-breeding range	Afr	Eu	Asia	Oc	Neo	NA	Estimate	Source	Trend	Source	1% level	Notes
regulorum	S Angola, N Namibia, Botswana, Zimbabwe, to SE S Africa		•						8,000–12,000	DO	STA	DO	100	
gibbericeps	Uganda, Kenya, D R Congo S to N Zimbabwe, N Mozambique		•						50,000–65,000	DO	DEC	MC	580	

Crowned Crane.

Johan Verbanck

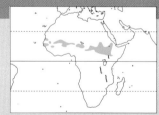

Balearica pavonina NT — Black Crowned Crane

Subspecies/Population	Breeding range	Wintering, or core non-breeding range	Afr	Eu	Asia	Oc	Neo	NA	Estimate	Source	Trend	Source	1% level	Notes
pavonina	Sub-Saharan W Africa, Senegambia E to Chad		•						15,000	B9	DEC	B9	150	
ceciliae	W Chad, Sudan, Ethiopia, Uganda, Kenya		•						25,000–55,000	DO	DEC	MC	400	

Grus virgo — Demoiselle Crane

Subspecies/Population	Breeding range	Wintering, or core non-breeding range	Afr	Eu	Asia	Oc	Neo	NA	Estimate	Source	Trend	Source	1% level	Notes
NW Africa (br)	Atlas Mts, NW Africa	Sub-Saharan Africa L Chad–Ethiopia	•						<30	B9			1	
Black Sea (br)	Black Sea, SE Russia	Sub-Saharan Africa L Chad–Ethiopia	•	•					450–510	HC	DEC	HC	5	HC estimate 150–170 pairs (450–510 individuals).
Turkey (br)	Turkey	Turkey?		•	•				60–90	BE			1	BE estimate 20–30 pairs (60–90 individuals) but this population may be close to extinction.
Kalmykia (br)	Kalmykia	Sudan via Saudi Arabia	•	•	•				30,000–35,000	MC	STA	MC	325	
W Central Asia (br)	W, Central Asia	Indian Subcontinent			•				100,000	MC	INC	MC	1,000	
E Asia (br)	E Asia	Indian Subcontinent			•				70,000–100,000	MC	STA	MC	850	

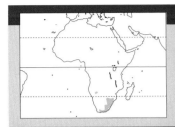

Grus paradisea VU — Blue Crane

Subspecies/Population	Breeding range	Wintering, or core non-breeding range	Afr	Eu	Asia	Oc	Neo	NA	Estimate	Source	Trend	Source	1% level	Notes
South Africa	E & S South Africa		•						20,000–21,000	M7	STA	M7	210	
N Namibia	Namibia: Etosha Pan		•						60	BC	DEC	BC	1	

Grus carunculatus VU — Wattled Crane

Subspecies/Population	Breeding range	Wintering, or core non-breeding range	Afr	Eu	Asia	Oc	Neo	NA	Estimate	Source	Trend	Source	1% level	Notes
Ethiopia	Ethiopian Highlands		•						200	MC	STA	DO	2	
South Africa	E South Africa		•						235	B8	DEC	BC	2	230 (BC) declining rapidly.
C–S Africa	D R Congo, Zambia, Tanzania to Botswana, Mozambique		•						8,000	DO	DEC	BC	80	

Grus leucogeranus CR — Siberian Crane

Subspecies/Population	Breeding range	Wintering, or core non-breeding range	Afr	Eu	Asia	Oc	Neo	NA	Estimate	Source	Trend	Source	1% level	Notes
Iran (non-br)	Tyumen district, NW Russia	Iran			•				3	IE	DEC	MC	1	Only 3 individuals returned to Iran in 2001–02.
India (non-br)	Kunovat River Basin, NW Russia	Bharatpur, India			•				2	IE	DEC	SR	1	
China (non-br)	NE Siberia Kolyma–Yana River	Poyang, China			•				3,000	LW	DEC	BC	30	

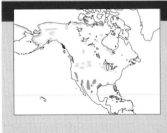

Grus canadensis — Sandhill Crane

Subspecies/Population	Breeding range	Wintering, or core non-breeding range	Afr	Eu	Asia	Oc	Neo	NA	Estimate	Source	Trend	Source	1% level	Notes
canadensis	Arctic & subarctic N America & E Siberia	SW USA, N Central Mexico			•			•						
rowani	Subarctic Canada	Texas coast, SW USA, N Central Mexico						•	450,000	MC	STA	MC	4,500	
tabida	Mid-Continental NW N America	N Central Mexico & S USA						•	65,000–75,000	MC	INC	MC	700	
pratensis	S Georgia, Florida (resident)							•	4,000–6,000	MC	STA	MC	50	
pulla	SE Mississippi							•	120	MC			1	
nesiotes	Cuba & Isle of Pines						•		650	SR	INC	SR	7	Information provided by George Archibald, October 2001.

Sandhill Cranes.

Nancy Camel

Grus antigone VU — Sarus Crane

Subspecies/Population	Breeding range	Wintering, or core non-breeding range	Afr	Eu	Asia	Oc	Neo	NA	Estimate	Source	Trend	Source	1% level	Notes
antigone	Pakistan, N India, Nepal	Pakistan, N India, Nepal			•				8,000–10,000	MC	DEC	SZ GP	90	Declines in Gujarat and Rajasthan possibly being balanced by increases in Uttar Pradesh (Gopi Sundar in litt.).
sharpii, Indochina	N Cambodia, Possibly S Laos, S Vietnam	Vietnam, Cambodia, Laos, possibly NE Thailand			•				1,000	B6	DEC	B6	10	
sharpii, Myanmar	Myanmar. Possibly disperses short distances into surrounding countries				•				1,000	B6	DEC	B6	10	
gilliae	N Australia					•			15,000	GC	STA	GC	150	GC estimate 10,000 breeding adults (15,000 individuals), This population is now given subspecific status.

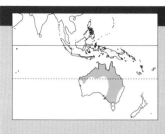

Grus rubicunda　　　　Brolga

Subspecies/Population	Breeding range	Wintering, or core non-breeding range	Afr	Eu	Asia	Oc	Neo	NA	Estimate	Source	Trend	Source	1% level	Notes
N Australia	N Australia					•			C	MC	STA	MC	1,000	Formerly assigned to *argentea* (Peters 1934).
S Australia	S Australia					•			1,000	MC	DEC	MC	10	Formerly assigned to *argentea* (Peters 1934).
New Guinea	S New Guinea					•								

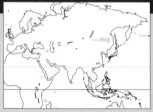

Grus vipio VU　　　　White-naped Crane

Subspecies/Population	Breeding range	Wintering, or core non-breeding range	Afr	Eu	Asia	Oc	Neo	NA	Estimate	Source	Trend	Source	1% level	Notes
China (non-br)	Mongolia, NE China, extreme SE Russia	*China (Yangtze Basin)*			•				4,000	WA	STA	WA	40	
Korea, Japan (non-br)	Mongolia, NE China, extreme SE Russia	*Korean Peninsula, Japan*			•				3,200	CE	STA	CE	30	c 2,700 winter in Japan and 500 in Korea.

Grus grus　　　　Common Crane, Eurasian Crane

Subspecies/Population	Breeding range	Wintering, or core non-breeding range	Afr	Eu	Asia	Oc	Neo	NA	Estimate	Source	Trend	Source	1% level	Notes
grus, NW Europe (br)	Scandinavia, N Continental Europe	*France, Iberia, Morocco*	•	•					75,000	HC	INC	MC	750	
grus, NE, C Europe (br)	NE Europe	*Algeria, Tunisia, Libya*	•	•					70,000	HC	STA	MC	600	
grus, SW Asia, NE Africa (non-br)	NE Europe, W Russia S & W of Urals	*Turkey, SW Asia to SW Iran, Iraq, NE Africa*	•	•					35,000	MC	DEC	MC	350	
(*lilfordi*), Black Sea	Black Sea, Turkey	*Black Sea, ?Turkey, ?NE Africa*	•	•					200–500	MC	DEC	MC	4	"*lilfordi*" not widely recognised.
(*lilfordi*), India (non-br)	W Siberia & Kazakhstan	*W & C India, E Iran, Afghanistan*			•	•			70,000	SR			700	Information provided by George Archibald, October 2001.
(*lilfordi*), C China (non-br)	Central Siberia, NE China	*China, Korea, Japan, Taiwan*			•				10,000–12,000	WA	DEC	MC	110	
(*lilfordi*), S China (non-br)	Tibetan plateau	*SW China & N Myanmar*			•				5,000–10,000	CE	STA	MC	75	Wintering area of Tibetan birds assumed with no strong basis.

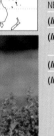

Common Crane.　　　*Johan Verbanck*

Grus monacha VU　　　　Hooded Crane

Subspecies/Population	Breeding range	Wintering, or core non-breeding range	Afr	Eu	Asia	Oc	Neo	NA	Estimate	Source	Trend	Source	1% level	Notes
C China (non-br)	NE China, SE Russia	*China*			•				1,000	WA	DEC	BC	10	
Korea, Japan (non-br)		*Korea, Japan*			•				8,500	CE	INC	BC	85	About 8,300 winter in Japan and 150 in South Korea.

104

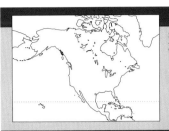

Grus americana EN — Whooping Crane

Subspecies/Population	Breeding range	Wintering, or core non-breeding range	Afr	Eu	Asia	Oc	Neo	NA	Estimate	Source	Trend	Source	1% level	Notes
W C Canada (br)	W Central Canada: Wood Buffalo National Park	Texas coast: Aransas National Wildlife Refuge						•	180	SR	INC	SR	2	Information provided by George Archibald, October 2001.
Florida (re-established)	Florida (re-established)							•	52	SR	INC	SR	1	Information provided by George Archibald, October 2001.
Wisconsin– Florida (re-established)	Wisconsin	Florida						•	8	SR			1	Information provided by George Archibald, October 2001.

Grus nigricollis VU — Black-necked Crane

Subspecies/Population	Breeding range	Wintering, or core non-breeding range	Afr	Eu	Asia	Oc	Neo	NA	Estimate	Source	Trend	Source	1% level	Notes
C & S Asia	Extreme NW India E to W & Central China	Bhutan, NE India, S Tibet E to SW China			•				6,000	WA	STA	CE	60	

Grus japonensis EN — Red-crowned Crane

Subspecies/Population	Breeding range	Wintering, or core non-breeding range	Afr	Eu	Asia	Oc	Neo	NA	Estimate	Source	Trend	Source	1% level	Notes
E China (non-br)	NE China, SE Russia	E China			•				1,200	BC	DEC	BC	10	
Korea (non-br)	NE China, SE Russia	Central Korea			•				400	BC	INC	BC	4	
Japan	Hokkaido, Japan				•				800	CE	INC	BC	8	

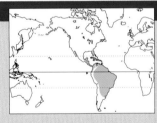

Aramus guarauna — Limpkin

Subspecies/Population	Breeding range	Wintering, or core non-breeding range	Afr	Eu	Asia	Oc	Neo	NA	Estimate	Source	Trend	Source	1% level	Notes
guarauna, South America	South America N & E of Andes						•		E	CC	STA	CC		
dolosus, Central America	Panama–SE Mexico						•	•						
elucus, Puerto Rico, Hispaniola	Puerto Rico, Hispaniola						•							
pictus, Florida, Cuba, Jamaica	Florida, Cuba, Jamaica						•	•						

Sarothrura pulchra — White-spotted Flufftail

Subspecies/Population	Breeding range	Wintering, or core non-breeding range	Afr	Eu	Asia	Oc	Neo	NA	Estimate	Source	Trend	Source	1% level	Notes
pulchra	Gambia & S Senegal E to SW Niger, Nigeria, N & C Cameroon		•								DEC	TB		
zenkeri	SE Nigeria, coastal Cameroon & Gabon		•								DEC	TB		
batesi	Interior S Cameroon		•								DEC	TB		
centralis	Congo basin E to Sudan, W Kenya, NW Tanzania		•								DEC	TB		

ARAMIDAE LIMPKIN

RALLIDAE RAILS, GALLINULES & COOTS

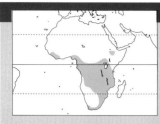

Sarothrura elegans — Buff-spotted Flufftail

Subspecies/Population	Breeding range	Wintering, or core non-breeding range	Afr	Eu	Asia	Oc	Neo	NA	Estimate	Source	Trend	Source	1% level	Notes
elegans	S Ethiopia, S Sudan, W Kenya S to N & E South Africa		•											
reichenovi	Sierra Leone E to D R Congo, Uganda, S to N Angola		•											

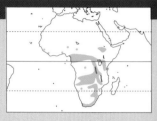

Sarothrura rufa — Red-chested Flufftail

Subspecies/Population	Breeding range	Wintering, or core non-breeding range	Afr	Eu	Asia	Oc	Neo	NA	Estimate	Source	Trend	Source	1% level	Notes
rufa	C Kenya, Tanzania, S DR Congo, Angola–South Africa		•									DEC	TB		
bonapartii	Sierra Leone E to Nigeria, Cameroon, Gabon, Congo		•									DEC	TB		
elizabethae	Ethiopia; Central African Republic & NE DR Congo E to Uganda, W Kenya		•									DEC	TB		

Sarothrura lugens — Long-toed Flufftail, Chestnut-headed Flufftail

Subspecies/Population	Breeding range	Wintering, or core non-breeding range	Afr	Eu	Asia	Oc	Neo	NA	Estimate	Source	Trend	Source	1% level	Notes
lugens	Cameroon to DR Congo, Rwanda, W Tanzania		•												
lynesi	C Angola & Zambia		•							A	SU			100	

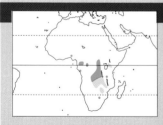

Sarothrura boehmi — Streaky-breasted Flufftail

Subspecies/Population	Breeding range	Wintering, or core non-breeding range	Afr	Eu	Asia	Oc	Neo	NA	Estimate	Source	Trend	Source	1% level	Notes
Africa	Scattered, Nigeria & Cameroon E to Kenya, S to E Angola, N South Africa	Some movement from tropical to equatorial zone	•						A	FE	DEC	TB	100	

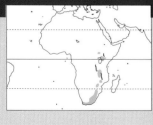

Sarothrura affinis — Striped Flufftail

Subspecies/Population	Breeding range	Wintering, or core non-breeding range	Afr	Eu	Asia	Oc	Neo	NA	Estimate	Source	Trend	Source	1% level	Notes
affinis	Highlands of E Zimbabwe, SW Mozambique, Malawi, NE Zambia, S Tanzania, SW Kenya		•									DEC	TB		
antonii, South Africa	South Africa		•									DEC	TB		
Unknown subspecies, E Rift Valley	Kenya highlands E of Rift Valley		•												Two new subspecies yet to be described (TB).
Unknown subspecies, W Rift Valley	Kenya highlands W of Rift Valley, SE Sudan		•												

Sarothrura insularis — Madagascar Flufftail

Subspecies/Population	Breeding range	*Wintering, or core non-breeding range*	Afr	Eu	Asia	Oc	Neo	NA	Estimate	Source	Trend	Source	1% level	Notes
Madagascar	E Madagascar		•						B/C	HJ			1,000	

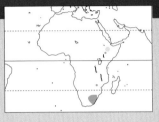

Sarothrura ayresi EN — White-winged Flufftail

Subspecies/Population	Breeding range	*Wintering, or core non-breeding range*	Afr	Eu	Asia	Oc	Neo	NA	Estimate	Source	Trend	Source	1% level	Notes
Ethiopia	Ethiopia		•						630–645	BC	DEC	BC	6	Migration between 2 widely separated distribution ranges in S & E Africa considered very unlikely (TB).
Southern Africa	Zimbabwe, South Africa		•						235	BC	DEC	BC	2	

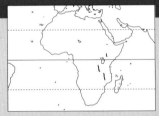

Sarothrura watersi EN — Slender-billed Flufftail

Subspecies/Population	Breeding range	*Wintering, or core non-breeding range*	Afr	Eu	Asia	Oc	Neo	NA	Estimate	Source	Trend	Source	1% level	Notes
Madagascar	E Madagascar (2+ localities)		•						250–1,000	BC	DEC	BC	6	

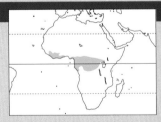

Himantornis haematopus — Nkulengu Rail

Subspecies/Population	Breeding range	*Wintering, or core non-breeding range*	Afr	Eu	Asia	Oc	Neo	NA	Estimate	Source	Trend	Source	1% level	Notes
Africa	Guinea E to W Uganda S to coastal & C DR Congo		•								DEC	TB		3 subspecies have been described but are not widely recognised (TB).

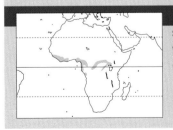

Canirallus oculeus — Grey-throated Rail

Subspecies/Population	Breeding range	*Wintering, or core non-breeding range*	Afr	Eu	Asia	Oc	Neo	NA	Estimate	Source	Trend	Source	1% level	Notes
W Africa	E Sierra Leone to SW Ghana		•								DEC	TB		
C & E Africa	SE Nigeria to Congo & DR Congo to W Uganda		•								DEC	TB		Birds from Cameroon eastward have been treated as a separate subspecies, *batesi*.

Canirallus kioloides — Madagascar Wood Rail

Subspecies/Population	Breeding range	Wintering, or core non-breeding range	Afr	Eu	Asia	Oc	Neo	NA	Estimate	Source	Trend	Source	1% level	Notes
kioloides	E Madagascar		•								DEC	TB		
berliozi	NW Madagascar		•								DEC	TB		
?bemaraha	Bemaraha Tsingy, W Madagascar		•						1,000–2,000	HJ	DEC	DO	15	

Coturnicops exquisitus VU — Swinhoe's Rail

Subspecies/Population	Breeding range	Wintering, or core non-breeding range	Afr	Eu	Asia	Oc	Neo	NA	Estimate	Source	Trend	Source	1% level	Notes
C & E Asia	SE Siberia, Mongolia, E China	S China to Korea, Japan			•				A	BC	DEC	BC	100	

Coturnicops noveboracensis — Yellow Rail

Subspecies/Population	Breeding range	Wintering, or core non-breeding range	Afr	Eu	Asia	Oc	Neo	NA	Estimate	Source	Trend	Source	1% level	Notes
noveboracensis	SC & SE Canada to NE USA, NW USA	SE & S USA						•	B	WC	STA	WC	250	
goldmani	Marshes of R Lerma, Central Mexico						•							Last record 1964.

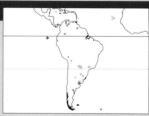

Coturnicops notatus — Speckled Rail

Subspecies/Population	Breeding range	Wintering, or core non-breeding range	Afr	Eu	Asia	Oc	Neo	NA	Estimate	Source	Trend	Source	1% level	Notes
S America	S Brazil to N Argentina	S Brazil to N Argentina. Colombia, Venezuela, Guyana					•							Probably also breeds in N South America; possibly therefore two or more populations.

Micropygia schomburgkii — Ocellated Crake

Subspecies/Population	Breeding range	Wintering, or core non-breeding range	Afr	Eu	Asia	Oc	Neo	NA	Estimate	Source	Trend	Source	1% level	Notes
schomburgkii	Costa Rica, Colombia, Venezuela, Guianas. SE Peru, Bolivia						•							
chapmani	C to SE Brazil						•							

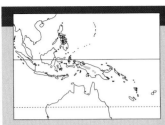

Rallina rubra — Chestnut Forest-Rail

Subspecies/Population	Breeding range	Wintering, or core non-breeding range	Afr	Eu	Asia	Oc	Neo	NA	Estimate	Source	Trend	Source	1% level	Notes
rubra	Arfak Mts, W New Guinea					•								
klossi	Weyland Mts to Oranje Mts, WC New Guinea					•								
telefolminensis	Victor Emmanuel & Hindenburg Mts, C New Guinea	Victor Emmanuel & Hindenburg Mts & Tari Gap, C New Guinea				•								

Rallina leucospila NT — White-striped Forest-Rail

Subspecies/Population	Breeding range	Wintering, or core non-breeding range	Afr	Eu	Asia	Oc	Neo	NA	Estimate	Source	Trend	Source	1% level	Notes
New Guinea	Tamrau, Arfak & Wandammen Mts, NW New Guinea					•								

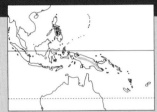

Rallina forbesi — Forbes's Forest-Rail

Subspecies/Population	Breeding range	Wintering, or core non-breeding range	Afr	Eu	Asia	Oc	Neo	NA	Estimate	Source	Trend	Source	1% level	Notes
forbesi	Herzog Mts to Owen Stanley Mts, SE New Guinea					•								
steini	Snow Mts to C Highlands, New Guinea					•								
parva	Adelbert Range, NE New Guinea					•								
dryas	Huon Peninsula, NE New Guinea					•								

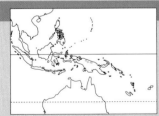

Rallina mayri DD — Mayr's Forest-Rail

Subspecies/Population	Breeding range	Wintering, or core non-breeding range	Afr	Eu	Asia	Oc	Neo	NA	Estimate	Source	Trend	Source	1% level	Notes
mayri	Cyclops Mts, NE Irian Jaya					•								
carmichaeli	Torricelli & Bewanni Mts, NW Papua New Guinea					•								

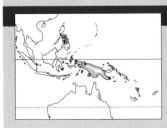

Rallina tricolor — Red-necked Crake

Subspecies/Population	Breeding range	Wintering, or core non-breeding range	Afr	Eu	Asia	Oc	Neo	NA	Estimate	Source	Trend	Source	1% level	Notes
New Guinea, NE Australia	New Guinea & offshore Is, NE Queensland (Australia), S Moluccas	New Guinea & offshore Is, NE Queensland (Australia)				•								Up to 6 subspecies have been described, but geographical variation not well understood (TB). Declining in Australian part of range (TB).

Rallina canningi DD — Andaman Crake

Subspecies/Population	Breeding range	Wintering, or core non-breeding range	Afr	Eu	Asia	Oc	Neo	NA	Estimate	Source	Trend	Source	1% level	Notes
Andaman Islands	Andaman Islands				•				A/B	BD			250	

Rallina fasciata — Red-legged Crake

Subspecies/Population	Breeding range	Wintering, or core non-breeding range	Afr	Eu	Asia	Oc	Neo	NA	Estimate	Source	Trend	Source	1% level	Notes
S & SE Asia	Lowlands NE India, SW Indochina E to Phillipiines, S to E Indonesia				•									

Rallina eurizonoides — Slaty-legged Crake

Subspecies/Population	Breeding range	Wintering, or core non-breeding range	Afr	Eu	Asia	Oc	Neo	NA	Estimate	Source	Trend	Source	1% level	Notes
eurizonoides	Philippines & Palau Is	S & SE Asia, Philippines, Sulawesi, Taiwan, Ryukyu Is, Sri Lanka, Indonesia			•									
amauroptera	Pakistan & India E to Assam	Pakistan, India, Sri Lanka, possibly Sumatra			•									
telmatophila	Myanmar & Thailand E to C Vietnam & SE China	S Thailand & Sumatra to W Java			•									
sepiaria	Ryukyu Is				•						DEC	HV		
formosana	Taiwan & Lanyu Is				•									
alvarezi	Batan Is (N Philippines)				•									
minahasa	Sulawesi & Sula Is				•									

Anurolimnas castaneiceps — Chestnut-headed Crake

Subspecies/Population	Breeding range	Wintering, or core non-breeding range	Afr	Eu	Asia	Oc	Neo	NA	Estimate	Source	Trend	Source	1% level	Notes
castaneiceps	E Ecuador & N Peru						•							
coccineipes	S Colombia & NE Ecuador						•							

Anurolimnas viridis — Russet-crowned Crake

Subspecies/Population	Breeding range	Wintering, or core non-breeding range	Afr	Eu	Asia	Oc	Neo	NA	Estimate	Source	Trend	Source	1% level	Notes
viridis	Tropical South America East of Andes						•							
brunnescens	Lower Cauca & Magdalena Valleys (E Colombia)						•							

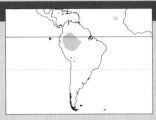

Anurolimnas fasciatus — Black-banded Crake

Subspecies/Population	Breeding range	Wintering, or core non-breeding range	Afr	Eu	Asia	Oc	Neo	NA	Estimate	Source	Trend	Source	1% level	Notes
NW South America	West Amazon Basin–Colombia, Ecuador, Peru, W Brazil						•							

Laterallus melanophaius — Rufous-sided Crake

Subspecies/Population	Breeding range	Wintering, or core non-breeding range	Afr	Eu	Asia	Oc	Neo	NA	Estimate	Source	Trend	Source	1% level	Notes
melanophaius	Venezuela E to Surinam, C & E Brazil, E Bolivia, Paraguay, Uruguay, N Argentina						•							
oenops	SE Colombia, E Ecuador, E Peru, W Brazil						•							

Laterallus levraudi EN — Rusty-flanked Crake

Subspecies/Population	Breeding range	Wintering, or core non-breeding range	Afr	Eu	Asia	Oc	Neo	NA	Estimate	Source	Trend	Source	1% level	Notes
N Venezuela	N Venezuela						•		250–1,000	BC	DEC	BC	6	

Laterallus ruber — Ruddy Crake

Subspecies/Population	Breeding range	Wintering, or core non-breeding range	Afr	Eu	Asia	Oc	Neo	NA	Estimate	Source	Trend	Source	1% level	Notes
C America	S & E Mexico S to Honduras, N Nicaragua, NW Costa Rica						•							

Laterallus albigularis — White-throated Crake

Subspecies/Population	Breeding range	Wintering, or core non-breeding range	Afr	Eu	Asia	Oc	Neo	NA	Estimate	Source	Trend	Source	1% level	Notes
albigularis	SW Costa Rica–Panama, N & W Colombia, W Ecuador						•							
cinereiceps	SE Honduras, E Nicaragua, Costa Rica, NW Panama						•							
cerdaleus	E Colombia						•							

Laterallus exilis — Grey-breasted Crake

Subspecies/Population	Breeding range	Wintering, or core non-breeding range	Afr	Eu	Asia	Oc	Neo	NA	Estimate	Source	Trend	Source	1% level	Notes
C America, N South America	Guatemala S to Venezuela, Guianas, Colombia, N Ecuador, E Peru, N Bolivia to SE Brazil						•							

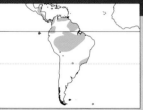

Laterallus jamaicensis NT — Black Rail

Subspecies/Population	Breeding range	Wintering, or core non-breeding range	Afr	Eu	Asia	Oc	Neo	NA	Estimate	Source	Trend	Source	1% level	Notes
jamaicensis	E & C USA & E Central America	S USA to Costa Rica & Greater Antilles					•	•	C	WC	DEC	BC	1,000	
coturniculus	Arizona, California & Baja California, C Sierra Nevada; most now along N San Fransisco Bay							•	A	EF	DEC	EF	100	EF gives an estimate for N San Fransisco Bay of 3,204–8,905. ET estimates 100–200 calling males along the lower Colorado River.
murivagans	Coastal Central Peru							•						
salinasi	C Chile, extreme W Argentina & extreme S coastal Peru							•						

Laterallus (j.) tuerosi EN — Junin Rail

Subspecies/Population	Breeding range	Wintering, or core non-breeding range	Afr	Eu	Asia	Oc	Neo	NA	Estimate	Source	Trend	Source	1% level	Notes
Lake Junin, Peru	Lake Junin, Peru						•		1,000–2,500	BC	DEC	BC	20	Full specific status recommended by TB and adopted by BC.

Laterallus spilonotus VU — Galapagos Rail

Subspecies/Population	Breeding range	Wintering, or core non-breeding range	Afr	Eu	Asia	Oc	Neo	NA	Estimate	Source	Trend	Source	1% level	Notes
Galapagos Islands	Galapagos Islands						•		5,000–10,000	BC	DEC	BC	75	

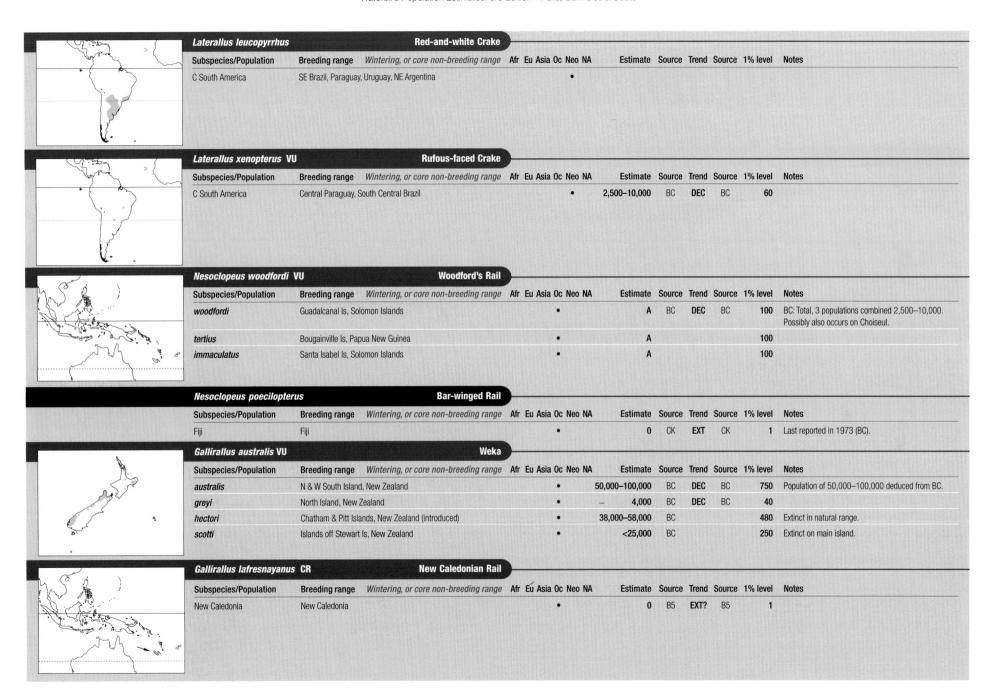

Laterallus leucopyrrhus — Red-and-white Crake

Subspecies/Population	Breeding range	Wintering, or core non-breeding range	Afr	Eu	Asia	Oc	Neo	NA	Estimate	Source	Trend	Source	1% level	Notes
C South America	SE Brazil, Paraguay, Uruguay, NE Argentina						•							

Laterallus xenopterus VU — Rufous-faced Crake

Subspecies/Population	Breeding range	Wintering, or core non-breeding range	Afr	Eu	Asia	Oc	Neo	NA	Estimate	Source	Trend	Source	1% level	Notes
C South America	Central Paraguay, South Central Brazil						•		2,500–10,000	BC	DEC	BC	60	

Nesoclopeus woodfordi VU — Woodford's Rail

Subspecies/Population	Breeding range	Wintering, or core non-breeding range	Afr	Eu	Asia	Oc	Neo	NA	Estimate	Source	Trend	Source	1% level	Notes
woodfordi	Guadalcanal Is, Solomon Islands					•			A	BC	DEC	BC	100	BC: Total, 3 populations combined 2,500–10,000. Possibly also occurs on Choiseul.
tertius	Bougainville Is, Papua New Guinea					•			A				100	
immaculatus	Santa Isabel Is, Solomon Islands					•			A				100	

Nesoclopeus poecilopterus — Bar-winged Rail

Subspecies/Population	Breeding range	Wintering, or core non-breeding range	Afr	Eu	Asia	Oc	Neo	NA	Estimate	Source	Trend	Source	1% level	Notes
Fiji	Fiji					•			0	CK	EXT	CK	1	Last reported in 1973 (BC).

Gallirallus australis VU — Weka

Subspecies/Population	Breeding range	Wintering, or core non-breeding range	Afr	Eu	Asia	Oc	Neo	NA	Estimate	Source	Trend	Source	1% level	Notes
australis	N & W South Island, New Zealand					•			50,000–100,000	BC	DEC	BC	750	Population of 50,000–100,000 deduced from BC.
greyi	North Island, New Zealand					•			— 4,000	BC	DEC	BC	40	
hectori	Chatham & Pitt Islands, New Zealand (introduced)					•			38,000–58,000	BC			480	Extinct in natural range.
scotti	Islands off Stewart Is, New Zealand					•			<25,000	BC			250	Extinct on main island.

Gallirallus lafresnayanus CR — New Caledonian Rail

Subspecies/Population	Breeding range	Wintering, or core non-breeding range	Afr	Eu	Asia	Oc	Neo	NA	Estimate	Source	Trend	Source	1% level	Notes
New Caledonia	New Caledonia					•			0	B5	EXT?	B5	1	

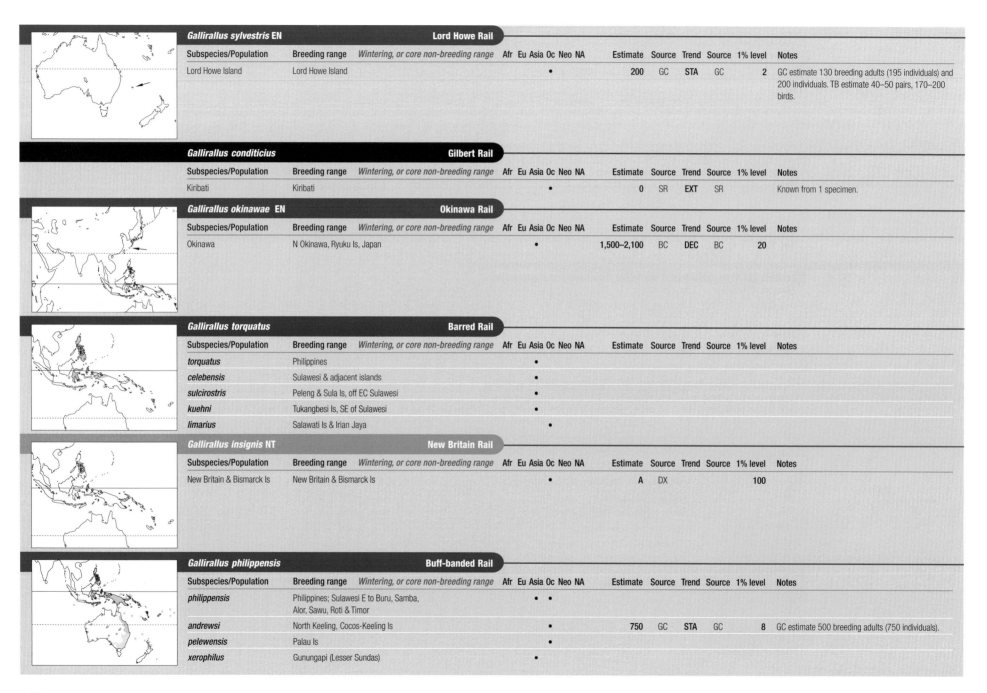

Gallirallus sylvestris EN — Lord Howe Rail

Subspecies/Population	Breeding range	Wintering, or core non-breeding range	Afr	Eu	Asia	Oc	Neo	NA	Estimate	Source	Trend	Source	1% level	Notes
Lord Howe Island	Lord Howe Island					•			200	GC	STA	GC	2	GC estimate 130 breeding adults (195 individuals) and 200 individuals. TB estimate 40–50 pairs, 170–200 birds.

Gallirallus conditicius — Gilbert Rail

Subspecies/Population	Breeding range	Wintering, or core non-breeding range	Afr	Eu	Asia	Oc	Neo	NA	Estimate	Source	Trend	Source	1% level	Notes
Kiribati	Kiribati					•			0	SR	EXT	SR		Known from 1 specimen.

Gallirallus okinawae EN — Okinawa Rail

Subspecies/Population	Breeding range	Wintering, or core non-breeding range	Afr	Eu	Asia	Oc	Neo	NA	Estimate	Source	Trend	Source	1% level	Notes
Okinawa	N Okinawa, Ryuku Is, Japan					•			1,500–2,100	BC	DEC	BC	20	

Gallirallus torquatus — Barred Rail

Subspecies/Population	Breeding range	Wintering, or core non-breeding range	Afr	Eu	Asia	Oc	Neo	NA	Estimate	Source	Trend	Source	1% level	Notes
torquatus	Philippines				•									
celebensis	Sulawesi & adjacent islands				•									
sulcirostris	Peleng & Sula Is, off EC Sulawesi				•									
kuehni	Tukangbesi Is, SE of Sulawesi				•									
limarius	Salawati Is & Irian Jaya					•								

Gallirallus insignis NT — New Britain Rail

Subspecies/Population	Breeding range	Wintering, or core non-breeding range	Afr	Eu	Asia	Oc	Neo	NA	Estimate	Source	Trend	Source	1% level	Notes
New Britain & Bismarck Is	New Britain & Bismarck Is					•			A	DX			100	

Gallirallus philippensis — Buff-banded Rail

Subspecies/Population	Breeding range	Wintering, or core non-breeding range	Afr	Eu	Asia	Oc	Neo	NA	Estimate	Source	Trend	Source	1% level	Notes
philippensis	Philippines; Sulawesi E to Buru, Samba, Alor, Sawu, Roti & Timor				•	•								
andrewsi	North Keeling, Cocos-Keeling Is					•			750	GC	STA	GC	8	GC estimate 500 breeding adults (750 individuals).
pelewensis	Palau Is					•								
xerophilus	Gunungapi (Lesser Sundas)					•								

Gallirallus philippensis... continued

Subspecies/Population	Breeding range	Wintering, or core non-breeding range	Afr	Eu	Asia	Oc	Neo	NA	Estimate	Source	Trend	Source	1% level	Notes
wilkinsoni	Flores, (Indonesia)					•								
lacustris	N New Guinea					•								
reductus	C Highlands & NE coastal New Guinea, Long Is					•								
anachoretae	Kaniet Is, NW of Ninigo Is	Kaniet Is, NW of Ninigo Is, Bismarck Archipelago				•			A	DX			100	
admiralitatis	Admiralty Is					•			A	DX			100	Probably <1,000 but data inadequate (DX).
praedo	Skoki (Admiralty Is)					•			A	DX			100	Very small size of island precludes a larger population (DX).
lesouefi	New Hanover, Tabar & Tanga Is, (Bismarck Archipelago)					•			A	DX			100	
meyeri	New Britain & Witu Is (Bismarck Archipelago)					•			A	DX			100	
christophori	Solomon Islands					•			A/B	DX			250	
mellori	S & SW New Guinea, Australia & Norfolk Is					•								
assimilis	New Zealand					•								
macquariensis	Macquarie Is					•			0	GC	EXT	GC		Extinction occurred between 1879 and 1894 (GC).
dieffenbachii	Chatham Island					•			0	GC	EXT	GC		
touneliere	SE New Guinea Archipelagos, Great Barrier Reef E to New Caledonia					•								Small size of islands makes A likely (DX). About 100 in New Caledonia on 2 islets in the north.
swindellsi	New Caledonia & Loyalty Is					•			5,000	B5			50	
sethsmithi	Vanuatu & Fiji					•			B/C	DX			1,000	
ecaudatus	Tonga					•			A	DX			100	
goodsoni	Samoa & Niue Is					•			A	DX			100	

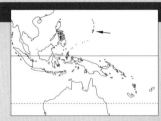

Gallirallus owstoni EW — Guam Rail

Subspecies/Population	Breeding range	Wintering, or core non-breeding range	Afr	Eu	Asia	Oc	Neo	NA	Estimate	Source	Trend	Source	1% level	Notes
Guam	Guam (introduced, Rota Is)					•				BC	EXT	BC		Extinct in wild by 1987, c.180 in captivity.

Gallirallus rovianae NT — Roviana Rail

Subspecies/Population	Breeding range	Wintering, or core non-breeding range	Afr	Eu	Asia	Oc	Neo	NA	Estimate	Source	Trend	Source	1% level	Notes
Kolumbangra	Kolombangra, Central Solomon Islands					•			A	DX			100	Flightlessness allows treatment as separate populations on possibly as many as 5 islands. Only apparently widespread on Kolombangra (BC).
New Georgia	New Georgia, Central Solomon Islands					•								

Gallirallus wakensis — Wake Rail

Subspecies/Population	Breeding range	Wintering, or core non-breeding range	Afr	Eu	Asia	Oc	Neo	NA	Estimate	Source	Trend	Source	1% level	Notes
Wake Is	Wake Island, C Pacific					•			0	GY	EXT	GY		Extinct between 1942 & 1945.

115

Gallirallus pacificus — Tahiti Rail

Subspecies/Population	Breeding range	Wintering, or core non-breeding range	Afr	Eu	Asia	Oc	Neo	NA	Estimate	Source	Trend	Source	1% level	Notes
Tahiti	Tahiti					•			0	GY	EXT	GY		Last reported in Tahiti in 1842, in Mehetia in 1930s (BC).

Gallirallus dieffenbachii — Dieffenbach's Rail

Subspecies/Population	Breeding range	Wintering, or core non-breeding range	Afr	Eu	Asia	Oc	Neo	NA	Estimate	Source	Trend	Source	1% level	Notes
Chatham Is	Chatham Island					•			0	GY	EXT	GY		Extinct by 1872 (BC).

Gallirallus modestus — Chatham Rail

Subspecies/Population	Breeding range	Wintering, or core non-breeding range	Afr	Eu	Asia	Oc	Neo	NA	Estimate	Source	Trend	Source	1% level	Notes
Chatham Is	Chatham Island					•			0	GY	EXT	GY		Extinct by 1900 (BC) Ascribed to genus Cabalus in BC.

Gallirallus sharpei — Sharpe's Rail

Subspecies/Population	Breeding range	Wintering, or core non-breeding range	Afr	Eu	Asia	Oc	Neo	NA	Estimate	Source	Trend	Source	1% level	Notes
Sundas	Possibly Sundas					•			0	SR	EXT?	SR		Known only from type specimen described in 1893 (BC).

Gallirallus striatus — Slaty-breasted Rail

Subspecies/Population	Breeding range	Wintering, or core non-breeding range	Afr	Eu	Asia	Oc	Neo	NA	Estimate	Source	Trend	Source	1% level	Notes
striatus	Philippines, Sulu Is, N Borneo, Sulawesi				•									
albiventer	India & Sri Lanka to SC China & Thailand	India & Sri Lanka to SC China, Thailand, Malaysia?			•									
obscurior	Andaman & Nicobar Is				•									
jouyi	Coastal SE China & Hainan				•									
taiwanus	Taiwan				•						INC	SC		
gularis	Vietnam & Cambodia, Malaysia, W Indonesia, S China				•									
paratermus	Samar Is, E C Philippines				•									

Rallus longirostris — Clapper Rail

Subspecies/Population	Breeding range	Wintering, or core non-breeding range	Afr	Eu	Asia	Oc	Neo	NA	Estimate	Source	Trend	Source	1% level	Notes
longirostris	Coasts of Guyana, Suriname, French Guiana						•	•						
obsoletus	C California, mainly San Fransisco Bay							•	400	HV	DEC	HV	4	
levipes	Coastal S California to N Baja California							•	970–1,170	EC	DEC	HV	10	EC estimates 970–1,170; HV gives 1990 US population of 190 pairs, Mexico population of 240 pairs, (1,290 individuals).
yumanensis	SE California, SW Arizona & NW Mexico						•	•	2,100	EC	DEC	HV	20	EC estimates 700+ calling males (2,100 individuals).
beldingi	S Baja California							•						
crepitans	Coastal Connecticut S to NE North Carolina							•			STA	EC		
waynei	Coastal SE North Carolina to E Florida							•			STA	EC		
saturatus	Gulf Coast SW Alabama to extreme NE Mexico						•	•						
pallidus	Coastal Yucatan (SE Mexico)							•						
grossi	Quintana Roo (SE Mexico)							•						

Rallus longirostris... continued

Subspecies/Population	Breeding range	Wintering, or core non-breeding range	Afr	Eu	Asia	Oc	Neo	NA	Estimate	Source	Trend	Source	1% level	Notes
belizensis	Ycacos Lagoon, Belize						•							
scotti	Coastal Florida							•						
insularum	Florida Keys, USA							•						
coryi	Bahamas							•						
leucophaeus	Is of Pines (Cuba)						•							
caribaeus	Cuba to Puerto Rico & Lesser Antilles E to Antigua; Guadeloupe						•							
cypereti	Coasts SW Colombia–Ecuador–NW Peru						•							
phelpsi	NE Colombia–NW Venezuela						•							
margaritae	Margarita Is (Venezuela)						•							
pelodramus	Trinidad						•							
crassirostris	Coastal Brazil Amazon Delta–Santa Catarina						•							

Rallus elegans King Rail

Subspecies/Population	Breeding range	Wintering, or core non-breeding range	Afr	Eu	Asia	Oc	Neo	NA	Estimate	Source	Trend	Source	1% level	Notes
elegans	E Canada & NE USA	SE USA, E Mexico					•	•			DEC	RD		
tenuirostris	Central Mexico						•							
ramsdeni	Cuba & Is of Pines						•							

Rallus wetmorei EN Plain-flanked Rail

Subspecies/Population	Breeding range	Wintering, or core non-breeding range	Afr	Eu	Asia	Oc	Neo	NA	Estimate	Source	Trend	Source	1% level	Notes
Venezuela	NW Venezuela coast						•		250–1,000	BC	DEC	BC	6	

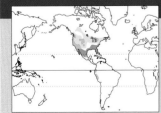

Rallus limicola Virginia Rail

Subspecies/Population	Breeding range	Wintering, or core non-breeding range	Afr	Eu	Asia	Oc	Neo	NA	Estimate	Source	Trend	Source	1% level	Notes
limicola	S Canada & W, C, NE USA	SW Canada & E Great Lakes S to Guatemala					•	•			INC	NB		
meyerdeschauneseei	Coastal Peru, La Libertad to Arequipa						•							Described in 1990 (TB).
friedmanni	CS Mexico to Guatemala						•							
aequatorialis	SW Colombia and Andes of Ecuador.						•							

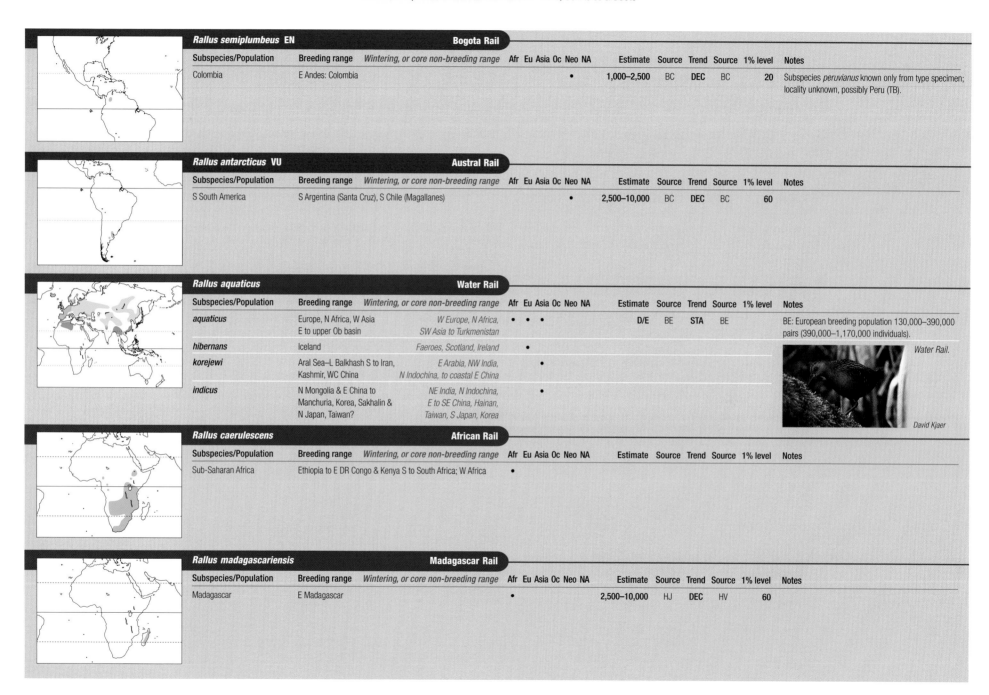

Rallus semiplumbeus EN — Bogota Rail

Subspecies/Population	Breeding range	Wintering, or core non-breeding range	Afr	Eu	Asia	Oc	Neo	NA	Estimate	Source	Trend	Source	1% level	Notes
Colombia	E Andes: Colombia						•		1,000–2,500	BC	DEC	BC	20	Subspecies *peruvianus* known only from type specimen; locality unknown, possibly Peru (TB).

Rallus antarcticus VU — Austral Rail

Subspecies/Population	Breeding range	Wintering, or core non-breeding range	Afr	Eu	Asia	Oc	Neo	NA	Estimate	Source	Trend	Source	1% level	Notes
S South America	S Argentina (Santa Cruz), S Chile (Magallanes)						•		2,500–10,000	BC	DEC	BC	60	

Rallus aquaticus — Water Rail

Subspecies/Population	Breeding range	Wintering, or core non-breeding range	Afr	Eu	Asia	Oc	Neo	NA	Estimate	Source	Trend	Source	1% level	Notes
aquaticus	Europe, N Africa, W Asia E to upper Ob basin	*W Europe, N Africa, SW Asia to Turkmenistan*	•	•	•				D/E	BE	STA	BE		BE: European breeding population 130,000–390,000 pairs (390,000–1,170,000 individuals).
hibernans	Iceland	*Faeroes, Scotland, Ireland*		•										
korejewi	Aral Sea–L Balkhash S to Iran, Kashmir, WC China	*E Arabia, NW India, N Indochina, to coastal E China*			•									
indicus	N Mongolia & E China to Manchuria, Korea, Sakhalin & N Japan, Taiwan?	*NE India, N Indochina, E to SE China, Hainan, Taiwan, S Japan, Korea*			•									

Water Rail.

David Kjaer

Rallus caerulescens — African Rail

Subspecies/Population	Breeding range	Wintering, or core non-breeding range	Afr	Eu	Asia	Oc	Neo	NA	Estimate	Source	Trend	Source	1% level	Notes
Sub-Saharan Africa	Ethiopia to E DR Congo & Kenya S to South Africa; W Africa		•											

Rallus madagascariensis — Madagascar Rail

Subspecies/Population	Breeding range	Wintering, or core non-breeding range	Afr	Eu	Asia	Oc	Neo	NA	Estimate	Source	Trend	Source	1% level	Notes
Madagascar	E Madagascar		•						2,500–10,000	HJ	DEC	HV	60	

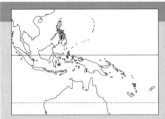

Lewinia mirificus DD — Brown-banded Rail, Luzon Rail

Subspecies/Population	Breeding range	Wintering, or core non-breeding range	Afr	Eu	Asia	Oc	Neo	NA	Estimate	Source	Trend	Source	1% level	Notes
N Philippines	Luzon (N Philippines)					•								

Lewinia pectoralis — Lewin's Rail

Subspecies/Population	Breeding range	Wintering, or core non-breeding range	Afr	Eu	Asia	Oc	Neo	NA	Estimate	Source	Trend	Source	1% level	Notes
pectoralis	E & SE Australia					•			30,000	GC	DEC	GC	300	GC estimates 20,000 breeding adults (30,000 individuals).
brachipus	Tasmania					•								This subspecies much more numerous than *pectoralis* (GC).
clelandi	SW Australia					•				HV	EXT?	HV		Last recorded in 1932.
exsul	Flores (Lesser Sundas, Indonesia)					•				HV	EXT?			Last recorded in 1959.
mayri	Arfak & Weyland Mts (W New Guinea)					•								
captus	Central New Guinea					•								
insulus	Herzog Mts (E New Guinea)					•								
alberti	Mts of SE New Guinea					•								

Lewinia muelleri VU — Auckland Island Rail

Subspecies/Population	Breeding range	Wintering, or core non-breeding range	Afr	Eu	Asia	Oc	Neo	NA	Estimate	Source	Trend	Source	1% level	Notes
Auckland Is	Adams & Disappointment Is (Auckland Islands)					•			2,000	BC	STA	BC	20	

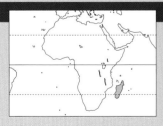

Dryolimnas cuvieri — White-throated Rail

Subspecies/Population	Breeding range	Wintering, or core non-breeding range	Afr	Eu	Asia	Oc	Neo	NA	Estimate	Source	Trend	Source	1% level	Notes
cuvieri	Madagascar lowlands		•											Subspecies *abboti* of Assumption Island recently extinct (TB).
aldabranus, Aldabra	Aldabra Is, Indian Ocean		•						5,000–7,000	SM	STA	HV	60	
aldabranus, Ile aux Cerdes, Aldabra	Ile aux Cerdes, Aldabra		•						100–500	SL	STA	HV	3	
abbotti	Cosmoledo, Astove, Assumption, Aldabra		•						0	SM	EXT	SM		

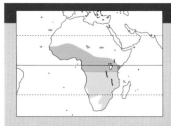

Crecopsis egregia African Crake

Subspecies/Population	Breeding range	Wintering, or core non-breeding range	Afr	Eu	Asia	Oc	Neo	NA	Estimate	Source	Trend	Source	1% level	Notes
Sub-Saharan Africa	Sub-Saharan Africa: Senegal E to Kenya, S to S Africa	*Complex movements within Sub-Saharan Africa*	•											

Crex crex VU Corncrake

Subspecies/Population	Breeding range	Wintering, or core non-breeding range	Afr	Eu	Asia	Oc	Neo	NA	Estimate	Source	Trend	Source	1% level	Notes
Sub-Saharan Africa (non-br)	W & NW Europe E to NW China & Central Siberia	*Sub-Saharan Africa (especially SE Africa)*	•	•	•				E	SA	DEC	HC BE BC		BE: European breeding population 1,100,000–1,800,000 "pairs" (3,300,000–5,400,000 individuals). Asian population unknown.

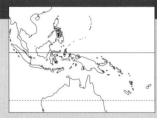

Rougetius rougetii NT Rouget's Rail

Subspecies/Population	Breeding range	Wintering, or core non-breeding range	Afr	Eu	Asia	Oc	Neo	NA	Estimate	Source	Trend	Source	1% level	Notes
Ethiopia, Eritrea	West & Central Ethiopia highlands, Eritrea		•								DEC	BC		

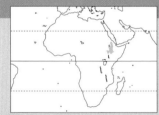

Aramidopsis plateni VU Snoring (Platen's) Rail

Subspecies/Population	Breeding range	Wintering, or core non-breeding range	Afr	Eu	Asia	Oc	Neo	NA	Estimate	Source	Trend	Source	1% level	Notes
Sulawesi	N, N Central & SE Sulawesi				•				2,500–10,000	BC	DEC	BC	60	

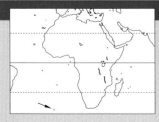

Atlantisia rogersi VU Inaccessible (Island) Rail

Subspecies/Population	Breeding range	Wintering, or core non-breeding range	Afr	Eu	Asia	Oc	Neo	NA	Estimate	Source	Trend	Source	1% level	Notes
Inaccessible Is	Inaccessible Is: Tristan da Cunha group		•						8,400	BC	STA	BC	85	

Atlantisia elpenor — Ascension Rail

Subspecies/Population	Breeding range	Wintering, or core non-breeding range	Afr	Eu	Asia	Oc	Neo	NA	Estimate	Source	Trend	Source	1% level	Notes
Ascension Is	Ascension Island		•						0	HV	EXT	HV		Probably extinct by 1656 (HV). May have survived until introduction of cats in 1815 (BC).

Atlantisia podarces — St Helena Crake

Subspecies/Population	Breeding range	Wintering, or core non-breeding range	Afr	Eu	Asia	Oc	Neo	NA	Estimate	Source	Trend	Source	1% level	Notes
St Helena Is	St Helena Island		•						0	BC	EXT	BC		Probably extinct soon after discovery of St Helena in 1502 (BC).

Aramides mangle — Little Wood Rail

Subspecies/Population	Breeding range	Wintering, or core non-breeding range	Afr	Eu	Asia	Oc	Neo	NA	Estimate	Source	Trend	Source	1% level	Notes
Brazil	E Brazil						•							

Aramides axillaris — Rufous-necked Wood Rail

Subspecies/Population	Breeding range	Wintering, or core non-breeding range	Afr	Eu	Asia	Oc	Neo	NA	Estimate	Source	Trend	Source	1% level	Notes
C America, N South America	Coasts of Central America & N South America						•							

Aramides cajanea — Grey-necked Wood Rail

Subspecies/Population	Breeding range	Wintering, or core non-breeding range	Afr	Eu	Asia	Oc	Neo	NA	Estimate	Source	Trend	Source	1% level	Notes
cajanea	Costa Rica to Colombia E & S to Brazil, N Argentina, Uruguay						•		D	CC	STA	CC	10,000	
mexicanus	Caribbean slope of SE Mexico						•							
albiventris	Yucatan to Belize & N Guatemala						•							
vanrossemi	Pacific coasts of S Mexico to S Guatemala & El Salvador						•							
pacificus	E Honduras, Nicaragua						•							
plumbeicollis	Caribbean lowlands of NE Costa Rica						•							
latens	San Miguel & Viveros (Pearl Is, Panama)						•							Known from only 4 specimens (HV).
morrisoni	San Jose & Pedro Gonzalez (Pearl Is, Panama)						•							

Aramides wolfi VU — Brown Wood Rail

Subspecies/Population	Breeding range	Wintering, or core non-breeding range	Afr	Eu	Asia	Oc	Neo	NA	Estimate	Source	Trend	Source	1% level	Notes
NW South America	W Colombia S to SW Ecuador, NW Peru?						•				DEC	BC		

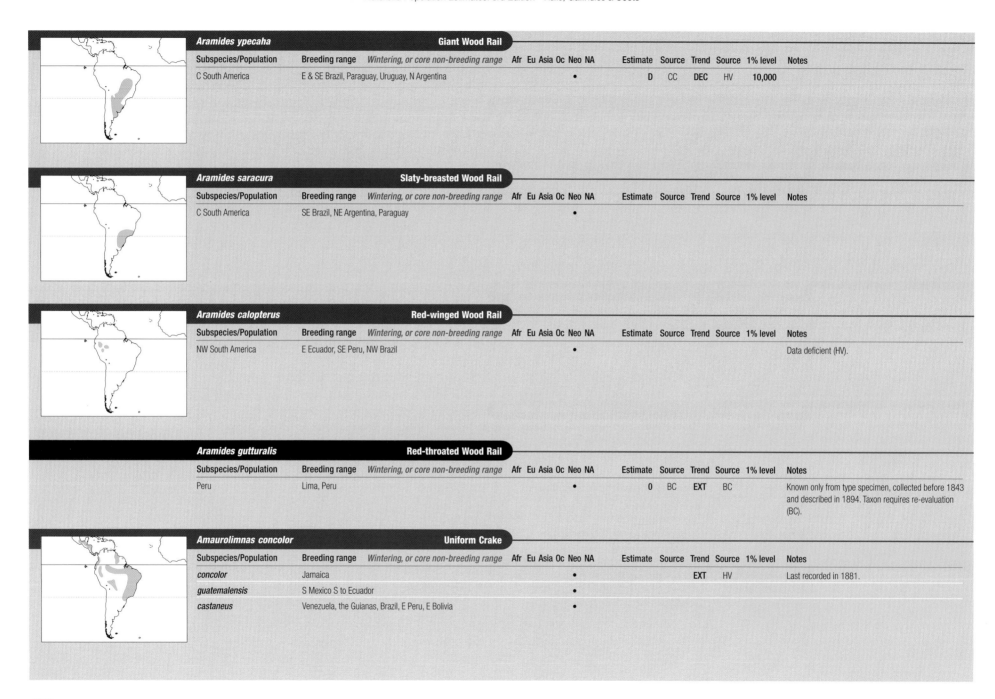

Aramides ypecaha — Giant Wood Rail

Subspecies/Population	Breeding range	Wintering, or core non-breeding range	Afr	Eu	Asia	Oc	Neo	NA	Estimate	Source	Trend	Source	1% level	Notes
C South America		E & SE Brazil, Paraguay, Uruguay, N Argentina					•		D	CC	DEC	HV	10,000	

Aramides saracura — Slaty-breasted Wood Rail

Subspecies/Population	Breeding range	Wintering, or core non-breeding range	Afr	Eu	Asia	Oc	Neo	NA	Estimate	Source	Trend	Source	1% level	Notes
C South America		SE Brazil, NE Argentina, Paraguay					•							

Aramides calopterus — Red-winged Wood Rail

Subspecies/Population	Breeding range	Wintering, or core non-breeding range	Afr	Eu	Asia	Oc	Neo	NA	Estimate	Source	Trend	Source	1% level	Notes
NW South America		E Ecuador, SE Peru, NW Brazil					•							Data deficient (HV).

Aramides gutturalis — Red-throated Wood Rail

Subspecies/Population	Breeding range	Wintering, or core non-breeding range	Afr	Eu	Asia	Oc	Neo	NA	Estimate	Source	Trend	Source	1% level	Notes
Peru	Lima, Peru						•		0	BC	EXT	BC		Known only from type specimen, collected before 1843 and described in 1894. Taxon requires re-evaluation (BC).

Amaurolimnas concolor — Uniform Crake

Subspecies/Population	Breeding range	Wintering, or core non-breeding range	Afr	Eu	Asia	Oc	Neo	NA	Estimate	Source	Trend	Source	1% level	Notes
concolor	Jamaica						•				EXT	HV		Last recorded in 1881.
guatemalensis	S Mexico S to Ecuador						•							
castaneus	Venezuela, the Guianas, Brazil, E Peru, E Bolivia						•							

Gymnocrex rosenbergii VU — Bald-faced Rail, Bare-faced Rail

Subspecies/Population	Breeding range	Wintering, or core non-breeding range	Afr	Eu	Asia	Oc	Neo	NA	Estimate	Source	Trend	Source	1% level	Notes
Sulawesi & Peleng	N & N Central Sulawesi & Peleng					•			2,500–10,000	BC	DEC	BC	60	Birds from Pelang may merit treatment as a separate subspecies.

Gymnocrex plumbeiventris — Bare-eyed Rail

Subspecies/Population	Breeding range	Wintering, or core non-breeding range	Afr	Eu	Asia	Oc	Neo	NA	Estimate	Source	Trend	Source	1% level	Notes
plumbeiventris	N Moluccas, Misool, Aru Is, New Guinea, Karkar, New Ireland				•	•								
hoeveni	Aru Is & S New Guinea					•								

Gymnocrex talaudensis EN — Talaud Rail

Subspecies/Population	Breeding range	Wintering, or core non-breeding range	Afr	Eu	Asia	Oc	Neo	NA	Estimate	Source	Trend	Source	1% level	Notes
Talaud Is	Karakelong I (Talaud Is) (N Moluccas)				•				1,000–2,500	BC	DEC	BC	20	Described in 1998 (TB).

Amaurornis akool — Brown Crake

Subspecies/Population	Breeding range	Wintering, or core non-breeding range	Afr	Eu	Asia	Oc	Neo	NA	Estimate	Source	Trend	Source	1% level	Notes
akool	India, Bangladesh, W Myanmar				•									
coccineipes	SE China to NE Vietnam				•									

Amaurornis isabellinus — Isabelline Bush-Hen

Subspecies/Population	Breeding range	Wintering, or core non-breeding range	Afr	Eu	Asia	Oc	Neo	NA	Estimate	Source	Trend	Source	1% level	Notes
Sulawesi	Sulawesi				•									

Amaurornis olivaceus — Plain Bush-Hen

Subspecies/Population	Breeding range	Wintering, or core non-breeding range	Afr	Eu	Asia	Oc	Neo	NA	Estimate	Source	Trend	Source	1% level	Notes
Philippines	Philippines except Palawan				•									

Amaurornis moluccanus — Rufous-tailed Bush-Hen

Subspecies/Population	Breeding range	Wintering, or core non-breeding range	Afr	Eu	Asia	Oc	Neo	NA	Estimate	Source	Trend	Source	1% level	Notes
moluccanus	Sangihe Is, Moluccas, Misool Is & W & N New Guinea				●	●								
nigrifrons	Bismarck Archipelago & Solomon Is					●			A/B	DX			250	
ultimus	E Solomon Is					●			A/B	DX			250	
ruficrissus	S & E New Guinea, NE & E Australia					●								

Amaurornis magnirostris — Talaud Bush-Hen

Subspecies/Population	Breeding range	Wintering, or core non-breeding range	Afr	Eu	Asia	Oc	Neo	NA	Estimate	Source	Trend	Source	1% level	Notes
Talaud Is	Karakelong Is, (Talaud Is) (N Moluccas)					●								Described in1998 (TA).

Amaurornis phoenicurus — White-breasted Waterhen

Subspecies/Population	Breeding range	Wintering, or core non-breeding range	Afr	Eu	Asia	Oc	Neo	NA	Estimate	Source	Trend	Source	1% level	Notes
phoenicurus	South Asia, Indochina to E China, Taiwan, Korea, S Japan, Malaysia, Philippines, Greater Sundas	South Asia, Indochina to E China, Taiwan, Japan, Malaysia, Philippines, Greater Sundas, E Arabia			●				D/E	CE				Sometimes ascribed to chinensis.
insularis	Andaman & Nicobar Is				●									
midnicobaricus	Central Nicobar Is				●									
leucomelanus	Sulawesi, W Moluccas & Lesser Sundas				●									

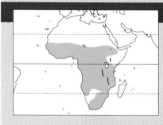

Amaurornis flavirostris — Black Crake

Subspecies/Population	Breeding range	Wintering, or core non-breeding range	Afr	Eu	Asia	Oc	Neo	NA	Estimate	Source	Trend	Source	1% level	Notes
Sub-Saharan Africa	Sub-Saharan Africa except deserts of NE & SW		●						E	RS				

Amaurornis olivieri CR — Sakalava Rail, Olivier's Crake

Subspecies/Population	Breeding range	Wintering, or core non-breeding range	Afr	Eu	Asia	Oc	Neo	NA	Estimate	Source	Trend	Source	1% level	Notes
Madagascar	W Central Madagascar		●						50–250	BC	DEC	BC	2	

Amaurornis bicolor — Black-tailed Crake, Elwes's Crake

Subspecies/Population	Breeding range	Wintering, or core non-breeding range	Afr	Eu	Asia	Oc	Neo	NA	Estimate	Source	Trend	Source	1% level	Notes
S & SE Asia	NE India & Myanmar E to S C China, NW Vietnam	NE India & Myanmar E to S C China			•									

Porzana parva — Little Crake

Subspecies/Population	Breeding range	Wintering, or core non-breeding range	Afr	Eu	Asia	Oc	Neo	NA	Estimate	Source	Trend	Source	1% level	Notes
parva	S, C & E Europe	Poorly known: Mediteranean basin, W & E Africa, Arabia	•	•	•				D	BE	DEC	HC	10,000	European breeding population 35,000–140,000 pairs (105,000–420,000 individuals) (BE).
(illustris)	Central Asia to W Xingjiang	W Pakistan, NW India			•									

Porzana pusilla — Baillon's Crake

Subspecies/Population	Breeding range	Wintering, or core non-breeding range	Afr	Eu	Asia	Oc	Neo	NA	Estimate	Source	Trend	Source	1% level	Notes
intermedia, Europe (br)	S & C Europe, N Africa	Poorly known: Mediteranean basin, Africa	•	•					10,000–20,000	SA	STA/DEC	BE	150	
obscura, Africa (br)	Ethiopia, NW, S & E Africa, Madagascar	Movements within Africa imperfectly known	•						B	DO			250	Sometimes included in intermedia.
pusilla	E Europe, C & E Asia to N China, N Korea, Japan, S to Iran, N India	SW Asia, India, Sri Lanka, Myanmar, Korea, S China, Taiwan to Indonesia, Philippines		•	•									
mira	SE Borneo	Unknown			•									
mayri	New Guinea	Unknown				•								Known only from type specimen (TB).
palustris	E New Guinea, Australia & Tasmania					•								
affinis	New Zealand & Chatham Island	Unknown				•			A	ON			100	

Porzana palmeri — Laysan Crake

Subspecies/Population	Breeding range	Wintering, or core non-breeding range	Afr	Eu	Asia	Oc	Neo	NA	Estimate	Source	Trend	Source	1% level	Notes
Laysan Is, Hawaii	Laysan Island, Hawaii					•			0	GY	EXT	GY		Extinct in wild between 1923 and 1936. Introduced populations extinct by 1944 (TB).

Porzana porzana — Spotted Crake

Subspecies/Population	Breeding range	Wintering, or core non-breeding range	Afr	Eu	Asia	Oc	Neo	NA	Estimate	Source	Trend	Source	1% level	Notes
S Asia (non-br)	N, Central Asia E to NW China, S to Iran	N India to W Myanmar			•									
Europe & W Asia (br)	Europe & W Asia	S Europe, Africa, mainly in E & S	•	•					D	BE	DEC	BI	10,000	European breeding population 52,000–170,000 pairs (156,000–510,000 individuals) (BE).

125

Porzana fluminea — Australian Crake

Subspecies/Population	Breeding range	Wintering, or core non-breeding range	Afr	Eu	Asia	Oc	Neo	NA	Estimate	Source	Trend	Source	1% level
Australia	Australia & Tasmania					•							

Australian Crake.

Ian Montgomery

Porzana carolina — Sora

Subspecies/Population	Breeding range	Wintering, or core non-breeding range	Afr	Eu	Asia	Oc	Neo	NA	Estimate	Source	Trend	Source	1% level	Notes
N America (br)	SE Alaska, Canada, USA	*S USA, C America, Caribbean, Peru to the Guianas*					•	•			INC	S5		

Porzana spiloptera VU — Dot-winged Crake

Subspecies/Population	Breeding range	Wintering, or core non-breeding range	Afr	Eu	Asia	Oc	Neo	NA	Estimate	Source	Trend	Source	1% level	Notes
C E South America	Uruguay, N Argentina, S Brazil						•		2,500–10,000	BC	DEC	BC	60	

Porzana albicollis — Ash-throated Crake

Subspecies/Population	Breeding range	Wintering, or core non-breeding range	Afr	Eu	Asia	Oc	Neo	NA	Estimate	Source	Trend	Source	1% level	Notes
albicollis	E & S Brazil, N & E Bolivia, Paraguay, N Argentina, SE Peru?						•							
olivacea	Colombia, Venezuela, Trinidad, the Guianas, N Brazil						•							

Porzana sandwichensis — Hawaiian Rail

Subspecies/Population	Breeding range	Wintering, or core non-breeding range	Afr	Eu	Asia	Oc	Neo	NA	Estimate	Source	Trend	Source	1% level	Notes
Hawaii	Hawaiian Islands					•			0	GY	EXT	GY		Last reported in 1884 (possibly 1893) (TB).

Porzana fusca — Ruddy-breasted Crake

Subspecies/Population	Breeding range	Wintering, or core non-breeding range	Afr	Eu	Asia	Oc	Neo	NA	Estimate	Source	Trend	Source	1% level	Notes
fusca	Pakistan, N India to Yunnan (SC China), Vietnam, Malay Peninsula, Philippines, W Indonesia					•								
zeylonica	W India & Sri Lanka					•					DEC	HT		Population in Sri Lanka 10,000–20,000 (HT).
erythrothorax	S Kuril Is, Japan, Korea, E & S China, E & S Indochina	S Japan, S China, E & S Indochina				•								
phaeopyga	Ryukyu Is (Japan)					•								

Porzana paykullii NT — Band-bellied Crake

Subspecies/Population	Breeding range	Wintering, or core non-breeding range	Afr	Eu	Asia	Oc	Neo	NA	Estimate	Source	Trend	Source	1% level	Notes
E, SE Asia	Far E Russia, NE China,	Indochina, Sumatra, Java, Borneo				•								

Porzana tabuensis — Spotless Crake

Subspecies/Population	Breeding range	Wintering, or core non-breeding range	Afr	Eu	Asia	Oc	Neo	NA	Estimate	Source	Trend	Source	1% level	Notes
tabuensis	Philippines, Micronesia, Polynesia, SW Pacific Islands, New Zealand, Australia				•	•								
edwardi	W & C New Guinea					•								
richardsoni	Oranje Mts, W New Guinea					•								

Porzana monasa — Kosrae Crake

Subspecies/Population	Breeding range	Wintering, or core non-breeding range	Afr	Eu	Asia	Oc	Neo	NA	Estimate	Source	Trend	Source	1% level	Notes
E Caroline Islands	Kosrae Island: E Caroline Islands					•				0	GY	EXT	GY		Known only from two specimens collected in 1827–28.

Porzana atra VU — Henderson Island Crake

Subspecies/Population	Breeding range	Wintering, or core non-breeding range	Afr	Eu	Asia	Oc	Neo	NA	Estimate	Source	Trend	Source	1% level	Notes
Henderson: Pitcairn Islands	Henderson: Pitcairn Islands					•				6,200	BC	STA	BC	60	

Porzana flaviventer — Yellow-breasted Crake

Subspecies/Population	Breeding range	Wintering, or core non-breeding range	Afr	Eu	Asia	Oc	Neo	NA	Estimate	Source	Trend	Source	1% level	Notes
flaviventer	Panama, Colombia, Venzuela, The Guianas, N, EC & S Brazil, E Bolivia, Paraguay, N Argentina							•						
gossii	Cuba & Jamaica							•						
hendersoni	Hispaniola & Puerto Rico							•						
woodi	S Mexico to NW Puerto Rico							•						
bangsi	N & E Colombia							•						

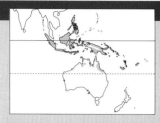

Porzana cinerea — White-browed Crake

Subspecies/Population	Breeding range	Wintering, or core non-breeding range	Afr	Eu	Asia	Oc	Neo	NA	Estimate	Source	Trend	Source	1% level	Notes
SE Asia, Australia, Micronesia	Taiwan, Indonesia, Malaysia, Philippines, New Guinea, N Australia, Micronesia, Melanesia, WC Polynesia				•	•								As many as 9 subspecies are recognised but differences are slight (TB).

Porzana nigra — Miller's Rail

Subspecies/Population	Breeding range	Wintering, or core non-breeding range	Afr	Eu	Asia	Oc	Neo	NA	Estimate	Source	Trend	Source	1% level	Notes
Tahiti	Tahiti					•			0	BC	EXT	BC		Known from 2 illustrations and subsequent descriptions by Latham and Gmelin. Presumably extinct in 18th Century (BC).

Aenigmatolimnas marginalis — Striped Crake

Subspecies/Population	Breeding range	Wintering, or core non-breeding range	Afr	Eu	Asia	Oc	Neo	NA	Estimate	Source	Trend	Source	1% level	Notes
Sub-Saharan Africa	Patchy distribution in Sub-Saharan Africa	Movements within Africa imperfectly known	•						A/B	DO	DEC	TB	250	

Cyanolimnas cerverai EN — Zapata Rail

Subspecies/Population	Breeding range	Wintering, or core non-breeding range	Afr	Eu	Asia	Oc	Neo	NA	Estimate	Source	Trend	Source	1% level	Notes
W Central Cuba	Zapata Swamp: W Central Cuba						•		250–1,000	BC	DEC	BC	6	

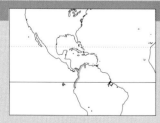

Neocrex colombianus DD — Colombian Crake

Subspecies/Population	Breeding range	Wintering, or core non-breeding range	Afr	Eu	Asia	Oc	Neo	NA	Estimate	Source	Trend	Source	1% level	Notes
columbianus	N & W Colombia, W Ecuador						•							
ripleyi	C & E Panama						•							Known only from 2 specimens in C Panama & NW Colombia, and one site in E Panama.

Neocrex erythrops — Paint-billed Crake

Subspecies/Population	Breeding range	Wintering, or core non-breeding range	Afr	Eu	Asia	Oc	Neo	NA	Estimate	Source	Trend	Source	1% level	Notes
erythrops	Coastal Peru & Galapagos Is						•							
olivascens	Panama, Colombia, Venezuela, the Guianas, E & C Brazil, Bolivia, Paraguay, N Argentina						•							

Pardirallus maculatus — Spotted Rail

Subspecies/Population	Breeding range	Wintering, or core non-breeding range	Afr	Eu	Asia	Oc	Neo	NA	Estimate	Source	Trend	Source	1% level	Notes
maculatus	N Caribbean, N Colombia E to Guianas, S to Peru; E Brazil S to N Argentina						•		A	NA			100	
insolitus	Mexico to Costa Rica						•							

Pardirallus nigricans — Blackish Rail

Subspecies/Population	Breeding range	Wintering, or core non-breeding range	Afr	Eu	Asia	Oc	Neo	NA	Estimate	Source	Trend	Source	1% level	Notes
nigricans	E Ecuador, E Peru, N Bolivia, W, SC & E Brazil, Paraguay, NE Argentina						•		B/C	NA			1,000	
caucae	SW Colombia						•							

Pardirallus sanguinolentus — Plumbeous Rail

Subspecies/Population	Breeding range	Wintering, or core non-breeding range	Afr	Eu	Asia	Oc	Neo	NA	Estimate	Source	Trend	Source	1% level	Notes
sanguinolentus	Paraguay, SE Brazil, Uruguay, Argentina S to Rio Negro						•		E	CC	STA	CC		
simonsi	W Peru S to N Chile						•							
tschudii	Temperate Peru to C & SE Bolivia						•							
zelebori	SE Brazil						•							
landbecki	C Chile & SW Argentina						•		C/D	S8				
luridus	S Chile & S Argentina to Tierra del Fuego						•		A	S8			100	

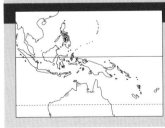

Eulabeornis castaneoventris — Chestnut Rail

Subspecies/Population	Breeding range	Wintering, or core non-breeding range	Afr	Eu	Asia	Oc	Neo	NA	Estimate	Source	Trend	Source	1% level	Notes
castaneoventris	Coasts N Western Australia–N Queensland						•							
sharpei	Aru Island, Indonesia						•							

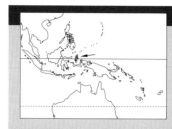

Habroptila wallacii VU — Invisible Rail

Subspecies/Population	Breeding range	Wintering, or core non-breeding range	Afr	Eu	Asia	Oc	Neo	NA	Estimate	Source	Trend	Source	1% level	Notes
Halmahera Is: N Moluccas	Halmahera Is: N Moluccas					•			2,500–10,000	BC	DEC	BC	60	

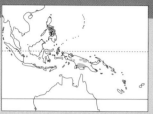

Megacrex inepta NT — New Guinea Flightless Rail

Subspecies/Population	Breeding range	Wintering, or core non-breeding range	Afr	Eu	Asia	Oc	Neo	NA	Estimate	Source	Trend	Source	1% level	Notes
inepta	SC New Guinea					•					STA?	BC		
pallida	NC New Guinea					•					STA?	BC		

Gallicrex cinerea — Watercock

Subspecies/Population	Breeding range	Wintering, or core non-breeding range	Afr	Eu	Asia	Oc	Neo	NA	Estimate	Source	Trend	Source	1% level	Notes
S, SE & E Asia	South Asia E to C & E China, Korea, Japan, Taiwan, S to Philippines, Indochina, Malaysia, W Indonesia				•						DEC	PE		

Aphanapteryx bonasia — Mauritian Red Rail

Subspecies/Population	Breeding range	Wintering, or core non-breeding range	Afr	Eu	Asia	Oc	Neo	NA	Estimate	Source	Trend	Source	1% level	Notes
Mauritius	Mauritius		•						0	HV	EXT	HV		Extinct 1675–1700 (HV).

Aphanapteryx leguati — Leguat's Rail

Subspecies/Population	Breeding range	Wintering, or core non-breeding range	Afr	Eu	Asia	Oc	Neo	NA	Estimate	Source	Trend	Source	1% level	Notes
Rodrigues	Rodrigues		•						0	HV	EXT	HV		Extinct c.1730 (HV).

Porphyrio porphyrio — Purple Swamphen

Subspecies/Population	Breeding range	Wintering, or core non-breeding range	Afr	Eu	Asia	Oc	Neo	NA	Estimate	Source	Trend	Source	1% level	Notes
porphyrio	Portugal, E & S Spain, S France, Sardinia, Morocco, Algeria, Tunisia		•	•					B	CP	INC	CP	250	CP: Totals for Portugal, Spain, France, Italy, Tunisia & Morocco combined: 4,165–5,404 breeding pairs (12,495–16,212 individuals). Algeria unknown.
madagascariensis	Egypt, sub-Saharan Africa, Madagascar		•						C	DO	STA?	DO	1,000	Possibly merits treatment as full species (TB).
caspius	Caspian Sea, NW Iran, Turkey, Syria & ?Azerbaijan			•	•									Probably this subspecies in Azerbaijan (TB).
seistanicus	Iraq, S Iran, Pakistan, Afghanistan, NW India				•									
poliocephalus	From S & E Pakistan through India, Sri Lanka, Bangladesh, N Myanmar to SW China & N Thailand				•				D/E	HT				

Porphyrio porphyrio... continued

Subspecies/Population	Breeding range	*Wintering, or core non-breeding range*	Afr	Eu	Asia	Oc	Neo	NA	Estimate	Source	Trend	Source	1% level	Notes
viridis	S Myanmar, S Thailand, Malay Peninsula, Indochina, S China				●									
indicus	Greater Sundas to Bali & Sulawesi				●									
pulverulentus	Philippines				●									Possibly merits treatment as full species (TB).
pelewensis	Palau Is					●								
melanopterus	Moluccas & Lesser Sundas to New Guinea				●	●								
bellus	SW Australia					●								
melanotus	N & E Australia, Tasmania, New Zealand, S & WC New Guinea					●			D	ON			10,000	Possibly merits treatment as full species (TB).
samoensis	Admiralty Is S to New Caledonia, E to Samoa					●			B/C	DX			1,000	B5: 2,000–3,000 in New Caledonia.

Porphyrio albus — White Gallinule, Lord Howe Swamphen

Subspecies/Population	Breeding range	*Wintering, or core non-breeding range*	Afr	Eu	Asia	Oc	Neo	NA	Estimate	Source	Trend	Source	1% level	Notes
Lord Howe Island	Lord Howe Island					●			0	GY	**EXT**	GY		Probably extinct by 1834.

Porphyrio coerulescens — Réunion Gallinule

Subspecies/Population	Breeding range	*Wintering, or core non-breeding range*	Afr	Eu	Asia	Oc	Neo	NA	Estimate	Source	Trend	Source	1% level	Notes
Réunion	Réunion		●						0	BC	**EXT**	BC		Probably extinct around 1730. Considered conspecific with *P porphyrio* by some, but very different habitat (montane forest) make this unlikely (BC).

Porphyrio mantelli hochstetteri EN — Takahe

Subspecies/Population	Breeding range	*Wintering, or core non-breeding range*	Afr	Eu	Asia	Oc	Neo	NA	Estimate	Source	Trend	Source	1% level	Notes
hochstetteri	S South Island, + translocated to 4 offshore islands, New Zealand					●			150–220	BC	**INC**	BC	2	Nominate subspecies of North Island long extinct. Sometimes considered a separate species, *Porphyrio hochstetteri*.

Porphyrio alleni — Allen's Gallinule

Subspecies/Population	Breeding range	*Wintering, or core non-breeding range*	Afr	Eu	Asia	Oc	Neo	NA	Estimate	Source	Trend	Source	1% level	Notes
Sub-Saharan Africa	Sub-Saharan Africa (not arid SW), Madagascar		●						C/D	DO				

Porphyrio martinicus — (American) Purple Gallinule

Subspecies/Population	Breeding range	*Wintering, or core non-breeding range*	Afr	Eu	Asia	Oc	Neo	NA	Estimate	Source	Trend	Source	1% level	Notes
N, C & N South America	E USA, Caribbean, Central America, South America S to N Argentina						●	●	D	WC CC	**STA**	CC	10,000	

American Purple Gallinule.

Johan Verbanck

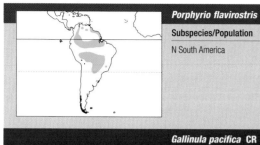

Porphyrio flavirostris — Azure Gallinule

Subspecies/Population	Breeding range	Wintering, or core non-breeding range	Afr	Eu	Asia	Oc	Neo	NA	Estimate	Source	Trend	Source	1% level	Notes
N South America	N South America East of Andes, S to Paraguay						•							

Gallinula pacifica CR — Samoan Moorhen

Subspecies/Population	Breeding range	Wintering, or core non-breeding range	Afr	Eu	Asia	Oc	Neo	NA	Estimate	Source	Trend	Source	1% level	Notes
Western Samoa	Western Samoa					•			<50	BC	EXT?	BC	1	Possibly extinct by 1907. 2 possible sightings in 1984

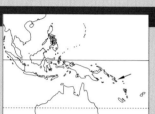

Gallinula silvestris CR — San Cristobal Moorhen

Subspecies/Population	Breeding range	Wintering, or core non-breeding range	Afr	Eu	Asia	Oc	Neo	NA	Estimate	Source	Trend	Source	1% level	Notes
Solomon Is	Makira (San Cristobal) Solomon Is					•			<50	BC	EXT?	BC	1	

Gallinula nesiotis VU — Tristan Moorhen

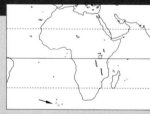

Subspecies/Population	Breeding range	Wintering, or core non-breeding range	Afr	Eu	Asia	Oc	Neo	NA	Estimate	Source	Trend	Source	1% level	Notes
"Tristan Moorhen" *nesiotis*	Tristan da Cunha island, South Atlantic Ocean		•						0	HV	EXT	HV		Nominate subspecies extinct by end of 19th Century.
"Gough Moorhen" *comeri*	Gough Is, introduced in Tristan da Cunha,		•						6,750–9,750	HV	INC	BC	85	HV estimates 2,250–3,250 pairs (6,750–9,750 individuals).

Gallinula chloropus — Common Moorhen, Common Gallinule

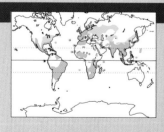

Subspecies/Population	Breeding range	Wintering, or core non-breeding range	Afr	Eu	Asia	Oc	Neo	NA	Estimate	Source	Trend	Source	1% level	Notes
chloropus, Europe, N Africa (br)	Europe, N Africa	*Europe, N & sub-Saharan Africa*	•	•					>2,600,000– 4,500,000	BE	STA	BE	20,000	BE: European breeding population 850,000–1,500,000 pairs (2,550,000–4,500,000 individuals). For populations over 2 million birds, Ramsar Convention criterion 5 (20,000 or more waterbirds) applies.
chloropus, SW Asia (non-br)	West & W Central Asia	*SW Asia, Caspian*		•	•				D	PE			10,000	
chloropus, South Asia (non-br)	Central & S Asia	*S Asia*			•						STA	PE		
chloropus, SE Asia (non-br)	E Asia, Indochina, C Malaysia	*Southern E Asia, Indochina, W Malaysia, W Indonesia*			•									Sometimes ascribed to *indica*.
meridionalis	Sub-Saharan Africa, St Helena		•						D	DO			10,000	
pyrrhorrhoa	Madagascar, Réunion, Mauritius, Comoros		•											
orientalis	Seychelles, Andamans, S Malaysia, Greater & Lesser Sundas to Philippines & Pulau		•		•									

Common Moorhen.   Nancy Camel

Gallinula chloropus... continued

Subspecies/Population	Breeding range	Wintering, or core non-breeding range	Afr	Eu	Asia	Oc	Neo	NA	Estimate	Source	Trend	Source	1% level	Notes
guami	Guam, N Marianas					•			300–375	ST	DEC	ST	3	ST estimate 100–125 pairs (300–400 individuals).
sandvicensis	Hawaiian islands					•			<1,000	RI	DEC	RI	10	
cachinnans	SE Canada &USA S to Panama, Bermuda, Galapagos	USA S to Panama, Bermuda, Galapagos					•	•	E	WC	INC	NB		Estimate from BBS for USA & Canada 436,174 pairs (1,308,522 individuals).
cerceris	Greater & Lesser Antilles						•							
barbadensis	Barbados						•							
pauxilla	C & E Panama, N & W Colombia, W Ecuador, NW Peru						•							
garmani	Andes of Peru, Bolivia, Chile, NW Argentina						•							
galeata	Trinidad & the Guianas S through Brazil to Uruguay, N Argentina						•							

Gallinula tenebrosa — Dusky Moorhen

Subspecies/Population	Breeding range	Wintering, or core non-breeding range	Afr	Eu	Asia	Oc	Neo	NA	Estimate	Source	Trend	Source	1% level	Notes
tenebrosa	Australia					•								B5: Recently established in New Caledonia where there are 100–200.
frontata	SE Borneo, Sulawesi, S Moluccas, Lesser Sundas, W & SE New Guinea				•	•								
neumanni	N New Guinea					•								

Gallinula angulata — Lesser Moorhen

Subspecies/Population	Breeding range	Wintering, or core non-breeding range	Afr	Eu	Asia	Oc	Neo	NA	Estimate	Source	Trend	Source	1% level	Notes
Sub-Saharan Africa	Sub-Saharan Africa except arid SW and NE		•						C/D	FE				

Gallinula melanops — Spot-flanked Gallinule

Subspecies/Population	Breeding range	Wintering, or core non-breeding range	Afr	Eu	Asia	Oc	Neo	NA	Estimate	Source	Trend	Source	1% level	Notes
melanops	E Bolivia & Paraguay, E & S Brazil, NE Argentina, Uruguay						•		D	CC	STA	CC	10,000	
bogotensis	E Andes of Colombia						•							
crassirostris	Chile & S Argentina (except extreme south)						•		B/C	S8			1,000	

Gallinula ventralis — Black-tailed Native-Hen

Subspecies/Population	Breeding range	Wintering, or core non-breeding range	Afr	Eu	Asia	Oc	Neo	NA	Estimate	Source	Trend	Source	1% level	Notes
Australia	Australia excluding Tasmania					•								

Gallinula mortierii — Tasmanian Native-Hen

Subspecies/Population	Breeding range	Wintering, or core non-breeding range	Afr	Eu	Asia	Oc	Neo	NA	Estimate	Source	Trend	Source	1% level	Notes
Tasmania	Tasmania					•								

Fulica cristata — Red-knobbed Coot, Crested Coot

Subspecies/Population	Breeding range	Wintering, or core non-breeding range	Afr	Eu	Asia	Oc	Neo	NA	Estimate	Source	Trend	Source	1% level	Notes
Morocco, Spain	N Morocco, S Spain		•	•					7,000–9,000	GX	DEC	GX	80	GX estimate a minimum of 7,762 in Morocco. AM estimates 90 pairs (270 individuals) in Spain.
E & S Africa	NE, E & S Africa, Madagascar		•						D	FE			10,000	Increasing in Southern Africa.

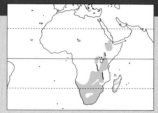

Fulica atra — Common Coot

Subspecies/Population	Breeding range	Wintering, or core non-breeding range	Afr	Eu	Asia	Oc	Neo	NA	Estimate	Source	Trend	Source	1% level	Notes
atra, NW Europe (non-br)	E, N & W Europe	*NW Europe*		•					1,750,000	DF	INC	DF	17,500	DF Report stable trend 1974–1996, but increasing trend 1987–96. Rate of increase 1987–96 applied to 1997 estimate results in 2002 estimate of 1,750,000.
atra, Black Sea, Mediterranean (non-br)	E Europe, W Asia	*Black Sea, Mediterranean, West Africa*	•	•	•				2,500,000	MN			20,000	For populations over 2 million birds, Ramsar criterion 5 (20,000 or more waterbirds), applies. Apparent increase in E Mediterranean and decrease in W Mediterranean in 1990s (DF).
atra, SW Asia (non-br)	W & Central Asia	*SW Asia*	•	•					2,000,000	PE			20,000	
atra, South Asia (non-br)	Central & S Asia	*S Asia*			•				1,500,000	PE	STA	PE	15,000	
atra, E, SE Asia (non-br)	East Asia	*E, SE Asia*			•				D/E	PE	DEC	CE		
lugubris	NW New Guinea, (E Java)					•	•							Formerly bred in E Java.
novaeguineae	Central New Guinea					•								
australis	Australia, New Zealand					•								

Fulica alai VU — Hawaiian Coot

Subspecies/Population	Breeding range	Wintering, or core non-breeding range	Afr	Eu	Asia	Oc	Neo	NA	Estimate	Source	Trend	Source	1% level	Notes
Hawaii	Hawaiian Islands					•			2,000–4,000	BC	STA	U2	30	

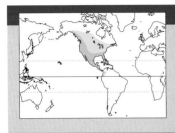

Fulica americana   American Coot

Subspecies/Population	Breeding range	Wintering, or core non-breeding range	Afr	Eu	Asia	Oc	Neo	NA	Estimate	Source	Trend	Source	1% level	Notes
americana	SE Alaska E to Nova Scotia, S to Caribbean, Costa Rica	*W & S North America, Central America, Hawaii*					•	•	>6,000,000	WC	STA	S5	20,000	Estimate from BBS 2,051,103 pairs (6,153,309 individuals). For populations over 2 million birds, Ramsar criterion 5 (20,000 or more waterbirds), applies.
columbiana	Colombia (& N Ecuador)						•							Apparently extinct in Ecuador (TB).

Fulica caribaea NT   Caribbean Coot

Subspecies/Population	Breeding range	Wintering, or core non-breeding range	Afr	Eu	Asia	Oc	Neo	NA	Estimate	Source	Trend	Source	1% level	Notes
Caribbean	Mostly N Caribbean, to Venezuela						•				DEC	BC		

Fulica leucoptera   White-winged Coot

Subspecies/Population	Breeding range	Wintering, or core non-breeding range	Afr	Eu	Asia	Oc	Neo	NA	Estimate	Source	Trend	Source	1% level	Notes
S South America	South America S of Paraguay						•		E	CC	STA	CC		

Fulica ardesiaca   Andean Coot, Slate-colored Coot

Subspecies/Population	Breeding range	Wintering, or core non-breeding range	Afr	Eu	Asia	Oc	Neo	NA	Estimate	Source	Trend	Source	1% level	Notes
ardesiaca	Interior Peru, C & W Bolivia, N Chile, NW Argentina						•							S8 gives total estimate for both subspecies of C/D.
atrura	S Colombia, Ecuador, Coastal Peru S to Lima						•							

Fulica armillata   Red-gartered Coot

Subspecies/Population	Breeding range	Wintering, or core non-breeding range	Afr	Eu	Asia	Oc	Neo	NA	Estimate	Source	Trend	Source	1% level	Notes
S South America	C & S Chile, Argentina, SE Brazil, Uruguay						•		E	CC				

Fulica rufifrons — Red-fronted Coot

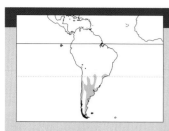

Subspecies/Population	Breeding range	Wintering, or core non-breeding range	Afr	Eu	Asia	Oc	Neo	NA	Estimate	Source	Trend	Source	1% level	Notes
W–C South America	Coastal S Peru & C Chile; SE Brazil, S Paraguay, NE Argentina & Uruguay, C & S Argentina						•		C	S8	STA	CC	1,000	

Fulica gigantea — Giant Coot

Subspecies/Population	Breeding range	Wintering, or core non-breeding range	Afr	Eu	Asia	Oc	Neo	NA	Estimate	Source	Trend	Source	1% level	Notes
C Andean South America	Andes of S Peru, W Bolivia, N Chile, NW Argentina						•		B/C	CC	STA	CC	1,000	

Fulica cornuta NT — Horned Coot

Subspecies/Population	Breeding range	Wintering, or core non-breeding range	Afr	Eu	Asia	Oc	Neo	NA	Estimate	Source	Trend	Source	1% level	Notes
C Andean South America	High Andes of SW Bolivia, N Chile, NW Argentina						•		A	(BC)	DEC	HV	100	BC cites a count of 8,988 in Argentina in Oct 1995.

Fulica newtoni — Mascarene Coot

Subspecies/Population	Breeding range	Wintering, or core non-breeding range	Afr	Eu	Asia	Oc	Neo	NA	Estimate	Source	Trend	Source	1% level	Notes
Réunion, Mauritius	Réunion, Mauritius						•		0	HV	EXT	HV		Last report on Réunion in 1672 and Mauritius in 1693 (BC).

HELIORNITHIDAE FINFOOTS

Podica senegalensis — African Finfoot

Subspecies/Population	Breeding range	Wintering, or core non-breeding range	Afr	Eu	Asia	Oc	Neo	NA	Estimate	Source	Trend	Source	1% level	Notes
senegalensis	Senegal–Uganda, NW Tanzania, Ethiopia		•						C/D	DO				
somerini	Coastal East Africa to the East Rift		•						A/B	DO			250	
camerunensis	S Cameroon, Gabon, Bioco Is, DR Congo?		•						B/C	DO			1,000	
(albipectus)	Angola		•						A	DO	DEC	DO	100	
petersii	E Angola, Caprivi, N Botswana to Zimbabwe, SE DR Congo, Zambia, Mozambique to E S Africa		•						B/C	DO			1,000	Declining in southern Africa (HF).

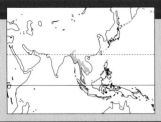

Heliopais personata VU — Masked Finfoot

Subspecies/Population	Breeding range	Wintering, or core non-breeding range	Afr	Eu	Asia	Oc	Neo	NA	Estimate	Source	Trend	Source	1% level	Notes
S, SE Asia	NE India SE to Vietnam, Malaysia, Sumatra				•				2,500–10,000	BC	DEC	BC	60	

Heliornis fulica — Sungrebe

Subspecies/Population	Breeding range	Wintering, or core non-breeding range	Afr	Eu	Asia	Oc	Neo	NA	Estimate	Source	Trend	Source	1% level	Notes
C America, N South America	SE Mexico S to Colombia & NE Argentina						•							

Eurypyga helias — Sunbittern

Subspecies/Population	Breeding range	Wintering, or core non-breeding range	Afr	Eu	Asia	Oc	Neo	NA	Estimate	Source	Trend	Source	1% level	Notes
helias	Colombia–Guyana S to E Bolivia, C Brazil						•							
major	Guatemala–W Ecuador						•							
meridionalis	SC Peru (Junin & Cuzco)						•							

EURYPYGIDAE SUNBITTERN

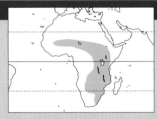

Microparra capensis — Lesser Jacana

Subspecies/Population	Breeding range	Wintering, or core non-breeding range	Afr	Eu	Asia	Oc	Neo	NA	Estimate	Source	Trend	Source	1% level	Notes
Sub-Saharan Africa	Mali E to Ethiopia, S to E Angola, E Namibia, E South Africa		•						C	FE			1,000	Declining in southern Africa (HF).

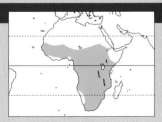

Actophilornis africana — African Jacana

Subspecies/Population	Breeding range	Wintering, or core non-breeding range	Afr	Eu	Asia	Oc	Neo	NA	Estimate	Source	Trend	Source	1% level	Notes
Sub-Saharan Africa	Sub-Saharan Africa		•						E	FE	STA	DO		

JACANIDAE JACANAS

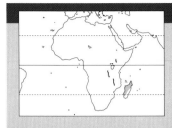

Actophilornis albinucha Madagascar Jacana

Subspecies/Population	Breeding range	Wintering, or core non-breeding range	Afr	Eu	Asia	Oc	Neo	NA	Estimate	Source	Trend	Source	1% level	Notes
Madagascar	N & W Madagascar		•						A	RB	DEC	RB	100	

Irediparra gallinacea Comb-crested Jacana

Subspecies/Population	Breeding range	Wintering, or core non-breeding range	Afr	Eu	Asia	Oc	Neo	NA	Estimate	Source	Trend	Source	1% level	Notes
gallinacea	S Philippines, E Indonesia					•								
novaeguinea	N-Central New Guinea, Misool & Aru Islands					•								
novaehollandiae	S New Guinea & N-E Australia					•								

Hydrophasianus chirurgus Pheasant-tailed Jacana

Subspecies/Population	Breeding range	Wintering, or core non-breeding range	Afr	Eu	Asia	Oc	Neo	NA	Estimate	Source	Trend	Source	1% level	Notes
S & SE Asia	S Asia, SE Asia, S China, Taiwan, Philippines	*S Asia, S Japan, Taiwan, SE Asia, Sumatra, Java, (Oman, Yemen)*			•				C	B3	DEC	CE	1,000	Declining in E Asia, but may be stable in S & SE Asia (CE).

Metopidius indicus Bronze-winged Jacana

Subspecies/Population	Breeding range	Wintering, or core non-breeding range	Afr	Eu	Asia	Oc	Neo	NA	Estimate	Source	Trend	Source	1% level	Notes
S & SE Asia	S Asia, Indochina, Sumatra				•									Birds in Sumatra may be a separate population (SH).

Jacana spinosa Northern Jacana

Subspecies/Population	Breeding range	Wintering, or core non-breeding range	Afr	Eu	Asia	Oc	Neo	NA	Estimate	Source	Trend	Source	1% level	Notes
spinosa	Belize & Guatemala S to W Panama						•							
gymnostoma	SW & E Mexico, S Texas	*Mexico, S Texas*					•							
violacea	Cuba, I of Pines, Jamaica, Hispaniola						•							

Jacana jacana — Wattled Jacana

Subspecies/Population	Breeding range	Wintering, or core non-breeding range	Afr	Eu	Asia	Oc	Neo	NA	Estimate	Source	Trend	Source	1% level	Notes
jacana	S Caribbean, W Cent America, South America N & E of Andes to N Argentina						•							
hypomelaena	W Central Panama to N Colombia						•							
melanopygia	W Colombia–W Venezuela						•				STA	NA		
intermedia	N & Central Venezuela						•							
scapularis	Lowland W Ecuador & NE Peru						•							
peruviana	NE Peru & adjacent NW Brazil						•							

Rostratula benghalensis — Greater Painted-Snipe

Subspecies/Population	Breeding range	Wintering, or core non-breeding range	Afr	Eu	Asia	Oc	Neo	NA	Estimate	Source	Trend	Source	1% level	Notes
benghalensis, Africa	Sub-Saharan Africa & Nile Delta		•						C/D	DO				
benghalensis, Asia	S & SE & E Asia, Indonesia				•									
australis	E Australia					•			A	B3	DEC	GC	100	GC estimate 5,000 breeding adults (7,500 individuals). LE present strong evidence that this is a separate and endangered species.

Rostratula semicollaris — South American Painted-Snipe

Subspecies/Population	Breeding range	Wintering, or core non-breeding range	Afr	Eu	Asia	Oc	Neo	NA	Estimate	Source	Trend	Source	1% level	Notes
semicollaris	Paraguay, SE Brazil, Uruguay, N Argentina, C Chile						•							Sometimes placed in the genus Nycticryphes.

Dromas ardeola — Crab Plover

Subspecies/Population	Breeding range	Wintering, or core non-breeding range	Afr	Eu	Asia	Oc	Neo	NA	Estimate	Source	Trend	Source	1% level	Notes
NW Indian Ocean	NW Indian Ocean, Red Sea, Persian Gulf	NW Indian Ocean, Red Sea, Persian Gulf, Coastal E Africa S to Madagascar, Coastal Pakistan, W India	•	•					60,000–80,000	DO SA	STA	DO	700	40,000–50,000 in Africa (DO); 20,000–30,000 in Asia (SW).

ROSTRATULIDAE PAINTED-SNIPES

DROMADIDAE CRAB PLOVER

139

HAEMATOPODIDAE OYSTERCATCHERS

Haematopus leucopodus — Magellanic Oystercatcher

Subspecies/Population	Breeding range	Wintering, or core non-breeding range	Afr	Eu	Asia	Oc	Neo	NA	Estimate	Source	Trend	Source	1% level	Notes
S South America	S American coasts SC Chile–SC Argentina,						•		C	S8			1,000	
Falkland/Malvinas Is	Falkland/Malvinas Is						•		21,000–39,000	WS			300	WS estimate 7,000–13,000 pairs (21,000–39,000 individuals).

Haematopus ater — Blackish Oystercatcher

Subspecies/Population	Breeding range	Wintering, or core non-breeding range	Afr	Eu	Asia	Oc	Neo	NA	Estimate	Source	Trend	Source	1% level	Notes
S South America	S American coasts S Peru–SC Argentina						•		B/C	S8			1,000	
Falkland/Malvinas Is	Falkland/Malvinas Is						•		12,000–24,000	WS			180	WS estimate 4,000–8,000 pairs (12,000–24,000 individuals).

Haematopus bachmani — American Black Oystercatcher

Subspecies/Population	Breeding range	Wintering, or core non-breeding range	Afr	Eu	Asia	Oc	Neo	NA	Estimate	Source	Trend	Source	1% level	Notes
Pacific N America	Pacific coast Aleutian Is to NW Mexico	Mostly S British Colombia to Baja California						•	6,900–10,800	A1	STA	MT	90	

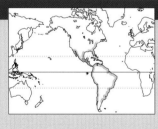

Haematopus palliatus — American Oystercatcher

Subspecies/Population	Breeding range	Wintering, or core non-breeding range	Afr	Eu	Asia	Oc	Neo	NA	Estimate	Source	Trend	Source	1% level	Notes
palliatus	Coasts E & S US, Caribbean							•	•	8,500	MU			85	NO estimate 7,700 from Georgia to Virginia, 9,000 for total Central & North American populations.
(frazari)	Gulf of California & W Mexico								•	350	MU			4	May refer to hybrid form between palliatus and bachmani.
(pitanay)	W South America, Ecuador to SC Chile							•		C	S8				Estimate refers to pitanay and durnfordi combined.
(durnfordi)	E South America, S Brazil to SC Argentina							•							
galapagensiss	Galapagos Islands							•		300	HV			3	HV estimates 100 pairs (300 individuals).

Haematopus meadewaldoi — Canarian Black Oystercatcher

Subspecies/Population	Breeding range	Wintering, or core non-breeding range	Afr	Eu	Asia	Oc	Neo	NA	Estimate	Source	Trend	Source	1% level	Notes
Canary Is	Eastern Canary Islands		•						0	CK	EXT	CK		Last Collected 1913, Probably became extinct in 1940s (BC).

Haematopus moquini NT — African Black Oystercatcher

Subspecies/Population	Breeding range	Wintering, or core non-breeding range	Afr	Eu	Asia	Oc	Neo	NA	Estimate	Source	Trend	Source	1% level	Notes
SE Africa	Coast N Namibia–SE South Africa	*Coast N Namibia–SE South Africa, S Angola*	•						5,000–6,000	DO	INC	DO	55	

Haematopus ostralegus — Eurasian Oystercatcher

Subspecies/Population	Breeding range	Wintering, or core non-breeding range	Afr	Eu	Asia	Oc	Neo	NA	Estimate	Source	Trend	Source	1% level	Notes
ostralegus, Europe, NW Africa	Europe & NE Russia	*Coastal W Europe, N & W Africa*	•	•					1,020,000	SW	INC	SW	10,200	
longipes	Black Sea, Asia Minor to W Siberia, NW Iran, Central Asia	*Coastal NE Africa, Arabian Peninsula, Persian, Arabian Gulf E to NW India*	•	•	•				100,000–200,000	SW	STA?	SW	1,500	
osculans	Kamchatka, Korea, NE & E China	*Japan, Korea, E China S to Taiwan*			•				10,000	B3 LK			100	B3 increased previous estimate of A on basis of additional data from Yellow Sea. LK reports 3,200 at Yubu Island, South Korea alone in December 1999.

Haematopus finschii — South Island Oystercatcher

Subspecies/Population	Breeding range	Wintering, or core non-breeding range	Afr	Eu	Asia	Oc	Neo	NA	Estimate	Source	Trend	Source	1% level	Notes
New Zealand	Coastal South Island, New Zealand	*Coastal New Zealand*				•			112,000	S1	INC	S1	1,100	Sometimes considered conspecific with *ostralegus*.

Haematopus longirostris — Australian Pied Oystercatcher

Subspecies/Population	Breeding range	Wintering, or core non-breeding range	Afr	Eu	Asia	Oc	Neo	NA	Estimate	Source	Trend	Source	1% level
Australia, S New Guinea, Aru Is	Coasts of Australia, Aru Is	*Coasts of Australia, S New Guinea, Aru Is*				•			11,000	WD			110

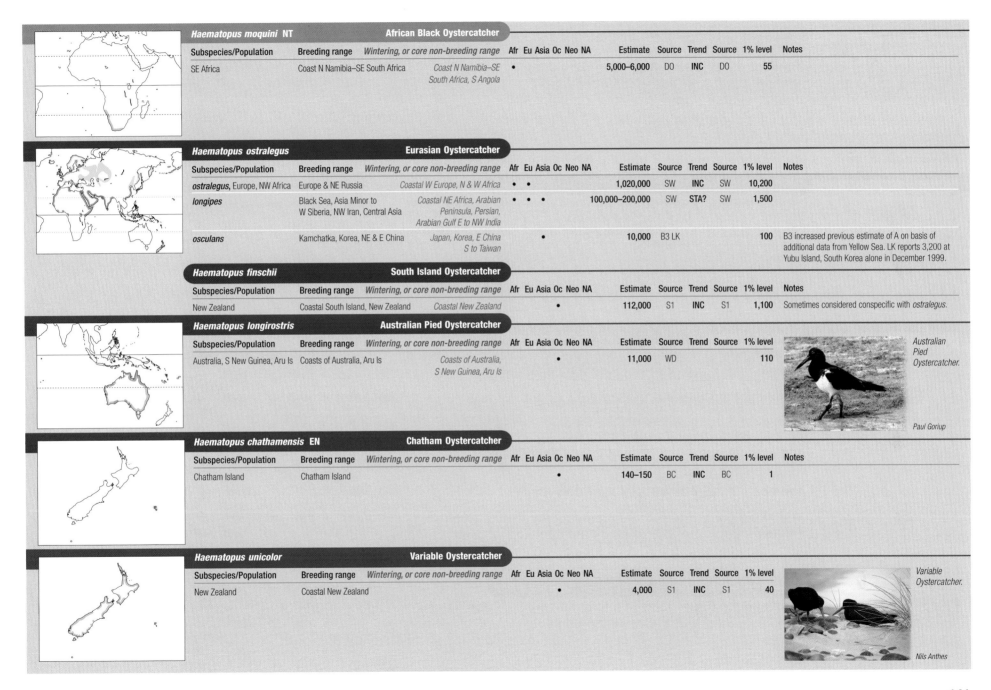

Australian Pied Oystercatcher.

Paul Goriup

Haematopus chathamensis EN — Chatham Oystercatcher

Subspecies/Population	Breeding range	Wintering, or core non-breeding range	Afr	Eu	Asia	Oc	Neo	NA	Estimate	Source	Trend	Source	1% level	Notes
Chatham Island	Chatham Island					•			140–150	BC	INC	BC	1	

Haematopus unicolor — Variable Oystercatcher

Subspecies/Population	Breeding range	Wintering, or core non-breeding range	Afr	Eu	Asia	Oc	Neo	NA	Estimate	Source	Trend	Source	1% level
New Zealand	Coastal New Zealand					•			4,000	S1	INC	S1	40

Variable Oystercatcher.

Nils Anthes

Haematopus fuliginosus — Sooty Oystercatcher

Subspecies/Population	Breeding range	Wintering, or core non-breeding range	Afr	Eu	Asia	Oc	Neo	NA	Estimate	Source	Trend	Source	1% level	Notes
fuliginosus	S Australia: SW, S & SE coasts of Australia					•			4,000	WD			40	
opthalmicus	N Australia: Coasts & islands CW Western Australia to SE Queensland.					•			7,500	GC	STA	GC	75	GC estimate 5,000 breeding adults (7,500 individuals).

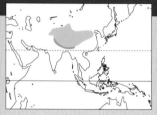

IBIDORHYNCHIDAE IBISBILL

Ibidorhyncha struthersii — Ibisbill

Subspecies/Population	Breeding range	Wintering, or core non-breeding range	Afr	Eu	Asia	Oc	Neo	NA	Estimate	Source	Trend	Source	1% level	Notes
Central Asia	High altitude rivers of Central Asian mountain systems N & NE of Himalayas. Partial short-distance altitudinal migrant.				•									

RECURVIROSTRIDAE STILTS & AVOCETS

Himantopus himantopus — Black-winged Stilt

Subspecies/Population	Breeding range	Wintering, or core non-breeding range	Afr	Eu	Asia	Oc	Neo	NA	Estimate	Source	Trend	Source	1% level	Notes
himantopus, Sub-Saharan Africa	Sub-Saharan Africa N of southern Africa		•						D	SW			10,000	
himantopus, Madagascar	Madagascar		•						5,000–10,000	DO			75	Madagascar birds appear to be morphologically distinct from those in mainland Africa (DO).
(meridionalis)	Southern Africa		•						15,000–30,000	UN	INC	HF	230	
himantopus, W & SW Europe, W Africa	SW Europe & NW Africa	Most W Africa, + SW Iberia	•	•					71,000–82,000	SW	STA	SW	770	
himantopus, Central & E Europe to E Mediterranean (br)	C Europe, E Mediterranean, Black Sea, Turkey	S to African Sahel	•	•	•				23,000–44,000	SW	STA	HC	340	
himantopus, SW Asia (wintering)	W, Central and SW Asia, Caspian	Iran, Iraq, Arabian Peninsula, NE Africa (to Sudan)	•	•	•				20,000–50,000	SW			350	
himantopus, S Asia	S Asia				•				D	PE	STA	PE	10,000	
himantopus, E & SE Asia	SE & E Asia including recent expansion of range into China, Taiwan, Korea, Japan				•				C	B3			1,000	Expanding range suggests increasing trend.
(ceylonensis)	Sri Lanka				•									6,680 counted by AWC in Sri Lanka in Jan 1997, 5,235 in Jan 2000 (HT).

Himantopus mexicanus — Black-necked Stilt

Subspecies/Population	Breeding range	Wintering, or core non-breeding range	Afr	Eu	Asia	Oc	Neo	NA	Estimate	Source	Trend	Source	1% level	Notes
mexicanus	W & S USA, C America, Caribbean, to SW Peru, E Ecuador, NE Brazil						•	•	D	MU	INC	S5	10,000	MU estimate 150,000 for North American portion of this population. Often considered conspecific with H himantopus.
knudseni "Hawaiian Stilt"	Hawaii					•			1,200–1,600	U2	STA	U2	15	Sometimes treated as separate species, H. knudseni.

Black-necked Stilt.   Paul Goriup

Himantopus melanurus — White-backed Stilt

Subspecies/Population	Breeding range	Wintering, or core non-breeding range	Afr	Eu	Asia	Oc	Neo	NA	Estimate	Source	Trend	Source	1% level	Notes
C South America	N Chile & EC Peru, Bolivia, Paraguay, SE Brazil, S to SC Argentina						•		D	MU	STA	AT	10,000	Often considered conspecific with *H himantopus*.

Himantopus leucocephalus — White-headed Stilt

Subspecies/Population	Breeding range	Wintering, or core non-breeding range	Afr	Eu	Asia	Oc	Neo	NA	Estimate	Source	Trend	Source	1% level	Notes
SE Asia–Australasia	Java E to New Guinea S to Australia, New Zealand	As breeding range + Philippines, Greater Sundas, Sulawesi				•			300,000	WD			3,000	Often considered conspecific with *H himantopus*.

Himantopus novaezelandiae CR — Black Stilt

Subspecies/Population	Breeding range	Wintering, or core non-breeding range	Afr	Eu	Asia	Oc	Neo	NA	Estimate	Source	Trend	Source	1% level	Notes
South Island New Zealand	Upper Waitaki Valley, C S Island, New Zealand	Central S Island, W N Island, New Zealand				•			40	BC	DEC	BC	1	An additional c.40 are in captivity.

Cladorhynchus leucocephalus — Banded Stilt

Subspecies/Population	Breeding range	Wintering, or core non-breeding range	Afr	Eu	Asia	Oc	Neo	NA	Estimate	Source	Trend	Source	1% level	Notes
Australia	Inland SW, Central & S Australia	Coastal SW & S Australia				•			206,000	WD			2,100	

Recurvirostra avosetta — Pied Avocet

Subspecies/Population	Breeding range	Wintering, or core non-breeding range	Afr	Eu	Asia	Oc	Neo	NA	Estimate	Source	Trend	Source	1% level	Notes
Southern Africa	Namibia, Botswana, South Africa		•						19,300	SW	INC	HF	190	
E Africa	Ethiopia, Kenya, Tanzania		•						C	SW			1,000	
W Europe (br)	NW Europe, W Mediterranean, NW Africa	Atlantic coast S to Mauritania, Senegal, Gambia	•	•					73,000	SW	STA	SW	730	
Mediterranean & SE Europe (br)	SE Europe, Black Sea, Turkey	E Mediterranean, E Sahel (Chad)	•	•	•				47,000	SW	STA (?DEC)	SW	470	
W, SW Asia & Eastern Africa	Caspian, Kazakhstan, Iran	Iran, Iraq, Arabian Peninsula, NE Africa (to Sudan)	•	•	•				B	PE SW	STA	SW	250	
Central & S Asia	Central Asia	South Asia			•				B/C	PE	INC	PE	1,000	
E Asia	SE Siberia, NE China	SE China, Taiwan, Korea, Japan			•				C	B3			1,000	

Recurvirostra americana — American Avocet

Subspecies/Population	Breeding range	Wintering, or core non-breeding range	Afr	Eu	Asia	Oc	Neo	NA	Estimate	Source	Trend	Source	1% level	Notes
N & C America	SW Canada, W USA, Coastal NE USA, W Mexico	SW & SE USA, Mexico–Guatemala, Bahamas, Cuba					•	•	450,000	MU	STA	S5	4,500	Great Salt Lake (Utah) Waterbird Survey recorded 204,878 in 1997 (PA).

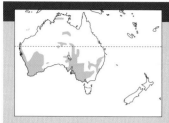

Recurvirostra novaehollandiae   Red-necked Avocet, Australian Avocet

Subspecies/Population	Breeding range	Wintering, or core non-breeding range	Afr	Eu	Asia	Oc	Neo	NA	Estimate	Source	Trend	Source	1% level	Notes
Australia	SW, SE, Central & N Australia					•			107,000	WD			1,100	

Recurvirostra andina   Andean Avocet

Subspecies/Population	Breeding range	Wintering, or core non-breeding range	Afr	Eu	Asia	Oc	Neo	NA	Estimate	Source	Trend	Source	1% level	Notes
Andean South America	Andes C Peru S to N Chile, NW Argentina						•							

BURHINIDAE THICK-KNEES

Burhinus oedicnemus   Stone-Curlew, Eurasian Thick-Knee

Subspecies/Population	Breeding range	Wintering, or core non-breeding range	Afr	Eu	Asia	Oc	Neo	NA	Estimate	Source	Trend	Source	1% level	Notes
oedicnemus, W Europe (br)	Europe W of Adriatic N to Denmark	Iberia, N Africa, Sahel	•	•					100,000–180,000	SW	DEC	SW	1,400	
oedicnemus, E Europe (br)	E Europe E of Adriatic N to Denmark, Russia	Mediterranean Basin & N Africa	•	•					25,000–51,000	SW	DEC	SW	380	
distinctus	Western Canary Islands		•						600	SW	DEC	SW	6	
insularum	Eastern Canary Islands		•						3,000	SW	DEC	SW	30	
saharae	E Mediterranean, SW Asia, N Africa		•	•	•				B/C	DO			1,000	
harterti	Central Asia. Iran, Pakistan, NW India	Mainly sedentary; some movement south in winter			•									
indicus	India & Sri Lanka E to Indochina				•									

Burhinus senegalensis   Senegal Thick-Knee

Subspecies/Population	Breeding range	Wintering, or core non-breeding range	Afr	Eu	Asia	Oc	Neo	NA	Estimate	Source	Trend	Source	1% level	Notes
senegalensis	W Africa S of Sahara E to Sudan		•						B	DO			250	
(inornatus)	Nile Valley Egypt to N Uganda, Ethiopia Kenya, Somalia		B						B	DO			250	

Burhinus vermiculatus — Water Dikkop, Water Thick-Knee

Subspecies/Population	Breeding range	Wintering, or core non-breeding range	Afr	Eu	Asia	Oc	Neo	NA	Estimate	Source	Trend	Source	1% level	Notes
vermiculatus	D R Congo E to Somalia, S to E & S South Africa		•						C	DO			1,000	
buttikoferi	W Africa Liberia–Nigeria–Gabon		•						A/B	DO			250	

Burhinus capensis — Spotted Dikkop

Subspecies/Population	Breeding range	Wintering, or core non-breeding range	Afr	Eu	Asia	Oc	Neo	NA	Estimate	Source	Trend	Source	1% level	Notes
capensis	Kenya–Southern Africa		•						C	DO			1,000	Increasing in Southern Africa (HF). >50,000 in Southern Africa (UN).
maculosus	Senegal E to NE Africa		•						B	DO			250	
damarensis	Namibia, W Botswana, SW South.Africa		•						A	DO			100	
dodsoni	Coastal Somalia, S Arabia		•		•				B	DO			250	

Burhinus bistriatus — Double-striped Thick-Knee

Subspecies/Population	Breeding range	Wintering, or core non-breeding range	Afr	Eu	Asia	Oc	Neo	NA	Estimate	Source	Trend	Source	1% level	Notes
bistriatus	S Mexico S to NW Costa Rica						•							
pediacus	N Colombia						•							
vocifer	Venezuela, Guyana, extreme N Brazil						•							
dominicensis	Hispaniola						•							

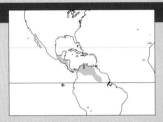

Burhinus superciliaris — Peruvian Thick-Knee

Subspecies/Population	Breeding range	Wintering, or core non-breeding range	Afr	Eu	Asia	Oc	Neo	NA	Estimate	Source	Trend	Source	1% level	Notes
Peru	Coast of Peru & extreme S Ecuador						•							

Burhinus grallarius NT — Bush Thick-Knee

Subspecies/Population	Breeding range	Wintering, or core non-breeding range	Afr	Eu	Asia	Oc	Neo	NA	Estimate	Source	Trend	Source	1% level	Notes
grallarius	S & E Australia,					•					DEC	GC		Total, 3 populations combined 150,000 (GC). Subspecies poorly defined (HV).
rufescens	NW & N C Australia	NW Australia				•								
ramsayi	N Queensland, S New Guinea					•								

Bush Thick-knee.

Ian Montgomery

145

Burhinus (Esacus) recurvirostris — Great Thick-Knee, Great Stone Plover

Subspecies/Population	Breeding range	Wintering, or core non-breeding range	Afr	Eu	Asia	Oc	Neo	NA	Estimate	Source	Trend	Source	1% level	Notes
SW, S & SE Asia		SE Iran, S Asia to Indochina & S China			●									

Burhinus gigantea (Esacus magnirostris) NT — Beach Thick-Knee

Subspecies/Population	Breeding range	Wintering, or core non-breeding range	Afr	Eu	Asia	Oc	Neo	NA	Estimate	Source	Trend	Source	1% level	Notes
SE Asia–Australia, Melanesia		Andaman Is, Malay Peninsula, Philippines, Indonesia, New Guinea, N Australia, SW Pacific Islands			●	●			A/B	GC (BC)			250	GC estimate 5,000 for Australia. Estimate for Melanesian islands, 1,000? (DX), and for New Caledonia 10–20 birds (B5).

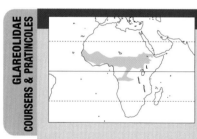

GLAREOLIDAE COURSERS & PRATINCOLES

Pluvianus aegyptius — Egyptian Plover, Egyptian Courser

Subspecies/Population	Breeding range	Wintering, or core non-breeding range	Afr	Eu	Asia	Oc	Neo	NA	Estimate	Source	Trend	Source	1% level	Notes
aegyptius, West Africa		Sub-Saharan West Africa	●						20,000–50,000	DO	STA	DO	350	
aegyptius, East Africa		Eastern Africa Ethiopia S to Uganda	●						A/B	DO	DEC	DO	250	
(angolae)		Lower Congo Basin DR Congo &, N Angola	●						A	DO			100	

Cursorius cursor — Cream-coloured Courser

Subspecies/Population	Breeding range	Wintering, or core non-breeding range	Afr	Eu	Asia	Oc	Neo	NA	Estimate	Source	Trend	Source	1% level	Notes
cursor	N Africa, Arabian Peninsula, Socotra	Africa S to Sahel & N Kenya, Saudi Arabia	●	●										
bogulubovi	SE Turkey, N Iran, E Caspian Basin	S Pakistan, NW India		●										
exsul	Cape Verde Islands		●						<5,000	DO			50	
(bannermani)	Canary Islands		●						600–750	BE	DEC	BE	7	BE: Breeding population 200–250 pairs (600–750 individuals). Often assigned to nominate race.
littoralis	Extreme SE Sudan, N Kenya, S Somalia		●						C	DO			1,000	littoralis and somaliensis sometimes treated as a separate species under name C somaliensis, Somali Courser.
somalensis	Eritrea, E Ethiopia, Somalia		●						C	DO			1,000	

146

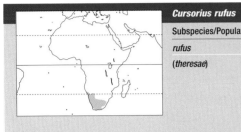

Cursorius rufus — Burchell's Courser

Subspecies/Population	Breeding range	Wintering, or core non-breeding range	Afr	Eu	Asia	Oc	Neo	NA	Estimate	Source	Trend	Source	1% level	Notes
rufus	S Botswana, & C S Africa E of 21 degrees		•											
(theresae)	SW Angola, South Africa W of 21 degrees & Namibia		•											

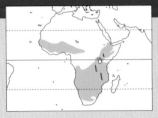

Cursorius teminckii — Temminck's Courser

Subspecies/Population	Breeding range	Wintering, or core non-breeding range	Afr	Eu	Asia	Oc	Neo	NA	Estimate	Source	Trend	Source	1% level	Notes
temminckii, W Africa	S Mauritania & Senegal to Nigeria, Chad & Central African Republic		•							B/C	DO			1,000	
temminckii, E & S Africa	Ethiopa S through C Africa to N South Africa		•							C/D	DO				
(damarensis)	Namibia, Kalahari Desert & Okavango		•							A/B	DO			250	Sometimes ascribed to aridus.

Cursorius coromandelicus — Indian Courser

Subspecies/Population	Breeding range	Wintering, or core non-breeding range	Afr	Eu	Asia	Oc	Neo	NA	Estimate	Source	Trend	Source	1% level
South Asia	Pakistan, India, Nepal, N Sri Lanka				•								

Indian Courser.

Paul Goriup

Rhinoptilus africanus — Double-banded Courser

Subspecies/Population	Breeding range	Wintering, or core non-breeding range	Afr	Eu	Asia	Oc	Neo	NA	Estimate	Source	Trend	Source	1% level	Notes
africanus	SW & C Kalahari, S Namib, N Cape Province		•									STA	HF		
raffertyi	E Ethiopia, Eritrea, Djibouti		•												
hartingi	SE Ethiopia & Somalia		•												
gracilis	Kenya & Tanzania		•												
traylori	Etosha (Namibia)–Makgadikgadi (Botswana)		•									STA	HF		
bisignatus	SW Angola		•												
sharpei	Central Namibia		•									STA	HF		
granti	W Cape Province & Karoo, South Africa		•									STA	HF		

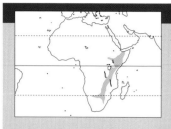

Rhinoptilus cinctus — Three-banded Courser

Subspecies/Population	Breeding range	Wintering, or core non-breeding range	Afr	Eu	Asia	Oc	Neo	NA	Estimate	Source	Trend	Source	1% level	Notes
cinctus	SE Sudan, E Ethiopia, Somalia & N Kenya		•						C/D	DO				
emini	S Kenya, Tanzania, N Zambia		•						B	DO			250	
seebohmi	N South Africa, Zimbabwe, Namibia, SE Angola		•						A/B	DO			250	

Rhinoptilus chalcopterus — Bronze-winged Courser

Subspecies/Population	Breeding range	Wintering, or core non-breeding range	Afr	Eu	Asia	Oc	Neo	NA	Estimate	Source	Trend	Source	1% level	Notes
chalcopterus	Senegal–S Sudan & W Ethiopia S to Kenya		•						C/D	DO			1,000	
(albofasciatus)	Tanzania S to southern Africa		•						C	DO			1,000	

Rhinoptilus bitorquatus CR — Jerdon's Courser

Subspecies/Population	Breeding range	Wintering, or core non-breeding range	Afr	Eu	Asia	Oc	Neo	NA	Estimate	Source	Trend	Source	1% level	Notes
SE India	Pennar Valley, S Andhra Pradesh, SE India				•				50–250	BC	DEC	BC	2	

Stiltia isabella — Australian Pratincole

Subspecies/Population	Breeding range	Wintering, or core non-breeding range	Afr	Eu	Asia	Oc	Neo	NA	Estimate	Source	Trend	Source	1% level	Notes
Australia	N & E & SE Australia	N & E Australia, New Guinea, E Indonesia			•	•			60,000	WD			600	

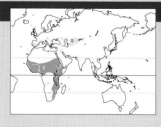

Glareola pratincola — Collared Pratincole

Subspecies/Population	Breeding range	Wintering, or core non-breeding range	Afr	Eu	Asia	Oc	Neo	NA	Estimate	Source	Trend	Source	1% level	Notes
pratincola, W Mediterranean (br)	SW Europe, NW Africa	S edge of Sahara: Senegal, Gambia to Nigeria	•	•					18,000–19,500	SW	STA	SW	190	
pratincola, Black Sea, E Mediterranean (br)	SE Europe, Black Sea, Asia Minor	Mainly E Sahel zone	•	•	•				16,000–31,000	SW	DEC	SW	240	
pratincola, SW Asia (br)	Caspian region, Iran, Iraq	NE Africa, Nile valley, Sudan, Ethiopia	•	•	•				B/C	SW			1,000	
erlangeri	Coastal S Somalia & N Kenya		•						A/B	DO			250	

Glareola pratincola... continued

Subspecies/Population	Breeding range	Wintering, or core non-breeding range	Afr	Eu	Asia	Oc	Neo	NA	Estimate	Source	Trend	Source	1% level	Notes
fuelleborni	Kenya to D R Congo, Namibia, E S Africa		•						100,000–300,000	DO			2,000	
(boweri)	Senegal to Lake Chad & Gabon		•						B	DO			250	
(limbata)	Eritrea, S Arabia, Sudan, Ethiopia & Somalia		•		•				B/C	DO			1,000	

Glareola maldivarum — Oriental Pratincole

Subspecies/Population	Breeding range	Wintering, or core non-breeding range	Afr	Eu	Asia	Oc	Neo	NA	Estimate	Source	Trend	Source	1% level	Notes
South Asia	India, Sri Lanka				•				C/D	PE				
E–SE Asia, Australia	S Siberia, NE Mongolia, E China, Taiwan, Japan, Indochina, Philippines	SE Asia, Indonesia, New Guinea, Australia, Philippines?			•	•			75,000	B3			750	

Glareola nordmanni DD — Black-winged Pratincole

Subspecies/Population	Breeding range	Wintering, or core non-breeding range	Afr	Eu	Asia	Oc	Neo	NA	Estimate	Source	Trend	Source	1% level	Notes
E Europe–Central Asia	Romania, Ukraine, SW Russia, N Kazakhstan	S Africa, Namibia, Botswana, Nigeria	•		•				29,000–45,000	B10 SW	DEC	B10	370	B10: World breeding population estimated at 9,700–14,900 pairs (29,100–44,700 individuals) and declining steeply.

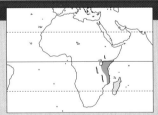

Glareola ocularis — Madagascar Pratincole

Subspecies/Population	Breeding range	Wintering, or core non-breeding range	Afr	Eu	Asia	Oc	Neo	NA	Estimate	Source	Trend	Source	1% level	Notes
Madagascar	Madagascar	E Africa coast N Mozambique N to S Somalia	•						5,000–10,000	DO	DEC	DO	75	

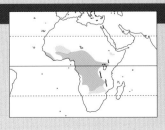

Glareola nuchalis — Rock Pratincole

Subspecies/Population	Breeding range	Wintering, or core non-breeding range	Afr	Eu	Asia	Oc	Neo	NA	Estimate	Source	Trend	Source	1% level	Notes
nuchalis	Chad E to Ethiopia, S to Mozambique & N Namibia	Some post-breeding dispersal	•						C	DO			1,000	Decreasing in Southern Africa (HF).
liberiae	W Africa Sierra Leone–W Cameroon	Some post-breeding dispersal	•						B	DO			250	

Glareola cinerea — Grey Pratincole

Subspecies/Population	Breeding range	Wintering, or core non-breeding range	Afr	Eu	Asia	Oc	Neo	NA	Estimate	Source	Trend	Source	1% level	Notes
cinerea	Niger to Ghana, Cameroon, W Zaire, NW Angola		•						B	DO			250	
(colorata)	Upper R Niger, Mali		•						A/B	DO			100	

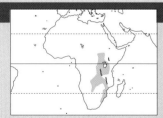

Glareola lactea — Small Pratincole

Subspecies/Population	Breeding range	Wintering, or core non-breeding range	Afr	Eu	Asia	Oc	Neo	NA	Estimate	Source	Trend	Source	1% level	Notes
S & SE Asia	S Asia N, W & C Indochina				•				B/C	PE			1,000	

CHARADRIIDAE PLOVERS

Vanellus vanellus — Northern Lapwing

Subspecies/Population	Breeding range	Wintering, or core non-breeding range	Afr	Eu	Asia	Oc	Neo	NA	Estimate	Source	Trend	Source	1% level	Notes
Europe (br)	Europe	Europe, Asia Minor, North Africa	•	•	•				2,800,000–4,000,000	SW	DEC	HC	20,000	For populations over 2 million birds, Ramsar criterion 5 (20,000 or more waterbirds), applies.
W Asia (br)	W Asia	SW Asia, Caspian	•	•	•				1,600,000–2,900,000	SW			20,000	For populations over 2 million birds, Ramsar criterion 5 (20,000 or more waterbirds), applies.
S Asia (non-br)	Central Asia	S Asia			•				B	PE			250	
E, SE Asia (non-br)	S & E Siberia, Mongolia, N China	E, SE Asia			•				C	PE			1,000	

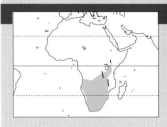

Vanellus crassirostris — Long-toed Lapwing

Subspecies/Population	Breeding range	Wintering, or core non-breeding range	Afr	Eu	Asia	Oc	Neo	NA	Estimate	Source	Trend	Source	1% level	Notes
crassirostris, E & C Africa	E & C Africa: S Sudan to N Malawi, W Angola		•						C	DO			1,000	
crassirostris, Lake Chad Basin	Lake Chad Basin		•						<5,000	DO			50	
leucopterus	S Africa: S Tanzania S to NE South Africa, W to Angola		•						25,000–50,000	DO			380	

Vanellus armatus — Blacksmith Lapwing

Subspecies/Population	Breeding range	Wintering, or core non-breeding range	Afr	Eu	Asia	Oc	Neo	NA	Estimate	Source	Trend	Source	1% level	Notes
S & E Africa	Southern, Eastern Africa		•						D	DO			10,000	Increasing in Southern Africa (HF).

Blacksmith Lapwing.

Paul Goriup

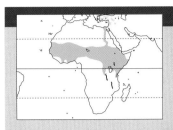

Vanellus spinosus — Spur-winged Lapwing

Subspecies/Population	Breeding range	Wintering, or core non-breeding range	Afr	Eu	Asia	Oc	Neo	NA	Estimate	Source	Trend	Source	1% level	Notes
Africa	Sub-Saharan Africa Senegal–Ethiopia, S to Kenya & Uganda; Nile Valley		•						100,000–700,000	DO			4,000	
SE Europe, Asia Minor	Greece, Turkey	Africa	•	•	•				C	SA	INC	SA	1,000	

Vanellus duvaucelli — River Lapwing

Subspecies/Population	Breeding range	Wintering, or core non-breeding range	Afr	Eu	Asia	Oc	Neo	NA	Estimate	Source	Trend	Source	1% level	Notes
S & SE Asia	NC India, Nepal, E to SC China, Indochina				•				A/B	PE			250	

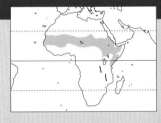

Vanellus tectus — Black-headed Lapwing

Subspecies/Population	Breeding range	Wintering, or core non-breeding range	Afr	Eu	Asia	Oc	Neo	NA	Estimate	Source	Trend	Source	1% level	Notes
tectus	S Mauritania, Senegal E to Ethiopia, Uganda, Kenya		•						C/D	DO				
latifrons	E Kenya to S Somalia		•						A/B	DO			250	

Vanellus malabaricus — Yellow-wattled Lapwing

Subspecies/Population	Breeding range	Wintering, or core non-breeding range	Afr	Eu	Asia	Oc	Neo	NA	Estimate	Source	Trend	Source	1% level	Notes
South Asia	S Pakistan, India, Bangladesh, Sri Lanka				•									

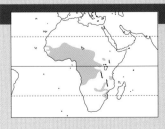

Vanellus albiceps — White-headed Lapwing

Subspecies/Population	Breeding range	Wintering, or core non-breeding range	Afr	Eu	Asia	Oc	Neo	NA	Estimate	Source	Trend	Source	1% level	Notes
W, C Africa	W, Central Africa		•						30,000–70,000	DO			500	
Tanzania	Tanzania		•						6,000–8,000	B1			70	
SE Africa	SE Africa		•						20,000–50,000	DO	STA	DO	350	

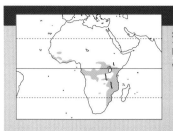

Vanellus lugubris — Lesser Black-winged Lapwing, Senegal Plover

Subspecies/Population	Breeding range	Wintering, or core non-breeding range	Afr	Eu	Asia	Oc	Neo	NA	Estimate	Source	Trend	Source	1% level	Notes
Equatorial, E & SE Africa	Equatorial Africa, E & SE Africa		•						20,000–50,000	P1			350	
West Africa	S West Africa								5,000–20,000	P1			130	

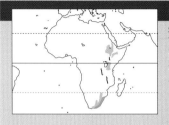

Vanellus melanopterus — Greater Black-winged Lapwing

Subspecies/Population	Breeding range	Wintering, or core non-breeding range	Afr	Eu	Asia	Oc	Neo	NA	Estimate	Source	Trend	Source	1% level	Notes
melanopterus, Ethiopia	Ethiopia, extreme E Sudan		•						10,000–50,000	DO			300	
minor, Kenya, Tanzania	SW Kenya to CN Tanzania		•							A	DO		100	
minor, Southern Africa	South Africa, NE Transvaal to E Cape Province	*Coastal Southern Africa, S Mozambique–E Cape*	•						2,000–3,000	UN	DEC	HF	25	

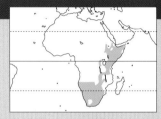

Vanellus coronatus — Crowned Lapwing

Subspecies/Population	Breeding range	Wintering, or core non-breeding range	Afr	Eu	Asia	Oc	Neo	NA	Estimate	Source	Trend	Source	1% level	Notes
coronatus, Eastern & Southern Africa	Ethiopia, Kenya, Tanzania to Zambia & Zimbabwe		•						400,000–900,000	DO			6,500	
coronatus, C Africa	SW Uganda, E D R Congo, Rwanda, Burundi		•							A/B	DO		250	
(*xerophilus*)	SW Angola, Namibia, Botswana, W Zimbabwe, SW Transvaal		•							B/C	DO	INC	HF	1,000	Often included in *coronatus*.
demissus	Somalia		•							B/C	P1			1,000	

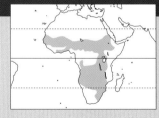

Vanellus senegallus — African Wattled Lapwing

Subspecies/Population	Breeding range	Wintering, or core non-breeding range	Afr	Eu	Asia	Oc	Neo	NA	Estimate	Source	Trend	Source	1% level	Notes
senegallus	SW Mauritania, Senegal, E to Sudan, N Uganda		•						25,000–60,000	DO			450	
(*solitaneus*)	S D R Congo & Angola		•							B/C	DO			1,000	
lateralis	S Uganda, S to NE South Africa		•							C	DO	STA	HF	1,000	10,000–20,000 in Southern Africa (UN).
major	W & C Ethiopia, Eritrea		•						5,000–15,000	P1			100	

Vanellus melanocephalus — Spot-breasted Lapwing

Subspecies/Population	Breeding range	Wintering, or core non-breeding range	Afr	Eu	Asia	Oc	Neo	NA	Estimate	Source	Trend	Source	1% level	Notes
Ethiopia	Ethiopian highlands		•							A	FE			100	

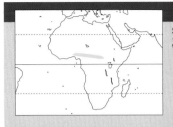

Vanellus superciliosus — Brown-chested Lapwing

Subspecies/Population	Breeding range	Wintering, or core non-breeding range	Afr	Eu	Asia	Oc	Neo	NA	Estimate	Source	Trend	Source	1% level	Notes
W, C & E Africa	Togo–NE D R Congo?	*E Ghana, Cameroon, S Chad, D R Congo, S Uganda, Tanzania*	•						A/B	DO			250	

Vanellus cinereus — Grey-headed Lapwing

Subspecies/Population	Breeding range	Wintering, or core non-breeding range	Afr	Eu	Asia	Oc	Neo	NA	Estimate	Source	Trend	Source	1% level	Notes
E, SE & S Asia	NE China, neighbouring Russia, Japan	*NE India, Nepal, Bangladesh, SE & E Asia*			•				C	CE	**DEC**	PE	1,000	

Vanellus indicus — Red-wattled Lapwing

Subspecies/Population	Breeding range	Wintering, or core non-breeding range	Afr	Eu	Asia	Oc	Neo	NA	Estimate	Source	Trend	Source	1% level
indicus	S Asia				•								
aigneri	SE Turkey, Iraq, Iran, E Arabia, Pakistan				•								
lankae	Sri Lanka				•				5,000–6,000	HT			55
atronuchalis	NE India & Myanmar to N Malaysia & Vietnam				•								

Red-wattled Lapwing.

Paul Goriup

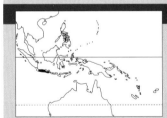

Vanellus macropterus CR — Javanese Wattled Lapwing, Sunda Lapwing

Subspecies/Population	Breeding range	Wintering, or core non-breeding range	Afr	Eu	Asia	Oc	Neo	NA	Estimate	Source	Trend	Source	1% level	Notes
Java	Java				•				<50	BC	**EXT?**	BC	1	Last recorded in 1940 (BC).

Vanellus tricolor — Banded Lapwing

Subspecies/Population	Breeding range	Wintering, or core non-breeding range	Afr	Eu	Asia	Oc	Neo	NA	Estimate	Source	Trend	Source	1% level
Australia	S Australia					•			27,000	WD			270

Banded Lapwing.

Johannes Wahl

Vanellus miles — Masked Lapwing

Subspecies/Population	Breeding range	Wintering, or core non-breeding range	Afr	Eu	Asia	Oc	Neo	NA	Estimate	Source	Trend	Source	1% level	Notes
miles	NE & S New Guinea, Aru Is, SE Wallacea, N Australia					•	•		170,000	B3			1,700	
novaehollandiae	E, SE Australia & New Zealand	E, S Australia & New Zealand				•			127,000	B3	INC	ON	1,300	This population reached New Zealand in 20th Century and is still increasing (HV). Also New Caledonia, where 50–100 birds (B5).

Vanellus gregarius VU — Sociable Lapwing

Subspecies/Population	Breeding range	Wintering, or core non-breeding range	Afr	Eu	Asia	Oc	Neo	NA	Estimate	Source	Trend	Source	1% level	Notes
NE Africa (Non-br)	S C Russia & Kazakhstan	Israel, Arabian Peninsula, Sudan, Eritrea	•	•	•				400–1,200	SW	DEC	SW	8	This species is in catastrophic decline. TP: World Population estimated in April 2002 to be 200–600 breeding pairs (600–1,800 individuals). Proportion of populations using the 2 wintering areas suggested by Lebedeva & Tomkovich in litt. Often assigned to genus *Chettusia*.
S Asia (Non-br)	S C Russia & Kazakhstan	NW India, Pakistan to Sri Lanka			•				200–600	SW	DEC	PE	2	

Vanellus leucurus — White-tailed Lapwing

Subspecies/Population	Breeding range	Wintering, or core non-breeding range	Afr	Eu	Asia	Oc	Neo	NA	Estimate	Source	Trend	Source	1% level	Notes
SW Asia, NE Africa (Non-br)	C & SE Turkey, E Syria, Caspian	SW Asia & NE Africa (Sudan)	•		•				B	SW	DEC?	SW	250	Often assigned to genus *Chettusia*.
S Asia (Non-br)	Central Asian Republics	C & E Pakistan, NC & NW India			•				B/C	PE	INC?	SW	1,000	

Vanellus cayanus — Pied Lapwing

Subspecies/Population	Breeding range	Wintering, or core non-breeding range	Afr	Eu	Asia	Oc	Neo	NA	Estimate	Source	Trend	Source	1% level	Notes
South America	S America E of Andes: Colombia-Amazon S to Misiones (Argentina)						•							Sometimes placed in genus *Hoploxypterus*.

Vanellus chilensis — Southern Lapwing

Subspecies/Population	Breeding range	Wintering, or core non-breeding range	Afr	Eu	Asia	Oc	Neo	NA	Estimate	Source	Trend	Source	1% level	Notes
chilensis	Argentina & Chile S to Chiloe Is & Comodora Rivadavia						•		E	S8	INC	S8		
fretensis	S Chile & S Argentina						•		E	S8	INC	S8		
cayennensis	South America E of Andes, N of R Amazon						•				STA	AT		
lampronotus	S of R Amazon–Brazil, N Chile, N Argentina						•				STA	AT		

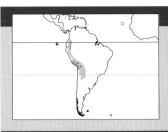

Vanellus resplendens — Andean Lapwing

Subspecies/Population	Breeding range	Wintering, or core non-breeding range	Afr	Eu	Asia	Oc	Neo	NA	Estimate	Source	Trend	Source	1% level	Notes
Andean South America	Andes, SW Colombia–N Chile, NW Argentina						•		A	S8	STA	S8	100	

Erythrogonys cinctus — Red-kneed Dotterel

Subspecies/Population	Breeding range	Wintering, or core non-breeding range	Afr	Eu	Asia	Oc	Neo	NA	Estimate	Source	Trend	Source	1% level	Notes
Australia	Australia, extreme S New Guinea					•			26,000	WD			260	Sometimes included in Vanellinae.

Red-kneed Dotterel.

Ian Montgomery

Pluvialis apricaria — Eurasian Golden Plover

Subspecies/Population	Breeding range	Wintering, or core non-breeding range	Afr	Eu	Asia	Oc	Neo	NA	Estimate	Source	Trend	Source	1% level	Notes
apricaria	Britain, Ireland, Denmark, Germany, Baltic States	*NW Europe*	•	•					69,000	SW	DEC	SW	650	SW prefer 1% level of 650 because estimate based on 1980s data and population declining.
altifrons, Iceland & Faeroes, E Atlantic	Iceland & Faeroes	*Ireland, W Britain, France, Iberia, NW Africa*	•	•					930,000	SW	STA?	SW	9,300	
altifrons, NW Europe, W Continental Europe, NW Africa	N Norway, Russia E to 70 °E	*W & S Continental Europe, NW Africa (Morocco to Tunisia)*	•	•					645,000–954,000	SW	STA	SW	8,000	
altifrons, N-Central Siberia (br)	N-Central Siberia E to 100° E	*Caspian Region, Asia Minor, E Mediterranean?*		•	•									

Pluvialis fulva — Pacific Golden Plover

Subspecies/Population	Breeding range	Wintering, or core non-breeding range	Afr	Eu	Asia	Oc	Neo	NA	Estimate	Source	Trend	Source	1% level	Notes
SW & S Asia, E Africa (non-br)	North C & E Siberia	*SW, S Asia & E Africa*	•		•				50,000–100,000	SW			750	
E, SE Asia Australia & Oceania (non-br)	North C & E Siberia	*E, SE Asia, Australia & Pacific islands*			•	•			100,000	B3			1,000	
Pacific Islands (non-br)	W Alaska	*Pacific Islands to New Zealand & E Australia*				•		•	16,000	MU			160	Alaska breeding population is 16,000 (MU). 3,500 winter in New Caledonia (B5).

Pluvialis dominica — American Golden Plover

Subspecies/Population	Breeding range	Wintering, or core non-breeding range	Afr	Eu	Asia	Oc	Neo	NA	Estimate	Source	Trend	Source	1% level	Notes
Americas	W Alaska E through N Canada to Baffin Is	*C & S South America*					•	•	150,000	MU	DEC	BO	1,500	

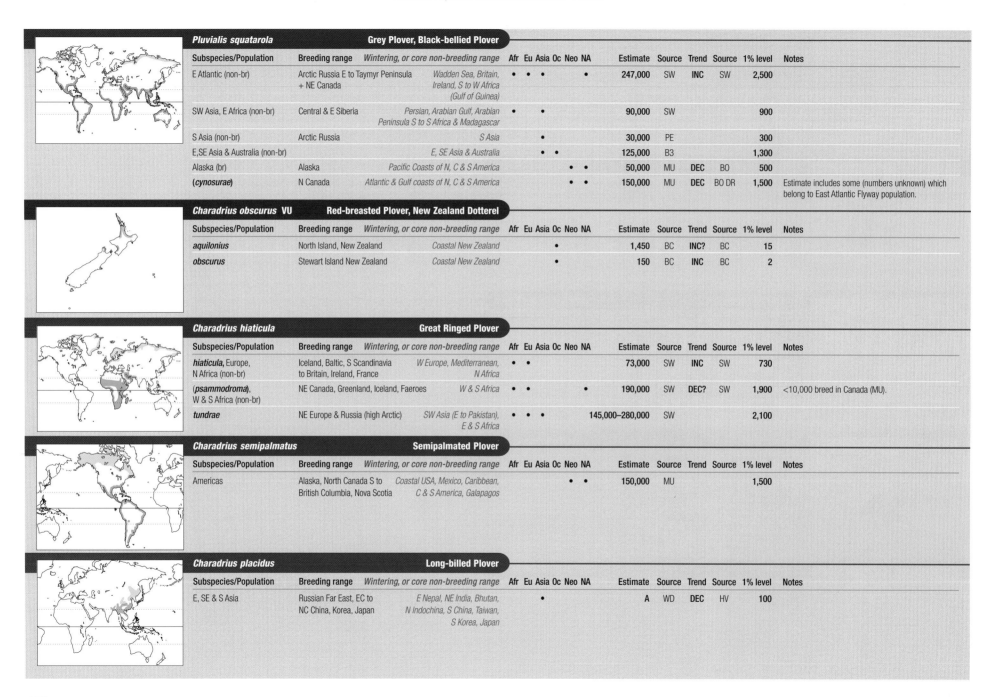

Pluvialis squatarola — Grey Plover, Black-bellied Plover

Subspecies/Population	Breeding range	Wintering, or core non-breeding range	Afr	Eu	Asia	Oc	Neo	NA	Estimate	Source	Trend	Source	1% level	Notes
E Atlantic (non-br)	Arctic Russia E to Taymyr Peninsula + NE Canada	Wadden Sea, Britain, Ireland, S to W Africa (Gulf of Guinea)	•	•	•			•	247,000	SW	INC	SW	2,500	
SW Asia, E Africa (non-br)	Central & E Siberia	Persian, Arabian Gulf, Arabian Peninsula S to S Africa & Madagascar	•		•				90,000	SW			900	
S Asia (non-br)	Arctic Russia	S Asia			•				30,000	PE			300	
E,SE Asia & Australia (non-br)		E, SE Asia & Australia			•	•			125,000	B3			1,300	
Alaska (br)	Alaska	Pacific Coasts of N, C & S America					•	•	50,000	MU	DEC	BO	500	
(cynosurae)	N Canada	Atlantic & Gulf coasts of N, C & S America					•	•	150,000	MU	DEC	BO DR	1,500	Estimate includes some (numbers unknown) which belong to East Atlantic Flyway population.

Charadrius obscurus VU — Red-breasted Plover, New Zealand Dotterel

Subspecies/Population	Breeding range	Wintering, or core non-breeding range	Afr	Eu	Asia	Oc	Neo	NA	Estimate	Source	Trend	Source	1% level	Notes
aquilonius	North Island, New Zealand	Coastal New Zealand				•			1,450	BC	INC?	BC	15	
obscurus	Stewart Island New Zealand	Coastal New Zealand				•			150	BC	INC	BC	2	

Charadrius hiaticula — Great Ringed Plover

Subspecies/Population	Breeding range	Wintering, or core non-breeding range	Afr	Eu	Asia	Oc	Neo	NA	Estimate	Source	Trend	Source	1% level	Notes
hiaticula, Europe, N Africa (non-br)	Iceland, Baltic, S Scandinavia to Britain, Ireland, France	W Europe, Mediterranean, N Africa	•	•					73,000	SW	INC	SW	730	
(psammodroma), W & S Africa (non-br)	NE Canada, Greenland, Iceland, Faeroes	W & S Africa	•	•				•	190,000	SW	DEC?	SW	1,900	<10,000 breed in Canada (MU).
tundrae	NE Europe & Russia (high Arctic)	SW Asia (E to Pakistan), E & S Africa	•	•	•				145,000–280,000	SW			2,100	

Charadrius semipalmatus — Semipalmated Plover

Subspecies/Population	Breeding range	Wintering, or core non-breeding range	Afr	Eu	Asia	Oc	Neo	NA	Estimate	Source	Trend	Source	1% level	Notes
Americas	Alaska, North Canada S to British Columbia, Nova Scotia	Coastal USA, Mexico, Caribbean, C & S America, Galapagos					•	•	150,000	MU			1,500	

Charadrius placidus — Long-billed Plover

Subspecies/Population	Breeding range	Wintering, or core non-breeding range	Afr	Eu	Asia	Oc	Neo	NA	Estimate	Source	Trend	Source	1% level	Notes
E, SE & S Asia	Russian Far East, EC to NC China, Korea, Japan	E Nepal, NE India, Bhutan, N Indochina, S China, Taiwan, S Korea, Japan			•				A	WD	DEC	HV	100	

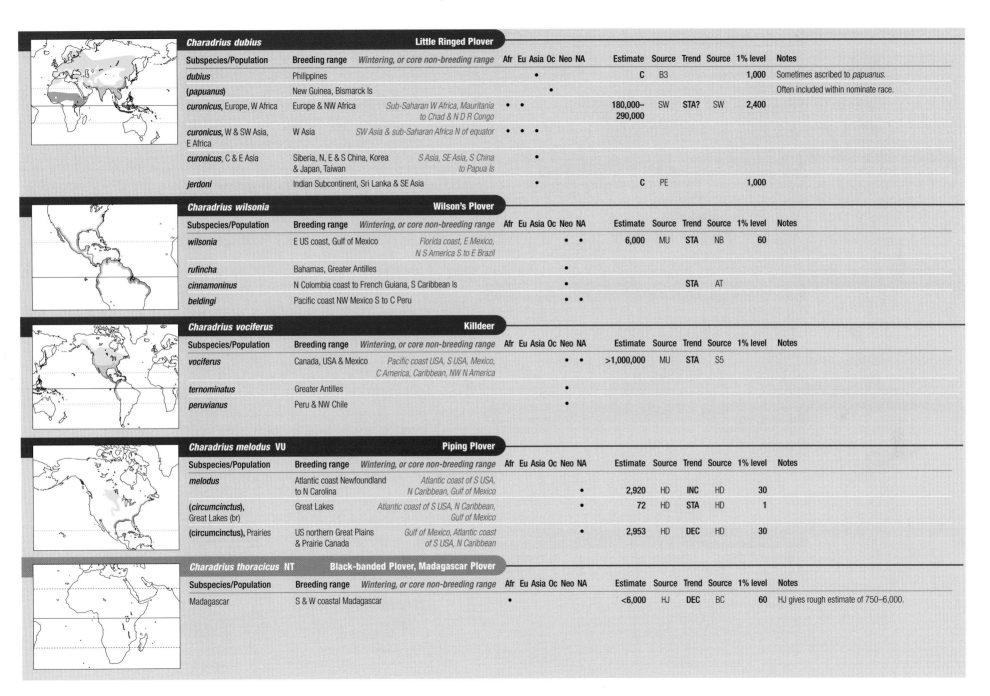

Charadrius dubius — Little Ringed Plover

Subspecies/Population	Breeding range	Wintering, or core non-breeding range	Afr	Eu	Asia	Oc	Neo	NA	Estimate	Source	Trend	Source	1% level	Notes
dubius	Philippines					•			C	B3			1,000	Sometimes ascribed to papuanus.
(papuanus)	New Guinea, Bismarck Is					•								Often included within nominate race.
curonicus, Europe, W Africa	Europe & NW Africa	Sub-Saharan W Africa, Mauritania to Chad & N D R Congo	•	•					180,000–290,000	SW	STA?	SW	2,400	
curonicus, W & SW Asia, E Africa	W Asia	SW Asia & sub-Saharan Africa N of equator	•	•	•									
curonicus, C & E Asia	Siberia, N, E & S China, Korea & Japan, Taiwan	S Asia, SE Asia, S China to Papua Is			•									
jerdoni	Indian Subcontinent, Sri Lanka & SE Asia				•				C	PE			1,000	

Charadrius wilsonia — Wilson's Plover

Subspecies/Population	Breeding range	Wintering, or core non-breeding range	Afr	Eu	Asia	Oc	Neo	NA	Estimate	Source	Trend	Source	1% level	Notes
wilsonia	E US coast, Gulf of Mexico	Florida coast, E Mexico, N S America S to E Brazil					•	•	6,000	MU	STA	NB	60	
rufincha	Bahamas, Greater Antilles						•							
cinnamoninus	N Colombia coast to French Guiana, S Caribbean Is						•				STA	AT		
beldingi	Pacific coast NW Mexico S to C Peru						•	•						

Charadrius vociferus — Killdeer

Subspecies/Population	Breeding range	Wintering, or core non-breeding range	Afr	Eu	Asia	Oc	Neo	NA	Estimate	Source	Trend	Source	1% level	Notes
vociferus	Canada, USA & Mexico	Pacific coast USA, S USA, Mexico, C America, Caribbean, NW N America					•	•	>1,000,000	MU	STA	S5		
ternominatus	Greater Antilles						•							
peruvianus	Peru & NW Chile						•							

Charadrius melodus VU — Piping Plover

Subspecies/Population	Breeding range	Wintering, or core non-breeding range	Afr	Eu	Asia	Oc	Neo	NA	Estimate	Source	Trend	Source	1% level	Notes
melodus	Atlantic coast Newfoundland to N Carolina	Atlantic coast of S USA, N Caribbean, Gulf of Mexico						•	2,920	HD	INC	HD	30	
(circumcinctus), Great Lakes (br)	Great Lakes	Atlantic coast of S USA, N Caribbean, Gulf of Mexico						•	72	HD	STA	HD	1	
(circumcinctus), Prairies	US northern Great Plains & Prairie Canada	Gulf of Mexico, Atlantic coast of S USA, N Caribbean						•	2,953	HD	DEC	HD	30	

Charadrius thoracicus NT — Black-banded Plover, Madagascar Plover

Subspecies/Population	Breeding range	Wintering, or core non-breeding range	Afr	Eu	Asia	Oc	Neo	NA	Estimate	Source	Trend	Source	1% level	Notes
Madagascar	S & W coastal Madagascar		•						<6,000	HJ	DEC	BC	60	HJ gives rough estimate of 750–6,000.

157

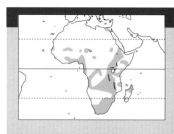

Charadrius pecuarius — Kittlitz's Plover

Subspecies/Population	Breeding range	Wintering, or core non-breeding range	Afr	Eu	Asia	Oc	Neo	NA	Estimate	Source	Trend	Source	1% level	Notes
pecuarius, E, C & S Africa	E, C & S Africa		•						>100,000	DO			1,000	
pecuarius, West Africa	West Africa								20,000–50,000	DO			350	
pecuarius, Madagascar	Madagascar								10,000–20,000	P1			150	
(allenbyi)	Nile Valley		•						1,000–5,000	P1			30	
(tephricolor)	SW Africa & N Botswana		•						A	DO			100	

Charadrius sanctaehelenae EN — St. Helena Plover

Subspecies/Population	Breeding range	Wintering, or core non-breeding range	Afr	Eu	Asia	Oc	Neo	NA	Estimate	Source	Trend	Source	1% level	Notes
Saint Helena	Saint Helena		•						435	DO	STA	DO	4	450 in 1988–1989, 315 in 1993 and 435 in 2001 (DO).

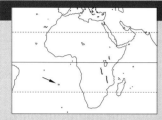

Charadrius tricollaris — Three-banded Plover

Subspecies/Population	Breeding range	Wintering, or core non-breeding range	Afr	Eu	Asia	Oc	Neo	NA	Estimate	Source	Trend	Source	1% level	Notes
tricollaris, E & S Africa	Ethiopia to Tanzania and Gabon, S to South Africa	*Ethiopia to Tanzania and Gabon, S to South Africa*	•						70,000–130,000	DO			1,000	Increasing in southern Africa (HF).
tricollaris, Lake Chad	Lake Chad basin		•						A	DO			100	
bifrontatus	Madagascar		•						10,000–30,000	P1			200	

Charadrius forbesi — Forbes's Plover

Subspecies/Population	Breeding range	Wintering, or core non-breeding range	Afr	Eu	Asia	Oc	Neo	NA	Estimate	Source	Trend	Source	1% level	Notes
Sub-Saharan Africa	Ghana E to S Sudan, S to C & S Angola, W Zambia	*Senegal E to S Sudan, S to C & S Angola, W Zambia*	•						B/C	DO			1,000	

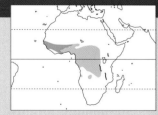

Charadrius marginatus — White-fronted Plover

Subspecies/Population	Breeding range	Wintering, or core non-breeding range	Afr	Eu	Asia	Oc	Neo	NA	Estimate	Source	Trend	Source	1% level	Notes
marginatus	S Angola to SW Cape		•						18,000	SX			180	
tenellus	Madagascar		•						5,000–15,000	HJ	DEC	HF	100	
mechowi, Inland E & C Africa	Inland E & C Africa S to N Angola, Botswana, Zimbabwe, N Mozambique		•						10,000–15,000	P1			130	
mechowi, Coastal E Africa	Coastal E Africa Somalia to Tanzania		•						15,000–25,000	DO			200	Includes "*pons*" in S Somalia.
arenaceus	S Mozambique to SW Cape		•						8,000–12,000	P1			100	
hesperius	W Africa to Central African Rep		•						10,000–15,000	P1			130	includes "*nigrius*" and "*spatzi*".

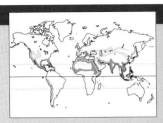

Charadrius alexandrinus — Kentish Plover, Snowy Plover

Subspecies/Population	Breeding range	Wintering, or core non-breeding range	Afr	Eu	Asia	Oc	Neo	NA	Estimate	Source	Trend	Source	1% level	Notes
alexandrinus, E Atlantic, W Mediterranean	Coastal W Mediterranean & W Europe N to Sweden	*Coastal SW Europe NW & W Africa*	•	•					62,000–70,000	SW	DEC	SW	660	
alexandrinus, Black Sea, E Mediterranean (Br)	Black Sea & E Mediterranean	*E Mediterranean & Red Seas & E Sahel zone*	•	•	•				32,000–49,000	SW	DEC?	SW	410	
alexandrinus, SW Asia, NE Africa (Non-br)	SW Asia	*S Caspian to Arabian Peninsula, NE Africa*	•		•				C	SW			1,000	
alexandrinus, S Asia (Non-br)	Central Asia	*S Asia*			•				C	PE			1,000	
dealbatus	Korea, Japan, Ryukyu Island to E & SE China, Taiwan	*Korea, E & SE China, Taiwan, S to Philippines & N Borneo*			•				100,000	B3			1,000	The birds breeding in Japan are sometimes ascribed to *C. a. nihonensis.*
seebohmi	Sri Lanka, SE India				•				5,000–10,000	HT			75	
nivosus, Interior Atlantic	Interior US & Atlantic coast	*S USA, Mexico, Caribbean*					•	•	13,200	BO DR	DEC	BO DR	130	P. Paton graduate study suggests 10,000 breeding adults at Great Salt Lake, Utah.
nivosus, Pacific	Pacific coast of Washington to California, Baja California, W Mexico	*California & Mexico*					•	•	2,000	BO DR	DEC	BO DR	20	
(tenuirostris)	Gulf of Mexico Coast & Caribbean	*Caribbean, Cuba, Bahamas*					•	•	2,200–2,800	GR	DEC	BO	25	GR estimate 200 pairs Florida–Alabama, possibly 500–700 pairs in Texas, 27 pairs on Puerto Rico, 17+ pairs in Cuba (all these pairs x 3 yield 2,232–2,832 individuals).
occidentalis	Coastal Peru to SC Chile						•		A	S8	DEC	S8	100	Sometimes considered a separate species: Peruvian Plover.

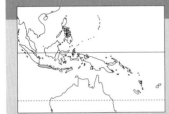

Charadrius javanicus NT — Javan Plover

Subspecies/Population	Breeding range	Wintering, or core non-breeding range	Afr	Eu	Asia	Oc	Neo	NA	Estimate	Source	Trend	Source	1% level	Notes
SE Asia	Java & Kangean Is					•								Data-deficient species (HV).

Charadrius ruficapillus — Red-capped Plover

Subspecies/Population	Breeding range	Wintering, or core non-breeding range	Afr	Eu	Asia	Oc	Neo	NA	Estimate	Source	Trend	Source	1% level	Notes
Australia	Australia					•			95,000	WD			950	

Charadrius peronii NT — Malaysian Plover

Subspecies/Population	Breeding range	Wintering, or core non-breeding range	Afr	Eu	Asia	Oc	Neo	NA	Estimate	Source	Trend	Source	1% level	Notes
SE Asia	SE Asia, Indonesia, Philippines					•			B	(BC)			250	

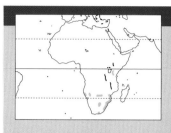

Charadrius pallidus — Chestnut-banded Plover

Subspecies/Population	Breeding range	Wintering, or core non-breeding range	Afr	Eu	Asia	Oc	Neo	NA	Estimate	Source	Trend	Source	1% level	Notes
pallidus	Coastal S Africa, Angola–Mozambique, N Namibia, N Botswana, N South Africa		•						11,200	SJ	STA	HF	110	SJ reports a simultaneous count in Namibia of 11,192 birds.
venustus	East African Rift Valley, Kenya–Tanzania	East African Rift Valley	•						4,000–5,000	P1			45	SJ reports a maximum coordinated count by AfWC from Kenya and Tanzania of <1,600 birds.

Charadrius collaris — Collared Plover

Subspecies/Population	Breeding range	Wintering, or core non-breeding range	Afr	Eu	Asia	Oc	Neo	NA	Estimate	Source	Trend	Source	1% level	Notes
collaris	C & S Brazil S to N Argentina; C Chile						•		A	S8	DEC	S8	100	
gracilis	Mexico S to N Brazil, W Ecuador						•	•						

Charadrius alticola — Puna Plover

Subspecies/Population	Breeding range	Wintering, or core non-breeding range	Afr	Eu	Asia	Oc	Neo	NA	Estimate	Source	Trend	Source	1% level	Notes
Andean South America	Andes of C Peru to N Chile, W Bolivia, N Argentina	Central Andes, S Peruvian coast					•		C/D	S8				

Charadrius falklandicus — Two-banded Plover

Subspecies/Population	Breeding range	Wintering, or core non-breeding range	Afr	Eu	Asia	Oc	Neo	NA	Estimate	Source	Trend	Source	1% level	Notes
S South America	C & S Chile & Argentina, S Brazil	N Chile & S Brazil S to S Chile, Argentina					•		C	BF	STA	AT	1,000	
Falkland/Malvinas Is	Falkland/Malvinas Is						•		21,000–39,000	WS			300	WS estimate 7,000–13,000 pairs (21,000–39,000 individuals). This population is possibly subspecifically distinct (HV).

Charadrius bicinctus — Double-banded Plover

Subspecies/Population	Breeding range	Wintering, or core non-breeding range	Afr	Eu	Asia	Oc	Neo	NA	Estimate	Source	Trend	Source	1% level	Notes
bicinctus	New Zealand & Chatham Is	N Zealand, S & E Australia, Tasmania, S Melanesia				•			50,000	S1			500	30,000 migrate to Australia.
exilis	Auckland Islands	Auckland Islands, Enderby Is				•			700	ON			7	

Charadrius mongolus — Lesser Sandplover, Mongolian Plover

Subspecies/Population	Breeding range	Wintering, or core non-breeding range	Afr	Eu	Asia	Oc	Neo	NA	Estimate	Source	Trend	Source	1% level	Notes
mongolus	Inland E Siberia, Russian Far East	Taiwan to Australia			•									
pamirensis	Central Asia	Coastal W India, SW Asia, E & SE Africa	•		•				30,000–50,000	SW			400	
atrifrons	Himalaya, S Tibet	India to Sumatra			•				100,000	PE			1,000	
schaeferi	E Tibet to S Mongolia	Coast Thailand to Greater Sunda Is			•									
stegmanni	Kolymskiy, Kamchatka, N Kuril Is N to Chukotskiy	Kyushu, Izu Bonin & Ryukyu Is (Japan) & Taiwan to Australia			•	•								

Charadrius leschenaultii — Greater Sandplover

Subspecies/Population	Breeding range	Wintering, or core non-breeding range	Afr	Eu	Asia	Oc	Neo	NA	Estimate	Source	Trend	Source	1% level	Notes
leschenaultii, South Asia (non-br)	Central Asia	Coastal S Asia			•				C	PE			1,000	
leschenaultii, E Africa (non-br)	E Kazakhstan, Kyrgyzstan & Xingjiang	S Somalia to S Africa, Madagascar	•		•				25,000–50,000	DO			380	
leschenaultii, SE Asia, Australia (non-br)	W China, S Mongolia, S Siberia & Altai Mts	Coastal Indochina, S Japan, Taiwan, Indonesia, Philippines, New Guinea, Australia			•	•			100,000	B3			1,000	
columbinus	Turkey, Syria, Jordan, S Afghanistan	Red Sea, Gulf of Aden, SE Mediterranean	•	•	•				A	RS			100	
crassirostris	Transcaspia E to SE Kazakhstan, Armenia, Azerbaijan	Shores of Red Sea, Gulf of Aden & Persian Gulf	•	•	•				C	SW			1,000	Birds in Azerbaijan & Armenia identified as belonging to this subspecies by HR.

Charadrius asiaticus — Caspian Plover

Subspecies/Population	Breeding range	Wintering, or core non-breeding range	Afr	Eu	Asia	Oc	Neo	NA	Estimate	Source	Trend	Source	1% level	Notes
Central Asia (br)	W N & E Caspian E to E Kazakhstan, NW China	NE, E & Southern Africa	•	•	•				40,000–55,000	DO	DEC	BE	480	

Charadrius veredus — Oriental Plover

Subspecies/Population	Breeding range	Wintering, or core non-breeding range	Afr	Eu	Asia	Oc	Neo	NA	Estimate	Source	Trend	Source	1% level	Notes
Central Asia (br)	S Siberia, W N & E Mongolia, NE China	Greater Sundas, Philippines to NW & NC Australia			•	•			70,000	B3			700	

Charadrius morinellus — Eurasian Dotterel

Subspecies/Population	Breeding range	Wintering, or core non-breeding range	Afr	Eu	Asia	Oc	Neo	NA	Estimate	Source	Trend	Source	1% level	Notes
Europe (br)	Europe (mostly Scandinavia, Scotland)	*NW Africa*	•	•					39,000–110,000	SW	STA/DEC	SW	750	Often placed in genus *Eudromias*.
Siberia, Central Asia (br)	N Siberia, Upland E C Asia	*SW Asia E to W Iran*			•				B/C	PE			1,000	

Charadrius modestus — Rufous-chested Dotterel

Subspecies/Population	Breeding range	Wintering, or core non-breeding range	Afr	Eu	Asia	Oc	Neo	NA	Estimate	Source	Trend	Source	1% level	Notes
S South America	SC & S Chile, WC & S Argentina	*Chile, S & E Argentina N to S Brazil*					•		D	S8			10,000	
Falkland/Malvinas Is	Falkland/Malvinas Is	*Chile, S & E Argentina N to S Brazil*					•		33,000–63,000	WS			480	WS estimate 11,000–21,000 pairs (33,000–63,000 individuals).

Charadrius montanus VU — Mountain Plover

Subspecies/Population	Breeding range	Wintering, or core non-breeding range	Afr	Eu	Asia	Oc	Neo	NA	Estimate	Source	Trend	Source	1% level	Notes
N America	C N America: S Canada to New Mexico & W Texas	*C & S California, E to S Texas, N Mexico*						•	8,000–9,000	BC MU	DEC	BC	85	

Charadrius rubricollis NT — Hooded Plover

Subspecies/Population	Breeding range	Wintering, or core non-breeding range	Afr	Eu	Asia	Oc	Neo	NA	Estimate	Source	Trend	Source	1% level	Notes
rubricollis	SE Australia					•			4,500	GC	DEC	BC	45	GC estimates 3,000 breeding adults (4,500 individuals). Sometimes ascribed to genus *Thinornis*.
(*tregellasi*)	Western Australia					•			6,000	GC	STA	GC	60	GC estimates 4,000 breeding adults (6,000 individuals). Sometimes ascribed to genus *Thinornis*.

Thinornis novaeseelandiae EN — Shore Plover

Subspecies/Population	Breeding range	Wintering, or core non-breeding range	Afr	Eu	Asia	Oc	Neo	NA	Estimate	Source	Trend	Source	1% level	Notes
Chatham Islands	Rangatira Is SE Chatham Islands + 2 introduced pops on offshore islands					•			159	BC	STA	BC	2	BC reports123 Rangatira, 21 on reef in Chatham group, 2 introduced populations of 5 and 10. KJ estimated 125.

Elseyornis melanops   Black-fronted Dotterel

Subspecies/Population	Breeding range	Wintering, or core non-breeding range	Afr	Eu	Asia	Oc	Neo	NA	Estimate	Source	Trend	Source	1% level	Notes
Australia	Australia					•			15,500	WD			160	WD estimates 17,000 for both populations combined.
New Zealand	New Zealand					•			1,600	HV			15	Colonised New Zealand in late 1950s; now c.1,600 individuals (HV).

Peltohyas australis   Inland Dotterel

Subspecies/Population	Breeding range	Wintering, or core non-breeding range	Afr	Eu	Asia	Oc	Neo	NA	Estimate	Source	Trend	Source	1% level	Notes
Australia	SW, SC & EC Australia					•			14,000	WD			140	

Anarhynchus frontalis VU   Wrybill

Subspecies/Population	Breeding range	Wintering, or core non-breeding range	Afr	Eu	Asia	Oc	Neo	NA	Estimate	Source	Trend	Source	1% level	Notes
New Zealand	Central South Island New Zealand	N North Island New Zealand				•			4,100–4,200	AO	DEC	BC	40	

Wrybill.

Nils Anthes

Phegornis mitchellii NT   Diademed Plover, Diademed Sandpiper-Plover

Subspecies/Population	Breeding range	Wintering, or core non-breeding range	Afr	Eu	Asia	Oc	Neo	NA	Estimate	Source	Trend	Source	1% level	Notes
Andean South America	Andes, NC Peru S to SC Chile & Argentina						•		A	S8	DEC	S8	100	

Oreopholus ruficollis   Tawny-throated Dotterel

Subspecies/Population	Breeding range	Wintering, or core non-breeding range	Afr	Eu	Asia	Oc	Neo	NA	Estimate	Source	Trend	Source	1% level	Notes
ruficollis	W S America: W C Peru S to Tierra del Fuego	Ecuador S to Chile, S & E Argentina, SE Brazil					•		A	S8			100	
pallidus	Coastal N Peru						•							

163

SCOLOPACIDAE SNIPES, SANDPIPERS & PHALAROPES

Pluvianellus socialis NT — Magellanic Plover

Subspecies/Population	Breeding range	Wintering, or core non-breeding range	Afr	Eu	Asia	Oc	Neo	NA	Estimate	Source	Trend	Source	1% level	Notes
S South America	Extreme S South America	*Extreme S South America N to Peninsula Valdez*					•		A	S8	DEC	S8	100	Now often placed in its own family Pluvianellidae.

Scolopax rusticola — Eurasian Woodcock

Subspecies/Population	Breeding range	Wintering, or core non-breeding range	Afr	Eu	Asia	Oc	Neo	NA	Estimate	Source	Trend	Source	1% level	Notes
Europe (Br)	N, E, C and parts of W Europe	*W & S Europe, N Africa*	•	•					>15,000,000	HR	STA	FB	20,000	For populations over 2 million birds, Ramsar Convention criterion 5 (20,000 or more waterbirds), applies.
W Asia (br)	W Siberia	*SW Asia (Caspian region)*		•	•									
C & E Asia (br)	Central Asia to Sakhalin & Japan	*N India, Indochina–SE China*			•				C/D	B3				

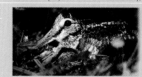

Eurasian Woodcock.

Dennis Bright

Scolopax mira VU — Amami Woodcock

Subspecies/Population	Breeding range	Wintering, or core non-breeding range	Afr	Eu	Asia	Oc	Neo	NA	Estimate	Source	Trend	Source	1% level	Notes
mira	Central Ryukyu Islands				•				2,500–10,000	BC	DEC	BC	60	

Scolopax saturata — Dusky Woodcock, Rufous Woodcock

Subspecies/Population	Breeding range	Wintering, or core non-breeding range	Afr	Eu	Asia	Oc	Neo	NA	Estimate	Source	Trend	Source	1% level	Notes
saturata	Mountains of N & SC Sumatra & W Java				•									
rosenbergi	Mountains of New Guinea					•								

Scolopax celebensis NT — Sulawesi Woodcock

Subspecies/Population	Breeding range	Wintering, or core non-breeding range	Afr	Eu	Asia	Oc	Neo	NA	Estimate	Source	Trend	Source	1% level	Notes
celebensis	NE & C Sulawesi				•									
(heinrichi)	N Sulawesi				•									Known from 3 specimens.

Scolopax bukidnonensis — Bukidnon Woodcock

Subspecies/Population	Breeding range	Wintering, or core non-breeding range	Afr	Eu	Asia	Oc	Neo	NA	Estimate	Source	Trend	Source	1% level	Notes
Philippines	Philippines (Central & N Luzon + parts of Mindanao)					•								Discovered in 1993 (KK).

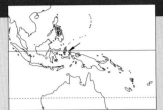

Scolopax rochussenii VU — Moluccan Woodcock

Subspecies/Population	Breeding range	Wintering, or core non-breeding range	Afr	Eu	Asia	Oc	Neo	NA	Estimate	Source	Trend	Source	1% level	Notes
N Moluccas	N Moluccas (Obi & Bacan Is)					•			2,500–10,000	BC	DEC	BC	60	

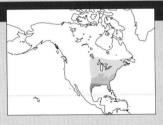

Scolopax minor — American Woodcock

Subspecies/Population	Breeding range	Wintering, or core non-breeding range	Afr	Eu	Asia	Oc	Neo	NA	Estimate	Source	Trend	Source	1% level	Notes
Atlantic N America (br)	SE Canada, NE & Atlantic USA	S Atlantic States SE USA						•			DEC	KI		Total, both populations, 5,000,000 (MU).
Inland E N America (br)	Inland E Canada & USA S of 51N	S Texas to S Florida						•			DEC	KI		

Coenocorypha pusilla VU — Chatham (Island) Snipe

Subspecies/Population	Breeding range	Wintering, or core non-breeding range	Afr	Eu	Asia	Oc	Neo	NA	Estimate	Source	Trend	Source	1% level	Notes
Chatham Islands	Chatham Islands					•			2,000	BC	STA	BC	20	

Coenocorypha aucklandica NT — Subantarctic Snipe

Subspecies/Population	Breeding range	Wintering, or core non-breeding range	Afr	Eu	Asia	Oc	Neo	NA	Estimate	Source	Trend	Source	1% level	Notes
aucklandica	Auckland Islands					•			20,000	BC			200	BC gives an estimate of 30,000 for all subspecies, with two thirds on the Auckland Is. Clements (2000) lists an undescribed subspecies on the Campbell Islands.
meinertzhagenae	Antipodes Islands					•			8,000	MI			80	
heugeli	Snares Islands					•			1,100	MI			11	
barrierensis	Little Barrier Island					•			0	NE	EXT	NE		
iredalei	Stewart Islands					•			0	NE	EXT?	NE	1	Still listed as extant by HV and Clements (2000).

165

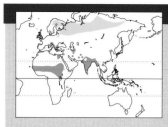

Lymnocryptes minimus — Jack Snipe

Subspecies/Population	Breeding range	Wintering, or core non-breeding range	Afr	Eu	Asia	Oc	Neo	NA	Estimate	Source	Trend	Source	1% level	Notes
NE Europe (br)	N European Russia, S Sweden, N Poland, N Belarus, Baltic States	*W & S Europe, N & W Africa*	•	•					E	SA KD	**STA**	KD		KD estimates 500,000 breeding pairs (1,500,000 individuals).
W Siberia (br)	W Siberia	*SW Asia, NE Africa*	•	•	•									
S Asia (non-br)	Central & E Siberia	*S Asia to Myanmar*			•									
E, SE Asia (non-br)		*S China, Vietnam*			•				A	CD			100	

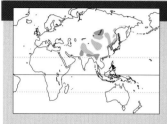

Gallinago solitaria — Solitary Snipe

Subspecies/Population	Breeding range	Wintering, or core non-breeding range	Afr	Eu	Asia	Oc	Neo	NA	Estimate	Source	Trend	Source	1% level	Notes
solitaria	Mountains of Central Asia– SC Siberia	*E Pakistan, N India, Myanmar*			•				B/C	B3			1,000	
japonica	SE Siberia, NE China, Sakhalin to Kamchatka	*Amurland to Kamchatka, Korea, Japan, E China*			•				A	B3			100	

Gallinago hardwickii — Latham's Snipe, Japanese Snipe

Subspecies/Population	Breeding range	Wintering, or core non-breeding range	Afr	Eu	Asia	Oc	Neo	NA	Estimate	Source	Trend	Source	1% level	Notes
E Asia (br)	Japan, Kuril Is, S Sakhalin, E Pimorskiy	*E Australia*			•	•			C	GC	**DEC**	GC	1,000	GC reports 37,000 adults breeding in Hokkaido, Japan (55,500 individuals) of which 15,000 reach SE Australia. Russian breeding population unknown.

Gallinago nemoricola VU — Wood Snipe

Subspecies/Population	Breeding range	Wintering, or core non-breeding range	Afr	Eu	Asia	Oc	Neo	NA	Estimate	Source	Trend	Source	1% level	Notes
S & SE Asia	Himalayas NW India, S & E Tibet, Nepal, Bhutan	*India, Bangladesh, Myanmar, N Laos, N Vietnam, N Thailand, S India*			•				2,500–10,000	BC	**DEC**	BC	60	

Gallinago stenura — Pintail Snipe

Subspecies/Population	Breeding range	Wintering, or core non-breeding range	Afr	Eu	Asia	Oc	Neo	NA	Estimate	Source	Trend	Source	1% level	Notes
S Asia, E Africa (non-br)	Urals to C Siberia	*Eastern Africa, Saudi Arabia, S Asia, Maldives*	•		•				C/D	PE				Presumed to breed predominantly in western half of Siberia.
E & SE Asia (non-br)	C Siberia–Sea of Okhotsk	*Indochina–SE China, Taiwan, S to Philippines, W Indonesia*			•				C/D	B3				Presumed to breed predominantly in eastern half of Siberia.

Gallinago megala — Swinhoe's Snipe

Subspecies/Population	Breeding range	Wintering, or core non-breeding range	Afr	Eu	Asia	Oc	Neo	NA	Estimate	Source	Trend	Source	1% level	Notes
Central Asia (br)	CS Siberia, N Mongolia, SE Russia & NE China	*S & E India E to S China, Taiwan, SE Asia to N Australia*			•	•			C	B3			1,000	

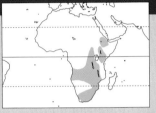

Gallinago nigripennis — African Snipe

Subspecies/Population	Breeding range	Wintering, or core non-breeding range	Afr	Eu	Asia	Oc	Neo	NA	Estimate	Source	Trend	Source	1% level	Notes
nigripennis	S Mozambique & South Africa		•						B	DO			250	DEC in SW Cape, South Africa (HF).
aequatoralis	Ethiopia S to E D R Congo & N Mozambique		•						B/C	DO			1,000	
angolensis	Angola, Namibia, Botswana, Zambia, W Zimbabwe		•						B/C	DO			1,000	

Gallinago macrodactyla NT — Madagascar Snipe

Subspecies/Population	Breeding range	Wintering, or core non-breeding range	Afr	Eu	Asia	Oc	Neo	NA	Estimate	Source	Trend	Source	1% level	Notes
Madagascar	E Madagascar		•						A	DO			100	HJ estimates 1,800–7,500.

Gallinago media NT — Great Snipe

Subspecies/Population	Breeding range	Wintering, or core non-breeding range	Afr	Eu	Asia	Oc	Neo	NA	Estimate	Source	Trend	Source	1% level	Notes
Scandinavia (br)	Scandinavia	*Sub-Saharan Africa*	•	•					18,000–51,000	SW	STA	SP	350	
W Siberia, NE Europe (br)	W Siberia, NE Europe	*Sub-Saharan Africa*	•	•	•				D	SA	DEC?	SA	10,000	KC estimates 250,000 for European part of range.

Gallinago gallinago — Common Snipe

Subspecies/Population	Breeding range	Wintering, or core non-breeding range	Afr	Eu	Asia	Oc	Neo	NA	Estimate	Source	Trend	Source	1% level	Notes
gallinago, Europe (br)	N Europe	*South & West Europe & West Africa*	•	•					>2,400,000	SW	STA	SW	20,000	Hunting bags suggest a population over 10,000,000 individuals but SW estimate 2.4–3.9 million. For populations over 2 million birds, Ramsar Convention criterion 5 (20,000 or more waterbirds), applies.
gallinago, W Siberia (br)	W Siberia	*SW Asia & Sub-Saharan Africa*	•	•	•				>1,500,000	SW			15,000	
gallinago, S Asia (non-br)	North Central Asia to Kamchatka, W Aleutians	*S Asia*			•				D/E	PE				

Gallinago gallinago... continued

Subspecies/Population	Breeding range	Wintering, or core non-breeding range	Afr	Eu	Asia	Oc	Neo	NA	Estimate	Source	Trend	Source	1% level	Notes
gallinago, E & SE Asia (non-br)	North Central Asia to Kamchatka, W Aleutians	*Indochina, E China, Taiwan, S Korea, S Japan, Philippines, W Indonesia*			•				D	B3			10,000	
faeroensis	Iceland, Fareoes, N Scotland	*Mainly Ireland, Britain*		•					570,000	SW	STA?	SW	5,700	
delicata	E Aleutians, Alaska to Newfoundland, S to C California, New Jersey	*NW & C USA, Central America, NW Caribbean, N Colombia & Venezuela*					•	•	1,000,000–3,000,000	MU	DEC	S5	20,000	

Gallinago paraguaiae — South American Snipe

Subspecies/Population	Breeding range	Wintering, or core non-breeding range	Afr	Eu	Asia	Oc	Neo	NA	Estimate	Source	Trend	Source	1% level	Notes
paraguaiae	South America E of Andes, S to N Argentina, Uruguay						•				STA	AT		
"Magellan Snipe" *magellanica*	C Chile, C Argentina S to Tierra del Fuego						•		C/D	S8	STA	AT		
magellanica	Falkland/Malvinas Is						•		15,000–27,000	WS			210	WS estimate 5,000–9,000 pairs (15,000–27,000 individuals). May merit treatment as a full species.

Gallinago andina — Puna Snipe

Subspecies/Population	Breeding range	Wintering, or core non-breeding range	Afr	Eu	Asia	Oc	Neo	NA	Estimate	Source	Trend	Source	1% level	Notes
Central Andes	S Peru, W Bolivia, N Chile, NW Argentina						•							Sometimes considered conspecific with *paraguaiae*.

Gallinago nobilis — Noble Snipe

Subspecies/Population	Breeding range	Wintering, or core non-breeding range	Afr	Eu	Asia	Oc	Neo	NA	Estimate	Source	Trend	Source	1% level	Notes
N South America	N Andes Venezuela, Colombia, Ecuador						•							

Gallinago undulata — Giant Snipe

Subspecies/Population	Breeding range	Wintering, or core non-breeding range	Afr	Eu	Asia	Oc	Neo	NA	Estimate	Source	Trend	Source	1% level	Notes
undulata	W & E Colombia, Venezuela, N Brazil, Guianas						•							
gigantea	E Bolivia, Paraguay, SE Brazil						•				DEC	AT		

Gallinago stricklandii NT — Fuegian Snipe

Subspecies/Population	Breeding range	Wintering, or core non-breeding range	Afr	Eu	Asia	Oc	Neo	NA	Estimate	Source	Trend	Source	1% level	Notes
S South America	SC Chile, SC Argentina–Tierra del Fuego						•		A	S8	DEC	S8	100	Often considered conspecific with *jamesoni*.

Gallinago jamesoni — Andean Snipe

Subspecies/Population	Breeding range	Wintering, or core non-breeding range	Afr	Eu	Asia	Oc	Neo	NA	Estimate	Source	Trend	Source	1% level	Notes
N Andes	Andes W Venezuela–WC Bolivia						•							

Gallinago imperialis NT — Imperial Snipe

Subspecies/Population	Breeding range	Wintering, or core non-breeding range	Afr	Eu	Asia	Oc	Neo	NA	Estimate	Source	Trend	Source	1% level	Notes
NW South America	Peru & Colombia (isolated sites)						•							

Limnodromus griseus — Short-billed Dowitcher

Subspecies/Population	Breeding range	Wintering, or core non-breeding range	Afr	Eu	Asia	Oc	Neo	NA	Estimate	Source	Trend	Source	1% level	Notes
griseus	C Quebec & W Labrador (E Canada)	Atlantic coast S USA to Brazil					•	•	110,000	MU	DEC	MS	1,100	
hendersoni	E British Colombia–SW Hudson Bay–Manitoba	SE USA to Panama					•	•	60,000	MU	DEC	MU	600	
caurinus	S Alaska & S Yukon	Pacific Coast C USA to S Peru					•	•	150,000	MU			1,500	

Limnodromus scolopaceus — Long-billed Dowitcher

Subspecies/Population	Breeding range	Wintering, or core non-breeding range	Afr	Eu	Asia	Oc	Neo	NA	Estimate	Source	Trend	Source	1% level	Notes
N & C America (non-br)	NE Siberia (E of R Yana), W Alaska, N Inuvik	W & S USA, Central America S to Guatemala			•			•	500,000	MU			5,000	TA describes apparent increases in Florida and Siberia, and an apparently stable population in Canada, which may represent changes in population or shifts in range.

Limnodromus semipalmatus NT — Asian Dowitcher

Subspecies/Population	Breeding range	Wintering, or core non-breeding range	Afr	Eu	Asia	Oc	Neo	NA	Estimate	Source	Trend	Source	1% level	Notes
C & E Asia (br)	W, C & E Siberia, Mongolia, N Manchuria	E India, SE Asia, Sumatra, Java, N Australia			•	•			23,000	B3			230	

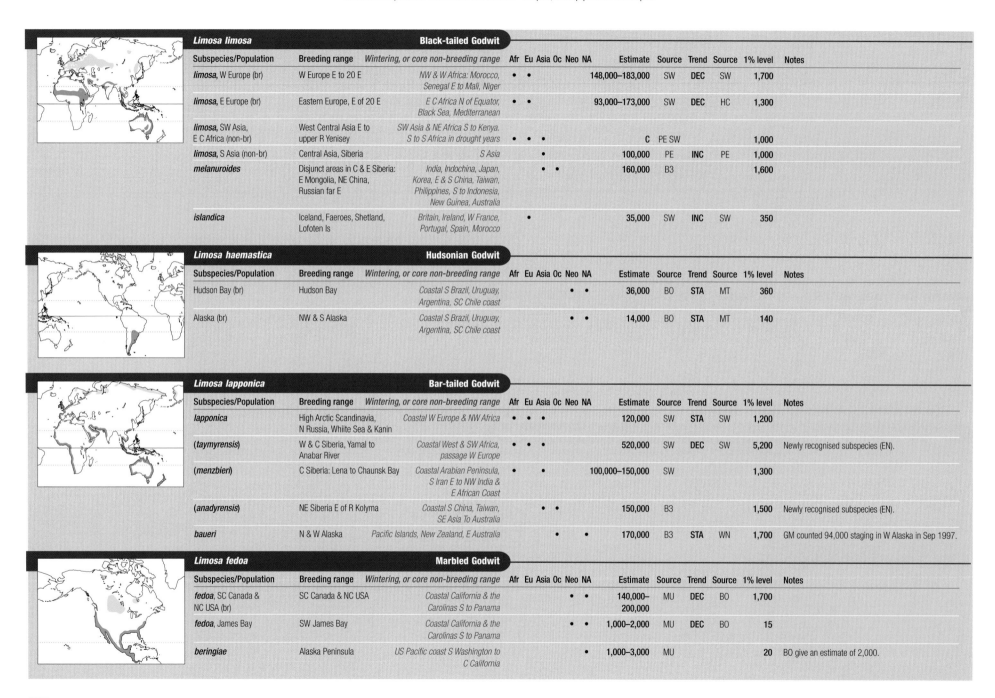

Limosa limosa — Black-tailed Godwit

Subspecies/Population	Breeding range	Wintering, or core non-breeding range	Afr	Eu	Asia	Oc	Neo	NA	Estimate	Source	Trend	Source	1% level	Notes
limosa, W Europe (br)	W Europe E to 20 E	*NW & W Africa: Morocco, Senegal E to Mali, Niger*	●	●					148,000–183,000	SW	DEC	SW	1,700	
limosa, E Europe (br)	Eastern Europe, E of 20 E	*E C Africa N of Equator, Black Sea, Mediterranean*	●	●					93,000–173,000	SW	DEC	HC	1,300	
limosa, SW Asia, E C Africa (non-br)	West Central Asia E to upper R Yenisey	*SW Asia & NE Africa S to Kenya. S to S Africa in drought years*	●	●	●				C	PE SW			1,000	
limosa, S Asia (non-br)	Central Asia, Siberia	*S Asia*			●				100,000	PE	INC	PE	1,000	
melanuroides	Disjunct areas in C & E Siberia: E Mongolia, NE China, Russian far E	*India, Indochina, Japan, Korea, E & S China, Taiwan, Philippines, S to Indonesia, New Guinea, Australia*			●	●			160,000	B3			1,600	
islandica	Iceland, Faeroes, Shetland, Lofoten Is	*Britain, Ireland, W France, Portugal, Spain, Morocco*		●					35,000	SW	INC	SW	350	

Limosa haemastica — Hudsonian Godwit

Subspecies/Population	Breeding range	Wintering, or core non-breeding range	Afr	Eu	Asia	Oc	Neo	NA	Estimate	Source	Trend	Source	1% level	Notes
Hudson Bay (br)	Hudson Bay	*Coastal S Brazil, Uruguay, Argentina, SC Chile coast*					●	●	36,000	BO	STA	MT	360	
Alaska (br)	NW & S Alaska	*Coastal S Brazil, Uruguay, Argentina, SC Chile coast*					●	●	14,000	BO	STA	MT	140	

Limosa lapponica — Bar-tailed Godwit

Subspecies/Population	Breeding range	Wintering, or core non-breeding range	Afr	Eu	Asia	Oc	Neo	NA	Estimate	Source	Trend	Source	1% level	Notes
lapponica	High Arctic Scandinavia, N Russia, Whiite Sea & Kanin	*Coastal W Europe & NW Africa*	●	●	●				120,000	SW	STA	SW	1,200	
(*taymyrensis*)	W & C Siberia, Yamal to Anabar River	*Coastal West & SW Africa, passage W Europe*	●	●	●				520,000	SW	DEC	SW	5,200	Newly recognised subspecies (EN).
(*menzbieri*)	C Siberia: Lena to Chaunsk Bay	*Coastal Arabian Peninsula, S Iran E to NW India & E African Coast*	●		●				100,000–150,000	SW			1,300	
(*anadyrensis*)	NE Siberia E of R Kolyma	*Coastal S China, Taiwan, SE Asia To Australia*			●	●			150,000	B3			1,500	Newly recognised subspecies (EN).
baueri	N & W Alaska	*Pacific Islands, New Zealand, E Australia*				●		●	170,000	B3	STA	WN	1,700	GM counted 94,000 staging in W Alaska in Sep 1997.

Limosa fedoa — Marbled Godwit

Subspecies/Population	Breeding range	Wintering, or core non-breeding range	Afr	Eu	Asia	Oc	Neo	NA	Estimate	Source	Trend	Source	1% level	Notes
fedoa, SC Canada & NC USA (br)	SC Canada & NC USA	*Coastal California & the Carolinas S to Panama*					●	●	140,000–200,000	MU	DEC	BO	1,700	
fedoa, James Bay	SW James Bay	*Coastal California & the Carolinas S to Panama*					●	●	1,000–2,000	MU	DEC	BO	15	
beringiae	Alaska Peninsula	*US Pacific coast S Washington to C California*					●		1,000–3,000	MU			20	BO give an estimate of 2,000.

Numenius minutus — Little Curlew

Subspecies/Population	Breeding range	Wintering, or core non-breeding range	Afr	Eu	Asia	Oc	Neo	NA	Estimate	Source	Trend	Source	1% level	Notes
N Siberia	North Central & NE Siberia	New Guinea, Australia			●	●			180,000	B3			1,800	

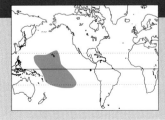

Numenius borealis CR — Eskimo Curlew

Subspecies/Population	Breeding range	Wintering, or core non-breeding range	Afr	Eu	Asia	Oc	Neo	NA	Estimate	Source	Trend	Source	1% level	Notes
N Canada	Central extreme N mainland Canada	E Central Argentina, Uruguay					●	●	<50	BC	EXT?	BC	1	

Numenius phaeopus — Whimbrel

Subspecies/Population	Breeding range	Wintering, or core non-breeding range	Afr	Eu	Asia	Oc	Neo	NA	Estimate	Source	Trend	Source	1% level	Notes
phaeopus, NE Europe (br)	Fennoscandia, Baltic States, NW Russia, Greenland	West Africa to Congo River (+ few W Europe)	●	●				●	160,000–300,000	SW	STA/ INC	SA	2,300	
phaeopus, W Siberia (br)	W Siberia	E & S Africa, Madagascar (via Caspian, SW Asia)	●		●				D	SW			10,000	
islandicus	Iceland, Faeroes, Scotland	West Africa	●	●					610,000	SW	STA	SW	6,100	Recently revived subspecies (EN).
variegatus, South Asia (non-br)	Central, E Siberia	S Asia			●				C	PE			1,000	
variegatus, E, SE Asia Asia (non-br)	Central, E Siberia	Coasts Indochina–Taiwan, Philippines, Indonesia, Australia			●	●			55,000	B3			550	
alboaxillaris	Lower Volga Steppe SE of Urals	Islands & coasts of W Indian Ocean	●	●					A	SA	DEC	MQ	100	
rufiventris	W, N Alaska to Yukon, Mackenzie	Pacific coasts S USA to S South America					●	●	39,000	MU	STA	NB	390	
hudsonicus	W Hudson Bay	Atlantic & Gulf coasts USA to NE South America					●	●	18,000	MU			180	

Numenius tahitiensis VU — Bristle-thighed Curlew

Subspecies/Population	Breeding range	Wintering, or core non-breeding range	Afr	Eu	Asia	Oc	Neo	NA	Estimate	Source	Trend	Source	1% level	Notes
W Alaska (br)	W Alaska	Central & S Pacific Islands				●		●	10,000	MU	DEC	BC	100	MU estimate 7,000 breeders + 3,000 immatures remaining on the winter range.

Numenius tenuirostris CR — Slender-billed Curlew

Subspecies/Population	Breeding range	Wintering, or core non-breeding range	Afr	Eu	Asia	Oc	Neo	NA	Estimate	Source	Trend	Source	1% level	Notes
Mediterranean basin (non-br)	SW Siberia?	NE, C & SW Mediterranean Basin, Morocco, Persian Gulf?	•	•	•				<50	BC	DEC	BC	1	

Numenius arquata — Eurasian Curlew

Subspecies/Population	Breeding range	Wintering, or core non-breeding range	Afr	Eu	Asia	Oc	Neo	NA	Estimate	Source	Trend	Source	1% level	Notes
arquata	W, Central & N Europe E to Urals	W Europe, Mediterranean, NW Africa (few SW Africa), E to Persian Gulf	•	•					420,000	SW	STA/INC	SW	4,200	
orientalis, SW Asia, E Africa (non-br)	SE Europe & Urals E to 120 E	SW Asia, E & S Africa (few SW Africa)	•	•	•				C	PE SW	DEC?	SW	1,000	Only 500 reach South Africa.
orientalis, S Asia (non-br)	Siberia	S & SW Asia			•				B/C	PE			1,000	
orientalis, E & SE Asia (non-br)	Siberia	E & SE Asia			•				35,000	B3 CD			350	
suschkini	S Urals & Kazakhstan	Eastern & Southern Africa?	•	•	•						DEC?	SA		

Numenius madagascariensis NT — Far Eastern Curlew, Australian Curlew

Subspecies/Population	Breeding range	Wintering, or core non-breeding range	Afr	Eu	Asia	Oc	Neo	NA	Estimate	Source	Trend	Source	1% level	Notes
C & E Asia (br)	NE Mongolia, NE China, E Siberia to Kamchatka	Australia, New Zealand, New Guinea, Indonesia			•	•			38,000	B3	DEC	WD	380	Estimate increased due to increased survey coverage.

Numenius americanus NT — Long-billed Curlew

Subspecies/Population	Breeding range	Wintering, or core non-breeding range	Afr	Eu	Asia	Oc	Neo	NA	Estimate	Source	Trend	Source	1% level	Notes
americanus	West Central USA	California & Texas S to Mexico & Guatemala						•	13,500	MR	DEC	S5	140	MU estimate 20,000 for both populations combined. Earlier, separate estimates remain valid.
parvus	W & N USA, SW & S Central Canada	California & Louisiana S to Mexico						•	6,500	MT	DEC	MT	65	

Bartramia longicauda — Upland Sandpiper

Subspecies/Population	Breeding range	Wintering, or core non-breeding range	Afr	Eu	Asia	Oc	Neo	NA	Estimate	Source	Trend	Source	1% level	Notes
Americas	C S Alaska, S Canada, N USA	Suriname, + Paraguay & S Brazil S to C Argentina					•	•	350,000	MU	DEC	MU	3,500	MU: the population increased 1966–79, declined 1980–1998.

Tringa erythropus — Spotted Redshank

Subspecies/Population	Breeding range	Wintering, or core non-breeding range	Afr	Eu	Asia	Oc	Neo	NA	Estimate	Source	Trend	Source	1% level	Notes
Europe (br)	N Scandinavia & NW Russia	W & NW Africa, S & W Europe	•	•					77,000–131,000	SA	STA	SW	1,000	
SW Asia, E Africa (non-br)	W Siberia	SW Asia, Eastern Africa	•	•	•				B/C	PE SW			1,000	
South Asia (non-br)	N Siberia	NW India, Pakistan, NE India, Bangladesh			•				B	PE			250	
E, SE Asia (non-br)	N Siberia	Taiwan, SE China, Indochina, Thailand, Myanmar, Malaysia			•				C	B3			1,000	

Tringa totanus — Common Redshank

Subspecies/Population	Breeding range	Wintering, or core non-breeding range	Afr	Eu	Asia	Oc	Neo	NA	Estimate	Source	Trend	Source	1% level	Notes
totanus, E Atlantic (non-br)	Fennoscandia, Baltic, W Central Europe	E Atlantic: Britain S to W Africa, W Mediterranean	•	•					250,000	SW DO	DEC	SW	2,500	
totanus, E Europe (br)	E Europe	East Mediterranean, Asia Minor, sub-Saharan Africa	•	•					223,000–464,000	SW	DEC	SW	3,400	
ussuriensis, SW Asia & E Africa (non-br)	Russia E of Urals	SW Asia, Eastern Africa, ?NW India	•	•	•				213,000–326,000	SW			2,700	
ussuriensis, S & SE Asia (non-br)	Mongolia E to Manchuria, Russian Far East	South & SE Asia			•				C	B3			1,000	
robusta	Iceland, Faeroes Islands	Britain, Ireland, North Sea, NW France		•					64,500	SW	STA/ INC?	SW	650	
brittanica	Britain, Ireland	Britain, Ireland, NW France		•					124,000–127,000	SW	DEC	SW	1,300	Included in *robusta* in WPE2.
terrignotae	E China (S Manchuria)	SE & E Asia			•				B/C	B3			1,000	
craggi	NW Xinjiang	?E China?			•				B/C	B3			1,000	
eurhinus	Pamirs, N India, C & S Tibet	India, Sri Lanka			•				D	HT			10,000	

Tringa stagnatilis — Marsh Sandpiper

Subspecies/Population	Breeding range	Wintering, or core non-breeding range	Afr	Eu	Asia	Oc	Neo	NA	Estimate	Source	Trend	Source	1% level
Europe (br)	W Russia, E Ukraine	North, West & Central Africa	•	•					21,000–52,000	SA			370
SW Asia, E & S Africa (non-br)	Siberia	SW Asia, E & S Africa	•	•	•				50,000–100,000	DO			750
S Asia (non-br)	Siberia	S Asia			•				C/D	PE			
E, SE Asia, Oceania (non-br)	Siberia to NE China	China, Taiwan, Indochina, Indonesia, Philippines, Australia			•	•			90,000	B3			900

Marsh Sandpiper.

Ian Montgomery

Tringa nebularia — Common Greenshank

Subspecies/Population	Breeding range	Wintering, or core non-breeding range	Afr	Eu	Asia	Oc	Neo	NA	Estimate	Source	Trend	Source	1% level	Notes
Europe (br)	Scotland, Scandinavia, NE Europe	W & SW Europe NW Africa, W Africa E to Chad & S to South Africa	•	•					234,000–395,000	SW	STA	BE	3,100	
SW Asia, E & S Africa (non-br	W Siberia, ?NE Europe	SW Asia, E & S Africa	•	•	•				D	SW			10,000	
South Asia (non-br)	Central Asia, Central & E Siberia	S Asia			•				B/C	PE			1,000	
E, SE Asia, Australia (non-br)	Central Asia, Central & E Siberia to Kamchatka	E, SE Asia Indonesia & Australia			•	•			55,000	B3			550	

Tringa guttifer EN — Nordmann's Greenshank

Subspecies/Population	Breeding range	Wintering, or core non-breeding range	Afr	Eu	Asia	Oc	Neo	NA	Estimate	Source	Trend	Source	1% level	Notes
NE Asia (br)	Sakhalin Is & W Okhotsk Sea	NE India, Bangladesh, Myanmar, Thailand, Malay Peninsula, Sumatra			•				250–1,000	BC	DEC	BC	6	

Tringa melanoleuca — Greater Yellowlegs

Subspecies/Population	Breeding range	Wintering, or core non-breeding range	Afr	Eu	Asia	Oc	Neo	NA	Estimate	Source	Trend	Source	1% level	Notes
Americas	S Alaska & British Colombia E to Labrador, Newfoundland	British Colombia and New England S through Central America, Caribbean, South America					•	•	100,000	MU			1,000	

Tringa flavipes — Lesser Yellowlegs

Subspecies/Population	Breeding range	Wintering, or core non-breeding range	Afr	Eu	Asia	Oc	Neo	NA	Estimate	Source	Trend	Source	1% level	Notes
Americas	Alaska to SC Canada E to James Bay	USA through Central America, SCaribbean, South America					•	•	300,000–800,000	MU	DEC	DR TM	5,500	

Tringa ochropus — Green Sandpiper

Subspecies/Population	Breeding range	Wintering, or core non-breeding range	Afr	Eu	Asia	Oc	Neo	NA	Estimate	Source	Trend	Source	1% level
Europe (br)	N Europe	W Europe, North & West Africa	•	•					1,000,000–1,890,000	SW	STA/ INC?	SA	14,500
SW Asia, E Africa (non-br)	W Siberia	Caspian, SW Asia, Eastern Africa to N southern Africa	•	•	•				D/E	SW			
South Asia (non-br)	Central Asia to E Siberia	S Asia, Tien Shan range, Tibet			•				C/D	PE			
E & SE Asia (non-br)	Central & E Siberia, NE China	Indochina, Malaysia, Philippines, SE China, Taiwan, S Japan, Korea			•				C	B3			1,000

Green Sandpiper.

Johan Verbanck

Tringa solitaria — Solitary Sandpiper

Subspecies/Population	Breeding range	Wintering, or core non-breeding range	Afr	Eu	Asia	Oc	Neo	NA	Estimate	Source	Trend	Source	1% level	Notes
solitaria	W Canada, Alaska	N S America S to C Argentina					•	•	<150,000	MU	STA	MT	1,500	
cinnamomea	Central and E Canada	Central America, Caribbean, S America S to Argentina					•	•	4,000	BO			40	

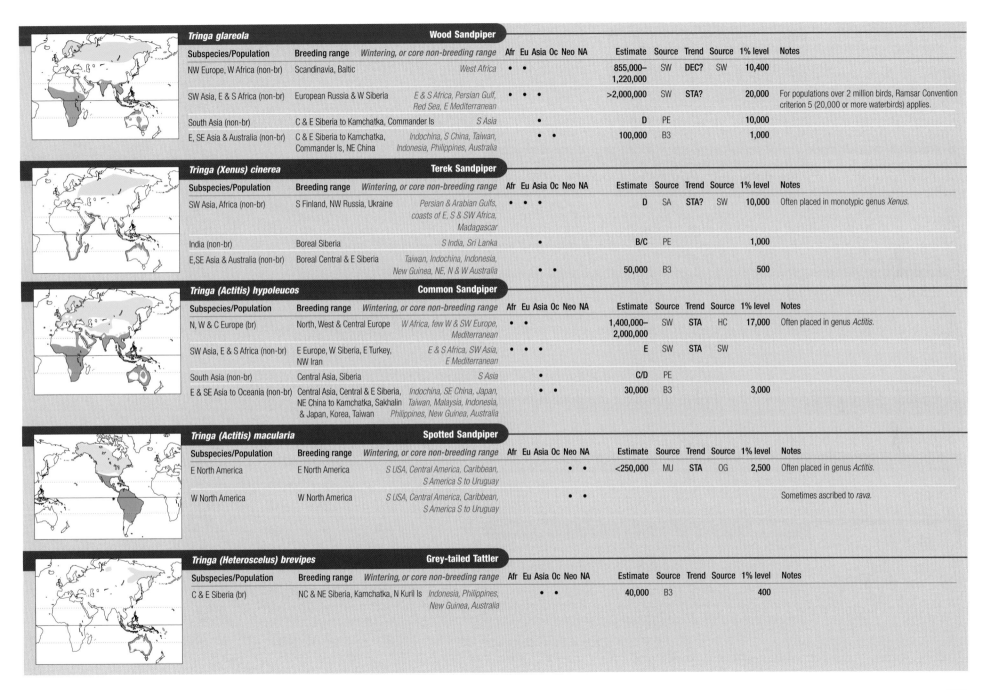

Tringa glareola — Wood Sandpiper

Subspecies/Population	Breeding range	Wintering, or core non-breeding range	Afr	Eu	Asia	Oc	Neo	NA	Estimate	Source	Trend	Source	1% level	Notes
NW Europe, W Africa (non-br)	Scandinavia, Baltic	West Africa	●	●					855,000–1,220,000	SW	DEC?	SW	10,400	
SW Asia, E & S Africa (non-br)	European Russia & W Siberia	E & S Africa, Persian Gulf, Red Sea, E Mediterranean	●	●	●				>2,000,000	SW	STA?		20,000	For populations over 2 million birds, Ramsar Convention criterion 5 (20,000 or more waterbirds) applies.
South Asia (non-br)	C & E Siberia to Kamchatka, Commander Is	S Asia			●				D	PE			10,000	
E, SE Asia & Australia (non-br)	C & E Siberia to Kamchatka, Commander Is, NE China	Indochina, S China, Taiwan, Indonesia, Philippines, Australia			●	●			100,000	B3			1,000	

Tringa (Xenus) cinerea — Terek Sandpiper

Subspecies/Population	Breeding range	Wintering, or core non-breeding range	Afr	Eu	Asia	Oc	Neo	NA	Estimate	Source	Trend	Source	1% level	Notes
SW Asia, Africa (non-br)	S Finland, NW Russia, Ukraine	Persian & Arabian Gulfs, coasts of E, S & SW Africa, Madagascar	●	●	●				D	SA	STA?	SW	10,000	Often placed in monotypic genus Xenus.
India (non-br)	Boreal Siberia	S India, Sri Lanka			●				B/C	PE			1,000	
E,SE Asia & Australia (non-br)	Boreal Central & E Siberia	Taiwan, Indochina, Indonesia, New Guinea, NE, N & W Australia			●	●			50,000	B3			500	

Tringa (Actitis) hypoleucos — Common Sandpiper

Subspecies/Population	Breeding range	Wintering, or core non-breeding range	Afr	Eu	Asia	Oc	Neo	NA	Estimate	Source	Trend	Source	1% level	Notes
N, W & C Europe (br)	North, West & Central Europe	W Africa, few W & SW Europe, Mediterranean	●	●					1,400,000–2,000,000	SW	STA	HC	17,000	Often placed in genus Actitis.
SW Asia, E & S Africa (non-br)	E Europe, W Siberia, E Turkey, NW Iran	E & S Africa, SW Asia, E Mediterranean	●	●	●				E	SW	STA	SW		
South Asia (non-br)	Central Asia, Siberia	S Asia			●				C/D	PE				
E & SE Asia to Oceania (non-br)	Central Asia, Central & E Siberia, NE China to Kamchatka, Sakhalin & Japan, Korea, Taiwan	Indochina, SE China, Japan, Taiwan, Malaysia, Indonesia, Philippines, New Guinea, Australia			●	●			30,000	B3			3,000	

Tringa (Actitis) macularia — Spotted Sandpiper

Subspecies/Population	Breeding range	Wintering, or core non-breeding range	Afr	Eu	Asia	Oc	Neo	NA	Estimate	Source	Trend	Source	1% level	Notes
E North America	E North America	S USA, Central America, Caribbean, S America S to Uruguay					●	●	<250,000	MU	STA	OG	2,500	Often placed in genus Actitis.
W North America	W North America	S USA, Central America, Caribbean, S America S to Uruguay					●	●						Sometimes ascribed to rava.

Tringa (Heteroscelus) brevipes — Grey-tailed Tattler

Subspecies/Population	Breeding range	Wintering, or core non-breeding range	Afr	Eu	Asia	Oc	Neo	NA	Estimate	Source	Trend	Source	1% level	Notes
C & E Siberia (br)	NC & NE Siberia, Kamchatka, N Kuril Is	Indonesia, Philippines, New Guinea, Australia			●	●			40,000	B3			400	

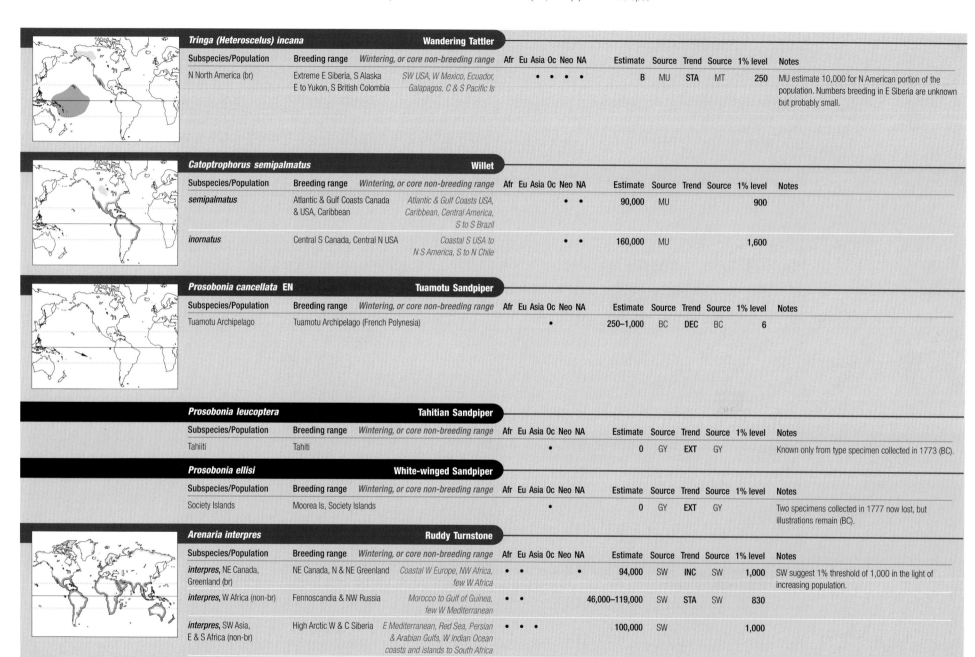

Tringa (Heteroscelus) incana — Wandering Tattler

Subspecies/Population	Breeding range	Wintering, or core non-breeding range	Afr	Eu	Asia	Oc	Neo	NA	Estimate	Source	Trend	Source	1% level	Notes
N North America (br)	Extreme E Siberia, S Alaska E to Yukon, S British Colombia	SW USA, W Mexico, Ecuador, Galapagos, C & S Pacific Is			•	•	•	•	B	MU	STA	MT	250	MU estimate 10,000 for N American portion of the population. Numbers breeding in E Siberia are unknown but probably small.

Catoptrophorus semipalmatus — Willet

Subspecies/Population	Breeding range	Wintering, or core non-breeding range	Afr	Eu	Asia	Oc	Neo	NA	Estimate	Source	Trend	Source	1% level	Notes
semipalmatus	Atlantic & Gulf Coasts Canada & USA, Caribbean	Atlantic & Gulf Coasts USA, Caribbean, Central America, S to S Brazil					•	•	90,000	MU			900	
inornatus	Central S Canada, Central N USA	Coastal S USA to N S America, S to N Chile					•	•	160,000	MU			1,600	

Prosobonia cancellata EN — Tuamotu Sandpiper

Subspecies/Population	Breeding range	Wintering, or core non-breeding range	Afr	Eu	Asia	Oc	Neo	NA	Estimate	Source	Trend	Source	1% level	Notes
Tuamotu Archipelago	Tuamotu Archipelago (French Polynesia)					•			250–1,000	BC	DEC	BC	6	

Prosobonia leucoptera — Tahitian Sandpiper

Subspecies/Population	Breeding range	Wintering, or core non-breeding range	Afr	Eu	Asia	Oc	Neo	NA	Estimate	Source	Trend	Source	1% level	Notes
Tahiiti	Tahiti					•			0	GY	EXT	GY		Known only from type specimen collected in 1773 (BC).

Prosobonia ellisi — White-winged Sandpiper

Subspecies/Population	Breeding range	Wintering, or core non-breeding range	Afr	Eu	Asia	Oc	Neo	NA	Estimate	Source	Trend	Source	1% level	Notes
Society Islands	Moorea Is, Society Islands					•			0	GY	EXT	GY		Two specimens collected in 1777 now lost, but illustrations remain (BC).

Arenaria interpres — Ruddy Turnstone

Subspecies/Population	Breeding range	Wintering, or core non-breeding range	Afr	Eu	Asia	Oc	Neo	NA	Estimate	Source	Trend	Source	1% level	Notes
interpres, NE Canada, Greenland (br)	NE Canada, N & NE Greenland	Coastal W Europe, NW Africa, few W Africa	•	•				•	94,000	SW	INC	SW	1,000	SW suggest 1% threshold of 1,000 in the light of increasing population.
interpres, W Africa (non-br)	Fennoscandia & NW Russia	Morocco to Gulf of Guinea, few W Mediterranean	•	•					46,000–119,000	SW	STA	SW	830	
interpres, SW Asia, E & S Africa (non-br)	High Arctic W & C Siberia	E Mediterranean, Red Sea, Persian & Arabian Gulfs, W Indian Ocean coasts and islands to South Africa	•	•	•				100,000	SW			1,000	
interpres, South Asia (non-br)	High Arctic Siberia	S Asia			•				B/C	PE			1,000	

Arenaria interpres... continued

Subspecies/Population	Breeding range	Wintering, or core non-breeding range	Afr	Eu	Asia	Oc	Neo	NA	Estimate	Source	Trend	Source	1% level	Notes
interpres, Pacific & SE Asia (non-br)	High Arctic Siberia, NW Alaska	*E & SE Asia, W & S Pacific Islands, Australasia, California, Mexico*			•	•		•	C	PE			1,000	Sometimes ascribed to *oahuensis*. B3 estimate 31,000 for population wintering in Asia–Oceania.
morinella	Low Arctic Canada & NE Alaska	*California & S Carolina S to SC Chile, N Argentina*					•	•	200,000	BO	INC	NB	1,800	MU estimates 180,000.

Arenaria melanocephala — Black Turnstone

Subspecies/Population	Breeding range	Wintering, or core non-breeding range	Afr	Eu	Asia	Oc	Neo	NA	Estimate	Source	Trend	Source	1% level	Notes
Alaska (br)	W & S Alaska	*Coast SE Alaska to NE Mexico*						•	61,000–99,000	H1			800	

Aphriza virgata — Surfbird

Subspecies/Population	Breeding range	Wintering, or core non-breeding range	Afr	Eu	Asia	Oc	Neo	NA	Estimate	Source	Trend	Source	1% level	Notes
Alaska, Yukon (br)	C & S Alaska, C Yukon	*E Pacific coasts, SE Alaska– Straits of Magellan*					•	•	70,000	MU	DEC	BO	700	

Calidris tenuirostris — Great Knot

Subspecies/Population	Breeding range	Wintering, or core non-breeding range	Afr	Eu	Asia	Oc	Neo	NA	Estimate	Source	Trend	Source	1% level	Notes
SW & W S Asia (non-br)	NE Siberia E of Verhoyansk Mts	*Oman, UAE, E Saudi Arabia, Pakistan, NW India, Sri Lanka*			•				2,000–5,000	SW			35	
SE Asia, Australia (non-br)	NE Siberia E of Verhoyansk Mts	*NE India, Bangladesh, SE Asia, New Guinea, Australia*			•	•			380,000	B3			3,800	

Calidris canutus — Red Knot

Subspecies/Population	Breeding range	Wintering, or core non-breeding range	Afr	Eu	Asia	Oc	Neo	NA	Estimate	Source	Trend	Source	1% level	Notes
canutus	Taymyr Peninsula (Central Siberia)	*W Africa Morocco–Gulf of Guinea, SW & S Africa, Sri Lanka*	•	•					340,000	SW	DEC	SW	3,400	
rogersi	Chukotskiy Peninsula, far NE Russia	*New Guinea, Australia, New Zealand*			•	•			220,000	B3			2,200	Estimate includes *piersmai*.
piersmai	New Siberian archipelago	*Australia, ?New Zealand*			•	•								Subspecies first described 2001 (TQ). Numbers unknown; should be subtracted from estimate for *rogersi*.
roselaari	Wrangel Is, NW Alaska	*?Florida, S Panama, N Venezuela?*			•		•	•	20,000	MU			200	Birds wintering from Florida through Caribbean to N South America thought to belong to this subspecies, but not proven (MU).
islandica	Islands of High Arctic Canada, Greenland	*W Europe, mainly Wadden Sea, Britain, Ireland*		•				•	450,000	SW	DEC	SW	4,500	Increase from late 1970s until 2000; steep decrease since 2000 (PM).
rufa	Canadian Low Arctic	*NE & S South America*					•	•	60,000	BA	DEC	HE BA BO	600	

Calidris alba — Sanderling

Subspecies/Population	Breeding range	Wintering, or core non-breeding range	Afr	Eu	Asia	Oc	Neo	NA	Estimate	Source	Trend	Source	1% level	Notes
E Atlantic, W&S Africa (non-br)	NE Canada, N & NE Greenland, Svalbard, W Taymyr	Atlantic coast Europe, W Africa S to S Africa	•	•	•				123,000	SW ME	STA/INC?	SW	1,200	
SW Asia, E & S Africa (non-br)	Severnaya Zemlya, Taymyr, Lena Delta, New Siberian Is	Red Sea, Persian & Arabian Gulfs, E African coast to Madagascar, South Africa	•		•				150,000	DO	STA?	SW	1,400	
S Asia (non-br)	Severnaya Zemlya, Taymyr, Lena Delta, New Siberian Is	Coasts of S Asia			•				C	PE			1,000	
E & SE Asia, Australia, New Zealand (non-br)	Severnaya Zemlya, Taymyr, Lena Delta, New Siberian Is, N Alaska	Coastal Australia, New Zealand, SW Pacific Is, Indonesia, Philippines, Indochina, S China, Taiwan, Korea			•	•			22,000	B3			220	
Nearctic and Neotropics (non-br)	High Arctic Canada	Coastal SW Canada & NE USA to Tierra del Fuego					•	•	300,000	MU	DEC	BA	3,000	The estimate includes some birds wintering in E Atlantic flyway.

Sanderling.

Nancy Camel

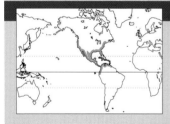

Calidris pusilla — Semipalmated Sandpiper

Subspecies/Population	Breeding range	Wintering, or core non-breeding range	Afr	Eu	Asia	Oc	Neo	NA	Estimate	Source	Trend	Source	1% level	Notes
Pacific	W & N Alaska	Pacific Coast Mexico to S Peru					•	•	3,500,000	MU	STA	MU		MU presents an estimate for the 3 populations combined of 2,000,000 to 5,000,000 and recommends use of a midpoint of 3,500,000.
E North Canada (br)	E North Canada	Atlantic Coast Yucatan & W Indies to C Argentina					•	•						
W North Canada (br)	W North Canada	Atlantic Coast Yucatan & W Indies to C Argentina					•	•						

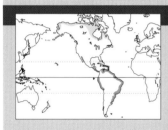

Calidris mauri — Western Sandpiper

Subspecies/Population	Breeding range	Wintering, or core non-breeding range	Afr	Eu	Asia	Oc	Neo	NA	Estimate	Source	Trend	Source	1% level	Notes
Alaska, Chukotskiy (br)	W & N Alaska, E Chukotskiy Peninsula	Coasts N California–S Peru, E USA, Caribbean to Surinam			•		•	•	3,500,000	MU	DEC	BO	20,000	For populations over 2 million birds, Ramsar Convention criterion 5 (20,000 or more waterbirds), applies.

Calidris ruficollis — Red-necked Stint

Subspecies/Population	Breeding range	Wintering, or core non-breeding range	Afr	Eu	Asia	Oc	Neo	NA	Estimate	Source	Trend	Source	1% level	Notes
NE Siberia (br)	N Siberia E of C & E Taymyr S to N Kamchatka; sporadic W & N Alaska	E India, Sri Lanka, through SE & E Asia to Australasia			•	•			315,000	B3	INC	SV	3,200	

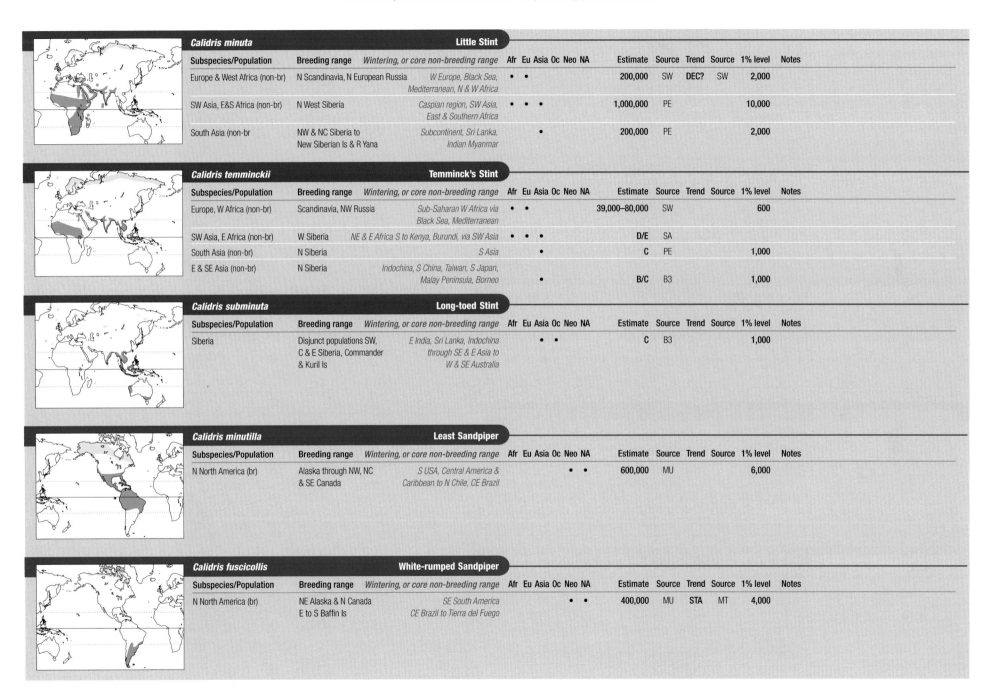

Calidris minuta — Little Stint

Subspecies/Population	Breeding range	Wintering, or core non-breeding range	Afr	Eu	Asia	Oc	Neo	NA	Estimate	Source	Trend	Source	1% level	Notes
Europe & West Africa (non-br)	N Scandinavia, N European Russia	W Europe, Black Sea, Mediterranean, N & W Africa	•	•					200,000	SW	DEC?	SW	2,000	
SW Asia, E&S Africa (non-br)	N West Siberia	Caspian region, SW Asia, East & Southern Africa	•	•	•				1,000,000	PE			10,000	
South Asia (non-br	NW & NC Siberia to New Siberian Is & R Yana	Subcontinent, Sri Lanka, Indian Myanmar			•				200,000	PE			2,000	

Calidris temminckii — Temminck's Stint

Subspecies/Population	Breeding range	Wintering, or core non-breeding range	Afr	Eu	Asia	Oc	Neo	NA	Estimate	Source	Trend	Source	1% level	Notes
Europe, W Africa (non-br)	Scandinavia, NW Russia	Sub-Saharan W Africa via Black Sea, Mediterranean	•	•					39,000–80,000	SW			600	
SW Asia, E Africa (non-br)	W Siberia	NE & E Africa S to Kenya, Burundi, via SW Asia	•	•	•				D/E	SA				
South Asia (non-br)	N Siberia	S Asia			•				C	PE			1,000	
E & SE Asia (non-br)	N Siberia	Indochina, S China, Taiwan, S Japan, Malay Peninsula, Borneo			•				B/C	B3			1,000	

Calidris subminuta — Long-toed Stint

Subspecies/Population	Breeding range	Wintering, or core non-breeding range	Afr	Eu	Asia	Oc	Neo	NA	Estimate	Source	Trend	Source	1% level	Notes
Siberia	Disjunct populations SW, C & E Siberia, Commander & Kuril Is	E India, Sri Lanka, Indochina through SE & E Asia to W & SE Australia			•	•			C	B3			1,000	

Calidris minutilla — Least Sandpiper

Subspecies/Population	Breeding range	Wintering, or core non-breeding range	Afr	Eu	Asia	Oc	Neo	NA	Estimate	Source	Trend	Source	1% level	Notes
N North America (br)	Alaska through NW, NC & SE Canada	S USA, Central America & Caribbean to N Chile, CE Brazil					•	•	600,000	MU			6,000	

Calidris fuscicollis — White-rumped Sandpiper

Subspecies/Population	Breeding range	Wintering, or core non-breeding range	Afr	Eu	Asia	Oc	Neo	NA	Estimate	Source	Trend	Source	1% level	Notes
N North America (br)	NE Alaska & N Canada E to S Baffin Is	SE South America CE Brazil to Tierra del Fuego					•	•	400,000	MU	STA	MT	4,000	

179

Calidris bairdii — Baird's Sandpiper

Subspecies/Population	Breeding range	Wintering, or core non-breeding range	Afr	Eu	Asia	Oc	Neo	NA	Estimate	Source	Trend	Source	1% level	Notes
E Siberia, N North America (br)	Wrangel Is & Chukotskiy Peninsula, N Alaska, N Canada to N Baffin Is, NW Greenland	Argentina, Chile, Paraguay, Bolivia, Peru, Ecuador					•	•	300,000	MU	STA	MT	3,000	

Calidris melanotos — Pectoral Sandpiper

Subspecies/Population	Breeding range	Wintering, or core non-breeding range	Afr	Eu	Asia	Oc	Neo	NA	Estimate	Source	Trend	Source	1% level	Notes
E Siberia, N North America (br)	E Siberia, W & N Alaska, NC Canada, W Hudson Bay	S Bolivia, Paraguay, Argentina, Chile		•			•	•	C	MU S8	STA	MT	1,000	MU: N American breeding population c.400,000 individuals. Regular in small numbers in Australasia and frequent vagrant to Europe.

Calidris acuminata — Sharp-tailed Sandpiper

Subspecies/Population	Breeding range	Wintering, or core non-breeding range	Afr	Eu	Asia	Oc	Neo	NA	Estimate	Source	Trend	Source	1% level	Notes
C & E Siberia (br)	NC & NE Siberia Lena Delta–Kolyma River	Taiwan, Philippines, New Guinea, Melanesia–New Caledonia, Tonga, Australia, New Zealand			•	•		•	160,000	B3			1,600	

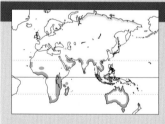

Calidris ferruginea — Curlew Sandpiper

Subspecies/Population	Breeding range	Wintering, or core non-breeding range	Afr	Eu	Asia	Oc	Neo	NA	Estimate	Source	Trend	Source	1% level	Notes
W Africa, (non-br)	Arctic Siberia Yamal Peninsula– N Chukotskiy Peninsula	Mainly W Africa, via Black Sea, Mediterranean	•	•					740,000	SW	INC	SW	7,400	
E & S Africa (non-br)	Arctic Siberia Yamal Peninsula– N Chukotskiy Peninsula	Mainly E & S Africa, via Caspian, SW Asia	•	•	•				330,000	SW	STA	SW	3,300	
South Asia (non-br)	Arctic Siberia Yamal Peninsula– N Chukotskiy Peninsula	South Asia, Myanmar			•				100,000	PE			1,000	
E, SE Asia & Australia (non-br)	Arctic Siberia Yamal Peninsula– N Chukotskiy Peninsula	Taiwan to SE Asia, Australasia			•	•			180,000	B3	DEC	B3	1,800	

Curlew Sandpiper.

Johan Verbanck

Calidris maritima — Purple Sandpiper

Subspecies/Population	Breeding range	Wintering, or core non-breeding range	Afr	Eu	Asia	Oc	Neo	NA	Estimate	Source	Trend	Source	1% level	Notes
maritima, E Atlantic	NE Canada, Greenland, Svalbard, N Scandinavia, N Russia, NW Siberia	Greenland, Iceland, Kola Peninsula, N Norway S to NW France: occasional Iberia	•	•					50,000–100,000	SW	STA	SW	750	SW: There is considerable variation in this form and there is potential to identify up to four populations.
maritima, E North America (non-br)	NE Canada, (Greenland)	E North America S to Maryland, USA						•	15,000	MU	INC	NB	150	Estimate of 15,000 includes all belcheri and unknown proportion of maritima from NE Canada.
belcheri	Belcher Islands, Hudson Bay, Canada	New Brunswick, E Canada						•	<15,000	MU			150	
littoralis	Iceland			•					90,000	SW	STA	SW	900	

Calidris ptilocnemis — Rock Sandpiper

Subspecies/Population	Breeding range	Wintering, or core non-breeding range	Afr	Eu	Asia	Oc	Neo	NA	Estimate	Source	Trend	Source	1% level	Notes
ptilocnemis	Pribilof Island, St Matthew & Hall Is	Alaska Peninsula						•	25,000	MU	DEC	MU	250	
tschuktschorum	E Chukotskiy Peninsula–W Alaska	Coastal NW North America, E Japan				•		•	60,000–70,000	MU	STA	MU	650	50,000 in Alaska, 10,000–20,000 in Chukotka.
couesi	Aleutian Islands & Alaska Peninsula							•	75,000	MU	STA	MU	750	
quarta	Kuril Islands, S Kamchatka & Commander Is					•								

Calidris alpina — Dunlin

Subspecies/Population	Breeding range	Wintering, or core non-breeding range	Afr	Eu	Asia	Oc	Neo	NA	Estimate	Source	Trend	Source	1% level	Notes
alpina, W Europe (non-br)	N Scandinavia, N Russia, NW Siberia	W Europe, Mediterranean N & W Africa	•	•	•				1,330,000	SW	STA	SW	13,300	
alpina, South Asia (non-br)	North Central Siberia	Pakistan, NW India, NE India, Bangladesh			•				C	PE			1,000	
centralis, SW Asia, E Africa (non-br)	North Central Siberia	Caspian, SW Asia, E Mediterranean, E,NE Africa	•		•				300,000	SW			3,000	
schinzii, Iceland, (br)	Iceland	SW Europe & NW Africa	•	•					940,000–960,000	SW	STA	SW	9,500	Occasional breeder in SE Greenland (BJ).
schinzii, Baltic (br)	Baltic, S Scandinavia	SW Europe & NW Africa	•	•					3,600–4,700	SW	DEC	SW	40	
schinzii, Britain & Ireland (br)	Britain & Ireland	SW Europe & (mostly) NW Africa	•	•					23,000–26,000	SW	DEC	SW	250	
arctica	NE Greenland	West Africa	•	•					21,000–45,000	SW ME	STA?	SW	330	
sakhalina	Kolyma River to Chukotskiy Peninsula	E China, Korea, Japan, Taiwan, W North America?			•			•	D	B3			10,000	
actites	N Sakhalin	unknown			•				900	NC			9	NC estimate 600 breeding adults (900 individuals).
kistchinskii	N Sea of Okhotsk, Kamchatka, Kuril Is	unknown			•				D	B3			10,000	
arcticola	N Alaska N of Seward Peninsula, NW Canada	East Asia						•	750,000	MU	DEC	WB	7,500	
pacifica	SW Alaska S of Seward Peninsula	British Colombia (Canada), W USA, W Mexico						•	500,000–600,000	MU	DEC	WB	5,500	
hudsonia	Central Canada	SE USA, E Mexico?					•	•	150,000–300,000	MU			2,300	

Eurynorhynchus pygmaeus VU — Spoon-billed Sandpiper

Subspecies/Population	Breeding range	Wintering, or core non-breeding range	Afr	Eu	Asia	Oc	Neo	NA	Estimate	Source	Trend	Source	1% level	Notes
E Siberia (br)	Chukotskiy Peninsula S to N Kamchatka	SE India, Bangladesh, Sri Lanka, Myanmar?			•				<3,000	TS	DEC	TS	30	TS present an estimate of <1,000 pairs (<3,000 individuals).

Limicola falcinellus — Broad-billed Sandpiper

Subspecies/Population	Breeding range	Wintering, or core non-breeding range	Afr	Eu	Asia	Oc	Neo	NA	Estimate	Source	Trend	Source	1% level	Notes
falcinellus, N Europe (br)	Scandinavia, NW Russia (& possibly W Siberia)	Coasts of Arabian Peninsula, E & S Africa, W & S India, Sri Lanka	•	•	•				61,000–64,000	SW			630	
sibirica	Taymyr Peninsula to NE Siberia	NE India, Japan, Taiwan, Malaysia, Indonesia, Philippines, Australia			•	•			B/C	PE			1,000	

Micropalama himantopus — Stilt Sandpiper

Subspecies/Population	Breeding range	Wintering, or core non-breeding range	Afr	Eu	Asia	Oc	Neo	NA	Estimate	Source	Trend	Source	1% level	Notes
N North America (br)	N Alaska E to S Victoria Is, W Hudson Bay	N Chile, Bolivia, SC Brazil, Paraguay, N Argentina, Uruguay					•	•	200,000	MU	STA	MT	2,000	

Tryngites subruficollis NT — Buff-breasted Sandpiper

Subspecies/Population	Breeding range	Wintering, or core non-breeding range	Afr	Eu	Asia	Oc	Neo	NA	Estimate	Source	Trend	Source	1% level	Notes
E Siberia, N North America (br)	Wrangel Is, Chukotskiy Peninsula, N Alaska, N Canada	S Brazil, Uruguay, C Argentina			•		•	•	15,000	MU	DEC	LB	150	

Philomachus pugnax — Ruff

Subspecies/Population	Breeding range	Wintering, or core non-breeding range	Afr	Eu	Asia	Oc	Neo	NA	Estimate	Source	Trend	Source	1% level	Notes
W Africa (non-br)	N & Central Europe, NW Russia, W & C Siberia	W Africa	•	•	•				E	SW	DEC	SW		Global total (all populations) estimated at 2,280,000 breeding females (ZC).
SW Asia E & S Africa (non-br)	W, C & E Siberia	E & S Africa, SW Asia	•	•	•				E	SW	DEC?	SW		
S Asia (non-br)	W, C & E Siberia	S Asia			•				C	PE			1,000	

Ruff.

Johan Verbanck

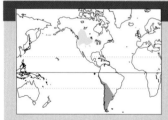

Steganopus (Phalaropus) tricolor — Wilson's Phalarope

Subspecies/Population	Breeding range	Wintering, or core non-breeding range	Afr	Eu	Asia	Oc	Neo	NA	Estimate	Source	Trend	Source	1% level	Notes
North America (br)	EC California N to N Alberta E to Great Lakes	N Peru to Uruguay S to Tierra del Fuego					•	•	1,500,000	MU	DEC	BO	15,000	Often placed in genus *Phalaropus*.

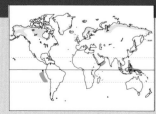

Phalaropus lobatus — Red-necked Phalarope, Northern Phalarope

Subspecies/Population	Breeding range	Wintering, or core non-breeding range	Afr	Eu	Asia	Oc	Neo	NA	Estimate	Source	Trend	Source	1% level	Notes
NW Eurasia	Arctic W Eurasia E to Taymyr, SW to Scotland	Pelagic, NW Arabian Sea	•	•					E	SW				
North America (br)	Arctic Greenland, Canada, Alaska	Pelagic, Pacific Ocean off South America					•	•	2,500,000	MU			20,000	For populations over 2 million birds, Ramsar Convention criterion 5 (20,000 or more waterbirds), applies.
NE Asia (br)	NE Siberia	Pelagic, C Indonesia to Philippines, W Melanesia												

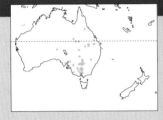

Phalaropus fulicaria — Grey Phalarope, Red Phalarope

Subspecies/Population	Breeding range	Wintering, or core non-breeding range	Afr	Eu	Asia	Oc	Neo	NA	Estimate	Source	Trend	Source	1% level	Notes
Canada, Greenland, Iceland (br)	High Arctic Canada, Greenland, Iceland	Pelagic off coasts of W & SW Africa	●	●				●	920,000	MU			9,200	MU estimate 920,000 in Canada. Only 50 pairs in Iceland, 250–500 pairs in Greenland (BE).
Alaska, North Siberia (br)	High Arctic Alaska, North Siberia	Pelagic off coast of Chile			●	●	●		D	MU			10,000	MU estimate 100,000 in Alaska.

Pedionomus torquatus EN — Plains-Wanderer

Subspecies/Population	Breeding range	Wintering, or core non-breeding range	Afr	Eu	Asia	Oc	Neo	NA	Estimate	Source	Trend	Source	1% level	Notes
E Australia	E Australia					●			2,500–8,000	GC	DEC	GC BC	55	Population fluctuates from 8,000 in good years to 2,500 after years with lower than average rainfall (GC).

PEDIONOMIDAE PLAINS-WANDERER

Attagis gayi — Rufous-bellied Seedsnipe

Subspecies/Population	Breeding range	Wintering, or core non-breeding range	Afr	Eu	Asia	Oc	Neo	NA	Estimate	Source	Trend	Source	1% level	Notes
gayi	Andean Chile & Argentina S of Antofagasta & Salta						●							
latreilli	Andes of N Ecuador						●							
simonsi	Central Peru to N Chile, W Bolivia, NW Argentina						●							

THINOCORIDAE SEEDSNIPES

Attagis malouinis — White-bellied Seedsnipe

Subspecies/Population	Breeding range	Wintering, or core non-breeding range	Afr	Eu	Asia	Oc	Neo	NA	Estimate	Source	Trend	Source	1% level	Notes
S South America	Far S South America						●							

Thinocorus orbignyianus — Grey-breasted Seedsnipe

Subspecies/Population	Breeding range	Wintering, or core non-breeding range	Afr	Eu	Asia	Oc	Neo	NA	Estimate	Source	Trend	Source	1% level	Notes
orbignyianus	Andean Chile, Argentina S of Antofagasta, La Rioja						●		B	S8			250	
ingae	Andean N Peru, W Bolivia, N Chile, NW Argentina						●							

Thinocorus rumicivorus — Least Seedsnipe

Subspecies/Population	Breeding range	Wintering, or core non-breeding range	Afr	Eu	Asia	Oc	Neo	NA	Estimate	Source	Trend	Source	1% level	Notes
rumicivorus	Patagonian Steppe S to N Tierra del Fuego						•		D	S8			10,000	
bolivianus	Altiplano S Peru, N Chile, W Bolivia, NW Argentina						•							
cuneicauda	Peruvian Desert						•		A/B	S8			250	
pallidus	Lowlands of SW Ecuador, extreme NW Peru						•							

Larus scoresbii — Dolphin Gull

Subspecies/Population	Breeding range	Wintering, or core non-breeding range	Afr	Eu	Asia	Oc	Neo	NA	Estimate	Source	Trend	Source	1% level	Notes
S South America	S South America, S of Chiloe Is, Chubut	S South America, extending slightly further N					•		B	YI			250	
Falkland/Malvinas Is	Falkland/Malvinas Is						•		9,000–18,000	WS			140	WS estimate 3,000–6,000 pairs (9,000–18,000 individuals).

Larus pacificus — Pacific Gull

Subspecies/Population	Breeding range	Wintering, or core non-breeding range	Afr	Eu	Asia	Oc	Neo	NA	Estimate	Source	Trend	Source	1% level	Notes
pacificus	Tasmania & Victoria	Tasmania, Victoria, New South Wales				•			4,950	GC	STA	GC	50	GC estimates 3,300 breeding adults (4,950 individuals).
georgii	Western Australia, South Australia					•			6,000	GC	STA	GC	60	GC estimates 4,000 breeding adults (6,000 individuals).

Larus belcheri — Band-tailed Gull, Belcher's Gull

Subspecies/Population	Breeding range	Wintering, or core non-breeding range	Afr	Eu	Asia	Oc	Neo	NA	Estimate	Source	Trend	Source	1% level	Notes
W South America	Pacific Coast N Peru to N Chile	Pacific Coast N Ecuador to C Chile					•		A	S8	INC	S8	100	

Larus atlanticus VU — Olrog's Gull

Subspecies/Population	Breeding range	Wintering, or core non-breeding range	Afr	Eu	Asia	Oc	Neo	NA	Estimate	Source	Trend	Source	1% level	Notes
SE South America	Atlantic coast C & N Argentina	Atlantic coast S Brazil, Uruguay S to C Argentina					•		4,600	BC	DEC	BC	45	Colony of 1,635 pairs (4,905 individuals) found in the Bahía Blanca Estuary during 1999 (YI). x3 multiplier to calculate population from number of breeding pairs not appropriate for this species (YI).

LARIDAE GULLS

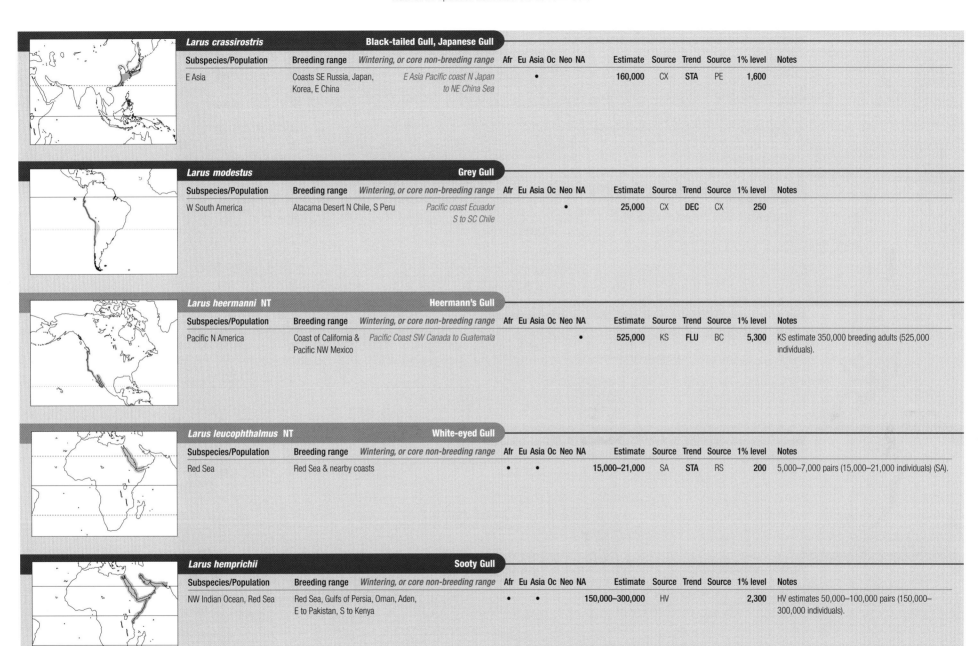

Larus crassirostris — Black-tailed Gull, Japanese Gull

Subspecies/Population	Breeding range	Wintering, or core non-breeding range	Afr	Eu	Asia	Oc	Neo	NA	Estimate	Source	Trend	Source	1% level	Notes
E Asia	Coasts SE Russia, Japan, Korea, E China	E Asia Pacific coast N Japan to NE China Sea			•				160,000	CX	STA	PE	1,600	

Larus modestus — Grey Gull

Subspecies/Population	Breeding range	Wintering, or core non-breeding range	Afr	Eu	Asia	Oc	Neo	NA	Estimate	Source	Trend	Source	1% level	Notes
W South America	Atacama Desert N Chile, S Peru	Pacific coast Ecuador S to SC Chile					•		25,000	CX	DEC	CX	250	

Larus heermanni NT — Heermann's Gull

Subspecies/Population	Breeding range	Wintering, or core non-breeding range	Afr	Eu	Asia	Oc	Neo	NA	Estimate	Source	Trend	Source	1% level	Notes
Pacific N America	Coast of California & Pacific NW Mexico	Pacific Coast SW Canada to Guatemala						•	525,000	KS	FLU	BC	5,300	KS estimate 350,000 breeding adults (525,000 individuals).

Larus leucophthalmus NT — White-eyed Gull

Subspecies/Population	Breeding range	Wintering, or core non-breeding range	Afr	Eu	Asia	Oc	Neo	NA	Estimate	Source	Trend	Source	1% level	Notes
Red Sea	Red Sea & nearby coasts		•	•					15,000–21,000	SA	STA	RS	200	5,000–7,000 pairs (15,000–21,000 individuals) (SA).

Larus hemprichii — Sooty Gull

Subspecies/Population	Breeding range	Wintering, or core non-breeding range	Afr	Eu	Asia	Oc	Neo	NA	Estimate	Source	Trend	Source	1% level	Notes
NW Indian Ocean, Red Sea	Red Sea, Gulfs of Persia, Oman, Aden, E to Pakistan, S to Kenya		•	•					150,000–300,000	HV			2,300	HV estimates 50,000–100,000 pairs (150,000–300,000 individuals).

Larus canus — Common Gull, Mew Gull

Subspecies/Population	Breeding range	Wintering, or core non-breeding range	Afr	Eu	Asia	Oc	Neo	NA	Estimate	Source	Trend	Source	1% level	Notes
canus	Iceland, Ireland, Britain, E to White Sea	Europe to N Africa	•	•					1,300,000–2,100,000	BE	DEC	BE	17,000	BE: European breeding population 430,000–690,000 pairs (1,290,000–2,070,000 individuals).
heinei	NW Russia, W & C Siberia E to R Lena	SE Europe, Black & Caspian Seas		•	•				D	SA	INC?	SA	10,000	
brachyrhynchus	N Alaska S to British Colombia, N Saskatchewan	W Canada & USA						•	240,000–360,000	KS	INC	CX	3,000	KS estimate 160,000–240,000 breeding adults (240,000–360,000 individuals).
kamtschatschensis	NE Siberia	Coasts E, SE Asia			•				D	CI			10,000	

Larus audouinii NT — Audouin's Gull

Subspecies/Population	Breeding range	Wintering, or core non-breeding range	Afr	Eu	Asia	Oc	Neo	NA	Estimate	Source	Trend	Source	1% level	Notes
Mediterranean (br)	Mediterranean coasts and islands	Mediterranean S to Mauritania, Senegambia, Gabon	•	•					57,600	BC	INC	BC	580	BC give estimate of 19,200 breeding pairs (57,600 individuals).

Larus delawarensis — Ring-billed Gull

Subspecies/Population	Breeding range	Wintering, or core non-breeding range	Afr	Eu	Asia	Oc	Neo	NA	Estimate	Source	Trend	Source	1% level	Notes
North America (br)	SW & S Canada, NW & NC USA, Great Lakes to Newfoundland	US Coasts, S USA, Central America, N Caribbean					•	•	2,550,000	KS	INC	S5	20,000	KS estimate 1,700,000 breeding adults (2,550,000 individuals). For populations over 2 million birds, Ramsar Convention criterion 5 (20,000 or more waterbirds), applies.

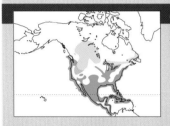

Larus californicus — California Gull

Subspecies/Population	Breeding range	Wintering, or core non-breeding range	Afr	Eu	Asia	Oc	Neo	NA	Estimate	Source	Trend	Source	1% level	Notes
W North America (br)	WC Canada, NW USA	SW Canada to SW Mexico						•	621,000	KS	STA	S5	6,200	KS estimate 414,000 breeding adults (621,000 individuals).

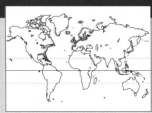

Larus marinus — Great Black-backed Gull

Subspecies/Population	Breeding range	Wintering, or core non-breeding range	Afr	Eu	Asia	Oc	Neo	NA	Estimate	Source	Trend	Source	1% level	Notes
NW Atlantic	Great Lakes, E Canada & USA N Carolina–S Greenland	W Atlantic coast S to West Indies						•	180,000	KS GQ	INC	LY	1,800	KS estimate 121,430 breeding adults (182,145 individuals). GQ estimate 60,000 breeding pairs (180,000 individuals).
Greenland	W & SE Greenland	SW Greenland						•	25,000	BI BJ	INC	BJ	250	
NE Atlantic	Coasts NW France, Ireland, Britain, Iceland E to Scandinavia, White Sea	E Atlantic coast S to Iberia		•					420,000–510,000	BE	STA	BE	4,700	European breeding population 140,000–170,000 pairs (420,000–510,000 individuals) (BE).

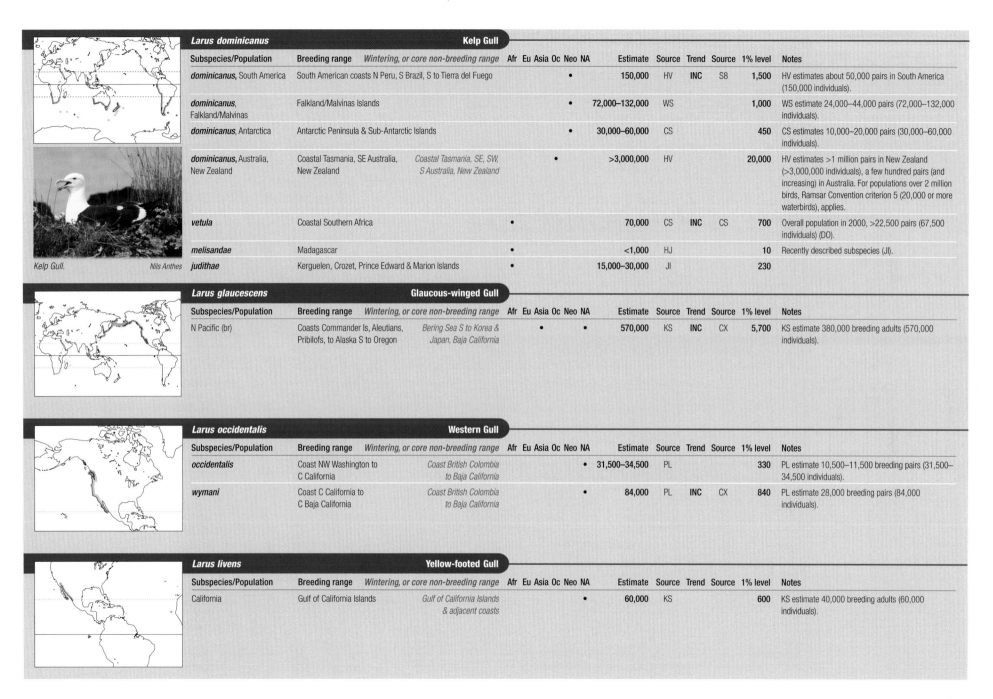

Larus dominicanus — Kelp Gull

Subspecies/Population	Breeding range	Wintering, or core non-breeding range	Afr	Eu	Asia	Oc	Neo	NA	Estimate	Source	Trend	Source	1% level	Notes
dominicanus, South America	South American coasts N Peru, S Brazil, S to Tierra del Fuego						•		150,000	HV	INC	S8	1,500	HV estimates about 50,000 pairs in South America (150,000 individuals).
dominicanus, Falkland/Malvinas	Falkland/Malvinas Islands						•		72,000–132,000	WS			1,000	WS estimate 24,000–44,000 pairs (72,000–132,000 individuals).
dominicanus, Antarctica	Antarctic Peninsula & Sub-Antarctic Islands						•		30,000–60,000	CS			450	CS estimates 10,000–20,000 pairs (30,000–60,000 individuals).
dominicanus, Australia, New Zealand	Coastal Tasmania, SE Australia, New Zealand	*Coastal Tasmania, SE, SW, S Australia, New Zealand*				•			>3,000,000	HV			20,000	HV estimates >1 million pairs in New Zealand (>3,000,000 individuals), a few hundred pairs (and increasing) in Australia. For populations over 2 million birds, Ramsar Convention criterion 5 (20,000 or more waterbirds), applies.
vetula	Coastal Southern Africa		•						70,000	CS	INC	CS	700	Overall population in 2000, >22,500 pairs (67,500 individuals) (DO).
melisandae	Madagascar		•						<1,000	HJ			10	Recently described subspecies (JI).
judithae	Kerguelen, Crozet, Prince Edward & Marion Islands		•						15,000–30,000	JI			230	

Kelp Gull.   Nils Anthes

Larus glaucescens — Glaucous-winged Gull

Subspecies/Population	Breeding range	Wintering, or core non-breeding range	Afr	Eu	Asia	Oc	Neo	NA	Estimate	Source	Trend	Source	1% level	Notes
N Pacific (br)	Coasts Commander Is, Aleutians, Pribilofs, to Alaska S to Oregon	*Bering Sea S to Korea & Japan, Baja California*			•			•	570,000	KS	INC	CX	5,700	KS estimate 380,000 breeding adults (570,000 individuals).

Larus occidentalis — Western Gull

Subspecies/Population	Breeding range	Wintering, or core non-breeding range	Afr	Eu	Asia	Oc	Neo	NA	Estimate	Source	Trend	Source	1% level	Notes
occidentalis	Coast NW Washington to C California	*Coast British Colombia to Baja California*						•	31,500–34,500	PL			330	PL estimate 10,500–11,500 breeding pairs (31,500–34,500 individuals).
wymani	Coast C California to C Baja California	*Coast British Colombia to Baja California*						•	84,000	PL	INC	CX	840	PL estimate 28,000 breeding pairs (84,000 individuals).

Larus livens — Yellow-footed Gull

Subspecies/Population	Breeding range	Wintering, or core non-breeding range	Afr	Eu	Asia	Oc	Neo	NA	Estimate	Source	Trend	Source	1% level	Notes
California	Gulf of California Islands	*Gulf of California Islands & adjacent coasts*						•	60,000	KS			600	KS estimate 40,000 breeding adults (60,000 individuals).

187

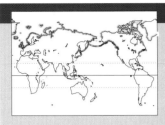

Larus hyperboreus — Glaucous Gull

Subspecies/Population	Breeding range	Wintering, or core non-breeding range	Afr	Eu	Asia	Oc	Neo	NA	Estimate	Source	Trend	Source	1% level	Notes
hyperboreus	Jan Mayen & Svalbard E to Taymyr Peninsula	to NW Europe		●	●									
pallidissimus	Taymyr Peninsula E to Bering Sea, Pribilof Is	to NE Asia			●									GH estimate 3,250 individuals breeding on Bering Sea islands, Alaska.
barrovianus	Alaska to W Canada	Aleutians to California						●			D		10,000	GH estimate 100,000 individuals breeding in Alaska (including 3,250 pallidissimus).
leuceretes	N Canada to Greenland & Iceland	to CE USA, SW Greenland, N Europe		●				●			D		10,000	GH estimate breeding population in Canada at 69,200 individuals. BE estimate W Greenland breeding population at 30,000–100,000 pairs (90,000–300,000 individuals). 8,000 pairs (24,000 individuals) in Iceland (BE).

Larus glaucoides — Iceland Gull

Subspecies/Population	Breeding range	Wintering, or core non-breeding range	Afr	Eu	Asia	Oc	Neo	NA	Estimate	Source	Trend	Source	1% level	Notes
glaucoides	S & W Greenland	N & W Europe		●				●	90,000–300,000	BE	STA	BI	2,000	Greenland breeding population 30,000–100,000 pairs (90,000–300,000 individuals) (BE).
"Kumlien's Gull" kumlieni	NE Canada–Baffin Is & NW Ungava	Labrdor S to E Great Lakes, Virginia						●	>100,000	KS			1,000	

Larus thayeri — Thayer's Gull

Subspecies/Population	Breeding range	Wintering, or core non-breeding range	Afr	Eu	Asia	Oc	Neo	NA	Estimate	Source	Trend	Source	1% level	Notes
N Canada (br)	Canadian Archipelago	Pacific Coast British Colombia–Baja California						●	<10,000	KS			100	KS estimate <10,000 individuals in Canada. Bred in Greenland until 1930s (BJ). Sometimes considered conspecific with L glaucoides.

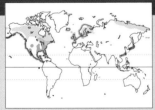

Larus argentatus — Herring Gull

Subspecies/Population	Breeding range	Wintering, or core non-breeding range	Afr	Eu	Asia	Oc	Neo	NA	Estimate	Source	Trend	Source	1% level	Notes
argentatus	Denmark & Fenno–Scandia to E Kola Peninsula	N & W Europe		●					1,100,000–1,500,000	BE	INC	BE	13,000	Includes the yellow-legged form referred to as L. a. omissus by some authors. BE estimates 357,000–486,000 pairs (1,071,000–1,458,000 individuals).
argenteus	Iceland, Ireland, Britain, NW France to Germany	NW Europe S to N Iberia		●					1,090,000	BE	STA?	BE	11,000	BE estimates 363,000–364,000 pairs (1,089,000–1,092,000 individuals).
vegae	Taymyr to Chukotka & Anadyr, NE China	W Pacific S to Japan, Korea, Taiwan, and S China			●									Possibly merits full specific status. Includes weakly defined birulai from W Taymyr to New Siberian Islands.
mongolicus	SE Altai & L Baykal to Mongolia	China & India			●				57,000–66,000	YE			620	Very close to Larus (argentatus) vegae; maybe best treated as subspecies of vegae, if vegae split from argentatus. YE estimated the population at 19,000–22,000 pairs (57,000–66,000 individuals).
smithsonianus	Alaska, Canada, Great Lakes, Atlantic coast S to Carolinas	Coastal Alaska & S Canada; USA & Central America						●	370,000	KS	DEC	S5	3,700	KS estimate >246,000 adults (369,000 individuals). Probably best treated as a separate species.

Larus heuglini — Heuglin's Gull

Subspecies/Population	Breeding range	Wintering, or core non-breeding range	Afr	Eu	Asia	Oc	Neo	NA	Estimate	Source	Trend	Source	1% level	Notes
heuglini	S Kola Peninsula E to Taymyr Peninsula	SW Asia S to E Africa & NW India, Sri Lanka	●	●	●									Sometimes treated as subspecies of fuscus or argentatus. Includes "taimyrensis", an intergrade between heuglinae and vegae (birulai) in W Taymyr.
barabensis	SW Siberia, N of L Balkhash	SW Asia, mainly shores of Persian Gulf, Arabian Sea			●									

Larus armenicus — Armenian Gull

Subspecies/Population	Breeding range	Wintering, or core non-breeding range	Afr	Eu	Asia	Oc	Neo	NA	Estimate	Source	Trend	Source	1% level	Notes
SE Europe, SW Asia	Caucasus through Armenia to E Turkey, NW Iran	SE Black Sea, E Mediterranean, N Red Sea		●	●				69,000–75,000	RT			720	RT estimate 23,000 to 25,000 pairs (69,000–75,000 individuals).

Larus schistisagus — Slaty-backed Gull

Subspecies/Population	Breeding range	Wintering, or core non-breeding range	Afr	Eu	Asia	Oc	Neo	NA	Estimate	Source	Trend	Source	1% level	Notes
NE Asia	Coast NE Siberia Cape Navarin–Kamchatka–N Japan–Vladivostok	NE Asia Pacific S to Taiwan			●				C/D	YA				

Larus cachinnans — Yellow-legged Gull

Subspecies/Population	Breeding range	Wintering, or core non-breeding range	Afr	Eu	Asia	Oc	Neo	NA	Estimate	Source	Trend	Source	1% level	Notes
cachinnans	Black Sea to Caspian & E Kazakhstan	Black & Caspian Seas, SW Asia, NE Africa, Sri Lanka		●	●				D	BE	INC?	BE	10,000	European breeding population (all races) 230,000–310,000 pairs (690,000–930,000 individuals) (BE).
michahellis	W & S Europe, NW Africa Mediterranean			●	●				630,000–768,000	VD	INC	BE	7,000	VD estimated the population at 210,000–256,000 pairs (630,000–768,000 individuals). Perhaps best treated as a separate species (YF).
atlantis	Azores to Madeira & Canary Is			●					37,500–48,000	BE			430	Best treated as subspecies of michahellis, if michahellis split from cachinnans (YF).

Larus fuscus — Lesser Black-backed Gull

Subspecies/Population	Breeding range	Wintering, or core non-breeding range	Afr	Eu	Asia	Oc	Neo	NA	Estimate	Source	Trend	Source	1% level	Notes
fuscus	Sweden, N Norway E to White Sea	E Africa S to Tanzania (+few SW Asia)	●	●	●				156,000–228,000	BE	DEC	BE	1,900	Summed BE data from relevant countries: 52,000–76,000 pairs (156,000–228,000 individuals).
graellsii	SW Greenland, Iceland, Faeroes, Ireland, Britain, France, Iberia	W Europe to W Africa	●	●					525,000	BE	INC	BE	5,300	Summed BE data from relevant countries: 174,650–174,965 pairs (523,950–524,895 individuals). Includes "intermedius", a hybrid population in The Netherlands, Denmark, S Norway, & Ebro Delta, Spain.

189

Larus ichthyaetus — Great Black-headed Gull

Subspecies/Population	Breeding range	Wintering, or core non-breeding range	Afr	Eu	Asia	Oc	Neo	NA	Estimate	Source	Trend	Source	1% level	Notes
E Europe, W Asia	Black & Caspian Seas	S Caspian, E Mediterranean, Red Sea, Persian, Oman & Arabian Gulfs, E Africa	•	•	•				72,000–120,000	BE	INC	HC	960	European breeding population 24,000–40,000 pairs (72,000–120,000 individuals) (BE).
Central Asia (br)	Central Asia E to L Balkash, S to Tibet	Coastal Pakistan, India, Sri Lanka, Bangladesh, Myanmar			•					C	PE LL			1,000	LL recorded a peak of 45,300 at one of the principal sites for this population, Qinghai Lake, in July–August 1997–2000.

Larus brunnicephalus — Brown-headed Gull

Subspecies/Population	Breeding range	Wintering, or core non-breeding range	Afr	Eu	Asia	Oc	Neo	NA	Estimate	Source	Trend	Source	1% level	Notes
Central Asia (br)	Mountains of S Central Asia	Coasts of S Asia, Indochina, S China & W to Arabian Peninsula			•					100,000	PE			1,000	

Larus cirrocephalus — Grey-headed Gull

Subspecies/Population	Breeding range	Wintering, or core non-breeding range	Afr	Eu	Asia	Oc	Neo	NA	Estimate	Source	Trend	Source	1% level	Notes
cirrocephalus, E South America	S America S & E of Amazonia to S Argentina						•								
cirrocephalus, W South America	Coasts of Peru & Ecuador						•								
poiocephalus, West Africa	W coast and rivers of West Africa		•							30,000	KF			300	KF estimate 10,000 pairs (30,000 individuals).
poiocephalus, C, E & S Africa	Coasts & rivers of E & S Africa,		•							200,000–400,000	DO			3,000	
poiocephalus, Madagascar	Madagascar		•							A	HJ			100	

Larus hartlaubii — Hartlaub's Gull

Subspecies/Population	Breeding range	Wintering, or core non-breeding range	Afr	Eu	Asia	Oc	Neo	NA	Estimate	Source	Trend	Source	1% level	Notes
Southern Africa	Coastal SW Africa C Namibia–SW Cape Province		•							30,000	TO	INC	TO	300	

Larus novaehollandiae — Silver Gull

Subspecies/Population	Breeding range	Wintering, or core non-breeding range	Afr	Eu	Asia	Oc	Neo	NA	Estimate	Source	Trend	Source	1% level	Notes
novaehollandiae	S Australia including Tasmania					•				E	CX				
forsteri	N Australia New Caledonia & Loyalty Is					•									B5: 2,500–3,500 in New Caledonia.

Larus scopulinus — Red-billed Gull

Subspecies/Population	Breeding range	Wintering, or core non-breeding range	Afr	Eu	Asia	Oc	Neo	NA	Estimate	Source	Trend	Source	1% level
New Zealand	New Zealand					•			D	CX			10,000

Red-billed Gull.

Nils Anthes

Larus bulleri VU — Black-billed Gull

Subspecies/Population	Breeding range	Wintering, or core non-breeding range	Afr	Eu	Asia	Oc	Neo	NA	Estimate	Source	Trend	Source	1% level	Notes
New Zealand	New Zealand					•			96,000	BC	DEC	BC	960	

Larus maculipennis — Brown-hooded Gull

Subspecies/Population	Breeding range	Wintering, or core non-breeding range	Afr	Eu	Asia	Oc	Neo	NA	Estimate	Source	Trend	Source	1% level	Notes
S South America	SC Chile & Uruguay S to Tierra del Fuego	N Chile & CE Brazil S to Tierra del Fuego					•		D	S8	INC	CX	10,000	
Falkland/Malvinas Is	Falkland/Malvinas Islands						•		4,200–7,500	WS			60	WS estimate 1,400–2,500 pairs (4,200–7,500 individuals).

Larus ridibundus — Common Black-headed Gull

Subspecies/Population	Breeding range	Wintering, or core non-breeding range	Afr	Eu	Asia	Oc	Neo	NA	Estimate	Source	Trend	Source	1% level	Notes
N & C Europe (br)	Most of Europe, S Greenland	S & W Europe		•					5,600,000–7,300,000	BE	INC	BE	20,000	European breeding population 1,855,000–2,424,000 pairs (5,565,000–7,272,000 individuals) (BE). For populations over 2 million birds, Ramsar Convention criterion 5 (20,000 or more waterbirds), applies.
Mediterranean (br)	SE Europe & Mediterranean	Mediterranean, N Africa	•	•					1,300,000–1,700,000	BE	INC	BE	15,000	European breeding population 445,000–576,000 pairs (1,335,000–1,728,000 individuals) (BE).
SW Asia, E Africa (non-br)	W Russia, Central Asia	SW Asia, Eastern Africa	•	•	•				250,000	PE			2,500	
South Asia (non-br)	Russia, Central Asia	S Asia			•				C/D	PE				
E & SE Asia (non-br)	Central Asia to Kamchatka, NE China	Japan, Korea, E & S China, Taiwan, Indochina, Philippines			•				D/E	CE				
NE North America	SE Canada, NE USA	NE North America						•	440	KS			4	KS estimate 40 breeders, 400 non-breeders. Colonised in 1950s.

Common Black-headed Gull. Johan Verbanck

191

Larus genei — **Slender-billed Gull**

Subspecies/Population	Breeding range	Wintering, or core non-breeding range	Afr	Eu	Asia	Oc	Neo	NA	Estimate	Source	Trend	Source	1% level	Notes
West Africa	Coasts of Senegal, Mauritania		•						22,500	KF	STA	DO	230	KF estimate 7,500 pairs (22,500 individuals).
Black Sea, Mediterranean	Black Sea and Mediterranean		•	•					123,000–237,000	BE	INC	HC	1,800	European breeding population 41,000–79,000 pairs (123,000–237,000 individuals) (BE).
W, SW & S Asia (br)	SW Asia to Caspian, E Kazakhstan, Afghanistan, Pakistan, NW India	*Coasts of Caspian & SW Asia*	•		•				150,000	PE	INC	PE	1,500	

Larus philadelphia — **Bonaparte's Gull**

Subspecies/Population	Breeding range	Wintering, or core non-breeding range	Afr	Eu	Asia	Oc	Neo	NA	Estimate	Source	Trend	Source	1% level	Notes
North America	W Alaska & S British Colombia E to Quebec	*Pacific SW Canada–C Mexico, Atlantic coast to Gulf of Mexico, N Caribbean*					•	•	255,000–525,000	HV	STA	CX	3,900	HV estimate 85,000–175,000 pairs (255,000–525,000 individuals).

Larus saundersi VU — **Saunders's Gull**

Subspecies/Population	Breeding range	Wintering, or core non-breeding range	Afr	Eu	Asia	Oc	Neo	NA	Estimate	Source	Trend	Source	1% level	Notes
NE Asia (br)	Coastal NE & E China, Korea	*S Japan, South Korea, E & S China, Taiwan, Vietnam*			•				7,100–9,600	BD	DEC	BC	85	

Larus serranus — **Andean Gull**

Subspecies/Population	Breeding range	Wintering, or core non-breeding range	Afr	Eu	Asia	Oc	Neo	NA	Estimate	Source	Trend	Source	1% level	Notes
Central Andes	Andes N Ecuador–N Chile, W Bolivia, N Argentina	*Andean range + coast Ecuador–SC Chile*					•		150,000	HV			1,500	HV estimates possibly fewer than 50,000 pairs (150,000 individuals).

Larus melanocephalus — **Mediterranean Gull**

Subspecies/Population	Breeding range	Wintering, or core non-breeding range	Afr	Eu	Asia	Oc	Neo	NA	Estimate	Source	Trend	Source	1% level	Notes
Europe	Most on Ukrainian Black Sea + scattered through C, S & W Europe & E to Azerbaijan	*Black Sea, Mediterranean, NW Europe, NW Africa*	•	•					570,000–1,110,000	BE	INC	BE	8,400	European breeding population 190,000–370,000 pairs (570,000–1,110,000 individuals) (BE).

Larus relictus VU — Relict Gull

Subspecies/Population	Breeding range	Wintering, or core non-breeding range	Afr	Eu	Asia	Oc	Neo	NA	Estimate	Source	Trend	Source	1% level	Notes
C Asia (br)	Isolated colonies on lakes C Asia–NC China	Few winter records; occasional in Japan, S Korea, Hong Kong			•				12,000	BC	DEC	BC	120	BC gives estimate of 12,000 individuals (<10,000 mature adults).

Larus fuliginosus VU — Lava Gull

Subspecies/Population	Breeding range	Wintering, or core non-breeding range	Afr	Eu	Asia	Oc	Neo	NA	Estimate	Source	Trend	Source	1% level	Notes
Galapagos Is	Galapagos Islands						•		900–1,200	BC	STA?	BC	10	BC estimates 300–400 pairs (900–1,200 individuals).

Larus atricilla — Laughing Gull

Subspecies/Population	Breeding range	Wintering, or core non-breeding range	Afr	Eu	Asia	Oc	Neo	NA	Estimate	Source	Trend	Source	1% level	Notes
(megalopterus) N & C America (br)	SE California to W Mexico, Nova Scotia to Florida, & Texas, locally E Central America	Carolinas & S Californria S to Central America & Pacific coast S to Peru					•	•	792,000–807,000	KS	INC	S5	8,000	KS estimate North American breeding population at 528,000–538,000 adults (792,000–807,000 individuals) BR estimated the US breeding population at 258,851 pairs (776,553 individuals).
atricilla, Caribbean (br)	Caribbean Islands	Caribbean S to N Brazil					•	•	15,000–30,000	CG			230	CG estimates 5,000–10,000 pairs (15,000–30,000 individuals).

Larus pipixcan — Franklin's Gull

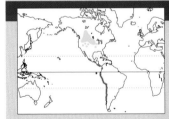

Subspecies/Population	Breeding range	Wintering, or core non-breeding range	Afr	Eu	Asia	Oc	Neo	NA	Estimate	Source	Trend	Source	1% level	Notes
Americas	SC Canada, NC USA	Pacific coasts Central & S America					•	•	470,000–1,490,000	KS			9,800	KS estimate 315,608–990,864 breeding adults (473,412–1,486,296 individuals. PJ estimate 365,800 breeding pairs (1,097,400 individuals).

Larus minutus — Little Gull

Subspecies/Population	Breeding range	Wintering, or core non-breeding range	Afr	Eu	Asia	Oc	Neo	NA	Estimate	Source	Trend	Source	1% level	Notes
N, C & E Europe (br)	N Scandinavia, Baltic States, W Russia, Belarus, Ukraine	W Europe, NW Africa	•	•					66,000–102,000	BE	STA?	HC	840	European breeding population 22,000–34,000 pairs (66,000–102,000 individuals) (BE).
Black, Caspian & E Mediterranean Seas (non-br)	W Siberia	Black & Caspian Seas, E Mediterranean		•	•				C	SA			1,000	Counts of 50,000 in the Nile Delta reported in HC.
E China (non-br)	E Siberia	East China			•				A	PE			100	
North America	Hudson Bay to the Great Lakes	SE Canada, NE USA						•	150–300	KS			2	KS estimate 100–200 breeding adults (150–300 individuals. Largest single concentration recorded in North America: 297 (EW).

Pagophila eburnea — Ivory Gull

Subspecies/Population	Breeding range	Wintering, or core non-breeding range	Afr	Eu	Asia	Oc	Neo	NA	Estimate	Source	Trend	Source	1% level	Notes
High Arctic	Very high Arctic, NE Canada, N & E Greenland, Svalbard to New Siberian Is		•	•				•	C	KS BE OP HV			1,000	KS estimate North American breeding population at >2,400 adults (>3,600 individuals). Greenland & European breeding population 3,600–5,500 pairs (10,800–16,500 individuals) (BE). OP records aerial estimates of up to 35,000+ between Canada and Greenland in 1978–79. HV estimate possibly 25,000 pairs (75,000 individuals).

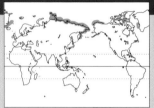

Rhodostethia rosea — Ross's Gull

Subspecies/Population	Breeding range	Wintering, or core non-breeding range	Afr	Eu	Asia	Oc	Neo	NA	Estimate	Source	Trend	Source	1% level	Notes
High Arctic	N Siberia Taymyr–Kolyma River, NE Canada	Arctic Ocean			•			•	C	HV DE			1,000	HV estimates 10,000–25,000 (possibly up to 50,000) pairs, and up to 38,000 off point Barrow in autumn. DE estimated c.50,000.

Ross's Gull.

Gerard Boere

Xema sabini — Sabine's Gull

Subspecies/Population	Breeding range	Wintering, or core non-breeding range	Afr	Eu	Asia	Oc	Neo	NA	Estimate	Source	Trend	Source	1% level	Notes
sabini	Arctic Canada to N & NE Greenland	SE Atlantic off SW Africa, E Pacific off NW South America	•	•				•	>300,000–600,000	KS			4,500	KS estimate North American breeding population at 200,000–400,000 individuals (300,000–600,000 individuals). 1990 Greenland breeding population 100–300 pairs (300–900 individuals).
(woznesenksii)	NE Siberia (Anadyr Gulf) to Alaska				•		•	•	C	DD HV	STA	CX	1,000	DD Estimate entire Pacific Ocean wintering population (which includes woznesenksii and tschuktschorum) at =<100,000. Alaska population several tens of thousands of pairs (HV).
(palaearctica)	Svalbard E to Taymyr & Lena Delta				•									4 pairs in Svalbard (Norway) (BE).
(tschuktschorum)	Chukchi Peninsula, E Siberia				•		•	•						

Creagurus furcatus — Swallow-tailed Gull

Subspecies/Population	Breeding range	Wintering, or core non-breeding range	Afr	Eu	Asia	Oc	Neo	NA	Estimate	Source	Trend	Source	1% level	Notes
Galapagos Is	Galapagos Is	Galapagos Is, coasts Ecuador to C Chile					•		35,000	CX			350	10,000–15,000 pairs (30,000–45,000 individuals) (HV).

Rissa tridactyla — Black-legged Kittiwake

Subspecies/Population	Breeding range	Wintering, or core non-breeding range	Afr	Eu	Asia	Oc	Neo	NA	Estimate	Source	Trend	Source	1% level	Notes
tridactyla, East Atlantic (br)	Coastal N & W Europe E to Taymyr Peninsula	E North Atlantic & North Seas	•	•					8,400,000	LY			20,000	European breeding population (minus Greenland) 2,200,000–2,600,000 pairs (6,600,000–7,800,000 individuals) (BE). For populations over 2 million birds, Ramsar Convention criterion 5 (20,000 or more waterbirds), applies.
tridactyla, Greenland (br)	E & W Greenland Coasts	North Atlantic	•					•	D/E	(BI)				W. Greenland breeding population 100,000–200,000 pairs (300,000–600,000 individuals (BI).
tridactyla, W Atlantic (br)	Arctic Canada S to Gulf of Lawrence	W North Atlantic						•	900,000	HV			9,000	HV estimates 300,000 pairs (900,000 individuals). KS estimate North American breeding population (all populations combined) at 3,126,000 adults (4,689,000 individuals).
pollicaris, E Pacific (br)	Bering Sea, W & S Alaska	North Pacific						•	2,500,000	CX	STA	CX	20,000	For populations over 2 million birds, Ramsar Convention criterion 5 (20,000 or more waterbirds), applies. 650,000 pairs in Alaska (HV).
pollicaris, W Pacific (br)	NE Siberia, Kamchatka, Sea of Okhotsk, Kuril Is	North Pacific			•				>4,800,000	HV			20,000	1,600,000 pairs (4,800,000 individuals) in Kamchatka alone (HV). For populations over 2 million birds, Ramsar Convention criterion 5 (20,000 or more waterbirds), applies.

Rissa brevirostris VU — Red-legged Kittiwake

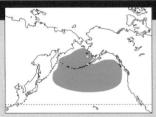

Subspecies/Population	Breeding range	Wintering, or core non-breeding range	Afr	Eu	Asia	Oc	Neo	NA	Estimate	Source	Trend	Source	1% level	Notes
North Pacific	Bering Sea, Commander, Pribilof & Aleutian Is	North Pacific			•			•	290,000–320,000	KS HV BC	DEC	BC	3,100	KS estimate 160,000–180,000 breeding adults in Alaska (240,000–270,000 individuals). HV estimates 17,000 pairs in Commander Is, Russia (51,000 individuals). Total, 291,000–321,000. HV estimates 100,000 pairs (300,000 individuals).

Sterna nilotica — Gull-billed Tern

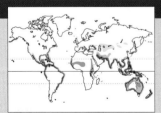

Subspecies/Population	Breeding range	Wintering, or core non-breeding range	Afr	Eu	Asia	Oc	Neo	NA	Estimate	Source	Trend	Source	1% level	Notes
nilotica, W Europe & W Africa (br)	W & SW Europe, NW & W Africa S to Mauritania	West Africa, E African Rift Valley & coast	•	•					10,000–16,000	BE DO	DEC	BE	130	Summed breeding populations of relevant European countries 2,376–2,803 pairs (7,128–8,409 individuals) (BE). DO calculates African total of 3,135–7,485 individuals. Overall total 10,263–15,894. Often placed in monotypic genus Gelochelidon.
nilotica, Black Sea, E Mediterranean (br)	Black Sea, E Mediterranean		•	•					14,000–39,000	BE	DEC	BE	270	Summed breeding populations of relevant countries 4,700–13,000 pairs (14,100–39,000 individuals) (BE).
nilotica, SW Asia (non-br)	Caspian region, Central Asia	SW Asia particularly Persian Gulf	•	•	•				B	PE			250	
nilotica, South Asia (non-br)	Central Asia	S Asia			•				C	PE	STA	PE	1,000	
addenda	E Central Asia, N & E China	Indochina, S China, Malaysia, Indonesia, Philippines			•				B/C	PE			1,000	
macrotarsa	E & S Australia	Australia, New Zealand?				•								
groenvoldi	Coast & rivers French Guiana–NE Argentina						•							

STERNIDAE TERNS

195

Sterna nilotica... continued

Subspecies/Population	Breeding range	Wintering, or core non-breeding range	Afr	Eu	Asia	Oc	Neo	NA	Estimate	Source	Trend	Source	1% level	Notes
vanrossemi	Coastal California to Mexico	*Unknown, Mexico & C America?*					•	•			STA	P2		P2: Taxonomy of W Mexico population uncertain. Definite colonies of this subspecies in S California and N Mexico total 260–350 pairs (780–1,050 individuals).
groenvoldi or *vanrossemi*	Coastal Ecuador & Peru						•							Subspecific status of this population uncertain.
aranea	E US coast S to Caribbean Islands, Yucatan	*Coasts of southern USA, Central America S to Peru & Brazil*					•	•	B	KS	STA?	P2	250	KS estimate 6,000–8,000 breeding adults (9,000–12,000 individuals including *vanrossemi*). Declining in NE parts of US range, but despite trends being locally erratic, probably stable overall in most parts of US (P2).

Sterna caspia — Caspian Tern

Subspecies/Population	Breeding range	Wintering, or core non-breeding range	Afr	Eu	Asia	Oc	Neo	NA	Estimate	Source	Trend	Source	1% level	Notes
Southern Africa (br)	Southern Africa		•						1,500	CM	STA	TO	15	Often assigned to monotypic genus Hydroprogne.
Madagascar (br)	Madagascar, Europa & Aldabra Group (Seychelles)		•						1,000–2,000	DO			15	Estimate for Madagascar 960–1900 (HJ).
W Africa (br)	W Africa		•						45,000–60,000	DO VE	STA	DO	530	
Europe (br)	Baltic & Black Seas, Turkey	*Mediterranean, W, N & E, Africa, SW Asia*	•	•					5,400–7,800	BE	DEC	KQ	65	European breeding population (excluding Volga) 1,800–2,600 pairs (5,400–7,800 individuals) (BE).
Caspian (br)	Caspian & Iran	*SW Asia, NE Africa*	•	•	•				9,000–16,500	SA			130	
South Asia (non-br)	Central Asia, Sri Lanka	*Pakistan, India, Sri Lanka*			•				B/C	PE	STA	PE	1,000	
E & SE Asia (non-br)	Central Asia, Central Siberia, E China	*E China, Taiwan, Indochina*			•				B	PE	INC	PE	250	
North America: Pacific Coast	Alaska through W USA, along coast to Baja California	*Pacific coast California–C America*					•	•	44,500–45,000	WO	INC	WO	450	WO estimates 14,846–14,982 pairs (44,538–44,946 individuals). KS combined estimate for all 5 North American populations: 66,000–70,000 breeding adults, (99,000–105,000 individuals).
North America: Central Canada (br)	Central Canada from Manitoba to Alberta	*Caribbean Basin & Pacific Coast?*					•	•	26,000–30,000	WO	INC	WO	280	WO estimates 8,780–9,980 pairs (26,340–29,940 individuals).
North America: Gulf Coast	Gulf of Mexico from Texas to Florida	*SE USA & across Caribbean Basin*					•	•	6,900	WO	INC	WO	70	WO estimates 2,303 pairs (6,909 individuals).
North America: Atlantic Coast	Atlantic coast Newfoundland to North Carolina	*SE USA & across Caribbean Basin*					•	•	420–426	WO	DEC	WO	4	WO estimates 140–142 pairs (420–426 individuals).
North America: Great Lakes	Great Lakes region of Canada & USA	*SE USA & across Caribbean Basin*					•	•	19,200	WO	INC	WO	190	WO estimates 6,416 pairs (19,248 individuals).
(strenua)	Australia, New Zealand					•			1,000–5,000	CX			30	

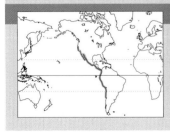

Sterna (Thalasseus) elegans NT — Elegant Tern

Subspecies/Population	Breeding range	Wintering, or core non-breeding range	Afr	Eu	Asia	Oc	Neo	NA	Estimate	Source	Trend	Source	1% level	Notes
Pacific N America	Pacific coast S California & Gulf of California, Mexico	*Pacific coast California to Chile*					•	•	51,00–90,000	KS	FLU	BS	700	KS estimates 34,000–60,000 breeding adults (51,000–90,000 individuals).

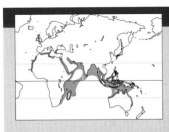

Sterna (Thalasseus) bengalensis — Lesser Crested Tern

Subspecies/Population	Breeding range	Wintering, or core non-breeding range	Afr	Eu	Asia	Oc	Neo	NA	Estimate	Source	Trend	Source	1% level	Notes
par, Mediterranean (br)	Libyan coast	*S Mediterannean, NW & W African coasts*	●	●					4,000	MD	STA	SP	40	Sometimes assigned to *emigrata* or *torresii*.
par, Red Sea & Gulf of Aden (br)	Red Sea & Gulf of Aden	*W Indian Ocean S to South Africa & Madagascar*	●		●				30,000	DO			300	Sometimes assigned to *bengalensis* or *arabica*.
bengalensis	Persian Gulf, Pakistan coast, Maldive & ?Laccadive Is	*Indian Ocean S to Sri Lanka and possibly South Africa*	●		●				150,000–180,000	SA			1,700	
torresii, SE Asia, Australia (br)	Sulawesi to New Guinea & N, NE Australia	*SW Pacific Ocean*				●	●							

Sterna (Thalasseus) sandvicensis — Sandwich Tern

Subspecies/Population	Breeding range	Wintering, or core non-breeding range	Afr	Eu	Asia	Oc	Neo	NA	Estimate	Source	Trend	Source	1% level	Notes
sandvicensis, W Europe (br)	Coasts of W & N Europe	*Mostly W & NW African coasts S to South Africa*	●	●					159,000–171,000	BE	INC	BE	1,700	BE estimate for relevant countries 53,000–57,000 pairs (159,000–174,000 individuals).
sandvicensis, Black Sea (br)	Black Sea coast	*Mediterranean & Black Sea coasts*	●	●	●				44,000–73,000	BE	DEC	HC	590	BE estimate for relevant countries 14,700–24,400 pairs (44,000–73,000 individuals).
sandvicensis, Caspian (br)	Caspian Sea	*Coasts Persian Gulf & S Red Sea to Pakistan, India, Sri Lanka*			●				110,000	LY			1,100	
acuflavidus	N & C American coast Virginia to Belize, Caribbean	*Caribbean to S Peru & Uruguay*					●	●	100,000	CX			1,000	KS estimates 75,000–100,000 individuals in Americas North of the equator (*acuflavidus* + part of *eurygnatha*). 45,000 pairs in E USA (HV).
eurygnatha, S Caribbean (br)	Netherlands Antilles–Venezuela	*S Caribbean, Atlantic coast S America to Argentina*					●		35,000–37,000	NT			360	NT estimates 11,600–12,200 pairs (34,800–36,600 individuals) in the Netherlands Antilles and off the coast of N South America. Additionally, only 10–100 pairs (30–300 individuals) are thought to nest elsewhere in the Caribbean.
eurygnatha, E Brazil–Argentina (br)	E Brazil–Argentina	*S Caribbean, Atlantic coast S America to Argentina*					●		10,000	CX			100	

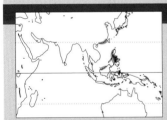

Sterna (Thalasseus) bernsteini CR — Chinese Crested Tern

Subspecies/Population	Breeding range	Wintering, or core non-breeding range	Afr	Eu	Asia	Oc	Neo	NA	Estimate	Source	Trend	Source	1% level	Notes
E China (br)	Poorly known; E China coast	*Taiwan & S China to Indonesia & Philippines*			●				<50	BC			1	

Sterna (Thalasseus) maxima — Royal Tern

Subspecies/Population	Breeding range	Wintering, or core non-breeding range	Afr	Eu	Asia	Oc	Neo	NA	Estimate	Source	Trend	Source	1% level	Notes
maxima, W Atlantic (br)	Coast of Maryland to Texas, West Indies, Guianas, S Brazil, Uruguay, N Patagonia	*Coast of S Carolina S to Brazil*					●	●	139,000	KS			1,400	Sum of North and Central American and Caribbean totals from relevant Bird Conservation Regions in KS, 139,490.
maxima, E Pacific (br)	Coast of S California to Sinaloa	*Coast of California S to Peru*					●	●	10,900	KS			110	Sum of North and Central American totals from relevant Bird Conservation Regions in KS, 10,870. Assumption that 2,700 birds in "Central America" split 50/50 between Atlantic and Pacific.
albididorsalis	Coast of W Africa Mauritania to Guinea	*Coast of W Africa Morocco to Namibia*	●						135,000–165,000	VE	STA/ INC	DO	1,500	>50,000 pairs (150,000 individuals) in Senegal & Mauritania in 1999. (VE)

197

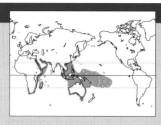

Sterna (Thalasseus) bergii — (Greater) Crested Tern

Subspecies/Population	Breeding range	Wintering, or core non-breeding range	Afr	Eu	Asia	Oc	Neo	NA	Estimate	Source	Trend	Source	1% level	Notes
bergii	Namibia to South Africa	Angola to S. Mozambique	•						20,000	HF	STA	TO	200	
(enigma), Madagascar (br)	Madagascar, ?Juan de Nova, Mozambique	Zambezi Delta, Mozambique, to Durban, South Africa	•						7,500–10,000	DO			90	Often assigned to bergii.
thalassina, Indian Ocean islands (br)	Tanzania, Seychelles, Chagos		•		•				1,300–1,700	DO			15	
velox, Red Sea & NE Africa (br)	Red Sea & NW Somalia	Red Sea & NW Somalia S to Kenya			•				C	SA			1,000	5,300 pairs (15,900 individuals) in Red Sea & NE Africa excluding Ethiopia (SA).
velox, Arabian Gulf & Indian Ocean (br)	Arabian Gulf, E to Maldives, Sri Lanka, Myanmar	Indian Ocean Kenya to Myanmar	•		•									
gwendolenae	W & NW Australia					•								
cristata	Japan, Taiwan, E. China, Indonesia–Philippines, E Australia, SW Pacific Is				•	•								

Crested Tern.

Johannes Wahl

Sterna aurantia — River Tern

Subspecies/Population	Breeding range	Wintering, or core non-breeding range	Afr	Eu	Asia	Oc	Neo	NA	Estimate	Source	Trend	Source	1% level	Notes
S & SE Asia	E Pakistan to S India, Nepal, SW China, Myanmar, C Indochina to Mekong Delta				•				B/C	PE	DEC	PE	1,000	

Sterna dougallii — Roseate Tern

Subspecies/Population	Breeding range	Wintering, or core non-breeding range	Afr	Eu	Asia	Oc	Neo	NA	Estimate	Source	Trend	Source	1% level	Notes
dougalli, South Africa (br)	S Cape Province South Africa		•						750	TO	INC	UN	8	
dougalli, E Africa (br)	S Somalia–Tanzania	E African seaboard (dispersive)	•						25,500	CM			260	Perhaps better assigned to bangsi (HV). 8,500 pairs (25,500 individuals) (CM).
dougalli, W Europe (br)	Azores, Ireland, Britain	Coasts of tropical W Africa	•	•					4,800–5,400	BE	DEC	BE	50	European breeding population 1,600–1,800 pairs (4,800–5,400 individuals) (BE).
dougalli, W Atlantic (br): Nova Scotia–New York	Nova Scotia, New York	N South America, Mid Atlantic Ocean?					•	•	11,700	KS	DEC	LY	120	KS estimate 7,800 breeding adults (11,700 individuals) in these bird conservation regions. GO estimates population at 3,000–4,000 pairs (9,000–12,000 individuals).
dougalli, W Atlantic (br): Florida Keys & Caribbean Basin	Florida Keys and Caribbean Basin	N South America, Mid Atlantic Ocean?					•	•	13,050	KS			130	KS estimate 8,700 breeding adults (13,050 individuals) in these bird conservation regions. S2 estimated Caribbean population at 4,000–6,000 pairs (12,000–18,000 individuals) and Florida Keys at 350 pairs (1,050 individuals).
arideensis	Seychelles S to Madagascar, E to Cargados Carajos (Mauritius)	W Indian Ocean	•						12,000–15,000	DO	DEC	DO	140	May not be distinct from bangsi (HV).
korustes	Sri Lanka Andaman Is, SW Myanmar	Indian & Pacific Oceans			•				A		LY		100	
gracilis	Australia & Moluccas Is	Indian & Pacific Oceans				•								
bangsi, Arabian Sea	Arabian Sea (islands off Oman)	Indian Ocean			•				<600	SA			6	The taxonomy of this subspecies needs revision. Two populations of "bangsi" are separated by korustes.
bangsi, SE Asia	Coasts Ryukyu Is, China Taiwan, S to Indonesia, E to Solomon Is, New Caledonia	Pacific Ocean S to Australia			•	•								B15 estimate 5,000 pairs (15,000 individuals) in New Caledonia.

Sterna striata — White-fronted Tern

Subspecies/Population	Breeding range	Wintering, or core non-breeding range	Afr	Eu	Asia	Oc	Neo	NA	Estimate	Source	Trend	Source	1% level	Notes
striata	New Zealand	SE Australia S Queensland–Tasmania–S Australia				•			1,500,000	HV			15,000	About 500,000 pairs (1,500,000 individuals) breed in New Zealand (HV).
incerta	Flinders & Cape Barren Is, NE Tasmania	SE Australia S Queensland–Tasmania–S Australia				•			135	GC	STA	GC	1	GC estimates 90 breeding adults (135 individuals). Breeding sites discovered 1979 (HV).
auklandorna	Chatham, Aukland and possibly Snares Is					•								

Sterna sumatrana — Black-naped Tern

Subspecies/Population	Breeding range	Wintering, or core non-breeding range	Afr	Eu	Asia	Oc	Neo	NA	Estimate	Source	Trend	Source	1% level	Notes
sumatrana	NE Indian Ocean, Malaysia, Indonesia, Philippines, S China, Taiwan, S Japan S to N & E Australia, SW Pacific Is				•	•								
mathewsi	Aldabra, Amirante, Chagos & Maldive Is				•	•								Estimate for Seychelles 250–350 (DO).

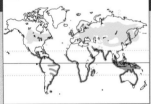

Sterna hirundinacea — South American Tern

Subspecies/Population	Breeding range	Wintering, or core non-breeding range	Afr	Eu	Asia	Oc	Neo	NA	Estimate	Source	Trend	Source	1% level	Notes
S South America	Coasts of S Peru & CE Brazil to Tierra del Fuego, Falkland/ Malvinas Is	Coasts Tierra del Fuego, Falkland/Malvinas Is to Ecuador & Bahia Brazil					•		C/D	CX	DEC	S8		WS estimate 6,000–12,000 pairs (18,000–36,000 individuals) in Falkland/Malvinas Is.

Sterna hirundo — Common Tern

Subspecies/Population	Breeding range	Wintering, or core non-breeding range	Afr	Eu	Asia	Oc	Neo	NA	Estimate	Source	Trend	Source	1% level	Notes
hirundo, W Africa (br)	Mauritania, Senegal, Nigeria, Gabon	Atlantic African coast	•						1,200	DO			10	
hirundo, S, W Europe (br)	S, W Europe	West African seaboard	•	•					170,000–200,000	SA	STA	SP BE	1,900	BE estimate from relevant countries 57,000–67,000 pairs (171,000–201,000 individuals).
hirundo, N, E Europe (br)	NE Europe, mainly countries around Baltic	Mainly Southern Africa	•	•					460,000–820,000	SA	STA	SP BE	6,400	BE estimate from relevant countries 153,000–273,000 pairs (459,000–819,000 individuals).
hirundo, W Asia (br)	W Asia	Indian Ocean	•		•				C/D	PE				
hirundo, North America: Atlantic coast (br)	Atlantic & Gulf of Mexico coasts, mostly S to the Carolinas	West Indies and South America S to S Peru, S Argentina					•	•	270,000	N1	STA	S5	2,700	N1 estimate 90,000 pairs (270,000 individuals).
hirundo, North America: Great Lakes (br)	Great Lakes of USA & Canada	West Indies and South America S to S Peru, S Argentina					•	•	27,000–30,000	N1			300	N1 estimate 9,000–10,000 pairs (27,000–30,000 individuals).
hirundo, North America: Interior (br)	Interior of C Canada and N USA	West Indies and South America S to S Peru, S Argentina					•	•	108,000	N1			1,100	N1 estimate 36,000 pairs (108,000 individuals).
hirundo, Caribbean (br)	6 scattered colonies Bermuda through Caribbean to Netherlands Antilles and Islets off Venezuela	West Indies and South America S to S Peru, S Argentina					•		870–1,470	BP			10	BP estimates 290–490 pairs (870–1,470 individuals) at 6 scattered locations.
tibetana	Mountains W Mongolia S to Kashmir, Tibet, Sichuan	Mostly E Indian Ocean			•				B/C	PE			1,000	
minussensis	Central Asia to N Mongolia, S Tibet	Mostly N Indian Ocean			•									
longipennis	NE Siberia S to NE China	SE Asia to Australia			•	•			C/D	PE				

Common Terns. Johan Verbanck

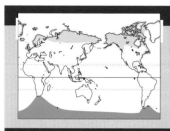

Sterna paradisaea — Arctic Tern

Subspecies/Population	Breeding range	Wintering, or core non-breeding range	Afr	Eu	Asia	Oc	Neo	NA	Estimate	Source	Trend	Source	1% level	Notes
N Eurasia (br)	Europe N of France, Scandinavia, Russia N of Arctic Circle	*Antarctic Ocean*	•	•	•	•	•	•	E	BE HV				European breeding population 440,000–760,000 pairs (1,320,000–2,280,000 individuals) (BE). Numbers breeding in Arctic Siberia unknown. Birds wintering off South Africa almost exclusively of European origin (to White Sea) (UN).
N North America (br)	Alaska, Canada, NE & NW USA, Greenland	*Antarctic Ocean*	•		•	•	•	•						

Sterna vittata — Antarctic Tern

Subspecies/Population	Breeding range	Wintering, or core non-breeding range	Afr	Eu	Asia	Oc	Neo	NA	Estimate	Source	Trend	Source	1% level	Notes
vittata	Prince Edward, Marion, Crozet, Kerguelen, Heard Is	*Prince Edward, Marion, Crozet, Kerguelen, Heard? Is, Coast of South Africa*	•						>6,700	TO			65	TO estimate 2,200 pairs (6,700 adults) of vittata on Kerguelen and Heard Is. Wintering population of these two subspecies in South Africa is >15,000 (HF & UN). GC estimates Australian population of *vittata*, principally on Heard Is, at 200 breeding adults (300 individuals). Bulk of population of *vittata*, 2,000 pairs, found on Kerguelen Is; numbers on Marion unknown (TO).
tristranensis	Tristan da Cunha, Gough Is, Amsterdam & St Paul?	*Coast of south Africa*	•						2,600–3,800	DO			30	
georgiae	South Georgia Is, S Orkney, S Sandwich & Bouvetoya?	*Coasts of Argentina, Falkland/Malvinas Is*	•				•		125,000	CX			1,250	3,000 pairs South Orkney, 2,500 pairs South Georgia (16,500 individuals) (HV).
bethunei	New Zealand Islands					•			1,500	HP			15	Up to 1,000 birds breed on New Zealand's sub-Antarctic islands (1,500 individuals).
gaini	S Shetland Is, Antarctic Peninsula?	*Coasts of Argentina, Falkland/Malvinas Is*					•							35,000 pairs in South Shetland Is (HV).
macquariensis	Macquarie Is					•			120	HV			1	40 pairs (HV) (120 individuals). Sometimes included in *bethunei*.

Sterna virgata NT — Kerguelen Tern

Subspecies/Population	Breeding range	Wintering, or core non-breeding range	Afr	Eu	Asia	Oc	Neo	NA	Estimate	Source	Trend	Source	1% level	Notes
S Indian Ocean	Kerguelen, Crozet, Prince Edward, Marion Is		•						3,500–6,500	TG			50	

Sterna forsteri — Forster's Tern

Subspecies/Population	Breeding range	Wintering, or core non-breeding range	Afr	Eu	Asia	Oc	Neo	NA	Estimate	Source	Trend	Source	1% level	Notes
Atlantic North America	Atlantic and Gulf coasts New England to Tamaulipas, Mexico	*Virginia S along Atlantic coast & E across Caribbean Basin*					•	•	86,600	MB			870	MB estimate 28,862 pairs (86,586 individuals) not including any birds in Mexico, so estimate slightly low.
Pacific North America	Pacific Coast, California–Baja California, Mexico	*California S to Guatemala*					•	•	24,400	MB			240	MB estimate 8,095 pairs + 30–35 pairs in Baja California, Mexico (24,390 individuals).
Interior: Great Lakes	Great Lakes–S Canada–C & W USA	*Atlantic & Gulf coasts E to Caribbean?*					•	•	9,100	MB			90	MB estimate 3,025 pairs (9,075 individuals).
Interior: Great Plains & W lowlands	Great Plains lowlands of W USA & Canada	*Pacific & Gulf coasts S to C America?*												KS estimate 47,000–51,500 breeding adults in all 4 populations breeding in North & Central America (70,500–77,250 individuals).

Sterna trudeaui — Trudeau's Tern, Snowy-crowned Tern

Subspecies/Population	Breeding range	Wintering, or core non-breeding range	Afr	Eu	Asia	Oc	Neo	NA	Estimate	Source	Trend	Source	1% level	Notes
SW South America	Central Chile	N Chile–S Peru					•		A	S8	STA	S8	100	
SE South America	SE Brazil & Uruguay to Patagonia	E coast S South America N to Rio de Janeiro					•							

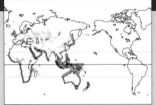

Sterna albifrons — Little Tern

Subspecies/Population	Breeding range	Wintering, or core non-breeding range	Afr	Eu	Asia	Oc	Neo	NA	Estimate	Source	Trend	Source	1% level	Notes
albifrons, W Europe (br)	W Europe–NW Africa	W & SW Africa	•	•					31,000–37,500	BE	STA	BE	340	BE estimate from relevant ocunties 10,450–12,500 pairs (31,350–37,500 individuals).
albifrons, E Europe (br)	E Europe, Black Sea, E Mediterranean	Red Sea, Arabia, E Africa	•	•					64,500–127,000	BE	DEC	BE	960	BE estimate from relevant ocunties 21,500–42,300 pairs (64,500–126,900 individuals).
albifrons, SW Asia (br)	SW Asia	Arabian Gulf & Indian Ocean	•	•	•				B	PE			250	Subspecies innominata listed in error by HV and Clements for islands in the Persian Gulf.
guineae	Mauritania–Senegal, Ghana to Gabon, Niger River	W & SW Africa	•						2,000–3,000	DO			25	
pusilla	NE India, Sri Lanka, Myanmar, Sumatra, Java	Indian Ocean & SE Asia			•				B/C	PE			1,000	
sinensis	E & SE Asia to Australia	SE Asia–Australia			•	•			B/C	PE	DEC	PE	1,000	GC estimate Australian population at 3,000 breeding adults (4,500 individuals). Australian population increasing in response to effective conservation management.
placens	E Australia & E Tasmania	Australia, Indonesia, New Guinea				•			15,000	CX	DEC	CX	150	

Sterna saundersi — Saunders's Tern

Subspecies/Population	Breeding range	Wintering, or core non-breeding range	Afr	Eu	Asia	Oc	Neo	NA	Estimate	Source	Trend	Source	1% level	Notes
N & W Indian Ocean, Red Sea	Red Sea S to S Somalia, Saudi, Omani coasts, Persian Gulf to NW India, Sri Lanka, Maldives	Red Sea S To Tanzania, Madagascar, E to India, Malaysian Peninsula	•		•				40,000	ES			400	

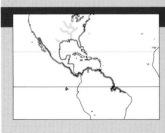

Sterna antillarum — Least Tern

Subspecies/Population	Breeding range	Wintering, or core non-breeding range	Afr	Eu	Asia	Oc	Neo	NA	Estimate	Source	Trend	Source	1% level	Notes
antillarum	W Atlantic Coast S of Maine, Gulf of Mexico, Caribbean	Coasts Colombia–N Brazil					•	•	50,000–55,000	TJ JA	DEC	S5	530	KS estimate 60,000–100,000 breeding adults (90,000–150,000 individuals) of all subspecies in North America & Caribbean. JA estimate 1,500–3,000 pairs (4,500–9,000 individuals) in West Indies.
athalassos	Inland rivers EC North America	Coasts Colombia–N Brazil					•	•	6,800	TJ	INC	TJ	70	Taxonomic status of this form uncertain.
browni	C California to Baja California & W Mexico	Most in Central America					•	•	8,250	TJ			85	TJ: estimate 2,750 pairs (8,250 individuals).

Sterna superciliaris — Yellow-billed Tern

Subspecies/Population	Breeding range	Wintering, or core non-breeding range	Afr	Eu	Asia	Oc	Neo	NA	Estimate	Source	Trend	Source	1% level	Notes
N South America	E Colombia to Guianas, NE Peru, C Argentina	Some movement to adjacent coasts					•		C	AT	STA	AT	1,000	

Sterna lorata NT — Peruvian Tern

Subspecies/Population	Breeding range	Wintering, or core non-breeding range	Afr	Eu	Asia	Oc	Neo	NA	Estimate	Source	Trend	Source	1% level	Notes
NW South America (br)	Coast C Ecuador, Peru, N Chile	Unknown					•		>15,000	BC	DEC	S8	150	BC estimate 5,000 pairs (15,000 individuals) in Peru. Also nests at 3 sites in Chile – numbers unknown (BC).

Sterna nereis LC — Fairy Tern

Subspecies/Population	Breeding range	Wintering, or core non-breeding range	Afr	Eu	Asia	Oc	Neo	NA	Estimate	Source	Trend	Source	1% level	Notes
nereis	S Australia, Victoria, Tasmania	S Australia, Victoria				•			2,580	BC	STA	BC	25	BC estimate 860 pairs (2,580 individuals). GC estimates 6,000 breeding adults (9,000 individuals) for nereis & horni combined.
horni	SW Western Australia	SW to NW Western Australia				•			6,060	BC	STA	BC	60	BC estimate 2,021 pairs (6,063 individuals).
exsul	New Caledonia					•			300	BC	DEC	BC	3	BC & B5 estimate 100 pairs (300 individuals).
davisae	N North Island New Zealand					•			25–30	BC	INC	BC	1	

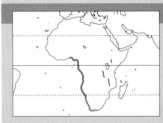

Sterna balaenarum NT — Damara Tern

Subspecies/Population	Breeding range	Wintering, or core non-breeding range	Afr	Eu	Asia	Oc	Neo	NA	Estimate	Source	Trend	Source	1% level	Notes
SW Africa (br)	Namibia to Cape Province South Africa	SW South Africa to Nigeria, W to Liberia	•						14,000	SI TO	STA	DO	140	13,500 in Namibia (SI); 120 pairs (360 individuals) in South Africa (TO); total 13,860.

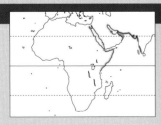

Sterna repressa — White-cheeked Tern

Subspecies/Population	Breeding range	Wintering, or core non-breeding range	Afr	Eu	Asia	Oc	Neo	NA	Estimate	Source	Trend	Source	1% level	Notes
N & W Indian Ocean, Red Sea	Red Sea S to S Somalia, Kenya, Persian Gulf to W India	Somalia & Kenya, Gulf of Oman, Pakistan & W Indian coasts	•		•				600,000	ES	DEC	ES	6,000	

Sterna acuticauda NT — Black-bellied Tern

Subspecies/Population	Breeding range	Wintering, or core non-breeding range	Afr	Eu	Asia	Oc	Neo	NA	Estimate	Source	Trend	Source	1% level	Notes
S & SE Asia	Pakistan, India, Nepal, E to SW China, S to S Vietnam				•				B	BC	DEC	PE	250	

Sterna aleutica — Aleutian Tern

Subspecies/Population	Breeding range	Wintering, or core non-breeding range	Afr	Eu	Asia	Oc	Neo	NA	Estimate	Source	Trend	Source	1% level	Notes
N Pacific (br)	Sakhalin, Sea of Okhotsk, Kamchatka, Aleutians, SW Alaska	Poorly known; S China Sea, Philippines to Malay Peninsula			•			•	30,000–35,000	KS NR	STA	CX	330	KS estimate 14,594 breeding adults in Alaska (21,891 individuals). NR estimates 12,949 in Alaska + 7,200–13,000 in Siberia.

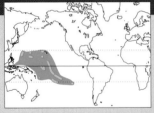

Sterna lunata — Grey-backed Tern

Subspecies/Population	Breeding range	Wintering, or core non-breeding range	Afr	Eu	Asia	Oc	Neo	NA	Estimate	Source	Trend	Source	1% level	Notes
Pacific Islands	Islands of tropical SW Pacific to Hawaii					•			D	CX			10,000	KS estimate Hawaiian population at 72,000–104,000 breeding adults (108,000–156,000 individuals).

Sterna anaethetus — Bridled Tern

Subspecies/Population	Breeding range	Wintering, or core non-breeding range	Afr	Eu	Asia	Oc	Neo	NA	Estimate	Source	Trend	Source	1% level	Notes
anaethetus	S Japan, Taiwan, Philippines, Indonesia, New Guinea, Australia	SW Pacific to NE Indian Ocean			•	•								
melanoptera	Gulf of Guinea Islands, Coastal Mauritania–Senegal	Tropical E Atlantic	•						1,500	DO	DEC	DO	15	
recognita	Caribbean, Venezuela	Caribbean, Tropical W Atlantic						•	12,000–18,000	CG			150	CG estimate 4,000–6,000 pairs (12,000–18,000 individuals). KS estimate *recognita* + *nelsoni* at 8,700–14,700 breeding adults (13,050–22,050 individuals).
antarctica	Maldives, Seychelles, Madagascar, Kenya coast	Tropical Indian Ocean	•		•				500,000	CX			5,000	
fuligula	Red Sea, Persian Gulf, Arabian Sea, W India	Arabian Sea, Tropical Indian Ocean	•		•				150,000	CX			1,500	
(*rogersi*)	N Western Australia	SW Pacific to NE Indian Ocean				•								
(*novaehollandiae*)	Queensland to S Australia, New Caledonia	SW Pacific to NE Indian Ocean				•								B5: 500–1,000 pairs (1,500–3,000) in New Caledonia.
nelsoni	W coast Mexico & Central America	Tropical E Pacific				•								

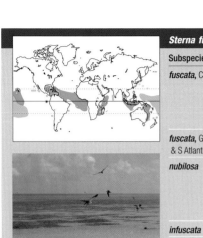

Sterna fuscata — Sooty Tern

Subspecies/Population	Breeding range	Wintering, or core non-breeding range	Afr	Eu	Asia	Oc	Neo	NA	Estimate	Source	Trend	Source	1% level	Notes
fuscata, Caribbean (br)	Caribbean, Gulf of Mexico, Venezuela	*Caribbean & Tropical Atlantic*					•	•	690,000–1,200,000	S3			9,500	S3 estimates 230,000–400,000 pairs (690,000–1,200,000 individuals). KS estimate 3,360,000–4,380,000 breeding adults (5,040,000–6,570,000 individuals) in all American subspecies N of equator (*fuscata, oahuensis, crissalis*).
fuscata, Gulf of Guinea & S Atlantic (br)	Tropical S Atlantic Is, Gulf of Guinea Is	*Tropical Atlantic*	•				•		900,000	DO			9,000	
nubilosa	Gulf of Aden, Coastal E Africa, Indian Ocean – Madagascar–Andaman Is; Philippines–S Japan	*Indian Ocean to W Pacific Ocean*	•		•	•			>13,500,000	DO			20,000	DO presents details of an estimate totalling 13,500,000 in the W Indian Ocean islands and E African coast alone. For populations over 2 million birds, Ramsar Convention criterion 5 (20,000 or more waterbirds), applies.
infuscata	C Indonesia (range uncertain)	*Indian to Pacific Oceans*				•								
serrata	New Guinea, Australia, New Caledonia	*Tropical Pacific Ocean*				•								5,500–12,500 pairs (16,500–37500) in New Caledonia (B5).
kermadeci	Kermadec Is	*Tropical Pacific Ocean*				•			>2,000,000	CX			20,000	For populations over 2 million birds, Ramsar Convention criterion 5 (20,000 or more waterbirds), applies.
oahuensis	Bonin Is to Hawaii Is & S through Pacific	*Tropical Pacific Ocean*				•			>2,000,000	CX			20,000	For populations over 2 million birds, Ramsar Convention criterion 5 (20,000 or more waterbirds), applies.
luctuosa	Juan Fernandez Is, Easter & Desventuradas Is, Chile	*Tropical Pacific Ocean*				•			A	S8			100	
crissalais	Islands W Mexico & C America, Galapagos Islands	*Tropical Pacific Ocean*				•			>2,000,000	CX			20,000	For populations over 2 million birds, Ramsar Convention criterion 5 (20,000 or more waterbirds), applies.

Sooty Tern colony. *Gerard Boere*

Chlidonias albostriatus/Sterna albostriata EN — Black-fronted Tern

Subspecies/Population	Breeding range	Wintering, or core non-breeding range	Afr	Eu	Asia	Oc	Neo	NA	Estimate	Source	Trend	Source	1% level	Notes
New Zealand	Interior South Island New Zealand	*Coastal South Island, S North Island New Zealand*				•			2,000–10,000	BC	**DEC**	BC	60	Often assigned to the genus *Sterna*.

Chlidonias hybridus — Whiskered Tern

Subspecies/Population	Breeding range	Wintering, or core non-breeding range	Afr	Eu	Asia	Oc	Neo	NA	Estimate	Source	Trend	Source	1% level	Notes
hybridus, W Europe, W Mediterranean (br)	W Europe, W Mediterranean	*West Africa*	•	•					21,500–31,000	SA	**DEC**	BE	260	Summed breeding populations of relevant countries 7,140–10,300 pairs (21,420–30,900 individuals) (BE). Very few in N Africa (SA).
hybridus, E Europe, E Mediterranean (br)	E Europe, Black Sea, E Mediterranean	*E Mediterranean, NE Africa*	•	•					80,000–120,000	BE	**STA / INC**	SA	1,000	Summed breeding populations of relevant countries 29,000–41,000 pairs (87,000–123,000 individuals) (BE) less 1,000–2,000 pairs (3,000–6,000 individuals) in Volga Delta.
hybridus, Central Asia (br)	Caspian, W Central Asia	*Iran–Pakistan, India, Sri Lanka*		•	•				C	PE			1,000	
sclateri, East Africa	Kenya, Tanzania		•						10,000–15,000	DO			130	*sclateri* is synonymous with *delalandii*.

Chlidonias hybridus... continued

Subspecies/Population	Breeding range	Wintering, or core non-breeding range	Afr	Eu	Asia	Oc	Neo	NA	Estimate	Source	Trend	Source	1% level	Notes
sclateri, Southern Africa	Southern Africa & Madagascar		•						5,000–15,000	DO			100	Possibly increasing in southern Africa (HF).
indicus	E Iran, Pakistan, N India	*S Asia*			•									
swinhoei	EC Asia, E China	*Poorly known: S China, Taiwan to SE Asia*			•									
javanicus	NE India, Sri Lanka	*Malaysia, Indonesia, Philippines*			•									
fluviatilis	Australia	*Australia, New Guinea, Moluccas*			•	•			D	PE			10,000	

Chlidonias leucopterus — White-winged (Black) Tern

Subspecies/Population	Breeding range	Wintering, or core non-breeding range	Afr	Eu	Asia	Oc	Neo	NA	Estimate	Source	Trend	Source	1% level	Notes
S & E Europe (br)	NW Italy–C & E Europe– W & W Central Asia	*Sub-Saharan Africa, Persian Gulf*	•	•	•				2,500,000– 3,500,000	BV			20,000	European breeding population 22,000–53,000 pairs (66,000–159,000 individuals) (BE).
Asia, Australasia	Central & E Siberia, N Mongolia– SE Russia, NE China	*India, Sri Lanka, Indochina, S & E China to Australia, New Zealand*			•	•			C/D	PE				

Chlidonias niger — Black Tern

Subspecies/Population	Breeding range	Wintering, or core non-breeding range	Afr	Eu	Asia	Oc	Neo	NA	Estimate	Source	Trend	Source	1% level	Notes
niger	W, C & S Europe, W & C Asia E to Altai Mts	*Coastal W, & C Africa to Namibia*	•	•	•				300,000– 500,000	SA	DEC	BE	4,000	European breeding population 47,000–88,000 pairs (141,000–264,000 individuals) (BE). W & C Asian population unknown, but perhaps of similar size.
surinamensis	S Canada, N USA	*Coasts S Mexico–Peru, Gulf of Mexico–Guianas*					•	•	150,000– 750,000	KS	DEC	S5	4,500	KS estimate 100,000–500,000 breeding adults (150,000–750,000 individuals). HV estimates possibly 100,000 pairs (300,000 individuals) in North America.

Phaetusa simplex — Large-billed Tern

Subspecies/Population	Breeding range	Wintering, or core non-breeding range	Afr	Eu	Asia	Oc	Neo	NA	Estimate	Source	Trend	Source	1% level	Notes
simplex	E Colombia–Trinidad, Amazonia	*Coasts & Rivers Colombia–Brazil*					•							
chloropoda	R Paraguay & R Parana basins S to NC Argentina	*Coasts & Rivers Brazil–Uruguay*					•		C	AT	STA	AT	1,000	

Anous stolidus — Brown Noddy

Subspecies/Population	Breeding range	Wintering, or core non-breeding range	Afr	Eu	Asia	Oc	Neo	NA	Estimate	Source	Trend	Source	1% level	Notes
stolidus	Caribbean, S Atlantic Islands, Gulf of Guinea Islands	*Caribbean and tropical Atlantic*	•				•	•	D	DO CF			10,000	CF estimate the Carribean breeding population at 12,000–18,000 pairs (36,000–54,000 individuals). KS estimate populations breeding in Americas N of the equator (*stolidus, galapagensis, ridgwayi*) at 286,000–298,000 adults (429,000–447,000).
plumbeigularis	S Red Sea and Gulf of Aden	*Indian Ocean*	•		•				75,000	DO			750	
pileatus	Seychelles & Madagascar E to N Australia, Polynesia, Hawaii, Easter Is, Bonin Is	*Indian & Pacific Oceans*	•		•	•								DO estimates 300,000–600,000 for E Afican Coast & W Indian Ocean Islands. Estimate for Melanesia is B (DX), of which 500 pairs (1,500) in New Caledonia (B5).

Anous stolidus... continued

Subspecies/Population	Breeding range	Wintering, or core non-breeding range	Afr	Eu	Asia	Oc	Neo	NA	Estimate	Source	Trend	Source	1% level	Notes
galapagensis	Galapagos Islands						•							
ridgwayi	W Mexico, W Central America to Cocos Is						•	•						

Anous minutus — **Black Noddy, White-capped Noddy**

Subspecies/Population	Breeding range	Wintering, or core non-breeding range	Afr	Eu	Asia	Oc	Neo	NA	Estimate	Source	Trend	Source	1% level	Notes
minutus	NE Australia, New Guinea, S & SW Pacific Islands					•								B5: Estimate for New Caledonia, 80,000 pairs (160,000).
worcesteri	Islands in Sulu Sea (Philippines, Borneo)	Sulu Sea (Philippines, Borneo)			•									
marcusi	Marcus Is & Wake Is–Micronesia–Caroline Is	Central Pacific				•								
melanogenys	Hawaiian Islands					•			60,000	HV			600	KS estimate melanogenys + americanus at >86,400 breeding individuals, >250,000 in total.
diamesus	E Cent Pacific (Cocos Is, Clipperton Is)	E Central Pacific				•								
americanus	Central America, Caribbean, Venezuelan Islands						•							CF estimate the Caribbean breeding population at 10–100 pairs (30–300 individuals).
atlanticus	Tropical Atlantic Is to Gulf of Guinea Islands		•				•							DO estimates 90,000–150,000 for Gulf of Guinea, Ascension & St Helena. 10,000 pairs (30,000 individuals) on Ascension Island (HV). Numbers on St Paul & Fernando de Noronha unknown.

Anous tenuirostris — **Lesser Noddy**

Subspecies/Population	Breeding range	Wintering, or core non-breeding range	Afr	Eu	Asia	Oc	Neo	NA	Estimate	Source	Trend	Source	1% level	Notes
tenuirostris	Seychelles, Mascarene Is, Maldives	Indian Ocean Madagascar–Maldives, Arabia	•	•					E	DO				DO estimates 1,050,000–1,350,000 for Seychelles and Mascarene Is. Numbers in Maldives unknown.
melanops	Houtman Abrolhos Is, Western Australia					•			150,000	GC	STA	GC	1,500	GC estimate 100,000 breeding adults (150,000 individuals).

Procelsterna cerulea — **Blue Noddy**

Subspecies/Population	Breeding range	Wintering, or core non-breeding range	Afr	Eu	Asia	Oc	Neo	NA	Estimate	Source	Trend	Source	1% level	Notes
cerulea	Marquesas Is, Kiritimati					•								2,000 pairs in Kiritimati (HV).
saxatilis	Marcus Is & N Marshall Is E to NW Hawaiian Is					•								
nebouxi	Tuvalu E to Phoenix Is, S to Fiji & Western Samoa					•								
teretirostris	Tuamotu Is, Cook, Austral & Society Is					•								
murphyi	Gambier Is, South Pacific, Easter & Desventuradas Is, Chile					•								Up to 1,000 breeding pairs (3,000 individuals) on Gambier (HV).

Procelsterna albivitta — **Grey Noddy**

Subspecies/Population	Breeding range	Wintering, or core non-breeding range	Afr	Eu	Asia	Oc	Neo	NA	Estimate	Source	Trend	Source	1% level	Notes
albivitta	Lord Howe Is, New Caledonia, Norfolk Is, Kermadec Is & Tonga					•			C	HV			1,000	Sometimes considered conspecific with P cerulea. Probably <25,000 pairs (<75,000 individuals) (HV). GC estimate 2,000 breeding adults (3,000 individuals) on Lord Howe & Norfolk Is; <20 on New Caledonia (B5).
skottsbergii	Henderson Is, Easter & Sala y Gomez Is					•			A	HV			100	Rare, probably endangered (HV).
imitatrix	San Ambrosio Is, San Felix Is (Central Chile)						•		A	HV			100	Rare, probably endangered (HV).

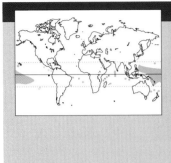

Gygis alba — White Tern

Subspecies/Population	Breeding range	Wintering, or core non-breeding range	Afr	Eu	Asia	Oc	Neo	NA	Estimate	Source	Trend	Source	1% level	Notes
alba	C American Is, tropical S Atlantic Is							•	A/B	CX			250	KS estimate American portion of *alba*, + *rothschildi* at 30,000 breeding individuals, with a total North American population of 80,700.
candida, Indian Ocean	Indian Ocean Islands		•		•				D	CX			10,000	
(royana)	Norfolk & Kermadec Is					•								GC estimate 6,500 breeding adults (9,750 individuals) on Norfolk, Cocos-Keeling & Lord Howe Is.
candida, SW Pacific	SW C Pacific Islands to Marquesas					•			15,000	CX			150	Estimate for Melanesian Islands 5,000–10,000 (DX), suggesting that overall estimate may be low.
(rothschildi)	Hawaiian Islands					•			20,000	CX			200	
(pacifica)	S Pacific: Caroline Island & Melanesia					•			15,000	CX			150	

Gygis microrhyncha — Little White Tern

Subspecies/Population	Breeding range	Wintering, or core non-breeding range	Afr	Eu	Asia	Oc	Neo	NA	Estimate	Source	Trend	Source	1% level	Notes
microrhyncha	Marquesas Islands, Phoenix & Line Is					•								Often considered conspecific with *G alba*.

Larosterna inca — Inca tern

Subspecies/Population	Breeding range	Wintering, or core non-breeding range	Afr	Eu	Asia	Oc	Neo	NA	Estimate	Source	Trend	Source	1% level	Notes
inca	Coast N Peru to C Chile						•		150,000	HV			1,500	HV estimates 50,000 pairs (150,000 individuals).

Rynchops niger — Black Skimmer

Subspecies/Population	Breeding range	Wintering, or core non-breeding range	Afr	Eu	Asia	Oc	Neo	NA	Estimate	Source	Trend	Source	1% level	Notes
niger, Pacific North America	S California and Pacific coast of Mexico						•	•	4,200	CL	INC	CL	40	CL estimate 1,350 pairs in California + 21 pairs in Baja California, Mexico (4,113 individuals). The number elsewhere along the Pacific coast of Mexico is unknown but small (KS).
niger, Atlantic North America	Atlantic & Gulf of Mexico coasts S from Massachussets	Florida and the Gulf of Mexico S to Panama					•	•	93,000–101,000	KS			970	KS estimate of both North American populations 65,000–70,000 breeding adults (97,500–105,000 individuals). Estimate derived by subtracting the Pacific estimate (4,200) from this range.
cinerascens	Amazon Delta–Colombia–Ecuador S to Bolivia, NW Argentina	Coasts Ecuador–S Chile, Panama–Trinidad–NC Brazil					•							
intercedens	Large Rivers of E Brazil, E Paraguay, Uruguay, NE Argentina	Coasts of E S America					•		C	AT	STA	AT	1,000	

RYNCHOPIDAE SKIMMERS

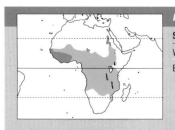

Rynchops flavirostris NT · African Skimmer

Subspecies/Population	Breeding range	Wintering, or core non-breeding range	Afr	Eu	Asia	Oc	Neo	NA	Estimate	Source	Trend	Source	1% level	Notes
West & Central Africa	Senegal E to Chad, S to DR Congo	West & W Central Africa	•						7,000–13,000	DO	DEC	DO	100	BC: estimates 10,000 >20,000.
East & Southern Africa	Sudan, SW Ethiopia S to Botswana, S Mozambique	Nile & Rift Valleys S to Botswana & South Africa	•						8,000–12,000	DO	DEC	HV	100	

African Skimmers.

Johan Verbanck

Rynchops albicollis VU · Indian Skimmer

Subspecies/Population	Breeding range	Wintering, or core non-breeding range	Afr	Eu	Asia	Oc	Neo	NA	Estimate	Source	Trend	Source	1% level	Notes
S & SE Asia	E Pakistan, N & E India, Bangladesh, Myanmar; possibly extinct along Mekong River				•				2,500–10,000	BC	DEC	BC	60	Now possibly <5,000 birds (HV).

References and other sources

References are presented in alphabetical order of first author. When this name includes an article or preposition (e.g. del Hoyo, van den Berg) the principal name has been used. The two symbol codes are those used in the "source" columns in the population estimates tables, also presented in a sequence very close to alphabetical (and numerical) order. References without codes appear in the text only, and not in the tables.

Code Reference

AG Aguilar, J.S. & Fernandez, G. 1999. *Species Action Plan for the Mediterranean Shag* Phalacracorax aristotelis desmarestii *in Europe.* BirdLife International.

AL Allen, George T., Caithamer, David F. and Otto, Mark. 1999. *A review of the status of greater and lesser scaup in North America.* DMBM unpublished report. 45pp.

AM Amat, Juan A. In litt. 2002.

AN Anderson, D. In litt. 1993. Summarised census data of New World Pelicans for Wetlands International.

A1 Andres, B.A. and Falxa, G.A. 1995. Black Oystercatcher (Haematopus bachmani). In: *The Birds of North America* No.155 (A. Poole and F. Gill, eds). Academy of Natural Sciences, Philadelphia, Pennsylvania, and American Ornithologists' Union, Washington, D.C.

AO Anon 2002. RHD: bad news for Wrybills? *World Birdwatch* 24 (1): 7.

AR Antas, P.T.Z. and Resende, S.M.L. 1983. First record of the South American pochard in Brazil. *Auk* 100: 220–221.

AT Antas, P.T.Z. In litt. 1993. Unpublished data concerning South American waterbirds.

AW Asian Waterbird Census unpublished data. 2002.

— Asia-Pacific Migratory Waterbird Conservation Committee, 2001. *Migratory Waterbird Conservation Strategy 2001–2005.* Wetlands International, Kuala Lumpur, Malaysia, 69 pp.

— Atkinson-Willes, G.L., Scott, D.A., and Prater, A.J. 1982. Criteria for selecting wetlands of international importance: Proposed amendments anfd guidelines on use. Pp 1017–1042 In: Spagnesi, M. (ed.) *Proceedings of the Conference on the conservation of wetlands of international importance, especially as waterfowl habitat (Cagliari, Italy).* Supplemento alle Ricerche di Biologia della Selvaggina. Vol VIII.

AZ Azafzaf, Hichem and Paul Isenmann. In litt. June–August, 2002.

BA Baker, A.J., Gonzalez, P.M., Minton, C.D.T., Carter, D.B., Niles, L., Nascimento, I.L.S., and Piersma, T. In press. 2000. Hemispheric problems in the conservation of Red Knots (Calidris canutus rufa). Proceedings of the 6th Neotropical Ornithological Congress, October 1999.

B1 Baker, N. E. 1996. *Tanzania Waterbird Count, January 1995: The first coordinated count of the major wetlands of Tanzania. January 1995.* Wildlife Conservation Society of Tanzania. Dar es Salaam.

B2 Baker, N. In press. 2002. The northern population of the Cape Teal *Anas capensis*. *Wildfowl*.

B3 Bamford, M.J., Watkins, D.G., Bancroft, W. and Tischler, G. In prep. 2002. *Migratory Shorebirds of the East Asian-Australasian Flyway; Population Estimates and Important Sites.* Wetlands International – Oceania.

B4 Barr, J.F., Eberl, C. and McIntyre, J.W. 2000. Red-throated Loon (Gavia stellata).

In: *The Birds of North America* No. 513 (A. Poole and F. Gill, eds). Academy of Natural Sciences, Philadelphia, Pennsylvania, and American Ornithologists' Union, Washington, D.C.

B5 Barré, N. and Dutson, G. 2000. Oiseaux de Nouvelle-Calédonie. Liste commentée. Suppl. *Alauda* (68) 3: 49pp.

B6 Barzen, J. and U.S. Seal (editors). 2000. *Eastern Sarus Crane PHVA Final Report.* CBSG, Apple Valley, MN, USA. Unpublished papers from Jeb Barzen and Tran Triet.

B7 Beekman, J.H. 1997. International censuses of the north-west European Bewick's Swan population, January 1990 and 1995. *Swan Specialist Group Newsletter* 6: 7–9.

B8 Beilfuss, R. In litt. 2002.

B9 Beilfuss, R., Williams, E. and Dodman, T. In prep. 2002. Status Survey and Conservation Action Plan for the Black Crowned Crane *Balearica pavonina*. Wetlands International, Dakar.

B10 Belik, V.P. and Lebedeva, E.A. 2002. *Draft International Action Plan for the Black-winged Pratincole* Glareola nordmanni. AEWA Secretariat/BirdLife International. 31 pp.

B11 Bellrose, F.C. 1980. *Ducks, geese and swans of North America. 3rd edn.* Stackpole Books, Harrisburg, USA.

B12 Bellrose, Frank C. and Holm, Daniel J. 1994. *Ecology and management of the wood duck.* Stackpole Books. 588pp.

B13 van den Berg, A. 2002. Western Palearctic Reports. *Dutch Birding* 24: 234–235.

B15 Benoit, M.P. and Bretagnolle, V. 2002. Seabirds of the southern lagoon of New Caledonia. Waterbirds 25 (2): 202–213.

BB BirdLife International Website.

BC BirdLife International. 2000. *Threatened Birds of the World.* Barcelona and Cambridge, Lynx Edicions and BirdLife International.

BD BirdLife International. 2001. *Threatened Birds of Asia: the BirdLife International Red Data Book.* Cambridge, UK. BirdLife International.

BE BirdLife International/European Bird Census Council. 2000. *European bird populations: estimates and trends.* Cambridge, UK. BirdLife International Conservation Series No. 10.

B14 BirdLife International/European Birds Census Council, European Birds Database. Accessed March 1994.

— Blanco, D. and Carbonell, M. (eds.) 2001. *The Neotropical Waterbird Census – the first 10 years: 1990–1999.* Wetlands International, Buenos Aires, Argentina, and Ducks Unlimited Inc, Memphis, USA.

BF Blanco, D. In litt. 2002. Unpublished information concerning Neotropical waterbirds.

BG Boertmann, D. 1994. *An annotated checklist to the birds of Greenland.* Meddr. Gronland Biosc. 38: 64 pp.

BH Boertmann, D. and Mosbech, A. 1997. Breeding distribution and abundance of the great cormorant *Phalacrocorax carbo carbo* in Greenland. *Polar Research* 16: 93–100.

BI Boertmann, D., Mosbech, A., Falk, K., and Kampp, K. 1996. *Seabird colonies in western Greenland*. NERI Technical Report 170: 148 pp.

BJ Boertmann, David. Unpublished data. 2002.

BK Bordage, D. and Savard, J.L.. 1995. Black Scoter (Melanitta nigra). In *The Birds of North America* No. 177 (A. Poole and F. Gill, eds). Academy of Natural Sciences, Philadelphia, Pennsylvania, and American Ornithologists' Union, Washington, D.C.

BL Bordage, D. Environment Canada – Canadian Wildlife Service. Personal Communication. 2002.

BM Bos, J. F. P., Essetti, I. and Gilissen, N. L. M. 2000. Record counts of Marbled Teal in Tunisia, October 1999: consequences for population estimates and distribution. *Threatened Waterfowl Spec. Group News* 12: 49–53.

— Boyd, H. 1999. Population modelling and management of Snow Geese. Occasional Paper No.102 Canadian Wildlife Service.

BN Brown, L.H., Urban, E.K. and Newman, K. 1982. *The Birds of Africa. Volume I*. Academic Press, London and New York.

BO Brown, S., Hickey, C. and Harrington, B. (eds.) 2000. *The U.S. Shorebird Conservation Plan*. Manomet Center for Conservation Sciences, Manomet, MA.

BP Buckley, P.A. and Buckley, F.G. 2000. Breeding Common Terns in the Greater West Indies: status and conservation priorities. In: Schreiber, E.A. and Lee, D.S. (eds.) *Status and Conservation of West Indian seabirds*. Soc. Caribbean Ornith. Spec. Pub. No.1.: 96–101.

BQ Burger, J. and Gochfeld, M. 1994. Franklin's Gull (Larus pipixcan). In: *The Birds of North America* No 116. (A. Poole and F. Gill, eds). The Academy of Natural Sciences, Philadelphia, PA and The American Ornithologists' Union, Washington D.C.

BR Burger, J. 1996. Laughing Gull (Larus atricilla). In: *The Birds of North America* No 225. (A. Poole and F. Gill, eds). The Academy of Natural Sciences, Philadelphia, PA and The American Ornithologists' Union, Washington D.C.

BS Burness, G., Lefevre, K. and Collins, C. 1999. Elegant Tern (Sterna elegans). In: *The Birds of North America* No 404. (A. Poole and F. Gill, eds). The Academy of Natural Sciences, Philadelphia, PA and The American Ornithologists' Union, Washington D.C.

BT Butler, R. W. 1992. Great Blue Heron (Ardea herodias). In: *The Birds of North America* No 25. (A. Poole and F. Gill, eds). The Academy of Natural Sciences, Philadelphia, PA and The American Ornithologists' Union, Washington D.C.

BU Butler, R.W., Kushlan, J.A. and Davidson, I.J. 2000. Herons in North America, Central America and the West Indies. Pp 151–175 in: *Heron Conservation* (James A. Kushlan and Heinz Hafner, Eds). Academic Press, London.

BV Byaruhanga, A., Arinaitwe, J. and Williams, C. 2002. Large concentrations of White-winged Black Terns Chlidonias leucopterus at Lutembe Bay, Lake Victoria. *Bull African Bird Club* 9 (1): 25–26.

BW Byers, O. (ed.) 1995. *Stork, Ibis, and Spoonbill Conservation Assessment and Management Plan: Working Document*. IUCN/SSC Conservation Breeding Specialist Group: Apple Valley, MN.

BX Byrkjedal, I. and Thompson, D. 1998. *Tundra Plovers: The Eurasian, Pacific and American Golden Plovers and Grey Plover*. T .and A.D. Poyser, London.

C1 Caithamer, D.F. (Compiler). 1995. *Survey of Trumpeter Swans in North America*. U.S. Fish and Wildlife Servic, Division of Migratory Bird Management, Patuxent Wildlife Research Center, Laurel, MD.

C2 Caithamer, D.F. (Compiler). 2001. *Trumpeter Swan population status, 2000*. U.S. Fish Wildlife Service, Division of Migratory Bird Managment, Laurel, MD.

C3 Callaghan, D.A. 1998. Conservation status of the Torrent Ducks Merganetta. *Wildfowl* 48: 166–173.

CA Callaghan, D.A. and Green, A.J. 1993. Wildfowl at risk, 1993. *Wildfowl* 44: 149–169.

CB Campredon, P. 1987. La reproduction des oiseaux d'eau sur le Parc National du Banc d'Arguin (Mauritanie) en 1984–1985. *Alauda* 55: 187–210.

CC Canevari, P. In litt. 1993. Unpublished information from Neotropical Wetlands Program.

CD Carey, Geoff. In litt. 2002.

CE Chan, Simba. In litt. 2002. Unpublished information on Asian waterbirds.

CF Chardine, J.W., Morris, R.D. and Norris R.C.. 2000. Status and Conservation needs of Brown Noddies and Black Noddies in the West Indies. In: Schreiber, E.A. and Lee, D.S. (eds). *Status and Conservation of West Indian seabirds*. Soc. Caribbean Ornith. Spec. Pub. No.1.: 118–125.

CG Chardine, J.W., Morris, R.D., Parnell, J.F. and Pierce, J. 2000. Status and Conservation of Laughing Gulls, Royal Terns and Bridled Terns in the West Indies. In: Schreiber, E.A. and Lee, D.S. (eds). *Status and Conservation of West Indian seabirds*. Soc. Caribbean Ornith. Spec. Pub. No.1.: 65–79.

CH Chaudhry, A.A. 2002. *White-headed Duck Survey in Pakistan: 2002*. Wetlands International Report, Kuala Lumpur. Malaysia.

CI Chinese Ornithological Society Waterbird Specialist Group. 1994. *Checklist of Waterbirds in China*. In: Chinese Ornithological Society Waterbird Specialist Group (ed). Waterbird Research in China. East China Normal University Press, Shanghai.

CJ Choudhury, A. 2000. *The Birds of Assam*. Gibbon Books and WWF – India, Guwahti, India.

CK Collar, N.J., Crosby, M.J. and Stattersfield, A.J. 1994. *Birds to Watch 2. The World List of Threatened Birds*. BirdLife Conservation series No. 4. BirdLife International, Cambridge, UK. 407 pp.

CL Collins, C.T. and Garrett, K.L. 1996. The Black Skimmer in California: an overview. *Western Birds* 27: 127–135.

CM Cooper, J., Williams, A.J. and Britton, P.L. 1984. *Distribution, population sizes and conservation of breeding seabirds in the Afrotropical region*. IUCN Technical Publication 2, 403–417.

CN Coulter, M.C., Rodgers, J.A., Ogden, J.C. and Depkin, F.C. 1999. Wood Stork (Mycteria americana). In: *The Birds of North America* No 409. (A. Poole and F. Gill, eds). The Academy of Natural Sciences, Philadelphia, PA and The American Ornithologists' Union, Washington D.C.

CO de le Court, Claudine. In litt. 2002.

CP Covadonga Viedma Gil de Vergara and Mario Giménez Ripoll (compilers). In review. 2002. *Species Action Plan for the Purple Gallinule* Porphyrio porphyrio. BirdLife International/Council of Europe.

MH Miller, Craig (2001). Notornis 48: 157–163.

CQ Cranswick, P.A., Colhoun, K., Einarsson, O., McElwaine, J. G., Gardarsson, A., Pollitt, M. S. and Rees E. C. In press. 2002. The Status and Distribution of the Icelandic Whooper Swan Population: Results of the International Whooper Swan Census 2000. *Waterbirds* 25, Special Edition 1.

CR Cranswick, P.A., Mitchell, C.R., Merne, O.J., Ogilvie, M.A., Kershaw, M., Delany, S.N., MacKay, M. and Lilley, R. 2000. *Status and distribution of the Greenland population* of Barnacle Goose Branta leucopsis *in Britain and Ireland, 1993 to 1999.* WWT report to JNCC.

CS Crawford, R. In prep. 2002. Species texts for: Cape Cormorant, *Phalacrocorax capensis*, Crowned Cormorant, *Phalacrocorax coronatus*, Great White Pelican, *Pelecanus onocrotalus* and Kelp Gull, *Larus dominicanus*. In: Hockey, P.A.R., et al. In prep. *Roberts' Birds of Southern Africa*, 7th edition.

CT Crivelli, A.J. and Schreiber, R.W. 1984. Status of the Pelecanidae. *Biol. Cons.* 30: 147–156.

CU Crivelli, A.J., Catsadorakis, G., Hatzilacou, D., Hulea, D., Malakou, M., Marinov, M., Michev, T., Nazirides, T., Peja, N., Sarigul, G. and Siki, M. 2000. Status and population development of Great White Pelican *Pelecanus onocrotalus* and Dalmatian Pelican *P. crispus* breeding in the Palearctic. Pp 38–46 In: Yésou, P. and Sultana, J. (eds.) *Proceedings of the 5th Medmaravis Symposium, Gozo, Malta.* Environment Protection Department, Malta.

CV Crivelli, A.J., Nazirides, T., Catsadorakis, G., Hulea, D., Malakou, M., Marinov, M. and Shogolev, I. 2000. Status and population development of Pygmy Cormorant *Phalacrocorax pygmeus* breeding in the Palearctic. Pp 49–60 In: Yésou, P. and Sultana, J. (eds.) *Proceedings of the 5th Medmaravis Symposium, Gozo, Malta.* Environment Protection Department, Malta.

CW Crosby, Michael. In litt. 2002.

CY Croxall, J.P. (ed) 1991. *Status and Conservation of the World's Seabirds: A Supplement.* ICBP Technical Publication No. 11. Cambridge, UK.

CX Croxall, J.P., Evans, P.G.H. and Schreiber, R.W. (eds). 1984. *Status and Conservation of the World's Seabirds.* ICBP Technical Publication No. 2. Cambridge, UK.

DA Dahmer, T.D. and Felley, M.L. In prep. *Global Population Estimates for Black-faced Sponbill,* Platalea minor*, 1988–2001.*

DB Davis Jr., W.E. and Krider, J. 2000. Glossy Ibis (Plegadis falcinellus). In: *The Birds of North America* No 545. (A. Poole and F. Gill, eds). The Academy of Natural Sciences, Philadelphia, PA and The American Ornithologists' Union, Washington D.C.

DC Davis Jr., W.E. 1993. Black-crowned Night-Heron (Nycticorax nycticorax). In: *The Birds of North America* No 74. (A. Poole and F. Gill, eds). The Academy of Natural Sciences, Philadelphia, PA and The American Ornithologists' Union, Washington D.C.

DD Day, R.H., Stenhouse, I.J. and Gilchrist, H.G. 2001. Sabine's Gull (Xema sabini) In: *The Birds of North America* No 593. (A. Poole and F. Gill, eds). The Academy of Natural Sciences, Philadelphia, PA and The American Ornithologists' Union, Washington D.C.

DE Degtyarev, A.G. 1991: Aerial Surveys of Ross's Gull (Rhodostethia rosea) in the tundra of Yakutia. *Zoologitski Zhurnal* 70: 81–85.

DF Delany, S.N., Reyes, C., Hubert, E., Pihl, S., Rees, E., Haanstra, L., and van Strien, A. *Results from the International Waterbird Census in the Western Palearctic and Southwest Asia, 1995 and 1996.* Wetlands International Publication No. 54. Wageningen, The Netherlands.

DG van Den Bossche, W. 2001. *Eastern European White Stork populations: migration studies and elaboration of conservation measures.* Report: German Federal Agency for Nature Conservation 2001. 202 pp.

DH Dodman, T. and Rose, P. 1997. Application of the African Waterfowl Census in estimating the distribution and abundance of African waterfowl. In: Dodman, T. (ed.) 1996. *A Preliminary Waterbird Monitoring strategy for Africa.* Wetlands International, Wageningen, The Netherlands.

D1 Dodman, T. and Taylor, V. 1996. *African waterfowl census 1996. Les Dénombrements Internationaux d'oiseaux d'eau en Afrique, 1996.* Wetlands International, Wageningen, The Netherlands. 206 pp.

DO Dodman, T. In review 2002. *Waterbird Population Estimates in Africa.* Wetlands International, Dakar.

DR Donaldson, G.M., Hyslop, C., Morrison, R.I.G., Dickson, H.L. and Davidson, I. 2000. *Canadian Shorebird Conservation Plan.* Canadian Wildlife Service, Environment Canada, Ottawa.

DU Duff, D.G., Bakewell, D.N. and Williams M.D. 1991. The Relict Gull (Larus relictus) in China and elsewhere. *Forktail* 6: 43–65.

DV Dugger, Bruce. In litt. 1999.

DW Dumas, J.V. 2000 Roseate Spoonbill (Ajaja ajaja). In: *The Birds of North America* No 490. (A. Poole and F. Gill, eds). The Academy of Natural Sciences, Philadelphia, PA and The American Ornithologists' Union, Washington D.C.

DX Dutson, Guy. In litt. 2002.

EB Ebbinge, B. 1991. Wild geese populations in northern Asia. *IWRB News* 5: 11.

EC Eddleman, W.R. and Conway, C.J. 1994. Clapper Rail. Pages 167–179 In: Migratory shorebird and upland game bird management in North America. (Tacha, T.C. and Braun, C.E. (eds.)

EF Eddleman, W.R., Flores, R.E. and Legare, M.L. 1994. Black Rail (Laterallus jamaicensis) In: *The Birds of North America* No 123. (A. Poole and F. Gill,

DH eds). The Academy of Natural Sciences, Philadelphia, PA and The American Ornithologists' Union, Washington D.C.

EJ Ellis-Joseph, S., Hewston, N. and Green, A. (compilers). 1992. *Global Waterfowl Conservation Assessment and Management Plan: First Review Draft.* Report by the IUCN Captive Breeding Specialist Group and The Wildfowl and Wetlands Trust. 1992. 77 pp.

EN Engelmoer, M. and Roselaar C.S. 1998. *Geographical variation in waders.* Kluwer Academic Publishers, Dordrecht, The Netherlands.

EP Espinoza, F., Parra, L., Aranguran, J., Martino, A., Quijada, M., Pirela, D., Rivero, R., Gutierrez, T., Jimenez, N., Leal, S. and Leon, E. 2000. Numbers and distribution of the Caribbean Flamingo in Venezuela. *Waterbirds* 23 Special Publication (1): 80–86.

EQ Ethiopian Wildlife and Natural History Society. 1996. Information supplied to BirdLife International.

ER Ethiopian Wildlife and Natural History Society. 2001. Ethiopia. In: Fishpool, L.D.C. and Evans, M.I. *Important Bird Areas in Africa and associated islands: Priority sites for conservation.* Newbury and Cambridge, UK: Pisces Publications and BirdLife International (BirdLife Conservation Series No. 11).

ES Evans, M. In litt. 1993. Data prepared for IWRB from BirdLife International/IWRB Middle East IBA project.

ET Evens, J.G., Page, G.W., Laymon, S.A. and Stallcup, R.W. 1991. Distribution, relative abundance and status of the California Black Rail in Western North America. *The Condor* 93: 952–966.

EV Evers, D. C. 2000. An update of North America's common loon breeding population. In J. W. McIntyre and D. C. Evers (eds). *Loons: Old history and new findings. Proceedings of a Symposium from the 1997 meeting, American Ornithologists' Union.* North American Loon Fund, Holderness, NH. pp 91–94.

EW Ewins, P.J. and Weseloh, D.V.C. 1999. Little Gull (Larus minutus) In: *The Birds of North America* No 428. (A. Poole and F. Gill, eds). The Academy of Natural Sciences, Philadelphia, PA and The American Ornithologists' Union, Washington D.C.

FA Falk, K., Hjort, C., Andreasen, C.,Christensen, K.D., Elander, M., Ericson, M., Kampp, K., Kristensen, R.M., Mobjerg, N., Moller, S. and Weslawski, J.M. 1997. Seabirds utilising the Northeast Water polynya. *Journal of Marine Systems* 10: 47–65.

FB Ferrand, Y. and Gossmann, F. 2001. Elements for a Woodcock (Scolopax rusticola) management plan. Game and Wildlife Science 18(1): 115–139.

FC Filchagov, A.V., Yésou, P. and Grabovsky, V.I. 1992. Le Goéland du Taimyr *Larus heuglini taimyrensis*: répartition et biologie estivales. *L'Oiseau et R.F.O.* 2(2):128–148.

FE Fishpool, L.D.C. and Evans, M.I.,(Eds). 2001. *Important Bird Areas in Africa and associated islands: Priority sites for conservation.* Newbury and Cambridge, UK: Pisces Publications and BirdLife International (BirdLife Conservation Series No. 11).

FF Fishpool, Lincoln. In litt. 2002.

FG Fjeldså, J. 1986b. Feeding Ecology and possible life-history tactics of the Hooded Grebe *Podiceps gallardoi*. Ardea 74: 40–58.

FH Fjeldså, J. 1988b. *Comparative ecology of Australian grebes* (Aves: Podicipedidae). RAOU Report 54: 1–30. Royal Australian Ornithological Union, Victoria.

FK Fjeldså, J. and Krabbe, N. 1990. *Birds of the high Andes.* Zoological Museum, University of Copenhagen, Denmark.

FO Fox, A.D. 2002. The Greenland White-fronted Goose study census network. *I-WeBS News* 7: 3–4.

FR Frederick, P.C. and Siegel-Causey, D. 2000. Anhinga (Anhinga anhinga). In: *The Birds of North America* No 522. (A. Poole and F. Gill, eds). The Academy of Natural Sciences, Philadelphia, PA and The American Ornithologists' Union, Washington D.C.

FS Frederick, P.C. 1997. Tricolored Heron (Egretta tricolor). In: *The Birds of North America* No 305. (A. Poole and F. Gill, eds). The Academy of Natural Sciences, Philadelphia, PA and The American Ornithologists' Union, Washington D.C.

FT Frederick, P.C., Morales, L.G., Spaans, A.L. and Luthin, C.S. (eds). 1990. *The Scarlet Ibis (Eudocimus ruber): Status Conservation and Recent Research.* IWRB Spec. Publ. No. 11. Slimbridge, UK. 194 pp.

FU Fukuda, M. 2002. Population changes of Great Cormorant. *Birder* 16(6): 16–17.

GA Gandini, P. and Frere, E. 1995. Distribución, abundancia y ciclo reproductivo del cormoran gris, *Phalacrocorax gaimardi*, en la costa patagónica, Argentina. *Hornero* 14: 57–60.

GC Garnett, S.T. and Crowley, G.M. 2000. *The Action Plan for Australian Birds 2000.* Environment Australia, Canberra.

GD Gerasimov, N.N. and Gerasimov, Yu.N. 1995. Investigation of waterfowl migration in Kamchatka. *Goose Study* 9: 1–7.

GE Gerasimov, N.N. and Gerasimov, Yu.N. 1995. Present status and perspective of geese in Kamchatka. *Goose Study* 9: 10–14.

GF Gerasimov, N.N. and Gerasimov, Yu.N. 1997. Observations of the Spring migration of divers and seaducks along the western coast of Kamchatka, Russia. *Wetlands International Seaduck Specialist Group Bulletin* No 6: 26–28.

GG Gilchrist, Grant. In litt. 2002.

GH Gilchrist, H.G. 2001. Glaucous Gull (Larus hyperboreus). In: *The Birds of North America* No 573. (A. Poole and F. Gill, eds). The Academy of Natural Sciences, Philadelphia, PA and The American Ornithologists' Union, Washington D.C.

GI Gilissen, N., Haanstra, L., Delany, S., Boere, G. and Hagemeijer, W. 2002. *Numbers and Distribution of Wintering Waterbirds in the Western Palearctic and Southwest Asia in 1997, 1998 and 1999 – Results from the International Waterbird Census.* Wetlands International Global Series No 11., Wageningen, The Netherlands.

GM Gill, R.E., and McCaffery, B.J. 1999. Bar-tailed Godwits *Limosa lapponica* in Alaska: a population estimate from staging grounds. *Wader Study Group Bull.* 88: 49–54.

GO Gochfield, M., Burger, J. and Nisbet, I.C.T. 1998. Roseate Tern (Sterna dougalli). In: *The Birds of North America* No 370. (A. Poole and F. Gill, eds). The Academy of Natural Sciences, Philadelphia, PA and The American Ornithologists' Union, Washington D.C.

GP Gole, P. 1990. *The Sarus Crane.* Unpublished manuscript. 48 pp.

GQ Good, T.P. 1998. Great Black-backed Gull (Larus marinus) In: *The Birds of North America* No 330. (A. Poole and F. Gill, eds). The Academy of Natural Sciences, Philadelphia, PA and The American Ornithologists' Union, Washington D.C.

GR Gorman, L.R. and Haig, S.M. 2002. Distribution and abundance of Snowy Plovers in eastern North America, the Caribbean and the Bahamas. *Journal of Field Ornithology* 73: 38–52.

GS Goudie, R.I., Robertson, G.J. and Reed, A. 2000. Common Eider (Somateria mollissima). In: *The Birds of North*

America No. 546 (A. Poole and F. Gill, eds). The Birds of North America, Inc., Philadelphia, PA.

GT Green, A.J. 1992. Wildfowl at Risk: 1992. *Wildfowl* 43: 160–184.

GU Green, A.J. 1993. *The status and conservation of the Marbled Teal (Marmaronetta angustirostris).* IWRB Special Publication No. 23. Slimbridge, UK. 107 pp.

GV Green, A.J. 2002. In prep. Porron Pardo Aythya nyroca. In: *Libro Rojo de las Aves en España*. Editors: SEO, publishers: Ministeria de Medio Ambiente.

GW Green, A.J. In litt. 2002.

GX Green, A.J., El Hamzaoui, M., El Agbani, M.A. and Franchimont, J. 2002. The Conservation Status of Moroccan wetlands with particular reference to waterbirds and to changes since 1978. *Biological Conservation* 104: 71–82.

GY Greenway, J.C. 1967. *Extinct and Vanishing Birds of the World.* Dover Publications, New York. 520 pp.

GZ Groves, D.J., Conant, B., King, R.J., Hodges, J.I. and King, J.G. 1996. Status and trends of loon populations summering in Alaska 1971–1993. *The Condor* 98: 189–195.

HA Hafner, H. 2000. Herons in The Mediterranean. Pp 32–54 in: *Heron Conservation* (James A. Kushlan and Heinz Hafner, Eds). Academic Press, London.

HB Hafner, Heinz and Kushlan, James A. (eds). In prep. 2002. *Action Plan for Conservation of the Herons of the World.* Heron Specialist Group. IUCN, Gland. Switzerland and Cambridge, UK and Station Biologique Tour du Valat, Arles, France.

HC Hagemeijer, W.J.M. and Blair, M.J. (eds). 1997. *The EBCC Atlas of European Breeding Birds: Their Distribution and Abundance.* T. and A.D. Poyser, London. 903 pp.

HD Haig, S.M., Ferland, C.L., Amirault, F., Cuthbert, J., Dingledine, A., Hecht, A. and McPhillips, N. In review. 2002. The importance of complete species censuses and evidence for regional declines in Piping Plovers. *Conservation Biology*.

H1 Handel, C.M., and Gill, R.E. 1992. Breeding distribution of the Black Turnstone. *Wilson Bulletin* 104:122–135.

HE Harrington, B.A. 2001. Red Knot (Calidris canutus). In: *The Birds of North America* No. 563 (A. Poole and F. Gill, eds). Academy of Natural Sciences, Philadelphia, Pennsylvania, and American Ornithologists' Union, Washington, D.C.

HF Harrison, J.A., Allan, D.G., Underhill, L.G., Herremans, M., Tree, A.J., Parker, V. and Brown, C.J. 1997. *The Atlas of Southern African Birds. Vol.1.* BirdLife South Africa, Johannesburg. 785 pp.

HG Hatch, J.J., K.M. Brown, G.G. Hogan, and R.D. Morris. 2000. Great Cormorant (*Phalacrocorax carbo*). In: *The Birds of North America* No. 553 (A. Poole and F. Gill, eds). Academy of Natural Sciences, Philadelphia, Pennsylvania, and American Ornithologists' Union, Washington, D.C.

HH Hatch, J.T. 1995. Changing populations of double-crested cormorants. *Colonial Waterbirds* 18 (Spec. Publ. 1): 8–24.

HI Haukos, D. 2002. Unpublished information from 2000 surveys of the FWS coordinated/State-run midwinter waterfowl inventories of the Central and Mississippi Flyways, and the triennial Mexico midwinter waterfowl inventory.

HJ Hawkins, F. In litt. 2002. Unpublished notes on waterbird population estimates of Madagascar.

HK Hawkins, F., Andriamasimanana, R., Sam The Seeing and Rabeony, Z. 2000. The sad story of the Alaotra Grebe *Tachybaptus rufolavatus*. *Bull African Bird Club* Vol 7, No 2: 115–117.

HM Hayman, P., Marchant, J. and Prater, A.J. 1986. *Shorebirds: An Identification Guide to the Waders of the World*. Croom-Helm, Beckenham, UK.

HN Hazevoet, C.J. 1992. A review of the Santiago Purple Heron (Ardea purpurea bournei) with a report of a new colony. *Bird Conservation International* 2: 15–23.

H2 Heath, M.F. and Evans, M.I. eds. (2000). *Important Bird Areas in Europe: Priority sites for conservation*. 2 vols. Cambridge, U.K.: BirdLife International (BirdLife Conservation Series No. 8).

HO Hepburn, I., Oldfield S. and Thompson, K. 1992. *UK Dependent Territories Ramsar Study: Stage 1*. Unpublished IWRB Report to the UK Department of Environment.

HR Hepburn, I.R. 1983. Hunting bags and populations of Woodcock in Europe. In: H. Kalchreuter (ed.). Proc. 2nd European Woodcock and Snipe Workshop, Fordingbridge, UK.

HP Higgins, P.J. and Davies, S.J.J.F. (eds). 1996. *Handbook of Australian, New Zealand and Antarctic Birds*. Oxford University Press, Melbourne.

— Hilton-Taylor, C. 2000. *2000 IUCN Red List of Threatened Species*. IUCN – The World Conservation Union, Cambridge, UK.

HR Hirschfield, E., Roselaar, C.S. and Shirihai, H. 2000. Identification, taxonomy and distribution of Greater and Lesser Sandplovers. *British Birds* 93 (4): 162–189.

HS Hobson, K.A. 1997. Pelagic Cormorant (Phalacrocorax pelagicus). In: *The Birds of North America* No 282. (A. Poole and F. Gill, eds). The Academy of Natural Sciences, Philadelphia, PA and The American Ornithologists' Union, Washington D.C.

HT Hoffman, T.W., Warakagoda, Deepal, and Sirivardena, U. In litt. 2002. Unpublished information on the birds of Sri Lanka.

HU Holmes, D. 1996. Sumatra Bird Report. *Kukila*. 8: 9–56.

HW del Hoyo, J., Elliott A. and Sargatal, J. (eds). 1992. *Handbook of the Birds of the World. Volume 1: Ostrich to Ducks*. Lynx Edicions, Barcelona.

HV del Hoyo, J., Elliot, A. and Sargatal, J. (eds). 1996. *Handbook of the Birds of the World. Volume 3: Hoatzin to Auks*. Lynx Edicions, Barcelona.

HX Hu Hongxing. 1999. Brief report on researches of cranes and waterbirds, Hubei. *China Crane News* 3(2): 13–14.

HY Hunter, L. 1988. Status of the endemic Atitlan Grebe of Guatemala: is it extinct? *The Condor* 90: 906–912.

HZ Hyslop, C. and Kennedy, J.A. (eds). 1996. *Bird Trends, No. 5*. Can. Wildl. Serv. Headquarters.

IE Ilyashenko, E. 2002. *Siberian Crane Flyway Newsletter*. CMS/ICF/CWGE.

IA Ingadóttir, Álfheidur (ed.). 2000. Válisti 2. Fuglar [Red list 2. Birds]. Icelandic Institute of Natural History. Reykjavík. 103 pp. In Icelandic with English summary.

JA Jackson, J.A. 2000. Distribution, population changes and threats to Least Terns in the Caribbean and adjacent waters of the Atlantic and Gulf of Mexico. In: Schreiber, E.A. and Lee, D.S. (eds) Status and Conservation of West Indian seabirds. Soc. Caribbean Ornith. Spec. Pub. No.1.: 109–117.

JD James, J.D. and Thompson, J.E. 2001. Black-bellied Whistling Duck (Dendrocygna autumnalis). In: *The Birds of North America* No. 578 (A.Poole and F. Gill, eds). Academy of Natural Sciences, Philadelphia, Pennsylvania, and American Ornithologists' Union, Washington, D.C.

JE Jehl, J.R. jr. 2001. The abundance of the Eared (Black-necked) Grebe as a recent phenomenon. *Waterbirds* 24: 245–249.

JI Jiguet, F. 2002. Taxonomy of the Kelp Gull, *Larus dominicanus* (Lichenstein) inferred from biometrics and wing plumage pattern, including two previously undescribed subspecies. *Bull. British Ornithologists' Club* 122 (1): 50–71.

JP Johnsgard, Paul A. and Carbonell, Montserrat. 1996. *Ruddy Ducks and Other Stifftails: Their Behavior and Biology*. University of Oklahoma Press. 291pp.

KA Kaatz, C. and M. 2001. The situation of the White Stork population in Germany and especially in Saxony-Anhalt. In: Kaatz, C and M. (Hrsg.) (2001): 2. *Jubiläumsband Weißstorch – 2 Jubilee Edition White Stork, 8 u. 9 Storchentag 1999/2000*. Tagungsbandreihe des Storchenhofes Loburg, 68–72.

KB Kahl, M.P. 1975. Distribution and Numbers – A summary. Pp. 93–102. In: Kear, J. and Duplaix-Hall, N. (eds), *Flamingos*. T. and A.D. Poyser, Berkhamstead.

KC Kalas, J.A. In review. 2002. *International Action Plan for the Great Snipe, Gallinago media (Latham 1787)*. BirdLife International.

KD Kalchreuter, H. 2002. *On the population status of the Jack Snipe Lymnocryptus minimus*. Report to the AEWA Secretariat. 20 pp.

KE Kehoe, F.P. 1996. Trends in seaduck numbers in eastern North America. In: Hyslop, C. and Kennedy, J.A. (eds). *Bird Trends No. 5*. Can. Wildl. Serv. headquarters.

KF Keijl, G.O., Brenninkmeijer, A., Schepers, F.J., Stienen, E.W.M., Veen, J. and Ndiaye, A. Breeding gulls and terns in Senegal in 1998 and proposal for new population estimates of gulls and terns in West Africa. *Atlantic Seabirds* 3 (2): 59–74.

213

KG   Keller, V. and J. Gremaud: Der Brutbestand des Gänsesägers *Mergus merganser* in der Schweiz 1998. *Ornithol. Beob.*

KH   Keller, V. 1999. Verbreitung und Bestandsentwicklung der Kolbenente *Netta rufina* ausserhalb der Brutzeit [Distribution and development of the southwest European population of the Red-crested Pochard *Netta rufina* outside the breeding season.] Report to the Swiss Agency for the Environment, Forests and Landscape, Federal Forest Agency, Section for Hunting and Wildlife Biology.

KI   Kelley, J.R. Jr. 2001. *American woodcock population status.* US Fish and Wildlife Service, Laurel, Maryland.

KJ   Kennedy, E., Reed, C. and Davis, A. 1997. *Draft New Zealand Shore Plover Recovery Plan.* Department of Conservation, Wellington.

KK   Kennedy, R.S., Fisher, T.H., Harrap, S.C.B., Diesmos, A.C. and Manamtam, A.S. 2001. A new species of woodcock from the Philippines and a re-evaluation of other Asian/Papuasian woodcock. *Forktail* 17: 1–12.

KL   Kerbes, R.H. and Caswell, F. D. Personal Comunication of Photoinventory survey results.

KM   Kerbes, R.H., Baranyuk, V.V. and Hines, J.E. 1999. *Estimated size of the western Canadian Arctic and Wrangel Island lesser snow goose populations on their breeding grounds and wintering grounds.* Pages 25 to 38 in: Kerbes, R.H., Meeres, K.M. and Hines, J.E. (eds.) Can. Wildl. Serv. Occas. Paper No. 98.

KN   Kershaw, M. and Cranswick, P.A. In press. 2002. Numbers of wildfowl and selected waterbirds wintering in Great Britain. *Biological Conservation.*

KO   Koffijberg, Kees. In litt. 2002.

KP   Kondratyev, A.V. 1995. Status of goose populations in North East Asia (Chukotka) and their conservation. *Goose Study* 9: 15–18.

KQ   Koskimies, P. 1992. Population sizes and recent trends of breeding birds in Nordic countries. *Bird Census News* 5 (3): 41–79.

KR   Krivenko, V.G., Crivelli, A.J. and Vinogradov, V.G. 1994. Historical changes and present status of pelicans in the former USSR: a synthesis with recommendations for their conservation. Pp. 132–151. In: Crivelli, A.J., Krivenko, V.G. and Vinogradov, V.G. (eds.) 1994. *Pelicans in the former USSR.* IWRB Publ. 27.

—   Kushlan, J.A. and Hancock, J.A. in press. 2002. *The Herons.* Oxford University Press.

KS   Kushlan, James, A., Melanie J. Steinkamp, Katharine Parsons, Jack Capp, Martin Acosta Cruz, Malcolm Coulter, Ian Davidson, Loney Dickson, Naomi Edelson, Richard Elliot, R. Michael Erwin, Scott Hatch, Stephen Kress, Robert Milko, Steve Miller, Kyra Mills, Richard Paul, Roberto Phillips, Jorge E. Saliva, Bill Sydeman, John Trapp, Jennifer Wheeler, and Kent Wohl. 2002. *The North American Waterbird Conservation Plan, Version 1.* Waterbird Conservation for the Americas, Washington, DC, USA. 78 pp.

LA   Lack, P. 1986. *The Atlas of Wintering Birds in Britain and Ireland.* T. and A.D. Poyser, Calton. 447 pp.

LB   Lanctot, R.B., Blanco, D.E., Dias, R.A., Isacch, J.P., Gill, V.A., Almeida, J.B., Delhey, K., Petracci, P.F., Bencke G.A. and Balbueno R. 2002. Conservation status of the Buff-breasted Sandpiper: Historic and contemporary distribution and abundance in South America. *Wilson Bulletin* 114(1): 44–72.

LD   Landesamt für Umweltschutz, Vogelschutzwarte Garmisch-Partenkirchen, Evaluation 1996–1999 for: In prep. 2002. *Atlas der Brutvögel Bayerns.*

LE   Lane, B.A. and Rogers, D.I. 2000. The Australian Painted Snipe *Rostratula (benghalensis) australis*: An Endangered Species? *The Stilt* 36: 26–34.

LF   Lansdown, R.V. 1986. *The status and ecology of the Sumatran Heron* (Ardea sumatrana). Interwader publ. No. 21. Kuala Lumpur.

LG   Lansdown, R.V. In litt. 1996. Data prepared for the Ardeidae Action Plan.

LH   Larned, W.W. and Tiplady, T. 1997. *Late winter population and distribution of spectacled eiders* (Somateria fischeri) *in the Bering Sea 1996–97.* Unpubl. Rep. U.S. Fish and Wildlife Service, Anchorage, Alaska.

LI   Laubeck, B., Nilsson, L., Wieloch, M., Koffijberg, K., Sudfelt, C. and Follestad, A. (1999). Distribution, number and habitat choice of the Northwest European Whooper Swan (Cygnus cygnus) population: results of an international Whooper Swan census, January 1995. *Vogelwelt* 120: ??–??

LJ   Laursen, K. 1992. New figures of seaduck winter populations in the Western Palearctic. *IWRB Seaduck Bulletin* No. 1. January 1992.

LK   Lee, H. S. (2002) Yubu Island, the Important Waterbird Habitat on the West Coast of Korea and Its Conservation. *Ocean and Polar Reserach* 24(1): ?–?

LL   Li Laixing, 2001. Survey results and new records of waterfowl at Qinghai Lake. *China Crane News* 5(1): 36–37.

LM   Li, David and Mundkur, Taej. In press. 2002. *Status Overview and Recommendations for the White-headed Duck Central Asian Population.* Wetlands International, Kuala Lumpur, Malaysia.

LW   Liu Binsheng, Ji Weitao, Ding Xiansheng and Wu Jiandong, 2002. Report of the monitoring of wintering waterbirds at Poyang Lake N.R. in 2001/2002. *China Crane News* 6 (1) June 2002.

LY   Lloyd, C., Tasker, M.L. and Partridge, K. 1991. *The status of seabirds in Britain and Ireland.* T. and A.D. Poyser, London, U.K. 355 pp.

LZ   Lopez, A. and Mundkur, T. (eds.) 1997. *The Asian Waterfowl Census 1994–1996. Results of the Coordinated Waterbird Census and an Overview of the Status of Wetlands in Asia.* Wetlands International, Kuala Lumpur.

MA   Ma Ming, 1993. Breeding Ecology of *Grus grus* and *Anthropoides virgo* in Xinjiang. *Arid Zone Research* 10(2): 56–60.

M1   Maddock, M. In litt. 1993. Literature on Australasian Ardeidae, summarised for IWRB.

M2   Madge, S. and Burn, H. 1988. *Wildfowl: An identification guide to ducks, geese and swans of the world.* Christopher Helm, Bromley, UK.

M3   Madsen, J., Cracknell, G. and Fox, A.D. (eds). 1999. *Goose populations of the Western Palearctic: A review of status and distribution.* Wetlands International Publication No.48. Wetlands International, Wageningen, The Netherlands; National Environmental Research Institute, Ronde, Denmark. 344 pp.

M4   Madsen, J., Matus, R., Benegas, L., Mateazzi, G., Blank O. and Blanco D.E. In press. 2002. Status of the population of ruddy-headed geese *Chloephaga rubidiceps* in Tierra del Fuego and mainland Patagonia (Chile and Argentina), December 1999–March 2000. *Neotropical Ornithology.*

M4a   Marchant, S.M. and Higgins, P.J. 1990. Handbook of Australian, New Zealand and Antarctic Birds. Volume 1: Ratites to Ducks. Oxford University Press, Melbourne, Australia.

M5   Marion, L., Ulenaers, P. and van Vessem, J. 2000. Herons in Europe. Pp 1–31 in:

Heron Conservation (James A. Kushlan and Heinz Hafner, Eds). Academic Press, London.

M6 Martindale, J. 1986. *The Freckled Duck*. RAOU Conservation Statement. RAOU Report 22.

M7 McCann, K., Morrison, K., Byres, A., Miller, P. and Friedman, Y. (eds). 2001. *Population and habitat viability assessment for the Blue Crane* Anthropoides paradiseus. *Final Workshop Report*. Conservation Breeding Specialist Group (SSC/IUCN), Apple Valley, MN.

— McCracken, K. G. and F. H. Sheldon, 2002, Phylogeny of the herons of the world. Abs. North American Ornithological Conference, New Orleans, LA, USA.

M8 McCrimmon Jr., D.A., Ogden, J.C. and Bancroft, G.T. 2001. Great Egret (Ardea alba) In: *The Birds of North America* No 570. (A. Poole and F. Gill, eds). The Academy of Natural Sciences, Philadelphia, PA and The American Ornithologists' Union, Washington D.C.

M9 McIntyre, J.W., and Barr, J.F.. 1997. Common Loon (Gavia immer). In: *The Birds of North America* No. 313 (A. Poole and F. Gill, eds). The Academy of Natural Sciences, Philadelphia, PA, and the American Ornithologists' Union, Washington, DC.

MB McNicholl, M.K., Lowther, P.E. and Hall, J.A. 2001. Forster's Tern (Sterna forsteri). In: *The Birds of North America* No 595. (A. Poole and F. Gill, eds). The Academy of Natural Sciences, Philadelphia, PA and The American Ornithologists' Union, Washington D.C.

MC Meine, C.D. and Archibald, G.W. (eds). 1996. *The Cranes: status survey and conservation Action Plan*. IUCN, Gland, Switzerland and Cambridge, UK. 294 pp.

— Meininger, P.L., Schekkerman, H., and van Roomen, M.W.J. 1995. Population estimates and 1% criteria for waterbird species occurring in the Netherlands: suggestions for standardization. Limosa 68 (2): 41–48.

MD Meininger, P.L., Wolf, P.A., Hadoud, D.A. and Essghaier, M.F.A. 1994. Rediscovery of Lesser Crested Terns breeding in Libya. *British Birds* 87: ?–?

ME Meltofte, H. 2001. Wader Population censuses in the Arctic: getting the timing right. *Arctic* 54: 367–376.

— Mendoza, Marlynn M. In litt. 2002. Unpublished information about birds of the Philippines.

MF Merkel, F.R., 2002. *Ederfugleoptællinger i Ilulissat, Ummannaq og Upernavik Kommuner, 1998–2001*. Pinngortitaleriffik, Grønlands Naturinstitut, teknisk rapport nr. 43.

MG Merkel, F.R., Mosbech, A., Boertmann, D., and Groendahl, L. In press. 2002. Winter seabird distribution and abundance off south-western Greenland, 1999. *Polar Research* 21: ?–?

MI Miskelly, C. In litt. 1993. Summary of unpublished data for IWRB.

MJ Mix, H.M. and Braunlich, A. 2000. Dalmatian Pelican. Pp 78–83, 332–333 in: Reading, R.P. and Miller, B. eds. *Endangered Animals. A Reference Guide to Conflicting Issues*. Westport, Connecticut and London, Greenwood Press.

MM Miyabayashi, Y. and Mundkur, T. 1999. *Atlas of Key Sites for Anatidae in the East Asian Flyway*. Wetlands International – Japan, Tokyo, and Wetlands International – Asia Pacific, Kuala Lumpur. 148 pp.

MN Monval, J-Y. and Pirot, J-Y. 1989. *Results of the IWRB International Waterfowl Census 1967–1986*. IWRB Spec. Publ. No. 8. Slimbridge, UK.

MO Morales Leal, J. 1996. El flamenco rosado caribeno. *Flora y Fauna* 0: 14–18.

MP Morales, G. 2000. Herons in South America. Pp 177–199 in: *Heron Conservation* (James A. Kushlan and Heinz Hafner, Eds). Academic Press, London.

MQ Morozov, V.V. 2000. Current status of the southern subspecies of the Whimbrel *Numenius phaeopus alboaxillaris* (Lowe 1921) in Russia and Kazakstan. *Wader Study Group Bulletin* 92: 30–37.

MR Morrison, G. In litt. 1999.

MS Morrison, R.G. et al. 1994. *Bird Trends No. 3*. Canadian Wildlife Service publication.

MT Morrison, R.I.G., Bourget, A., Butler, R., Dickson, H.L., Gratto-Trevor, C., Hicklin, P., Hyslop, C. and Ross, R.K. 1994. *A preliminary assessment of the status of shorebird populations in Canada*. Can. Wildl. Serv. Progress Notes No. 28. March 1994. 19pp.

MU Morrison, R.I.G., Gill, Jr., R.E., Harrington, B.A., Skagen, S., Page, G.W., Gratto-Trevor, C.L. and Haig, S.M. 2001. *Estimates of shorebird populations in North America*. Occasional Paper No. 104, Canadian Wildlife Service, Ottawa, Ontario. 64pp.

MV Mosbech, A. and Boertmann, D. 1999. Distribution and reaction to aerial surveys of post-breeding king eiders (Somateria spectabilis) in western Greenland. *Arctic* 52: 188–203.

MW Mosbech, A. and Johnson, S. 1999. Late winter distribution and abundance of sea-associated birds in Southwest Greenland, Davis Strait and southern Baffin Bay. *Polar Research* 18: 1–17.

MX Moser, T. J. (Editor.) 2001. *The status of Ross's geese*. Arctic Goose Joint Venture Publication. US Fish and Wildlife Service and Canadian Wildlife Service.

NA Naranjo, L. In litt. 1993. Unpublished data summarised for IWRB.

NC Nechaev, V.A. and Tomkovich, P.S. 1987. A new sub-species of the Dunlin, *Calidris alpina actites* ssp.n (Charadriidae, Aves), from Sakhalin Island. *Zoologicheskii Zhurnal*, 66 (7): 110–113.

NE New Zealand Checklist Committee. 1990. *Checklist of the birds of New Zealand and the Ross Dependancy, Antarctica. Third edition*. Ornithological Society of New Zealand Inc. Auckland. 247 pp.

NN Newton, S. In litt. 2002.

N1 Nisbet, I.C.T. 2002. Common Tern (Sterna hirundo). In: *The birds of North America*, No 618. (A. Poole and F. Gill, eds). The Academy of Natural Sciences, Philadelphia, PA and The American Ornithologists' Union, Washington D.C.

NO Nol, E., Truitt, B., Allen, D., Winn, B., and Murphy, T. 2000. A survey of wintering American Oystercatchers from Georgia to Virginia, USA, 1999. *Wader Study Group Bulletin* 93: 46–50.

NR North, M.R. 1997. Aleutian Tern (Sterna aleutica). In: *The Birds of North America* No 291. (A. Poole and F. Gill, eds). The Academy of Natural Sciences, Philadelphia, PA and The American Ornithologists' Union, Washington D.C.

NT Norton, R.L. 2000. Status and Conservation of Sandwich and Cayenne Terns in the West Indies. In: Schreiber, E.A. and Lee, D.S. (eds) *Status and Conservation of West Indian seabirds*. Soc. Caribbean Ornith. Spec. Pub. No.1.: 65–79.

OF O'Donnell, C.F.J. and Fjeldså, J. 1995. *Grebes: a global action plan for their conservation*. IUCN.

OG Oring, L.W., Gray, E.M. and Reed, J.M. 1997. Spotted Sandpiper (Actitis macularia). In: *The Birds of North America* No 289 (A. Poole and F. Gill, eds). The Academy of Natural Sciences, Philadelphia, PA, and the American Ornithologists' Union, Washington, DC.

ON Ornithological Society of New Zealand. In litt. 1993. Unpublished data compiled for IWRB.

OP   Orr, C.P. and Parsons, J.L.1982. Ivory Gulls *Pagophila eburnea* and ice-edges in Davis Strait and the Labrador Sea. *Can. Field-Nat.* 96: 323–328.

OT   Orthmeyer, D.L., J.Y. Takekawa, C. R. Ely, J.L. Yee, T.R. Rothe, and M. St. Louis. In review. 2002. *Estimating the population size of the Tule Greater White-fronted Goose* (Anser albifrons gambeli)*: A comparison of three estimation techniques.*

OZ   Overdijk, O. and Zwarts, F. In prep. 2002. *Proceedings of the fourth Eurosite Spoonbill workshop, Texel, The Netherlands, April 2002.*

P1   Parker, Vincent. In litt. 2002. Information provided for draft Atlas of Wader Populations in Africa and West Eurasia.

P2   Parnell, J.F., Erwin, R.M. and Molina, K.C. 1995. Gull-billed Tern (Sterna nilotica). In: *The Birds of North America* No 140. (A. Poole and F. Gill, eds). The Academy of Natural Sciences, Philadelphia, PA and The American Ornithologists' Union, Washington D.C.

P3   Parrish, R. and Williams, M. (2001) Decline of brown teal (Anas chlorotis) in Northland, New Zealand, 1988–99. *Notornis* 48: 131–136.

P4   Parsons, K.C. and Master, T.L. 2000. Snowy Egret (Egretta thula). In: *The Birds of North America* No 489. (A. Poole and F. Gill, eds). The Academy of Natural Sciences, Philadelphia, PA and The American Ornithologists' Union, Washington D.C.

PA   Paul, Don S. in litt., 2002.

PB   Paynter, D., Aarvak, T. and Sultanov, E. (1996). *Conservation of wetland reserves in Azerbaijan: counts of wintering birds, January–February 1996.* Flora and Fauna International, Wildfowl and Wetlands Trust, Norsk Ornitologisk Forening. Unpublished report.

PC   Perennou, C. 1991. *Les recensements internationaux d'oiseaux d'eau en Afrique*

Tropicale. IWRB Spec. Publ. No. 15. Slimbridge, UK. 140 pp.

PD   Perennou, C. 1992. *African waterfowl census 1992. Les Dénombrements Internationaux d'oiseaux d'eau en Afrique, 1992.* IWRB, Slimbridge, U.K. 87 pp.

PE   Perennou, C.P., Mundkur, T. and Scott, D.A. 1994. *The Asian Waterfowl Census 1987–1991: distribution and status of Asian waterfowl.* IWRB Spec. Publ. No. 24; AWB Spec. Publ. No. 86. Slimbridge, UK and Kuala Lumpur, Malaysia.

PG   Perez-Arteaga, A., Gaston, K.J. and Kershaw, M. 2002. Population trends and priority conservation sites for Mexican Duck *Anas diazi*. Bird Conservation International 12: 35–52.

PJ   Peterjohn, Bruce. In litt. April 2002.

PL   Pierotti, R.J. and Annett, C.A. 1995. Western Gull (Larus occidentalis). In: *The Birds of North America* No 174. (A. Poole and F. Gill, eds). The Academy of Natural Sciences, Philadelphia, PA and The American Ornithologists' Union, Washington D.C.

PM   Piersma, Theunis. In litt. 2002.

PP   Pihl, S. 1997. European Species Action Plan: Steller's Eider *Polysticta stelleri*. In: Final Technical Report and Claim, 1 March 1996 – 30 November 1997. *Species Action Plans for eight European Threatened Bird Species*. RSPB, Sandy, U.K.

PR   Pihl, S. 2002. Revision of the estimate for the Baltic/Wadden Sea Common Eider population. *Wetlands International Seaduck Specialist Group Bulletin* 9: 13–16.

PS   Pihl, S. and Laursen, K. 1996. A re-estimation of Western Palearctic seaduck numbers from the Baltic Sea 1993 Survey. In: *Proceedings of Anatidae 2000*. Birkan, M., van Vessem, J., Havet, P., Madsen, J., Trolliet, B. and Moser M. (eds.) *Gibier Faune Sauvage, Game Wildl*. 13.

PT   Pirot, J-Y., Laursen, K., Madsen, J. and Monval, J-Y. 1989. Population estimates of swans, geese, ducks, and Eurasian Coot (Fulica atra) in the Western Palearctic and Sahelian Africa. In: Boyd, H. and Pirot, J.-Y. (eds) *Flyways and Reserves Networks*. IWRB Spec. Publ. No. 9. Slimbridge, UK.

PW   Powlesland, R. In litt. 1993. New Zealand Department of Conservation unpublished data.

RA   Rabarisoa, R. 2001. Variation de la population des oiseaux d'eau dans le complexe des lacs Manambolomaty, un site Ramsar de Madagascar. In: Lens, L. (ed). Proceedings of the Tenth Pan-African Ornithological Congress. *Ostrich* Supplement No.15 (July 2001): 83–87.

RB   Rabarisoa, Rivo. In litt. 1999.

RC   Rahmani, A.R. 1989. Status of the Black-necked Stork (*Ephippiorhynchus asiaticus*) in the Indian subcontinent. *Forktail* 5: 99–110.

RD   Reid, F.A., Meanly, B. and Fredrickson, L.H. 1994 King Rail. Pp 181–191 In: *Migratory shorebird and upland game bird management in North America.* (Tacha, T.C. and Braun, C.E., eds.)

RE   Robert E. Trost and Martin S. Drut. 2001. *2001 Pacific Flyway Data Book.* 127pp.

RF   Robert, M., Benoit, R., and Savard, J.-P.L. 2000. *COSEWIC Status Report on the Eastern Population of the Barrow's Goldeneye* (Bucephala islandica) *in Canada.* Report prepared for the Committee on the Status of Endangered Wildlife in Canada (COSEWIC), Ottawa, Ontario.

RM   Robert, M., Bordage, D., Savard, J-P.L., Fitzgerald, D., and Morneau, F. 2000. The breeding range of the Barrow's Goldeneye in Eastern North America. *Wilson Bull.* 112: 1–7.

RO   Rocamora, G. and Skerrett, A. 2001. Seychelles. Pp 751–768. In L.D.C.

Fishpool and M.I. Evans, eds. *Important Bird Areas in Africa and associated islands: Priority sites for conservation.* Newbury and Cambridge, UK: Pisces Publications and BirdLife International (BirdLife Conservation Series No. 11).

RR   Rodgers Jr., J.A. and Smith, H.T. 1995. Little Blue Heron (Egretta caerulea). In: *The Birds of North America* No 145. (A. Poole and F. Gill, eds). The Academy of Natural Sciences, Philadelphia, PA and The American Ornithologists' Union, Washington D.C.

RS   Rose, P.M. and Scott, D.A. 1994. *Waterfowl Population Estimates.* IWRB Publication 29. Slimbridge, UK.

—   Rose, P.M. and Scott, D.A. 1997. *Waterfowl Population Estimates – Second Edition.* Wetlands International Publication 44. Wageningen, The Netherlands.

RT   Rufray, X. 2000. Present knowledge on the distribution and ecology of the Armenian Gull *Larus armenicus*. In Yésou, P. & Sultana, J. (eds). *Proceedings of the 5th MEDMARAVIS Symposium, Floriana, Malta.* Environment Protection Department.

RU   Rüger, A., Prentice, C. and Owen, M. 1986. *Results of the International Waterfowl Census 1967–1983.* IWRB Spec. Publ. No. 6. Slimbridge, UK.

S1   Sagar, P.M., Shankar, U.D.E., and Brown, S. 1999. Distribution and numbers of waders in New Zealand, 1983–1994. In: Robertson, H. A. (ed). Wader Studies in New Zealand. *Notornis* 46: Part 1.

S2   Saliva, J. E. 2000. Conservation priorities for Roseate Terns in the West Indies. In: Schreiber, E.A. and Lee, D.S. (eds). *Status and Conservation of West Indian seabirds.* Soc. Caribbean Ornith. Spec. Pub. No.1.: 87–95.

S3   Saliva, J. E. 2000. Conservation priorities for Sooty Terns in the West Indies. In:

Schreiber, E.A. and Lee, D.S. (eds). *Status and Conservation of West Indian seabirds.* Soc. Caribbean Ornith. Spec. Pub. No.1.: 103–117.

S4 Sargeant, D. 1994. Recent ornithological observation from São Tomé and Príncipe Islands. *Bull African Bird Club* 1(2): 96–102.

S5 Sauer, J.R., Hines, J.E. and Fallon, J. 2001. *The North American Breeding Bird Survey, Results and Analysis 1966 – 2000. Version 2001.2.* USGS Patuxent Wildlife Research Center, Laurel, MD.

S6 Sauer, J.R., Schwartz, S., and Hoover, B. 1996. *The Christmas Bird Count Home Page. Version 95.1* Natl. Biol. Serv., Patuxent Wildlife Research Center, Laurel MD.

S7 Scheuhammer, A.M., Money, S.L., Kirk, D.A., and Donaldson, G.A. In prep. 2002. *Review of the Use, and Toxic Impacts on Wildlife, of Lead Fishing Sinkers and Jigs in Canada.*

S8 Schlatter, R. In litt. 2002. Unpublished information on South American waterbirds.

S9 Schulz, H. 1999. The world Population of the White Stork (Ciconia ciconia) – results of the 5th International White Stork Census 1994/95. Pp 351–367 in: Schulz H. (ed). *Weissstorch im Aufwind? White Storks on the up? Proceedings Internat. Symp. on the White Stork, Hamburg,* 1996. NABU, Bonn.

S10 Scott, D.A. and Carbonnell, M. (compilers). 1986. *A Directory of Neotropical Wetlands.* IUCN, Cambridge, UK and IWRB, Slimbridge, UK.

S11 Scott, D.A. and Rose, P.M. 1996. *Atlas of Anatidae populations in Africa and western Eurasia.* Wetlands International Publication No. 41. Wetlands International, Wageningen, The Netherlands. 336 pp.

SA Scott, D.A. In press. 2002. *Report on the Conservation Status of Migratory Waterbirds in the Agreement Area.* Update Report to African Eurasian Migratory Waterbird Agreement Secretariat.

SB Sea Duck Joint Venture Management Board. 2001. *Sea Duck Joint Venture Strategic Plan: 2001–2006.* SDJV Continental Technical Team. Unpubl. rept. (c/o USFWS, Anchorage, Alaska; CWS Sackville, New Brunswick). 14 pp. + appendices.

SC Sha Chien – Chung. In litt. to Simba Chan. 1998.

SD Sharpe, C. In litt. 1996. Information supplied to the Wildfowl and Wetlands Trust for the Anatidae Action Plan.

SE Shepherd, R. 1993. *Ireland's Wetland Wealth: the birdlife of the estuaries, lakes, rivers, bogs and turloughs of Ireland. The report of the winter wetlands survey 1984/85 to 1986/87.* Irish Wildbird Conservancy, Dublin.

SF Shernazarov, E. 1999. Distribution and Numbers of *Ciconia c. asiatica* in Central Asia. Pp 331–334 in: Schulz, H. (ed). *Weissstorch im Aufwind? – White Storks on the up? Proc. Int. Symp. on the White Stork, Hamburg* 1996 – NABU (Naturschutzbund Deutschland e.V.), Bonn.

SG Sibley, C.G. and Monroe, B.L. 1990. *Distribution and Taxonomy of Birds of the World.* Yale University Press, New Haven and London.

SH Silvius, Marcel. In litt. 2002. Unpublished information about birds of Indonesia and Malaysia.

SI Simmons, R. E. Cordes, I., and Braby, R. 1998. Latitudinal trends, population size and habitat preferences of the Damara Tern *Sterna balaenarum* on Namibia's desert coast. Ibis 140: 439–445.

SJ Simmons, R.E. 2000. What is the world population of the Chestnutbanded Plover? *Bird Numbers* 9 (2): 45.

SK Simmons, Rob. In litt. 1999.

SL Skerrett, A. In litt. 2002.

SM Skerrett, A., Bullock, I. and Disley, T. 2001. *Birds of the Seychelles.* Christopher Helm, London.

SN Smith, G. W. 1995. *A critical review of the aerial and ground surveys of breeding waterfowl in North America.* Biological Science Report 5. USDI, National Biological Service. 252pp.

SO Smith, Graham. US Fish and Wildlife Service. In litt. 2002.

SP Snow, D.W. and Perrins, C.M. 1998. *The Birds of the Western Palearctic. Concise Edition. Volume 1: Non-Passerines.* Oxford University Press, Oxford and New York. 1008 pp.

SQ SOVON Ganzen- en zwanenwerkgroep. 2001. *Ganzen- en zwanentellingen in Nederland in 1999/2000.* SOVON Monitoringrapport 2001/06, RIZA-rapport BM01.17. SOVON Vogelonderzoek Nederland, Beek-Ubbergen.

SR Unpublished information supplied by Wetlands International Specialist Groups.

SS Standring, K. 1982: *Application of the Ramsar Convention to the Falkland Islands.* RSPB Report, Sandy, UK.

ST Stinson, D.W., Ritter, M.W. and Reichel, J.D. 1991. The Mariana common moorhen: decline of an island endemic. *Condor* 93: 38–43.

SU Stjernstedt, R. In litt. 2002.

S12 Storer, R. W. and G. L. Nuechterlein. 1992. Western and Clark's Grebe. In: *The Birds of North America,* No. 26 (A. Poole, P. Stettenheim, and F. Gill, eds.). Academy Natural Sci., Philadelphia, and Amer. Ornith. Union, Washington, D.C.

SV Straw, P. 2002. Red-necked Stint and Curlew Sandpiper – longer term population trends. *The Tattler* 31: 2.

SW Stroud, D.A., Davidson, N.C., West, R., Scott, D.A., Haanstra, L., Thorup, O., Ganter, B. and Delany, S. (compilers) on behalf of the International Wader Study Group. In review. 2002. Status of migratory wader populations in Africa and Western Eurasia in the 1990s. *International Wader Studies 15.*

— Stroud, D.A., Mudge, G.P. and Pienkowski, M.W. 1990. *Protecting Internationally Important Bird Sites.* Nature Conservancy Council, Peterborough, UK.

SX Summers, R.W., Underhill, L.G., Pearson, D.J. and Scott, D.A. 1987. Wader migration systems in southern and eastern Africa and western Asia. In: Davidson, N.C. and Pienkowski, M.W. (eds.) The Conservation of International Flyway Populations of Waders: 15–34. *Wader Study Group Bull.* 49 Supplement. IWRB Special Publication No 7. IWRB, Slimbridge, U.K.

SY Sundar, Gopi. In litt. 2002. Unpublished information about the birds of India.

SZ Sundar, K. S. G., Kaur, J. and Choudhury, B. C. 2000. Distribution, demography and conservation status of the Indian Sarus Crane (Grus antigone antigone) *J. Bombay Nat. Hist. Soc.* 97: 319–339.

TA Takekawa, J.Y., and Warnock., N. 2000. Long-billed Dowitcher (Limnodromus scolopaceus). In: *The Birds of North America,* No. 493 (A. Poole and F. Gill, eds.) The Academy of Natural Sciences, Philadelphia, PA, and the American Ornithologists' Union, Washington, DC.

TB Taylor, P.B. and van Perlo, B. 1998. *Rails: a Guide to the Rails, Crakes, Gallinules and Coots of the World.* Pica Press, Mountfield, Sussex.

TC Telfair II, R.C. and Morrison, M.L . 1995. Neotropic Cormorant (Phalacrocorax brasilianus). In: *The Birds of North America* No 137. (A. Poole and F. Gill, eds). The Academy of Natural Sciences,

Philadelphia, PA and The American Ornithologists' Union, Washington D.C.

TG Thibault, J.C. and Guyst, I. 1993. *Livre rouge des oiseaux menacés des régions Françaises d'outre mer.* ICBP Monograph No. 5. CIPO, Saint-Claude, France.

TH Thomas, P. W. and Robert, M. 2002. *COSEWIC Status Report of the Eastern Canada Harlequin Duck* (Histrionicus histrionicus). Report prepared for the Committee on the Status of Endangered Wildlife in Canada (COSEWIC), Ottawa, Ontario.

TJ Thompson, B.C., Jackson, J.A., Burger, J., Kirsch, E.M. and Atwood, J.C. 1997. Least Tern (Sterna antillarum). In: *The Birds of North America* No 290. (A. Poole and F. Gill, eds). The Academy of Natural Sciences, Philadelphia, PA and The American Ornithologists' Union, Washington D.C.

— Thorup, O. In review 2002. Breeding Waders in Europe, 2000.

TK Threatened Waterfowl Specialist Group e-mail newsgroup.

TL Threatened Waterfowl Specialist Group. In prep. 2002. Global Action Plan for the Conservation of Anseriformes (Ducks, Geese, Swans and Screamers). IUCN, Gland, Switzerland.

TM Tibbits, T.L. and Maskoff, W. 1999. Lesser Yellowlegs (Tringa flavipes). In: *The Birds of North America*, No. 427 (A. Poole and F. Gill, eds). The Academy of Natural Sciences, Philadelphia, PA, and the American Ornithologists' Union, Washington, DC.

TN Titman, R.D. 1999. Red-breasted Merganser (Mergus serrator). In: *The Birds of North America* No 443 (A. Poole and F. Gill, eds). The Academy of Natural Sciences, Philadelphia, PA and The American Ornithologists' Union, Washington D.C.

TO du Toit, M., Boere, G.C., Cooper, J., Kemper, J., Lenten, B., Simmons, R.S., Whittington, P.A. and Byers, O. (eds). 2002. *Conservation assessment and management plan for southern African coastal seabirds. Workshop Report, Cape Town, South Africa, 4–8 February 2002.* Avian Demography Unit, Cape Town and Conservation Breeding Specialist Group, IUCN/SSC.

TP Tomkovich, P.S. and Lebedeva, E.A. 2002. *International Action Plan for the Sociable Lapwing* Chettusia gregaria. AEWA Secretariat/BirdLife International. 32 pp.

TQ Tomkovich, P.S. 2001. A new subspecies of Red Knot Calidris canutus from the New Siberian Islands. *British Ornithologists' Club Bulletin* 121 (4): 257–263.

TS Tomkovich, P.S., Syroechkovski, Jr., E.E., Lappo, E.G. and Zöckler, C. 2002. First indications of a sharp population decline in the globally threatened Spoon-billed Sandpiper *Eurynorhynchus pygmeus. Bird Conservation International* 12: 1–18.

T1 Torres Esquivias, J.A. and Andy Green. In litt. June 2002.

TT Torres, J.A. and Moreno-Arroyo, B. 2000. La recuperación de la Malvasia cabeciblanca (Oxyura leucocephala) en España durante el último decenio del siglo XX. *Oxyura* 10: 69–78.

TW Troillet, B. and Girard, O. 2001. Record counts of Ferruginous Ducks in Sahelian Africa. *TWSG News* 13: 56.

U1 U.S. Fish and Wildlife Service. 2001. *Waterfowl Population Status, 2001.* US Department of the Interior, Washington, D.C. 50pp.

U2 U.S. Fish and Wildlife Service. 2002. *Draft Revised Recovery Plan for Hawaiian Waterbirds, Second Revision.* USFWS Region 1., Portland, Oregon, Code U9.

U3 U.S. Fish and Wildlife Service. 2002. *Draft Revised Recovery Plan for Nene or Hawaiian Goose* (Branta sandvicensis). USFWS Region 1., Portland, Oregon, Code U8.

U4 U.S. Fish and Wildlife Service. 2002. *Draft Revised Recovery Plan for The Laysan Duck* (Anas laysanensis). USFWS Region 1., Portland, Oregon, Code U7.

U5 U.S. Fish and Wildlife Service. 2002. *Waterfowl Population Status, 2002.* US Department of the Interior, Washington, D.C. 50pp.

UH Ul Haque, Enam and Halder, R. 2002. News from Bangladesh. *AWC Newsletter* No.3, May 2002. Information posted on the Oriental Birding Forum, 19 Feb 2002.

UL Underhill, L. In litt. 2002.

UN Underhill, L.G., Tree, A.J., Oschadleus, H.D. and Parker, V. 1999. *Review of Ring Recoveries of Waterbirds in Southern Africa.* Cape Town: Avian Demography Unit, University of Cape Town, South Africa. 119 pp.

UR Urban, E.K., Fry, C.H. and Keith, S. 1986. *The Birds of Africa. Volume II.* Academic Press, London and Orlando.

VA Valqui, M., Caziani, S. M., Rocha, O. and Rodriguez, E. 2000. Abundance and distribution of the South American altiplano flamingos. *Waterbirds 23 Special Publication* 1: 110–113.

VE Veen, J., Peeters, J., Leopold, M., van Damme, C. and Veen, P. In press. 2002. Effecten van visserij op natuurwarden langs de kust van West Afrika: visetende vogels als graadmeters voor de kwaliteit van het mariene milieu. Alterra rapport, Wageningen, The Netherlands.

VD Vidal, E., Duhem, C., Beaubrun, P.C. and Yésou, P. In press. 2002. Goéland leucophée *Larus michahallis.* In: Cadiou, B., Pons, J.M. and Yésou, P. (eds). Oiseaux marins nicheurs de France métropolitaine. Report to Ministère de l'aménagement du territoire et de l'environnement. GISOM, Muséum National d'Histoire Naturelle, Paris, 166pp.

WA Wang, Qishang. In litt. 2002. Unpublished data concerning Chinese waterbirds.

WB Warnock, N.D., and Gill, R.E. 1996. Dunlin (Calidris alpina). In: *The Birds of North America* No. 203 (A. Poole and F. Gill, eds.) The Academy of Natural Sciences, Philadelphia, PA, and the American Ornithologists' Union, Washington, DC.

WC Waterbird Conservation for the Americas. 2001. *Continental Marshbird Conservation Planning Workshop, August 2001,* Denver, Colorado.

WD Watkins, D. 1993. *A National Plan for Shorebird Conservation in Australia.* Report to World Wide Fund for Nature. Prepared by the Australasian Wader Studies Group.

WE Weitao, Ji, Wu Jiandong, Yi Wusheng, Huang Zuyou and Wu Xudong. 2001. Aerial survey of waterbirds at Poyang Lake conducted by the Poyang Lake N.R. *China Crane News* 5(1):16–17.

WI Wild Bird Society of Japan: Unpublished results of national surveys undertaken on behalf of the Ministry of the Environment, Japan.

WJ Williams, Jeff (Alaska Maritime Refuge). Pers. comm. 2002.

WK Williams, M.D., McKinney, F. and Norman, F.I. 1991. Ecological and behavioural responses of Austral teal to island life. *Proceedings of the International Ornithological Congress* 20: 876–884.

WM Williams, M.J. In litt. 1993. Unpublished information from New Zealand, summarised for IWRB.

WN Wilson JR. 2001. *Victoria Wader Surveys. January and February 2001.*

Australasian Wader Studies Group Report. Birds Australia, Melbourne.

WO Wires, L.R. and Cuthbert, F.C. 2000.Trends in Caspian Tern numbers and distribution in North America: a review. *Waterbirds* 23: 388–404.

WP Wong, F.K.O. 1994. Status and distribution of Saunders's Gull (Larus saundersii). In: Chinese Ornithological Society Waterbird Specialist Group (ed). *Waterbird Research in China*. East China Normal University Press, Shanghai.

WS Woods, R. and Woods, A. 1997. Atlas of the Breeding Birds of the Falkland Islands. Anthony Nelson, Oswestry, England.

XL Xinzhong, Liu, 1999. Preliminary Analysis of Wintering Waterbird Survey in Poyang

Lake. *Newsletter For Wetlands* No.4, July 1999. Wetlands International China Programme Publication.

YA Yanagisawa, N., Fujimaki, Y. and Higuchi, H., In litt., 1993. Japanese data on waterbird population sizes, summarised for IWRB.

YB Yaremchenko, O.A. and Rybachuk, K.I. 1999. Concerning the Black Sea population of the Common Eider. (In Russian). *Berkut*. 8 (2): 155–159.

YC Yeap Chin Aik. In litt. 2002. Information provided on behalf of Malaysia Nature Society.

YE Yésou, P. 2001. Phenotypic variations and systematics of Mongolian Gull. *Dutch Birding* 23: 65–82.

YF Yésou, Pierre. In litt. 1999.

YG Yorio, P., Frere, E., Gandini, P. and Harris G. (eds). 1998. *Atlas de la distribución reproductiva de aves marinas en el litoral patagónico argentino*. PMIZCP. FPN and WCS. 222 pp.

YI Yorio, P.M. In litt. 2002.

YO Young, Glyn. In litt. 2002. Durrell Wildlife Madagascar Project.

YS Yuan-Hsun, Sun. National Pingtung Univeristy of Science and Technology, Taiwan. In litt. 2002.

YU Yus Noor Rusila. In litt. 2002. Unpublished information on the birds of Indonesia.

ZJ Zhao, Jisheng. 2002. An extremely large wintering group of Swan Goose found at

Poyang Lake. *China Crane News*. Vol.6 No.1 June 2002.

ZL Zhiyong, Liu, Zhou, Fujun and Zheng, Weidong, 1999. An Observation on wintering waterbirds in Linchong Lake and bird count in whole area of Poyong Lake. *China Crane News* Vol.3 No.1 June 1999.

ZC Zöckler, C. 2002. A Comparison between Tundra and Wet Grassland Breeding Waders with Special Reference to the Ruff (Philomachus pugnax). Bundesamt für Nuturschutz, Bonn, Germany.

Index